M000118320

Rendering Nature

NATURE AND CULTURE IN AMERICA

Marguerite S. Shaffer, Series Editor

Volumes in the series explore the intersections between the construction of cultural meaning and perception and the history of human interaction with the natural world. The series is meant to highlight the complex relationship between nature and culture and provide a distinct position for interdisciplinary scholarship that brings together environmental and cultural history.

Rendering Nature

Animals, Bodies, Places, Politics

Edited by

Marguerite S. Shaffer *and* Phoebe S. K. Young

PENN

UNIVERSITY OF PENNSYLVANIA PRESS

PHILADELPHIA

Published by
University of Pennsylvania Press
Philadelphia, Pennsylvania 19104-4112
www.upenn.edu/pennpress

Printed in the United States of America
on acid-free paper

10 9 8 7 6 5 4 3 2 1

A Cataloging-in-Publication record is available from the Library of Congress
ISBN 978-0-8122-4725-1

Contents

Chapter 1

The Nature-Culture Paradox

Marguerite S. Shaffer and Phoebe S. K. Young

In 2000 the Nobel laureate and atmospheric chemist Paul Crutzen coined the term "Anthropocene" to mark the emergence of a new geologic epoch in which humans have become the most "globally potent biogeophysical force" on the planet.[1] As Crutzen and his fellow authors Will Steffen, a climate scientist, and John R. McNeill, an environmental historian, have explained it, "The term *Anthropocene* suggests that the Earth has now left its natural geological epoch, the present interglacial state called the Holocene. Human activities have become so pervasive and profound that they rival the great forces of Nature and are pushing the Earth into planetary *terra incognita*."[2] Crutzen and his fellow authors argue that in the two centuries shaped by the Industrial Revolution, humans have transformed the environment on a global scale: altering the chemical composition of the atmosphere and the oceans, significantly modifying the terrestrial landscape, consuming substantial quantities of freshwater, and impacting species biodiversity at incomparable levels.[3] These transformative changes in the cycles and systems that support all life on Earth, according to Steffen, Crutzen, and McNeill, demonstrate that "humans are not an outside force perturbing an otherwise natural system but rather an integral and interacting part of the Earth System itself."[4] Although the Anthropocene has yet to be officially sanctioned as a new era in Earth's history, it signals a paradigm shift in the sciences that has widespread implications for a diverse array of scholars interested in nature and culture.[5]

Interestingly, three decades ago the cultural historian Raymond Williams identified the Industrial Revolution as the moment when the concepts of "nature" and "culture" diverged as disparate and opposing realms. By the mid- to late eighteenth century, Williams noted, "Nature was where industry was not."[6] As scientific and technological advances transformed nature into something that could be systematically and extensively improved and made over through human and mechanized labor, nature emerged as a place apart, separate from human civilization and outside of human history, a pristine place of refuge unsullied by human activity. For Williams, this philosophical separation between man and nature was "a function of an increasing real interaction." In other words, tighter bonds between human culture and material nature accelerated the attempts to conceptualize and inhabit them as separate domains. Williams concluded, "In this actual world there is then not much point in counterposing or restating the great abstractions of Man and Nature. We have mixed our labour with the earth, our forces with its forces too deeply to be able to draw back and separate either out."[7] Through a different route Williams arrived at a similar conclusion to that of Crutzen and his colleagues: in the modern world nature and culture are inextricably entangled.

The recognition that nature and culture are fundamentally linked is perhaps nothing new. As these interpretations show, scholars have interrogated this dyad from different cultural, scientific, and environmental standpoints. One might argue, however, that both accounts assume some essential or romantic view of nature: the Anthropocene idealizing its predecessor, the Holocene, as the geologic moment during which the "great forces of Nature" both sustained and constrained human life to create a relatively stable Earth system and where it seemed possible to separate out human influence; and in Williams's case, the notion of a preindustrial, or more accurately a precapitalist, moment when human labor mixed with nature in a more balanced relationship. Yet these are also divergent trajectories; they chart the decline either from healthy separation to hazardous meddling or from organic reciprocity to ideological division. And yet pairing these two interpretations suggests a more nuanced understanding of the interconnections between nature and culture. These contrasting paradigms call to mind the theorist Donna Haraway's concept of "naturecultures," which, as she explains it, refuses "typological thinking, binary dualisms, and both relativisms and universalisms of many flavors" in favor of "relational categories" focused on "process, historicity, difference, specificity, co-habitation, co-constitution, and contingency."[8]

By focusing on the relational dynamic, Crutzen and his coauthors, Williams, and Haraway all point to a critical paradox: how might we both account for the fundamental entanglement of nature and culture and understand the persistent modern attempts to divide, define, and categorize them separately? To describe the hybridity of nature and culture or clarify the distinctions between them sheds little light on this question. More revealing, perhaps, are the ways in which we render those relationships meaningful in place, time, and context. The process of rendering exposes how nature and culture are transformed into categorical narratives and frameworks, material and philosophical products that might point to either separation or integration. It is in this spirit that we have put together this volume of essays: we want to identify and interrogate the ways that the relationship between nature and culture has been rendered in the last two centuries of American life. Favoring neither nature nor culture, we instead seek to foreground the complex interconnections between them—what the environmental historian Gregg Mitman has recently referred to as a "relational ontology" that integrally links these two realms and concepts.[9]

As the Anthropocene suggests, we exist in a world where entangled issues of nature and culture confront us at every turn, whether it be at the most basic level of survival—food, shelter, health, energy, work—or in connection to our more comfort-driven desires—consumption, media, recreation, travel. We believe that understanding how nature and culture are coconstituted matters more than ever as globalization expands its reach, as commodity chains become more complex, as the world population grows, as demand for resources both necessary and unnecessary increases, and as we become more implicated and interconnected by all of these things. We also believe that exposing the ways in which nature and culture are and have been rendered as meaningful categories—both cultural and material—is central to understanding the ways in which power, identity, and survival are implicated in the entanglement of nature and culture. The fields we represent, environmental history and American studies, are conducive to thinking through the interconnections between nature and culture in a more integrated way.[10] Yet each of these fields has an established practice and history of prioritizing one side of the nature-culture relationship over the other.

The field of American studies emphasizes culture as an independent realm. This prioritization emerged from the complicated and problematic origins and evolution of the field. As American studies developed in the early 1930s, evolving out of an insecure cultural nationalism and in some ways responding to the looming threat of the Great Depression to the future of American society, scholars sought to identify and define a distinct American character, a national identity rooted in American history and traditions and defined by America as a place and nation. In the aftermath of World War II, as a Cold War consensus sought to promulgate a democratic and capitalist American way in the face of communist aggression, American studies scholars looked to literature, art, and intellectual history to define a cultural nationalism, legitimize American exceptionalism, and explain the American character (specifically the core values of democracy, freedom, and individualism). Interestingly, the route to explicating American culture during this era often seemed to go through nature, implicitly drawing on theories of nationalism linking nature and culture. Leaders in the field—Perry Miller, Henry Nash Smith, and Leo Marx—connected American identity and values to American wilderness, the frontier, the pastoral landscape. This early body of interdisciplinary scholarship established a rich tradition of examining conceptions of nature and its impact on culture. Specifically, wilderness became, in the words of Richard White, "the highway to the American psyche most favored by intellectual historians" who identified with American studies.[11]

However, the focus on a unified American character grounded in wilderness and nature began to crumble as political, social, and racial divisions of the 1960s exposed deep fissures in American society. As civil rights activists, anti–Vietnam War protesters, feminist advocates, and other socially disenfranchised groups demanded rights, recognition, and change, American studies scholars called into question the idea of a unified America. They abandoned the study of the American character and began to examine the deep divisions that cut across American society in every direction. Race, gender, ethnicity, and class displaced wilderness and nature as defining categories in the field. Simultaneously scholars turned to anthropological theories of culture to define an interdisciplinary method that would address issues of identity and difference that expanded beyond an elite white male perspective to give voice to everyday actors including women, working-class laborers, immigrants, and African Americans. Nature as a subject of study became suspect, associated with an old-fashioned, elitist, nationalist, intellectual, and literary history and a mythology of American exceptionalism that sought to legitimize imperialism abroad and at home. The growing prominence of cultural studies during the late 1980s and early 1990s further emphasized and expanded the cultural focus of the field by providing new ways of thinking about issues of identity, difference, and power. Cultural studies brought new attention to situating the object of study in context—social, historical, political, and geographical—which in part has revived fledgling interest in topics related to environmental issues and cultural geography. Ecocriticism, the analysis of texts from an ecological perspective and topics related to environmental justice, has gained ground in American studies as well. But the field of cultural studies has predominantly served to legitimize an understanding of nature as a social and cultural construction. In other words, to study nature in the field of American studies is still another way of getting at culture—and for many scholars, a more marginal route than other pathways to understanding identity and power.

Environmental history, on the other hand, prioritizes the material integrity of nature.[12] The environmental historian Ellen Stroud states this succinctly: "Environmental history is sometimes about power, sometimes about place, occasionally about space, and more rarely about all three, but it is always about nature."[13] Or as Linda Nash recently put it, "What binds [environmental historians] together is a strongly held belief that material environments—for all their sociality, historicity, and constructedness—always matter to history."[14] This commitment to the biological and physical materiality of history—nature, environments, landscapes, ecological systems, and natural resources—as significant historical actors and forces stems from the complicated origins of the field and in that way is not unlike American studies. One of the founding figures in the field, Donald Worster, acknowledged this emphasis early on in a 1990 essay tellingly titled "Seeing Beyond Culture": "If I seem to be pushing the agency of nature a little hard, it is because I believe that nature ought to be valued a little more highly in our society, given more credit in our list of civilization's achievements, and respected as a self-managing set of patterns and processes."[15] At the very moment when American studies scholars were beginning to flee from nature, wilderness, and the garden, those who would call themselves environmental historians began to turn to those areas. While the social upheaval of the 1960s brought increased interest in issues of race, ethnicity, gender, and class, it also sparked a growing concern for the natural environment. Concern about pollution, resource use, energy policy, and wilderness conservation coalesced around an emerging politics of environmentalism. As the historian Richard White has noted, "environmental history as a self-proclaimed new field emerged on the academic scene deeply involved with, if not married to, modern environmentalism."[16] Although environmental historians drew from a wealth of established scholarship that extended from the work of U.S. intellectual, political, and regional historians, to historical and cultural geographers and to French historians connected to the Annales School, the field sought to distinguish itself through an approach that foregrounded the role of the physical world as a crucial context for understanding human history.

This scholarly turn toward nature, defined originally as "the nonhuman world," rested on an implicit vision of equilibrium: that humans and nature could be in or out of balance, where humans might historically have worked to preserve or degrade nature. As a result, the earliest works in the field focused on issues of environmental policy, conservation, and conceptions of nature.[17] Those scholars leading the field, including Donald Worster and William Cronon, identified three distinct levels through which one might track environmental historical change. As Cronon summarized, "First, the dynamics of natural ecosystems in time; second the political economies people erect within those natural ecosystems; and third, the cognitive lenses through which people perceive their relationships to the other two. Nature, political economy, and belief—these, in varying mixes, have been the chief fascinations of environmental historians' work"; and quickly, as Cronon went on to note, the issue became "how to best integrate the three."[18] Environmental historians worked to bring nature on par with human actors in the historical narrative—to give nature historical agency and define what that meant. In the process they understandably questioned, challenged, and mitigated the role and power of culture and mapped out the many ways in which the physical world exerted unrecognized influence on historical events. Nature established limits, reacted to human efforts, and shaped the possibilities for culture. Culture, in this formulation, became a subsidiary product of nature. The environmental historian Ted Steinberg, drawing on the authority of science, made this case in point: "humankind 'survives biologically or not at all.'"[19] The first generation of environmental historians endeavored to give these biological, ecological, geographical, climatic forces in history their due. The result was a growing collection of compelling histories that foregrounded rivers, grasslands, farming, wilderness, fire, water, disease, pollution, smog, and garbage. What people thought about them, what they meant in culture, followed the material fact.

By the 1990s a number of environmental historians had begun to borrow from a range of fields influenced by cultural studies and the history of science to challenge the holistic tendencies in environmental history, which implicitly, sometimes explicitly, leaned toward idealized social and ecological communities. Challenging the fixed categorization of nature and culture, they turned their attention to "hybrid environments"—landscapes, both natural and human, shaped by "interweaving the natural and the cultural in complex ways."[20] This second wave of environmental history critically interrogated the dualistic opposition between nature and culture. Specifically scholars have focused on contesting and deconstructing the category of nature in an effort to challenge and problematize earlier conceptions of nature as an objective, idyllic, uncontaminated realm beyond the human. Recent work has explored the ways in which social inequities and conflict connected to race, gender, class, and power impact and complicate human interactions with the physical world.[21] Scholars have also begun to probe the notion of normative biology by examining issues related to the body and health, genetic engineering, and environmental science.[22] In addition there is a significant body of scholarship in the field that has sought to highlight the power of culture—shopping malls, ski resorts, photographs, film, recreation, tourism—to frame nature and our relationship to it.[23] Through this work environmental historians have found a range of new terms to reflect a more complex give-and-take between nature and culture: "second nature," "organic machines," "ecotechnological systems," "workscapes," "industrial organisms," "creole ecosystems," "novel ecosystems."[24] Nature has increasingly become "contested terrain."[25] Despite the growing attention to the existence of spaces that contain both nature and culture, such terms presume that there are some spaces that might contain only one or the other, and thus posit hybridity as endproduct rather than first principle. If environmental historians had to choose, the field overall has sought to privilege the role and agency of nature within the historical narrative.[26]

In some ways over the past three decades, environmental historians have been more troubled by culture than American studies scholars have been concerned with nature. Early on, scholars in the field struggled to articulate where culture fit and how to integrate it. Donald Worster and William Cronon debated the issue as they sought to outline a defining methodological approach in the early 1990s.[27] As a body of scholarship in environmental history grew, critics upbraided the field for essentializing and depoliticizing nature. For example, the social historian Elizabeth Blackmar questioned the way in which environmental historians early on "appropriated the language of nature . . . to project and promote normative concepts of social equilibrium."[28] Similarly the Dutch historian Kristen Adsal has asserted that environmental history has depended too heavily on a conception of nature grounded in a scientific method that claims neutrality and objectivity.[29] However, the heated response to William Cronon's essay "The Trouble with Wilderness" and the ensuing critique of his edited volume *Uncommon Ground,* which further elaborated the cultural construction of nature, perhaps best exposed the broader discomfort with culture. *Uncommon Ground* elicited strong responses from scholars who criticized "the tendency of many contributors to treat *nature* as a mere linguistic bauble whose meaning can be constructed—and deconstructed—at will."[30] The book provoked outrage from environmental groups such as EarthFirst! and others who worried about the consequences if nature ceased to be a "real thing" to be managed, preserved, or destroyed. Although many environmental historians turned their attention to culture after Cronon's controversial challenge, the ecological paradigm, given the support it lends to the primacy and agency of nature, remains.[31]

Efforts to discount cultural understandings of nature as "not real" attempt to sidestep the thorny paradox that results when we acknowledge that "[b]iophysical and human nature are incomprehensible outside of culturally-based knowledge schemes," as the geographer James Proctor asserted. Once we do that, then "the vision of nature as culture cannot be readily dismissed as merely a vision of ideas of nature versus nature itself."[32] Acknowledging the power of "culturally-based knowledge schemes" is not a concession to the power of culture over nature. Rather it is an invitation to probe how concepts and categories of knowledge have been used to render both nature and culture. For example, as the anthropologists Ann Grodzins Gold and Bhoju Ram Gujar suggest, the term "environment" serves to "avoid the cultural baggage of 'nature'" and thus provide "a more neutral and prosaic [that is, scientific] way of saying almost the same thing." But in so doing, it produces "something flatter and more instrumental than the view of nature as inevitably mixed with human labor"—or, we would argue, culture. Taking "environment" as the object thus constrains scholars from moving "beyond . . . the functionalist/materialist"; whereas nature may suggest less "accuracy," it also affords greater "ambiguity, complexity, and uncertainty."[33] Precisely for such reasons, environmental historians have been more comfortable with concepts of environment, material products, and natural resources and have danced around the analytical primacy of nature and the natural. They have questioned theories and methods, debated concepts of agency versus structure, defined hybrid categories, and begun to ask questions about whose nature, what nature, and which nature. But as these criticisms suggest, nature and the natural have retained much of their material power as "autonomous, independent energies that do not derive from the drives and intentions of any culture."[34]

The most recent state of the field round table reaffirms this commitment to the physical materiality of nature as an organizing principle. Tracing recent historiography, the round table highlights the persistence of "many of the methodological and analytical tensions laid bare in the 1990 roundtable [*sic*]."[35] Paul Sutter documents the turn toward "hybrid environments," explaining that "[t]he hybrid turn has not only been a cultural shift . . . hybridity also implies that human history and culture cannot be easily isolated from environmental forces and circumstances."[36] Sutter traces a significant body of scholarly work that has sought to explore the complex intersections between nature and culture, identifying four prominent categories of recent scholarship: "the environmental management state"; "agroenvironmental history"; "environmental history of disease and health"; and "the human-built world." Yet even in celebrating the analytical and theoretical nuance of this more complicated give-and-take between nature and culture, Sutter expresses concern about the relativity of this perspective. Hybridity, he laments, "has not always offered analytical or normative clarity";[37] and he goes on to note that "scholars have found this world, without Eden or sin—without a pure nature or universal human transgression against it—a disorienting place." He concludes with a plea for the field to return to its commitment to "environmental prescription."[38] One of the round-table respondents, Linda Nash, makes this case even more emphatically: "If the second generation of environmental history successfully demonstrated how what was presumed natural was already intertwined with culture, now is the time for scholars to return to the material—to show how what is presumed to be social or cultural is thoroughly intertwined with the natural."[39]

In American studies, the ways in which nature has crept back into the field exhibits similar, if less obvious, quandaries about the underlying assumptions of the discipline. As issues of globalization, transnationalism, and border crossing have become increasingly significant in an expanded vision for the field, scholars have returned to explore the intersections of place, identity, and power more critically. Postmodern and postcolonial geography, diasporic studies, and global studies have called into question the fixed materiality/physicality of the nation-state and provided new ways for examining the social construction of place, global commodity chains, and transnational identity. In this way nature has gained ground to the degree that it is imagined in terms of politicized geography, environmental resources, and commodity flows. Ecocriticism, animal studies, queer studies, and a growing focus on the body have raised questions about the liberal enlightenment vision of humanity, the centrality of human agency as a cultural historical force, and the anthropocentric worldview and interpretive stance that go with it. For example, the *American Quarterly* recently published a special issue focused on what it means "to think and act in a multispecies world." The issue examines species as an organizing framework of difference in relation to other "categories of human difference" in an effort not only to "bring the animal into fuller visibility" but also to articulate a posthumanist, planetary perspective that seeks to expand the established conceptual boundaries of social justice, ethical behavior, and "taxonomies of power." In their introduction the editors note that the field of American studies "has yet to engage species/race/sex fully."[40] While these recent turns in the field have largely served to open up new theoretical territory on which to deconstruct systems of human power and normative cultural frameworks of identity and meaning, there has been no broader attempt to connect and organize new interpretive approaches around the concept of nature or to hypothesize an integrated understanding of nature-in-culture.

As the debates in both of these fields reveal, it is difficult to unpack the entanglement of nature and culture, possibly because we have become so deeply immersed in the separation between the two realms. Whether it be the legacy of the enlightenment mind-set and the related scientific worldview, which signified "the death of nature"; or the analytical remnants of Hegelian philosophy, which distinguishes the ideal from the real; or its spin-off, Marxist theory, which so clearly separates modes of production and the material world from ideology and culture; or just the intellectual, methodological, and professional boundaries that have sharply divided scholarly disciplines related to science and the humanities—as scholars we inhabit a conceptual and material world that predisposes us to understand nature and culture as distinct and separate domains that inhabit a seemingly fixed relationship to each other.

Recent works in the fields of posthumanist studies and animal studies offer new frameworks for rethinking well-established nature-culture binaries. By situating the concept of humanness in historical context, posthumanism challenges the naturalized and reductive ideal of the human as an independent, contained organic being. Building on Foucault's work detailing the connections between science and structures of power, posthumanism examines the process by which humans have defined themselves as a distinct biological species. Specifically, posthumanist scholars have highlighted the ways in which humanness is the product of a complex array of performed, constructed, historically situated relationships between humans and technologies, humans and nonhumans (both animate and inanimate), humans and "Others." "Within such webs," argue the scholars Julie Livingston and Jasbir Puar, "the human becomes one of many nodes, certainly not the originator of categories, matter, or meaning."[41] In a related approach, the field of animal studies positions the nonhuman animal as the organizing object of study. Scholars in the field have sought to contest the naturalized logic of human exceptionalism by historicizing and deconstructing the "shifting boundaries between humans and nonhuman animals."[42] Exploring issues of nonhuman agency, animal cognition, consciousness, communication, and the hierarchies of human-animal relationships, the field explores the ideologically charged oppositions that have long legitimized human exploitation and exoticization of animals. Specifically, animal studies scholars have embraced the concept of "interspecies," referring "to the relationships *between* different forms of biosocial life and their political effects," to examine the construction and ideological implications of species difference.[43]

In questioning taxonomies, species, and naturalized biological categories, both posthumanism and animal studies seek to provide an interpretative approach that recognizes relationships and processes over fixed types and finalized products. They offer new analytical tools with which to explore the relationship between nature and culture. Just as William Cronon's deconstruction of the concept of wilderness recalibrated the ways in which scholars defined and approached the concept of nature, posthumanism is poised to reframe the fundamental categories of humanness central to conceptions of culture. Where Cronon opened up wilderness to new lines of inquiry by understanding it as a mutable, material, and cultural space, posthumanism disaggregates the standard unit of historical agency—the human—into an ongoing product of a complex network of relationships of biology, politics, and power. This approach draws attention to "the moment human bodies are . . . rendered available for biological qualification through population construction."[44] This process of rendering that frames concepts of nature, culture, human, and animal then becomes the central concern. Through what means, what processes, and what kinds of relationships are such concepts and products rendered historically?

Animal Capital: Rendering Life in Biopolitical Times, by the animal studies scholar Nicole Shukin, offers a useful theoretical model for examining human-animal relationships by focusing on this process of rendering. Building on the multiple and conflicted meanings of the verb "to render" (to represent, to perform, to surrender, to return or restore, to process or melt down, to cover, to translate into a computer image or Web page),[45] Shukin argues, "[t]he rubric of rendering encompasses a cacophony of logics." These logics signify "both the mimetic act of making a copy, that is, reproducing or interpreting an object in linguistic, painterly, musical, filmic, or other media (new technologies of 3-D digital animation are, for instance, called 'renders') [,] *and* the industrial boiling down and recycling of animal remains."[46] Although focused specifically on the cultural work of animals, both economic and ideological, Shukin's framework shows how the multiple meanings of the term suggest provocative ways for thinking through the interconnections and boundaries between representation and materiality. The process of rendering offers a useful conceptual tool to interrogate the entanglement of nature and culture without presuming either to solve or to sidestep the paradox. That is, an inquiry into how we render nature and culture in conjunction contains more points of entry than asking, for example, what nature or whose culture. Such an inquiry sheds light on both the dynamic processes that link the two categories and the layers of thought, practice, and history that have served to divide nature and culture into distinct realms. The essays in this volume all speak to the multiple ways in which nature is rendered. Together they show that rendered nature brings us back to the complex interplay—the "relational ontologies"—of nature and culture.

The authors in this volume operate from a core assumption that nature and culture exist not as distinct realms but as a reciprocal give-and-take that blurs the boundaries of each and rejects the prioritization of either. Each of us works to situate nature in history and open it up as a negotiated process that involves a constant shifting of relations between people, places, animals, resources, images, and texts. We share a desire to experiment with the way in which we tell stories about nature and culture and what stories are told.[47] We rely on hybrid intellectual traditions—American studies, animal studies, cultural history, environmental history, labor history, public history, visual studies—that are premised on questioning normative categories and unpacking core assumptions, such as concepts of nationhood, identity, agency, audience, and representation. We agree that nature and culture could benefit from this same kind of critical approach. We want to carve out space to place this work at the center of inquiry rather than on the margins of several fields. The rubric of rendering encompasses our individual analytical approaches to nature-culture relationships and embodies the conceptual themes of the volume.

In seeking to interrogate the way nature is rendered, the essays in this book explore a diverse array of physical spaces and historical moments—from antebellum slave society to atomic testing sites, from gorillas in Central Africa to river runners in the Grand Canyon, from white sun tanners to Japanese American incarcerees, from taxidermists at the 1893 World's Fair to tents on Wall Street in 2011. Understood neither as perversions of nature (or culture) nor as hybrid products of the two realms, these topics present scholars with valuable opportunities to explore and understand how nature and culture manifest in tandem around some pivotal issues in the American past and present. They demonstrate the variety of ways nature and culture are rendered as meaningful categories—both separate and connected—in historical context. As such, these essays seek to model new approaches, to showcase new topics, and to explore the intricacies of how we have lived and live out nature and culture in relationships rendered in time, place, and context.

While the connections between the essays are multiple and will emerge in whichever order one might read them, they cluster into four categories: animals, bodies, places, and politics. This thematic structure highlights the multiplicity of renderings that precede apparently related topics and subjects. In the opening set of essays, for example, the horse that opens Thomas Andrews's chapter manifests as a different sort of animal from the horse that stands in John Herron's essay; and the dog, gorilla, bison, and moose discussed by Andrews, Herron, and Marguerite Shaffer speak to very distinct renderings of animals in relation to humans. Yet all these authors explore how animals play material and historical roles in the construction of human power, knowledge, and culture. Thomas Andrews begins with the often overlooked but striking fact of the ubiquity of animals in antebellum America. By revisiting the 1836 slave narrative of Charles Ball, Andrews pays close attention to the relationship between humans and animals in the slave system in a way that prompts a rethinking of key conceptual junctures. Learning how slaves, slave owners, and animals interacted in these moments, as Andrews importantly highlights, begins not only to dismantle the nature/culture binary but also to reveal the ways in which other such pivotal divisions have been rendered: namely energy and power, animals and humans, freedom and slavery.

John Herron moves forward to the late nineteenth century to examine the physical and intellectual developments that made taxidermy and museum displays of animal forms a potent mode for negotiating human relationships to animals and to each other. Taxidermy combined nature, art, craft, science, and culture in carefully curated displays that spoke to viewers' conception of narratives of "the ideal" and "the authentic." Gathered in a panorama at the 1893 World's Columbian Exposition, these scenes, of course, reflected gendered, racialized, and nationalist assumptions of the era. But more than a prop to insist on the natural basis of such hierarchies, the choreographed poses and communities on the other side of the glass engaged visitors in practicing how to see nature—not as pristine space absent of humans but as space that fostered active reflection on the organization of human society, politics, and sense of belonging.

Marguerite Shaffer reminds us of the famous tale of Digit the Gorilla and Dian Fossey, his primate girl, and their star-crossed love story calls attention to an animal encounter that renders both connection and separation. A charismatic animal and a celebrity scientist, portrayed as intermediaries between the worlds of nature and culture, became emblematic creatures for the 1970s, when stories about nature reflected much about American anomie, desires for redemption, and deeply personal experiences. The afterlives of Fossey and Digit echoed a broader social and economic trajectory, which commoditized that very desire for authenticity, connection, and innocence through nature. All three essays in Part I suggest that what we portray about animals (and about ourselves) hides as much as it reveals, concealing the great cultural (and physical) work that produces animals as natural objects apart from humans while making them available to claim as instruments of power and identity, ideal specimens of social life, or innocent experiences of authentic contact.

The essays in Part II move from the animal to the human to examine the body as a powerful site (or sieve) for rendering nature, whether through the forces that shape bodies or as embodiments of environmental vulnerability. Susan Miller provides useful perspective on tensions between ways of understanding the body as a sealed, unified container and those envisioning it as a mutable, porous entity constituted of both nature and culture. Adolescence, a concept that emerged at the turn of the twentieth century, became a consequential medium for sifting the influence of nature and culture. The members of a single, significant family, the Gulicks—among them natural scientists, Progressive reformers, and religious missionaries—envisioned adolescents' developing bodies as a crucible for natural forces and cultural imperatives. Though they evinced a modern confidence in their ability to manipulate the environment to produce healthier youths, cultural change, and a better race of Americans, along the way their suggestions about the malleability of adolescent bodies posited a view of humans-in-nature as fundamentally "in a state of becoming." If nature and culture together rendered this stage we define as adolescence, then so also has adolescence become a powerful source for the way we categorize and correlate nature, culture, and the human body.

Progressives such as the Gulicks shared a faith in the environment to influence cultural and material transformation, but as Catherine Cocks argues, the emergence of tanning as a popular practice represented a simultaneous but contrasting intellectual trend—one that sought to divest nature of its power to determine cultural identity. The general acceptance by the mid-twentieth-century of white people's deliberate pursuit of "skin darkening" was predicated on seeing "the tan" as a cultural affect rather than material transformation, even if it is seen and sensed on the body itself. Shifting beliefs in the permeability of skin and identity had everything to do with a complex relationship of race and nature to culture and history. Cocks traces a new path through the complex thicket that separated nineteenth-century notions of race as social destiny into the seemingly independent variables of biology and culture—which all the while continued to generate deep and complex physical connections.

Finis Dunaway examines a different nexus of biology and culture: emotions. In particular he demonstrates the emotional power wielded through images of vulnerable bodies that became central to the making of American environmentalism in the Cold War era and leading into its 1970s high point. Invoking the body at risk tapped into Americans' worries about the potential destructive transformations of nuclear energy and stimulated a transformation in attitudes regarding the uses of the environment. Dunaway reveals the covert links between biological, emotional, irrational responses and public actions in defense of nature. Human bodies as permeable hosts for genes, color, and emotions are thus transformational sites where nature and culture mingle on molecular, social, rhetorical, visual, and imaginative planes.

The essays that comprise Part III address the multivalent ways we know places of nature: through sensory experiences of landscapes as well as by narratives realized through text, time, and art and through the archives that collect them. Andrew Kirk examines how nature is rendered through a medium of tools, both things and images, art and technology. Using a place typically rendered as destroyed or absent of nature—the atomic landscape of the

Nevada Test Site (NTS)—Kirk eschews a focus on the material impacts of atomic testing or the symbolism of the nuclear reaction as a moment of both mastery and destruction of nature. Instead he reveals the complex relationships that people who worked on the ground forged with the material landscape they inhabited, which, rather than blasted clean, was surprisingly full of flora, fauna, and human structures. Alternately participating in and resisting federal attempts to publicize the NTS as a blank spot and advertise the invisibility of its nature, they struggled to reconcile their destructive labors with often-insightful comprehension of the places they inhabited.

Annie Gilbert Coleman asks what it means to know the Colorado River as an environmental palimpsest of sensation, text, place, and archive. River runners from John Wesley Powell to Barry Goldwater to Dock Marston made their marks on a river that has not remained fixed in time, place, or substance. By examining these layers of physical and textual attempts to organize the experience of the river, Coleman challenges the division between material and representational modes, between words and water, between real and written.

Frieda Knobloch establishes a framework for thinking about the desert not only in terms of place but also in terms of time. She proposes that we deepen landscapes into "chronotopes," places propagating particular senses of time. What renders an arid place into "the desert" are the relational bridges between modern consciousness, concepts of decadence, visions of geologic time, rainfall patterns, literary imagination, and wilderness expectations. Her formulation challenges us to see yet another binary—time and place—as deeply entangled as nature and culture. These essays share a focus on a place that American environmental historians have highlighted frequently, the arid West, but their inquiries examine this region in ways that augment our understanding of it as a definable geographic zone with a view into how its nature is rendered through multiple ways of knowing.

The essays in Part IV concern the political implications of rendering nature. Connie Chiang examines the relationship of nature to nation as articulated through the politics and practices of discrimination, nationalism, and control made manifest by the incarceration of Japanese Americans during World War II. Within a broader framework of what she terms "environmental patriotism" during the war, the incarceration mobilized the rhetoric of conservation alongside positive and negative versions of scientific racism to frame the war effort in environmental terms. Chiang looks beneath the victory-garden narrative of war-time conservation to see a multiplicity of contradictory purposes for environmental debates and manipulations, even as a fundamentally undemocratic place could, by way of nature, get a patriotic spin. This highlights not only the transformation of resources by way of ideology but also the ways Americans sought to envision nature through nation.

Brett Mizelle looks at the political dynamics embedded in human relationships to pigs, pork, and bacon. The stories of slaughter that humans tell and do not tell and how we idealize the domesticated pig but deliberately unknow the realities of the mass-production process every time we eat illuminate the political structures that sustain investments in separating animals and humans, nature and culture. The relationship between invisibility and hypervisibility exposes not only our assumptions about the differences and relationships between species but also the politics of the meat industrial complex.

Phoebe Young argues that the tents of Occupy Wall Street tapped into some of these latent connections, employing narratives of nature to frame a political protest. Camping for a political cause highlights how the outdoors has acted as a critical space for negotiating civic belonging and national identity. Physical and symbolic uses of tents generated competing modes of citizenship and dramatized a key connection between access to public spaces and the ability to participate in public life. Drawing upon a thick history that has associated camping with the nation as well as an ideal of behaved middle-class citizenship, examining Occupy Wall Street reveals how we render relationships between nature, culture, and the public. Looking for nature in incarceration facilities, slaughterhouses, and protest movements prompts us to rethink our assumptions about how and where nature has political, national, or public meaning.

In sum these essays reveal humans rendered into animals and animals rendered into humans; nature rendered as innocent, invisible, and elemental; environments rendered through race and race rendered through environment; nature rendered through time, text, and archive, while also making visible the politics of rendering nature as patriotic, as product, and as a form of protest. Portraying a broad range from enslaved peoples of the nineteenth century to encamped protesters of the twenty-first century, these essays neither coalesce around a singular theme in American history nor present a unified theory of how nature and culture finally relate. A dozen among many possible examples, together they offer new perspectives and conceptual tools that foreground the complicated and crucial relationships that render nature and culture: perspectives and tools that we believe can help us better negotiate and understand the paradoxes of our new epoch.

PART I

Animals

Chapter 2

Beasts of the Southern Wild: Slaveholders, Slaves, and Other Animals in Charles Ball's *Slavery in the United States*

Thomas G. Andrews

On a Maryland road in 1785, a slave family was torn apart. We might be tempted to tell the story of its sudden dissolution simply as a human drama acted out by a Maryland planter, a "Georgia trader," an enslaved woman, and her four-year-old son. Even half a century later the boy, who published his life story in 1836 under the pseudonym Charles Ball, winced at how "the terrors of the scene return[ed]" to him "with painful vividness."[1] Yet Ball could recollect neither the scene nor its terrors without introducing a fifth and more surprising player: a horse.[2]

The animal was hardly the agent of Ball's suffering. Yet it populated Ball's narrative nonetheless. The horse mattered, not just because it was present but also because it lent the Maryland slaveholder the power he needed to rip Charles Ball away from his mother, who had just been purchased by the Georgia trader along with Ball's siblings. Charles, too young to survive the journey south, was instead sold to the local man whose horse Ball could never forget. The boy's new owner picked Charles up, hoisted the boy onto his saddle, "and started home." Charles's grief-stricken mother "ran after me, took me down from the horse, clasped me in her arms, and wept loudly and bitterly over me." She begged Ball's master "to buy her and the rest of her children" instead of letting them "be carried away by the negro buyers." The Georgia trader, fearful that the Maryland planter might accede to the woman's wishes, hustled over to Ball's mother, "told her he was her master now, and ordered her to give that little negro to its owner, and come back with him." As she begged for the slave driver's mercy, he began to beat her. To protect her son, she thrust him back into his new owner's arms. The man "quickened the pace of his horse; and as we advanced, the cries of my poor parent became more and more indistinct." Eventually the woman's shrieks "died away in the distance, and I never again heard the voice of my poor mother."[3]

Charles Ball rode into an uncertain future perched atop a trotting horse in his new master's clutch. The creature that bore him away from his mother was but the first of many animals to inhabit *Slavery in the United States: A Narrative of the Life and Adventures of Charles Ball, a Black Man . . .* , first published in Lewistown, Pennsylvania in 1836. Animals figured in this narrative as meat and motive power, predators and prey, instruments of plantation discipline and essential adjuncts in the struggles Ball waged to stave off hunger, establish a human community, assert his autonomy, and gain his freedom.[4]

It should come as no surprise to historians of antebellum slavery in the United States that nonhuman creatures figured centrally in one slave's experience of bondage. Indeed animals have long occupied a niche in slavery studies.[5] The scholarly literature contains innumerable references to bloodhounds, mules, hogs, chickens, opossums, and a veritable menagerie of other creatures. Yet a systematic analysis of human-animal relationships during the heyday of America's "peculiar institution" remains long overdue.

Charles Ball understood that the story of *Slavery in the United States* could never be retold as an exclusively human drama. Animals played pivotal roles in the power struggles, social bonds, and acts of resistance through which Ball fashioned a life. Serving both documentary and rhetorical functions, nonhuman creatures shaped Charles Ball's travails as a slave and a fugitive, as well as the narrative acts by which this escaped slave sought to uphold and voice his own irreducible humanity.

Slavery in the United States, like the other fugitive slave narratives that began to appear in the mid-1830s, functioned simultaneously as testimony and literature, an exercise in self-making and a political intervention—a record, a performance, and a negotiation.[6] Unfortunately only limited evidence remains to document its production. No one has ever determined the identity of the fugitive whose story the narrative purported to tell.[7] The pseudonymous

Charles Ball never embarked upon the lecture circuit that turned Josiah Henson, Sojourner Truth, Frederick Douglass, and other slave narrators into public figures. The narrative's editor (and presumably its amanuensis) was Isaac Fisher, an irascible Delaware-born Quaker and respected attorney in Mifflin County, Pennsylvania.[8] Fisher played little role in formal abolition movements, and his only other known publications focused on local geology.[9] *Slavery in the United States,* the story of an anonymous fugitive as set down by an obscure lawyer, remains among the most enigmatic of all American slave narratives.[10]

From its first edition to the present day, the book has loomed as one of the most influential accounts of American slavery ever published. It was the "first book-length slave narrative published under the aegis of the abolitionists," and quite possibly the longest slave narrative ever published in the English-speaking world.[11] Its publication marked "the beginnings of the classic fugitive slave narrative genre in the United States."[12] By the end of 1836, the first edition of *Slavery in the United States* had sold out. American and English publishers printed several more editions in the following decades, including an abridged volume melodramatically (and inaccurately) titled *Fifty Years in Chains.*[13] The book even directly inspired the production of at least one other published narrative. When Rev. Charles E. Lester asked a fugitive named Peter Wheeler to commit his story to print, Wheeler replied by invoking *Slavery in the United States*: "You've got an idee of makin' out some sich a book as Charles Ball, and that has done a sight of good."[14]

In recent decades legions of scholars have mined Ball's narrative to great effect.[15] Yet for all the rich evidence historians have extracted from the pages of *Slavery in the United States,* they have mostly overlooked the animals that populate almost every part of Ball's narrative. This essay tracks the beasts of the southern wild—as well as those that stalked the plantation landscape and the slave quarters—through one slave's story. It demonstrates how paying closer attention to the animals dwelling within historical documents can help us better understand the experiences, struggles, and strategies of slaves such as Charles Ball. In the process it posits an unlikely genealogy for latter-day animal rights movements—one that originates with Ball and other black abolitionists.

Animal Passages and Plantation Metabolisms

The core of *Slavery in the United States* begins in 1804 or 1805, when several white men apprehended Charles Ball while he was working to hitch oxen to a cart. As Ball, newly married and roughly twenty years old at the time, would soon discover, his master had sold him to a slave trader. Ball's new owner placed "a strong iron collar" on his neck, handcuffed him, and chained him to thirty-two other men. Rounding out Ball's coffle were nineteen women, "merely tied together with a rope." The trader then forced Ball and his unfortunate companions to march south—just one brigade among the one million or so African Americans sold south in the massive forced migration that the historian Ira Berlin has aptly described as "a second Middle Passage."[16]

Ball told the story of his passage from the Chesapeake to the cotton kingdom of the Deep South as a journey from a landscape where work and food animals were abundant to one alarmingly deficient in livestock. He described a Virginia farm where the slave trader boarded his coffle as "the picture of sterility," with "neither barn nor stable." Farther south barns, hay, and corn all seemed to disappear entirely; "little attention," Ball huffed, "was paid to the cultivation of anything but cotton." The size and condition of the herds Ball saw as he entered the Carolinas decreased apace. Only "small numbers of cattle" grazed in the occasional fallow field, Ball noted, "and these were thin and meager." His coffle "had met with no flocks of sheep of late, and the hogs that we saw on the road-side were in bad condition. The horses and mules that I saw in the cotton-fields, were poor and badly harnessed, and the half-naked condition of the negroes, who drove them, or followed with the hoe, together with their wan complexions, proved to me that they had too much work, or not enough food."[17]

Ball soon discovered that this caloric gap was, in truth, a double bind, not an either/or proposition: slaves labored too much *and* ate too little. Charles Ball recounted his journey from the comparatively gentle margins of slavery in the Chesapeake to the Deep South heart of darkness as a story of separation, dislocation, and violence. Yet because of the far-reaching consequences of the energetic shortfall between the labor that slaves in the cotton-producing South were compelled to exert and the scant, overwhelmingly vegetarian rations that their masters fed them, Ball chose to tell the story of *his* middle passage as a tale of absent animals, hungry slaves, and the perverse systems of production and domination that bound them together.[18]

Ball developed this analysis by repeatedly comparing the different material realities of his native Chesapeake with plantation life in South Carolina. In Ball's Maryland the livestock, the feed crops that sustained them, and the barns, fences, and other improvements that sheltered and confined domesticated animals structured the rural landscape.[19] Draft animals provided both motive power and fertilizer in the form of manure. They also transformed work regimes on the region's farms, increasing the productivity of slaves on larger plantations in particular. As progressive planters devoted more of their land to feed crops and pasture, they needed fewer slaves.[20] Planters hired out some of their hands and reassigned others to nonfarming tasks. Many Chesapeake masters, though, determined that the most profitable way to dispose of slaves that mixed husbandry had displaced was by selling them to traders—the diabolical dynamic that led first Ball's mother and siblings and then Charles Ball himself into the internal slave trade.[21] As flesh peddlers drove Chesapeake slaves south and west, their coffles pushed into new plantation belts where livestock were scarce and human chattel fetched the highest prices in the Union. Together agricultural diversification, the substitution of animal energy for human power and skill, and the intertwined markets in human chattel and livestock had dire consequences for Charles Ball and the million other slaves forced to abandon families, communities, and homelands they and their forebears had painstakingly built in the Upper South and border states.[22]

As Ball intuited but never fully articulated, the production of enslaved labor, and hence the reproduction of slavery itself, depended on sustenance provided by animals whose lives often began—and ended—far beyond the Deep South. After claiming that a "description of one great cotton plantation will give a correct idea of all others," Ball explicitly pointed out that on the South Carolina estate where his first exodus southward had led, "there was no smoke-house, nor any place for curing meat, and while I was on this plantation no food was ever salted for the use of the slaves."[23] The plantation on which Ball would spend the next several years of his life, like most others in the Carolina upcountry, maximized the production of cotton and other cash crops by importing hogs and pork from other producers. Many Deep South planters obtained some meat for their slaves from local suppliers, including white yeomen, Native American women, and even enslaved blacks. Most planters, though, also purchased animals and meat from farmers and packers in Kentucky, Tennessee, Ohio, and beyond.[24] The traffic in pork and hogs on the hoof bound the border states and even the Old Northwest to the Deep South.[25] Some planters recognized that the metabolic connections linking imported meat, slave labor, and cash-crop production rendered them exceedingly vulnerable: "The great curse of this country," a Louisiana sugar planter griped, was "that we are all planters and no farmers."[26] But slaves such as Charles Ball felt the pangs of this "great curse" in ways their masters never did.

The ominous undertones of Ball's observations about the scarcity of livestock in the Deep South reflected his grasp of the far-reaching consequences of animal absence for enslaved peoples. In Maryland, Ball had eaten meat regularly. He had also worked frequently with livestock, yoking, harnessing, and commanding oxen to do the work that Ball, his overseers, and his masters demanded. In South Carolina, by contrast, the only livestock Ball saw working in the fields looked like "moving skeletons."[27] Whatever labor these gaunt and malnourished creatures were unable to perform, Ball recognized, would become the obligation of human chattel. But given the scarcity and poor condition of hogs, sheep, and cows in the Deep South, Ball recognized that he and his fellow slaves would have to complete these travails on a diet almost totally lacking in meat.

A very particular kind of animalization thus characterized the dehumanization experienced and narrated by Charles Ball on his forced remove from Maryland to South Carolina. He obsessed over the paucity of livestock in the cotton kingdom because without draft animals, he would have to rely even more on his own muscles and wits than he had in Maryland. Without meat to eat, though, he would find it much harder to muster the vital energy to labor or even to live. In the Chesapeake, Ball had mastered livestock and eaten fish, bacon, and wild game. Getting sold south, though, reduced him to a mere beast of burden: an herbivorous reserve of motive power to be dominated; a commodity to be examined, prodded, bought, and sold.[28]

Ball detailed how the market could reduce a slave to an object of exchange—"a person with a price," in Walter Johnson's devastatingly succinct phrase.[29] Ball could not conclude his initial impressions of South Carolina without remarking, "I was now in a country where the life of a black man was no more regarded than that of an ox, except as far as the man was worth the more money in the market." He noted with disdain how his master "talked of selling us." Ball overheard conversations in which his master and another slaveholder bantered about "the price we would bring, with as little compunction of conscience as they would have talked of the sale of so many mules." The trader, Ball noted elsewhere, "never spoke of us, except to order us to be fed or watered, as he would have directed the same offices to be performed for so many horses, or to inquire where the best prices could be obtained for us. He regarded us only as objects of traffic and the materials of his commerce." When Ball and two young male comrades were placed on a Columbia auction block amid Independence Day festivities, "the crier . . . said, 'These three fellows are as strong as horses, and as patient as mules.'"[30]

Because Charles Ball understood that agricultural production required immense inputs of muscle power, he recognized that in the Cotton Belt, slaves were not just traded *like* livestock; they *were* livestock: "On all the plantations that we passed," Ball had portentously observed as his coffle shuffled toward Carolina, "there was a want of live stock of every description, except slaves, and they were deplorably abundant."[31]

The Politics and Infrapolitics of Meat

Mentions of food—its presence and absence, its quality and its poverty—permeate Ball's narrative.[32] Indeed, Ball's narrative reminds us of just how large hunger loomed in the black experience under bondage.[33] Ball's near-constant search for food joined his drive to reunite with his family and his quest to achieve freedom as the three main themes of *Slavery in the United States*. Ball recognized that his passage south threatened to knock him down the food chain. As Ball's head and heart grappled with the destruction of the family ties he had forged in the Chesapeake, the rest of his body struggled to reverse his forced displacement from omnivore to herbivore—from a man to a plant-eating draft animal.

Ball's sale south brought dietary changes in its wake. At the last of his Maryland homes, Ball and his fellow slaves "had a tolerable supply of meat for a short time" after the December hog-killing season. In spring Ball also enjoyed "an abundance of fish" from the Patuxent River and Chesapeake Bay. Through the end of fishing season, the slaves on Ball's plantation received "one salt herring every day." Ball had even greater access to meat and other animal products during his forced march south. After crossing into South Carolina, Ball's owner upped his slaves' meat intake to "two rations" a day. Some of Ball's companions expressed themselves as "much surprised at the kindness of our master." But Ball knew that "kindness" was not what motivated the trader: "I had no doubt that his object was to make us look fat and hearty, to enable him to obtain better prices for us." Indeed the soul driver soon distributed butter to his charges "as an extraordinary ration" that would not only "strengthen and recruit us after our long march" but also "give us a healthy and expert appearance at the time of our future sale."[34]

Ball ate more meat while enmeshed in the slave market as a human commodity than at any other period of his enslavement—far more than he initially received after the trader sold him "to one of the most wealthy planters in Carolina, who planted cotton, rice, indigo, corn, and potatoes."[35] The plantation's 260 slaves, like its livestock, received a vegetarian diet, though unlike livestock, the slaves were expected to mill and cook their own food. The near-total reliance of Ball and his fellow slaves on plant foods (chiefly maize, with occasional supplements of peaches, greens, and sweet potatoes) marked their degradation as chattel.

Ball intuited how rations served to domesticate him and his fellow slaves. Slaves, like dogs or oxen, depended on their masters for sustenance. Skimping on rations—especially imported meat, which was much more costly than locally raised plant foods—offered slaveholders undeniable economic benefits. Ball's narrative, though, also shows that planters and overseers astutely parlayed their control of meat into power over the enslaved.[36] Through occasional, highly strategic departures from routinized deprivation, white masters and managers cast themselves as benevolent patriarchs. "Whatever was given to us beyond the corn," Ball explained, "was considered in the light of a bounty bestowed upon us, over and beyond what we were entitled to, or had a right to expect to receive."[37]

Ball's master and overseer used meat to demonstrate their "generosity."[38] Ten days after Ball's arrival on the plantation, "a great feast at the quarter" was held to celebrate one of the seasonal milestones in the yearly round of labor on the estate. On his overseer's command, Ball selected, roped, drove, and butchered a beef cow to serve as the master's gift to "his" people.[39] The overseer then told each family of slaves to send a representative to the big house with a bowl to carry home that household's share of the beef.

Ball recalled his fellow slaves' groveling behavior on meat days with palpable scorn. News of the master's munificence "diffused as much joy amongst us, as if each one had drawn a prize in a lottery. At the assurance of a meat dinner, the old people smiled and showed their teeth and returned thanks to master overseer." Ball could not stop his own mouth from watering, but to his chagrin he discovered that "the meat dinner of this day was made up of the basket of tripe, and other offal . . . boiled in four great iron kettles, until the flesh had disappeared from the bones, which were broken in small pieces." This stew of viscera and marrow delighted Ball's fellow slaves: "I doubt if there was in the world a happier assemblage than ours, on this Saturday evening. We had finished one of the grand divisions of the labors of a cotton plantation, and were supplied with a dinner, which to the most of my fellow slaves appeared to be a great luxury, and most liberal donation on the part of our master, whom they regarded with sentiments of gratitude for this manifestation by his bounty." Imagine these slaves' delight, then, the following day, when the overseer distributed choicer cuts from the beef's forequarters accompanied by a boiled pudding of cornmeal and lard. The taste of animal flesh and the anticipation of the nutrition it would imbue to the plantation's work-worn hands triggered ecstasy in the slave quarters, inaugurating what Ball remembered as "a day of uninterrupted happiness."[40]

Calculated distributions of meat enabled slaveholders to manipulate slaves. Because the taste of flesh could temporarily reconcile bondspeople to their lot as chattel, it figured centrally in the plantation's regime of social control. "A man cannot well be miserable," Ball remarked, "when he sees every one about him immersed in pleasure; . . . I forgot for a time all the subjects of grief that were stored in my memory, all the acts of wrong that had been perpetrated against me, and entered with the most sincere and earnest sentiments in the participation of the felicity of our community." The master class then withdrew the material basis of the slaves' happiness. "After the feat of laying by the corn and cotton," Ball lamented, "we had no meat for several weeks."[41] Masters and overseers deliberately kept slaves hungry. Deprivation, after all, enabled slaveholders to deploy meat at their fancy, and thus to choreograph the "pleasure," forgetfulness, and quiescence that meat eating engendered.

Charles Ball realized that to limit his vulnerability to meat as social control, he had to obtain his own supply of flesh. He began to scheme soon after arriving on the South Carolina plantation. He "proposed" to the slave family with whom he was quartered that "whilst I should remain a member of the family, I would contribute as much towards its support" as Nero, the putative head of the household. Ball agreed to "bring all my earnings into the family stock, provided I might be treated as one of its members, and be allowed a portion of the proceeds of their patch or garden." After his hut mates accepted, Ball and the family "constituted one community."[42] Ball subsequently began "making wooden trays, and such other wooden vessels as were most in demand," using the money thus earned to buy "three coarse blankets," molasses, "and some other luxuries" for the family with whom he lodged.[43] Ball also began to venture into the woods at night to set snares.[44] He discovered that trapping and hunting provided not just food but also furs and hides, which Ball traded to local storekeepers to obtain goods that he and his household desired, "sometimes with, and at other times without, the consent of the overseer."[45]

By the end of his first winter in Carolina, Ball "had . . . become in some measure acquainted with the country, and began to lay and execute plans to procure supplies of such things as were not allowed me by my master." Ball "understood various methods of entrapping rackoons [*sic*], and other wild animals" from the forests and swamps abutting the fields in which he labored. He knew that "besides the skins, which were worth something," he could harvest enough "rackoons, opossums, and rabbits" to provide his household with "two or three meals a week. The woman with whom I lived," Ball remembered, "understood the way of dressing an opossum, and I was careful to provide one for our Sunday dinner every week, so long as these animals continued fat and in good condition."[46] By killing wild animals, Ball gained purchasing power and sustenance. Hunting and trapping enabled him to avoid the worst pangs of hunger and deprivation, and thus to parry attempts by his master and overseer to translate their control over livestock and meat into power over Charles Ball.

Not all slaves were able or willing to take wild game, as Ball learned. Hunting and trapping, like other forms of independent economic production by slaves, not only complicated power relationships between slaves and masters but also sustained inequalities within slave communities.[47] "Many of the families in the quarter caught no game," Ball reported, either because "the men did not understand trapping game" or they "were too indolent to go far enough from home to find good places for setting their traps." Prior to Ball's arrival, the family he joined had "seldom tasted animal food, or even fish, except on meat-days, as they were called"—the six or seven occasions each year "when meat was given to the people by the overseer, under the orders of our master." Most slave households "had no meat" save what they "received from the overseer."[48]

Ball could neither protect nor provide meat for his wife and children back in Maryland, yet he could still don the mantle of manly provider by bringing the beasts of the southern wild into his new home. Ball described Nero, "the head of the family" with whom he lived, as "a very quiet, worthy man; but slothful and inactive in his habits." Though Nero made baskets to sell and picked cotton for wages on Sunday, his labors had not "enable[d] him to provide any kind of meat for his family." Ball supplied flesh to Nero and the other fictive kin with whom he lodged, as well as to a consumption-ridden slave named Lydia. Lydia's husband, Ball contended, "had never been taught to do any kind of labor" because he had been a priest in his African home-land. By giving "a quarter of a rackoon or a small opossum" to Lydia, Ball offset the emasculating effects of enslavement by helping a woman in need.[49] Exchanges of meat thus solidified social bonds within the slave community.

Ball appealed to his readers' maternal sentiments, using moral suasion to highlight the violence that a diet poor in meat inflicted on slave families: "A mother will imagine the painful feelings experienced by a parent, in the cabin of a slave, when a small portion of animal food is procured, dressed and made ready for the table." Enslaved mothers and fathers saw even the smallest, poorest pieces of meat as "not only food, but medicine." Though an enslaved man remained "dependant [sic] at all times upon the arbitrary will of his master, or yet more fickle caprice of the overseer," the slave's children would nonetheless continue to "look up to him . . . as their protector and supporter." Since vegetarian rations proved "quite inadequate to sustain the body in the full and powerful tone of muscular action"—especially for chil-dren who had grown old enough to be "obliged to labour hard"—enslaved children expressed a "ravenous craving for fresh meat" that Ball found "pain-ful to witness, without being able to gratify it." Harvesting wild animals en-abled Ball to save himself and his household from such anguish, for "during the whole of this fall and winter, we usually had something to roast, at least twice a week, in our cabin."[50]

Crimes of the Flesh

The inevitable changing of the seasons forced Ball to devise new ways of get-ting animal protein—and thus new strategies for parlaying animals taken from the southern wilds into social power. With spring's approach, "game became scarce, and both rackoons and opossums grew poor and worthless." Ball realized that he had "to discover some new mode of improving the al-lowance allotted to me by the overseer." Setting his sights on the Congaree River, which flowed through the plantation on which he lived, Ball resolved to transubstantiate fish into bacon, leveraging his muscle power and knowl-edge of nature into a modicum of freedom from the control his master and overseer wielded via their command over meat.[51]

Ball's fishery scheme began one late winter day after Ball walked three miles to the river to inspect its surface. "From the appearance of the stream," Ball recounted, "I felt confident that it must contain many fish; and I went immediately to work to make a weir." He set the device in the river and soon "took as many fish from my weir as filled a half bushel measure." Ball called this catch "a real treasure," for it yielded a kind of currency that constituted "the most fortunate circumstance . . . since I came to the country."[52]

From the outset Ball sought to achieve larger ends through his skill at fishing: relief from fieldwork; control over the labor of others; and not least, an ample supply of bacon, his favorite meat of all. Thanks to his half bushel of shad, Ball "was enabled to show my generosity, but, like all mankind, even in my liberality, I kept myself in mind." He gave fish to his overlords—three "to the great house," with "a large fish to the overseer" for good measure. Ball's gifts brought thanks, but he described himself as "not only disappointed, but chagrined" that "this was all the advantage I received from this effort to court the favor of the great. . . . [I]f my master and young mistresses had nothing but words to give me for my fish, we should not carry on a very large traffic." Just as Ball was about to seek other outlets for vending his shad, though, the master called Ball back to the big house and asked Ball to account for his prowess as a fisherman. Ball told him that he "had been employed at a fisher on the Patuxent, every spring, for several years." Impressed, Ball's owner replied that "he had a thought of having a seine made; and of placing me at the head of a fishing party, for the purpose of trying to take a supply of fish for his hands." Ball could barely contain his delight: "I now began to hope that there would be some respite from the labors of the cotton field, and that I should not be doomed to drag out a dull and monotonous existence, within the confines of the enclosures of the plantation."[53]

Ball spent the next two weeks knitting a seine while enjoying a house servant's privilege of "a little cold meat every day." Ball then took three other slaves "to the river to clear out a fishery," "a disagreeable job" that required the men to wade shoulder deep into cold water to remove snags and trunks from the river bottom. The work was so unpleasant, Ball remembered, that it gave him "cause to regret my removal from the plantation." Ball was troubled by the work he had undertaken but he also resented the terms his master had proposed. Ball's owner had suggested that Ball "should be able to gain some advantage to myself, by disposing of a part of the small fish that might be taken at the fishery." The arrival of "an ill-looking stranger" at the fishing ground, sent by Ball's master "to take charge of the fishery, and superintend all the work that was to be done at it," threatened to undermine Ball's chances of turning shad into "advantage."[54]

It did not take long, though, for the irrepressible Ball to cut a deal with the white yeoman he called "the fish master." With the yeoman's permission,

Ball resumed effective management of the fishery. Historians have often found it useful to partition the quest of slaves for autonomy into discrete categories of action. Charles Ball, however, inhabited a world in which a slave's expertise at fishing could simultaneously give him control over his labor, protect him from punishment, *and* make him the master of his own destiny. Ball sensed opportunity in the fact that his new boss "knew nothing of fishing with a seine," the tackle on which the fishery's success hinged. Ball took charge of "laying out and drawing in the seine." By laboring dutifully and productively, Ball and his fellow slaves gained the fish master's trust. Eventually the yeoman, who seemed to desire nothing more than a good night's sleep, "proposed to us all that if we would not let the affair be known to our master, he would leave us to manage the fishery at night according to our discretion." Ball thereby achieved "the object that I had held very near my heart ever since we began to fish at this place": the "authority to keep the other hands at work." Thereafter, Ball claimed, all the slaves at the fishery "lived well, and did not perform more work than we were able to bear." Equally important, the men now had "no fear of being punished." The fish master, Ball explained, "was now at least as much in my power as I was in his." If betrayed by Ball or the others, he could lose both his job and "all the profits of his share of the fishery."[55]

Even after Ball "obtained the virtual command of the fishery," a further goal beckoned: turning fish into flesh. "Since my arrival in Carolina," Ball bemoaned, "I had never enjoyed a full meal of bacon." Having become de facto overseer of the fishery, Ball now endeavored "to procure such a supply of that luxury, as would enable me and all my fellow-slaves at the fishery to regale ourselves at pleasure." Keelboats plying the Congaree River regularly hauled salt pork and bacon imported from the Upper South into the cotton kingdom. Such boats mostly traveled during the day, so when Ball saw one such vessel "working up the river about sundown" to anchor for the night across the river from Ball's fish camp, he suspected that fortune was smiling on him. Ball paddled over and forthrightly asked the ship's captain if he would be willing to swap bacon for shad.[56]

The keelboat captain told Ball that "he had a little" bacon, "but, as the risk he would run in dealing with a slave was great," Ball would have "to pay him more than the usual price"—"at least twice as much," it turned out, "as the bacon was worth." Ball disliked dealing on such unfavorable terms, but his "keen appetite for the bacon . . . settled the controversy." Ball and his companions paddled back across the river, hauled in their seine, counted out three hundred shad, and loaded the fish into their canoe. Racing back to the keelboat "with all possible dispatch," they completed the transaction. The captain gave the slaves "good weight," and then Ball and his companions returned to their camp. Over the previous months Ball had employed trapping, hunting, and fishing to obtain the animal protein his master and overseer had intentionally denied him. Now he had turned the shad that he and his comrades yanked from the river by the sweat of their brows into bacon, the meat they coveted above all others.[57]

Because the fish legally belonged to the master, and trading with slaves violated state law, Ball felt compelled to justify this doubly illicit exchange to his readers: "I was never acquainted with a slave who believed that he violated any rule of morality by appropriating to himself any thing that belonged to his master, if it was necessary to his comfort." Food, Ball claimed, occupied a special position in the slaves' moral economy: it fulfilled basic human needs, solidified communal relationships among "equally needy" slaves, drew upon common resources, and represented a product of the slaves' own labors. Ball claimed never to have deprived any of the masters he had served "of anything against his consent, unless it was some kind of food," which he invariably shared with other slaves.[58]

Ball described himself and his guiltless companions as "much rejoiced at being in possession of a hundred pounds of good flitch bacon." The men's triumph, though, meant that they now had a secret to keep. Ball and his coconspirators hid their newly acquired bacon "in an old salt barrel, and safely deposited in a hole dug for the purpose in the floor of my cabin." Since "fried flitch can be smelled a mile by a good nose," they also agreed always to mask the characteristic odor of their contraband by boiling the bacon instead of frying it.[59]

The ensuing section of *Slavery in the United States* illustrated the wisdom of these precautions. After another slave at the fishery began to trade cotton stolen from the plantation warehouses with the same boat captain, Ball's master swiftly called "a general meeting" in which he and neighboring planters resolved to unleash a pogrom against "the many white men who, residing in the district without property, or without interest in preserving the morals of the slaves, were believed to carry on an unlawful and criminal traffic with the negroes."[60] Even more alarming to Ball, though, was a maudlin incident Ball recounted at great length.

When the daughter of a neighboring planter was kidnapped, raped, and murdered, two house servants accused Ball of the crime. Ball then used his woodsman's knowledge of the countryside beyond the plantation's bound-aries to locate the criminals—the same two house servants who had tried to pin blame for the crime on Ball. Patrollers shot and wounded one of the servants as he fled. A bloodhound "mangled" the other "in a shocking manner" by shearing "a large piece of flesh entirely away from one side of his breast." The assembled whites then "unanimously sentenced" the two slaves to death, or-dering them to be stripped "and bound down securely upon their backs, on the naked earth, . . . to be left to be devoured alive by the carrion crows and buzzards, which swarm in every part of South Carolina." Years later, Ball claimed, the "exceedingly superstitious" slaves in the neighborhood still "re-ported and believed" that they could hear "the panting breath of the ago-nized suffer, quivering under the beaks of his tormentors, as they consumed his vitals."[61] The planter class, as Ball knew full well, adroitly conscripted animals—horses, dogs, and even scavenging birds—to maintain their power over enslaved African Americans.[62]

It is easy to dismiss this part of *Slavery in the United States* as simply a novelistic digression—gothic melodrama of the sort Edgar Allan Poe would begin to publish just a few years after Ball's narrative appeared. These pas-sages, however, also offered an extended meditation on guilt and punishment. Ball left no doubt that the slaves he helped catch were indeed guilty of raping and killing a neighboring planter's daughter; the men's attempt to pin blame on Ball shattered whatever sympathy he might have felt for them. Yet some thirty years after crows and buzzards had carried out the planters' sentence of death by avian torture, Ball remained haunted by the ease and ferocity with which masters enlisted wild animals to inflict terror on the enslaved—and so to make manifest the inhuman discipline on which human bondage depended.

Ball expressed not a shred of remorse for the instrumental role he played in the two killers' capture. Yet he also knew that he was guilty of other crimes of the flesh: of colluding with the fish master to superintend the fishery him-self, treating his master's shad as if it were his own, and surreptitiously swap-ping those fish for bacon. Ball understood, moreover, that slaveholders who had seen fit to sentence other slaves to be pecked to death by crows and buz-zards were capable of anything. Imagine his horror, then, when just minutes after leaving the place where the murderers had been stripped and bound, his overseer suddenly shouted for Ball "to come forward and let the gentlemen see me." After inspecting Ball's visage "with a kind of leer or side glance," a planter whom Ball "had never before seen, said, 'Boy, you appear to live well; how much meat does your master allow you in a week?'"[63] Ball found himself "almost totally confounded at the name of meat."[64] The very word dripped with blood and reeked of power. Its mention in this supercharged context instantaneously transformed Charles Ball from the hunter into the hunted. The overseers and planters whose eyes had all turned on Ball, after all, were fresh from the kill. They were, moreover, hell-bent on stomping out the shadowy exchange networks through which Charles Ball and other slaves vied to escape their subjugation as chattel—as quiescent, plant-eating livestock whose value inhered in their muscles instead of their minds.

Yet Ball was not easily cowed. He regained his composure, forced "a sort of smile," and donned a mask of calculated subservience. "My master," he told his interrogator, "has been very kind to all his people of late, but has not allowed us any meat for some weeks. . . . If master would please to give us a little meat now and then, we should be very thankful for it." Ball's overseer, though, responded to this performance with skepticism: "Charles, you need not tell lies about it; you have been eating meat, I know you have." The overseer cited Ball's appearance as proof of his guilt: "No negro could look as fat, and sleek, and black, and greasy, as you, if he had nothing to eat but corn bread and river chubs. You do not look at all as you did before you went to the fishery; and all the hands on the plantation have had as many chubs and other river fish as they could eat, . . . and yet they are as poor as snakes in comparison with you. Come, tell the truth, let us know where you get the meat that you have been eating and you shall not be whipped." Ball tried to duck these charges by emphasizing that he had done nothing to transgress the plantation's dietary order. He cast himself as "a poor slave . . . obliged to live on bread and fresh water fish." The overseer dismissed this "palaver" with an ominous declaration: "I smell the meat in you this moment. Do I not see the grease as it runs out of your face?"[65]

Ball, desperate to save himself, boldly challenged the overseer to examine the faces of every other slave at the fishery. The assembled masters and overseers accepted Ball's reasoning that if Ball's companions looked less healthy—less "fat, and sleek"—than Charles Ball, then Ball's gig was up. Miraculously the ruse worked. The overseer stood down, and Ball resumed fishing.[66] The slaves kept their secret—and their bacon. Had Ball been caught, he would have faced brutal punishment. As it was, though, he had managed to elude one of the most palpable consequences of having been sold south: the hunger for meat that, among other characteristics, distinguished human chattel from other livestock.

In Ball's telling, animals rendered into meat embodied an economy of energy and power. As Ball penetrated Deep South landscapes increasingly bereft of domesticated animals, he literally and figuratively descended to a lower level of animal being. The degeneration of his body and his stature went hand in hand. By trapping wild animals, fishing, and trading for meat summoned the physical energy to maintain his wits—and thus his humanity.

Hunter and Hunted

Had Charles Ball continued living along the Congaree, where he had adroitly carved out ecological and social niches for himself, he might never have escaped from bondage. As it was, events soon conspired to change the course of his life. Animals continued to play leading roles in the second half of Ball's narrative. Indeed as *Slavery in the United States* turned from Ball's final months in South Carolina to his forced migration to Georgia and finally to a succession of perilous escapes interspersed with stints of uncertain freedom, the menagerie of nonhuman creatures populating Ball's narrative grew both larger and more dangerous still.

The waning of the shad runs in mid-April forced two significant changes. Ball, having lost his access to fish (and hence to bacon), fell back on his "own expedients for the purpose of procuring something in the shape of animal food." Raccoons, opossums, and other wild mammals were too thin to eat, so he resorted to catching turtles.[67] More important, Ball left the fishery, where he had overseen his own work and that of his fellow slaves, for the fields, where he exerted much less control over his own labor.

In a small decision that had monumental implications for Ball's future, the overseer commanded him to take charge of a two-mule plow. Ball had experience with oxen, but he encountered "much trouble" with the mules. It did not take long, however, for Ball to master these famously stubborn animals.[68] Ball's freshly acquired competence with mules combined with his newfound skill at picking cotton to make him an ideal gift upon the marriage of one of his master's daughters. Ball and about a dozen other slaves became the property of the bridegroom, a man of humble means who brought no slaves of his own to the marriage. Ball's new master, like so many upwardly mobile but landless white men of the day, set his sights on rich agricultural lands in the West, on a parcel ceded by the Creek Nation in the 1802 Treaty of Fort Wilkinson. With Ball's account of driving a six-mule team through

Augusta and into the new American settlements of north-central Georgia in the fall of 1806, *Slavery in the United States* accelerated toward an enthralling, ultimately tragic conclusion.[69]

Ball's new life in the burgeoning cotton kingdom began prosaically. He found the labor of establishing a new plantation grueling but also rewarding. One of his first jobs upon arrival was to build "a stable for the mules." Soon, Ball's master purchased "several cows and more than twenty hogs," none of which "required any feeding at our hands," since "the woods were full of nuts, and the grass was abundant." Ball recalled that he and his fellow slaves "now lived very differently from what we did on my old master's plantation. We had as much bacon every day as we could eat."[70]

This comparatively idyllic phase in Ball's bondage, however, quickly ended after Ball's master and mistress died in close succession, he in a duel, she in childbirth. Ball consequently found himself attached to "an estate . . . advertised to be rented for the term of seven years, with all the stock of mules, cattle, and so forth, upon it—together with seventeen slaves."[71] The man who leased this estate—and with it Charles Ball—was kindly but consumption-stricken.

His wife immediately impressed Ball as "the worst woman I ever saw amongst the southern people. Her temper was as bad as that of a speckled viper; and her language, when she was enraged, was a mere vocabulary of profanity and virulence." This hissing serpent of a woman soon inflicted a change of rations on Ball and his fellow slaves: "Our allowance of meat was withdrawn," Ball lamented—a drastic change since the slaves heretofore "had meat in abundance."[72] With his master's health declining, Ball knew that his mistress was bound to assume greater control over his day-to-day life.

Ball responded to the elimination of meat from his rations by again turning to the woods. He fondly recalled how his ailing master "gave me an old gun that had seen much hard service, for the stock was quite shattered to pieces, and the lock would not strike fire." Though Georgia law forbade slaves from carrying guns, Ball took the weapon "to a blacksmith in the neighborhood, and he repaired the lock, so that my musket was as sure fire as any piece need be." Ball remembered how the weapon made him feel like a new kind of man. "For the first time in my life," he became "a hunter, in the proper sense of the word," vested with the force not simply to lure small game into traps, but to blast away any of God's creatures with a single pull of the trigger. As for "the country" Ball now inhabited, it "was new," a hunter's paradise, "abound[ing] with every sort of game common to a new settlement," including snakes, "panthers, wolves, and other beasts of prey."[73]

Charles Ball swiftly sought to establish himself as the alpha predator in these Georgia woods. By laboring tirelessly on the plantation all week, Ball was able "to get the half of Saturday to myself." He "appropriated" this and any other free time he could muster "to hunting, . . . and I soon became pretty expert in the use of my gun." Ball also learned to "ma[k]e salt licks in the woods, to which the deer came at night, and I shot them from a seat of clap-boards that was placed on the branches of a tree."[74] To chase deer and "tree rackoons and bears," Ball enlisted Trueman, whom he described as "a dog of my own which I had brought with me from Carolina, and which was an ex-cellent hunting dog."[75]

The dog's name hinted at the depths of Ball's affection even as it offered an implicit rebuke to the presumptions of human mastery that undergirded American slavery. Ball celebrated Trueman as "so faithful, that I thought he would lose his life, if necessary, in my defence." The dog's trustworthiness and virility suffice to explain the name Ball bestowed upon him. Yet the mon-iker also crackled with irony: What did it mean for Charles Ball to own a dog whose name embodied Ball's own aspirations—his own quest to show that he was more than a piece of property or a draft animal, but was himself a true man? Did it feel wrong or right for Ball to command the dog, to pun-ish him, to use meat to reduce him to domesticated subservience? Ball left such questions unanswered, leaving no clues other than the poignancy of the dog's name, and a remarkable scene of parting to which we will soon turn.

Torture and Companionship

Aided by Trueman, the gun, and his own wits, Ball "began to live well, not-withstanding the persecution that my mistress still directed against me, and to feel myself, in some measure, an independent man." The collapsing health of Ball's master, though, jeopardized the independent manliness that Ball had managed to stake out. Ball's master confided in late autumn "that he believed he should not live long, as he already felt the symptoms of approaching decay and death."[76]

A strange incident that Ball witnessed on a visit to another plantation caused him to revisit the master class's resort to animals as instruments of torture; the same incident also foreshadowed trouble ahead for Charles Ball.

God, as Ball's readers well knew, gave man dominion over the rest of his creation in Genesis 1:26. Ball cast chattel slavery as blasphemy by portraying how white Georgians flouted God's command by using a cat to punish and dominate their human slaves. As Ball looked on in horror, an overseer informed the hands under his command that someone had taken and slaughtered "a fat hog from the pen." The overseer threatened the slaves "that if they did not confess, and tell who the perpetrators of this theft were, they would all be whipped in the severest manner." Not a soul made a peep. The overseer ordered everyone to lie down and then dispensed "a share of the lash" to each. The rawhide failed to force a confession. Then a "well-dressed gentleman" from another plantation asked the overseer if he "had ever tried cat-hauling, upon an obstinate negro."[77] The overseer dispatched a boy to fetch "a large gray tom-cat," which the visitor "placed upon the bare back of the prostrate black man, near the shoulder, and forcibly dragged by the tail down the back, and along the bare thighs of the sufferer." The cat "sunk his nails into the flesh, and tore off pieces of the skin with his teeth" as the "gentleman" heaved the cat up and down the man's back and legs.

The unfortunate slave "roared with the pain of this punishment" and then admitted that he and three accomplices had taken the master's swine. The overseer rewarded the confessor by subjecting him to "another touch of the cat." Each of his supposed accomplices were then "compelled to lie down, and have the cat twice drawn along his back; first downwards, and then upwards." A final mortification completed the torture, as "each of the sufferers was washed with salt water."[78]

Ball declared cat-hauling "the most excruciating punishment that I ever saw inflicted on black people."[79] Forcing a cat to torture slaves epitomized the dehumanization at the heart of *Slavery in the United States*. To Ball, cat-hauling demonstrated the abomination of a system in which white men deployed beasts to break the will of "black people" whose only offense was to act on their yearning for meat—a yearning that their master had fostered by systematically depriving them of animal flesh.

Soon thereafter Ball resolved to run away after suffering a more conventional but equally brutal punishment. His mistress's brothers laid a "full three hundred lashes" on Ball's back for no other reason than "they thought a good whipping would be good for me." Ball, "indignant at the barbarity with which I had been treated," immediately began to lay plans to escape home to the Chesapeake. Loyalty to his master prompted Ball to bide his time until the man perished, three months later. With his master's death, Ball "felt the parting of the last tie that bound me to the place where I then was, and my heart yearned for my wife and children, from whom I had now been separated more than four years."[80]

By running away, Ball would break every social bond he had forged since moving to Georgia, but he found only one farewell worth recounting in *Slavery in the United States*: his parting with Trueman. At first Ball was "anxious" to take his dog along, but he soon had second thoughts. His "success" as a runaway, after all, "depended on secrecy and silence," exigencies that the dog, despite his many virtues, could not reliably fulfill. After much anguish Ball deemed "it safest to abandon my last friend, and engage in my perilous enterprise alone." Ball and Trueman shared a final supper. Then Ball tied the dog up "with a rope to a small tree." Beside the dog Ball leaned his musket, reckoning that he would "be better without the gun than with it."[81]

Just as Ball was about to depart, though, he noticed his "poor dog . . . looking wistfully" at him. Ball turned back toward Trueman, who "licked [Ball's] hands." After "rising on his hind feet and placing his fore paws on my breast," Trueman "uttered a long howl, which thrilled through my heart." Ball thought it was "as if he had said, 'My master, do not leave me behind you.'"[82]

Across the species divide, the man heard Trueman clearly voice his sentiments. Ball judged it only reasonable to answer the dog's pleas. He spoke back to Trueman, "talk[ing] to him as to a creature that understood language, and was sensible of the dangers I was going to meet." In what was almost certainly the strangest passage in Ball's entire narrative, he recounted a touching farewell speech in which Ball addressed his dog directly, using the formal second-person voice peculiar to Quakers such as Isaac Fisher, the country lawyer who edited *Slavery in the United States*:

Poor Trueman, faithful Trueman, fare thee well. Thou hast been an honest dog, and sure friend to thy master in all his shades of fortune. When my basket was well filled, how cheerfully we have partaken together of its contents. I did not then upbraid thee, that thou atest in idleness the proceeds of my labour, for I knew that thy heart was devoted to thy protector. In the day of my adversity, when all the world had forsaken me, when my master was dead, and I had no friend to protect me, still, poor Trueman, thou wert the same. . . . When I had no crumbs in my basket to give thee, nor crust in my pocket to divide with thee, thy faithful heart failed not; and a glance from the eye of thy hungry master filled thee with gratitude and joy.[83]

Ball explicitly upheld Trueman's moral superiority: "Man is selfish and heartless," he told the dog. "The richest of them all are as wretched slaves as I am, and are only minions of fear and avarice. Could pride and ambition witness thy fidelity and gratitude to thy forsaken master, and learn humility from thy example," Ball marveled, "how many tears would be wiped from the eyes of sorrow."[84] There is no sign that Ball ever regretted the mastery he had exercised over Trueman. It seems telling nonetheless that at the very instant Ball stood poised to consummate his metamorphosis from slave to true man, he implicitly questioned the justice of one creature owning and commanding another, even as he proceeded to leave Trueman tied to a tree to await an unknown fate.

Fugitive Creatures and the Vagaries of Freedom

Having exchanged words and feelings with his companion, Ball "took to the forest," using the stars to pursue a "north course." The hunter, having cast off his dog and gun, became the hunted. Ball perceived his ensuing encounters with dangerous wild beasts such as a "large alligator . . . moving in full pursuit" as omens "of the dangers that I must encounter on my journey to the north."[85] Yet Ball soon learned that animals under human command posed even greater dangers.

On the first morning of his flight north, Ball narrowly avoided two white men hunting deer on horseback as they discussed "an advertisement at the store, which offered a hundred dollars reward for the runaway, whose name was Charles." Ball experienced an even closer brush a few days later, this time with mounted patrollers who stopped to water their horses "not more than ten yards from me." Ball overheard the patrollers say that they were searching for a runaway "called Charles, in the advertisement." A few harrowing moments elapsed. Then the horsemen moved on, leaving Ball to count his blessings. Ball, "now certain, that the whole country had been advised of my flight," vowed henceforth to control his "movements, [so] as to wrap my very existence, in a veil of impenetrable secrecy."[86]

Mounting hunger, however, eventually forced Ball to take chances. About a week after he first ran away, the "loud growl of a dog" greeted Ball as he stole peaches from an orchard. Ball tried to escape, but two dogs followed, forcing Ball to slay "the largest and fiercest of the dogs." Ball got away by walking all night, but trouble soon caught up to him. As Ball was slumbering in a thicket the next day he awoke and "heard the noise of men's voices, and soon after the tramping of horses on the ground." The "troop," Ball reckoned, included "at least twenty horsemen" and more dogs than Ball "could count." He later remembered how "horses and voices were at my back, around me, and over me." For a few heart-stopping moments, the human and animal embodiments of white southern mastery seemed to surround Ball. "If they could find me," Ball realized, he would "be hunted down like a wild beast." Fortunately, though, the dogs on Ball's trail "had not been trained to hunt negroes." As for the patrollers, they dismissed their horses' clear "alarm" at Ball's presence.[87]

To protect himself from horses, dogs, and the men who harnessed and leached these creatures to police the plantation order, Ball resolved to travel only between midnight and 3:00 A.M. This decision slowed his progress considerably. By mid-October, after two months of flight, he had made it just to Columbia, South Carolina—an easy week's walk from the Georgia plantation on which he had started. With winter bearing down, Ball steeled himself for the long and grueling journey still before him.[88]

Trekking across the South Carolina upcountry, "a sensation of hunger harassed [him] constantly," for Ball had found no meat to eat since leaving Georgia. Ball had no qualms about dispatching any creature who crossed his path. In short order, the fugitive used his walking stick to slay a "very fat" opossum, a rabbit, and a groundhog. By the time Ball crossed into North Carolina in early December, he had feasted on a second opossum—"as fat as a well-fed pig"—and "several fowls" stolen by a fellow runaway.[89]

Famine followed this procession of feasts. "The means of subsistence," Ball lamented, "became every day more difficult to be obtained." Just as his deprivation was growing unbearable, Ball ran across "several pigs which appeared to be wild, having no marks on their ears." Ball killed one of the hogs with a stone and then "regale[d]" his famished body "with the flesh of the pig." Ball ate his fill and then roasted the remaining pork and packed it in his knapsack. The meat lasted for weeks. By the time Ball reached Virginia in March, though, he had again been "reduced to the utmost extremity for want of provisions."[90]

Weeks of gnawing hunger and Ball's mounting impatience together led him to commit a "great indiscretion." Nearing Maryland, Ball neglected to find a suitable hiding place before nightfall. As the road carried him beside a house, "a white man opened the door" and ordered Ball to halt. Ball refused to obey, so the man "set his dog upon me." Ball tried to defend himself with his walking stick, but the white man shot him in the legs. "A party of patrollers" soon arrived, tied Ball up, and "dragged [him] by the feet back to the house." They then "threw" the wounded slave "into the kitchen, like a dead dog." The vital fugitive, it seemed, had been reduced to an insensible beast.[91]

In time, though, Ball would resurrect himself. He had suffered too much on his seven-month journey and come too close to reuniting with his wife and children to relent. Patrollers could treat Ball "like a dead dog," but he remained a true man. He nursed his wounds and bided his time until opportunity arrived. Angered one morning by his jailer's failure to bring him breakfast, Ball pounded against his cell door, which he "discovered by its sound, to be a mere hollow shell, encrusted with a thin coat of sound timber." Ball kept quiet until nightfall and then busted out.[92]

After crossing the Potomac, he hastened to his wife's cabin. Even as the runaway reunited with his family, food and hunger continued to gnaw at him. Ball recounted how his children "had forgotten me. When I attempted to take them in my arms, they fled from me." Only Ball's eldest child, "who was four years old when I was carried away, still retained some recollections of once having had a father, but could not believe that I was that father." Ball described how his wife "seemed to awake from a dream; and gathering all three of her children in her arms, thrust them into my lap, as I sat in the corner, clapped her hands, laughed, and cried by turns." But nourishment was never far from Charles Ball's mind. "In her ecstasy," Ball recounted in *Slavery in the United States,* his wife forgot to feed him "until I at length told her that I was hungry." She made a meal and served it to Ball, but food could not give Ball the kind of sustenance he really needed. The famished fugitive had returned home thinking that he "could eat anything in the shape of food; but now that I attempted to eat, my appetite had fled, and I sat up all night with my wife and children." Ball recalled how with "the object of my labors attained, . . . that firmness of resolution which had so long sustained me, suddenly vanished from my bosom." Throughout a sleepless night, the "melancholy foreboding of [his] future destiny" weighed Ball down. "The idea that I was utterly unable to afford protection and safeguard to my own family . . . tormented my bosom with alternate throbs of affection and fear, until the dawn broke in the east, and summoned me to decide upon my future conduct."[93]

Ball placed his fate in the hands of the master and mistress who had sold him south four years earlier. They advised Ball to hide out until suspicion had passed, then to find "work in the neighborhood for wages . . . among the farmers." Ball did as he was told. He remained with his family in Calvert County and fought valiantly against the British in the War of 1812. At war's end in 1814, he "went to work in Baltimore, as a free black man." Over the course of the next sixteen years, Ball labored in Baltimore, Annapolis, "and frequently in Washington." His first wife died in 1816; four years later Ball used $350 accumulated through hard work and "constant economy" to buy twelve acres of land outside Baltimore. In *Slavery in the United States,* Ball told with pride how he built "a small house, and became a farmer on my own account, and upon my own property."[94]

Ball's quest for landed independence relied on his skills husbanding livestock. He "purchased a yoke of oxen and two cows, and became a regular attendant of the Baltimore market, where I sold the products of my own farm and dairy." Within just a few years Ball had brought the farm "into very good culture, and had increased my stock of cattle to four cows and several younger animals."[95] His family grew apace with his herds; Ball remarried, and his second wife bore four children.

Had *Slavery in the United States* concluded there, it might have read like a paean to American fecundity, freedom, and upward mobility. "I now lived very happily," Ball recounted, "and had an abundance of all the necessaries of life around me. . . . I now looked forward to an old age of comfort, if not of ease; but I was soon to be awakened from this dream."[96]

As Ball was plowing the Maryland soil in June 1830, some two decades after his remarkable flight home across the southern upcountry, a man identifying himself as Baltimore's sheriff rode up to his fence and claimed to have a writ for Ball's arrest. Ball was subsequently jailed and returned to Georgia. Once back in the bonds of slavery, he redoubled his struggle for liberty. First Ball tried to win his freedom in court. When that failed, he attempted to run away only to be recaptured. Eventually he escaped, hid in the hold of a northbound cotton vessel, and alighted in Philadelphia. He immediately set out for his old Maryland farm to find his wife and children. On arrival Ball learned the horrible news: during his absence his wife and children has been ripped from their beds in the night and sold to a slave dealer in Baltimore.

Charles Ball lived on. *Slavery in the United States,* though, drew to a peremptory close. Ball's silence spoke volumes. He spent just two short paragraphs on the time that had passed since discovering that his family had been sold south: "For the last few years," Ball blandly remarked, "I have resided about fifty miles from Philadelphia, where I expect to pass the evening of my life, working hard for my subsistence, without the least hope of ever again seeing my wife and children:—fearful, at this day, to let my place of residence be known, lest even yet it may be supposed, that as an article of property, I am of sufficient value to be worth pursuing in my old age."[97]

Black Freedom and Animal Rights

Tracking animals through *Slavery in the United States* reveals slaves literally and figuratively rendered into animals; it also exposes the material and cultural implications of animals rendered into meat. In the process of unmasking the physical, economic, and ideological dynamics of power, this intertwined story of slaves, slaveholders, and other creatures sheds new light on the familiar history of bondage and freedom. The lived experience of Charles Ball—a man whose world was inhabited by other slaves and pigs, overseers and mules, slaveholders and shad and, not least, a dog named Trueman—illuminates the pressing need for studies of slavery that transcend human/animal, nature/culture binaries. At the same time, however, *Slavery in the United States* never allows its readers to forget that the most ferocious beasts in all the southern wild assumed human form. Even in Pennsylvania, Charles Ball sensed them stalking. So the fugitive hid, and remembered, and told his story.

Through the act of narrative, Ball asserted his personhood. By bearing witness to slavery's pervasive inhumanity, he proved beyond a doubt that he was more than a beast of burden, an alpha predator, or a species of prey to be tracked, flushed out, and destroyed. Ball staked his claim to humanity by telling stories in which animals and animalization made and maintained the South's slave society. Even as the fugitive secreted away his real identity, Charles Ball materialized on the printed page as narrator and tragic hero— undeniably human kinds of being.

Read as an interspecies slave narrative, Charles Ball's telling of his unrelenting push for power, freedom, and humanity implores scholars to forsake the human exceptionalism that has too long constrained slavery studies. Ball's inability to relate his experiences and understandings of *Slavery in the United States* without repeatedly returning to the capacity of nonhuman creatures to shape his life's journey, and his life story, should inspire scholars to reconsider the entanglements and contradictions binding two fields of analysis: first, the fraught material and cultural relationships between human and nonhuman animals in slave societies; and second, the narrative and rhetorical acts by which fugitive slaves and their allies sought to undermine the prevailing justifications for reducing human beings to a species of property.

Viewed in this light, Ball's narrative raises an unexpected and tantalizing question: Why have scholars and activists alike assumed that the roots of contemporary animal-rights philosophies and politics must have originated with white abolitionists, but not with their black counterparts? Most animal-rights advocates, ethicists, and historians agree that organized movements to prevent cruelty to animals began with the abolitionist campaigns that began to shake the Atlantic world in the late 1700s and early 1800s.[98] But what if we look beyond the white moral crusaders widely regarded as the founding mothers and fathers of the animal-welfare and animal-liberation movements? These movements, after all, emerged from the great struggles for human rights galvanized by Charles Ball and the many other fugitive slaves who courageously testified about the injustices they had suffered and witnessed. At the very least, Ball's *Slavery in the United States* should convince us just how much we can learn about the past by contemplating the nonhuman animals who have always lurked near the heart of histories too blithely misconstrued as exclusively human dramas.

Chapter 3

Stuffed: Nature and Science on Display

John Herron

If you wish to see the lone survivor of the 1876 Battle of Little Bighorn, visit the Natural History Museum at the University of Kansas. Tucked into a dark corner on the fourth floor is a humidity-controlled glass case containing the stuffed remains of a twenty-nine-year-old decorated veteran from Custer's Last Stand. Nicknamed "Comanche" because of his bravery in past Indian engagements, he was found two days after the battle by a military recovery and burial team; he was still bleeding from a severe shoulder wound. A steamer rushed him to North Dakota's Fort Abraham Lincoln, where army surgeons removed three bullets from his broken body. A fourth bullet, too deep and too dangerous to be removed, remained. Weakened by the experience, this soldier remained in the service but would never see active duty again. After he succumbed to colic in 1891, the army marked his death with full military honors. At the museum, however, the St. Louis native is in top form: he stands erect, head held high, hair combed, shoes polished, and dressed in the full military uniform of the famous Seventh Cavalry Regiment. If the display of a soldier's cadaver seems a little morbid, know that Comanche is a horse.[1]

"The Brave Horse" Comanche is impressive, but he is not the star attraction of the museum. That honor goes to the Panorama of North American Plants and Animals. The panorama is a massive, multistory diorama containing more than 120 stuffed animals. As visitors walk around the circular dis-

Figure 3.1. Panorama of North American Plants and Animals at the Chicago World's Fair. Photo courtesy of University Archives, Spencer Research Library, University of Kansas.

play, they travel through the continent's divergent ecosystems. Starting in the rain forest of Central America, guests see tapirs and toucans grouped amid fig trees, arrowroot bushes, and patches of wild cacao. At the opposite end of the panorama, jungle gives way to ice as harbor seals and polar bears search for food amid stands of black spruce and arctic willow. The largest sections of the panorama are devoted to the Great Plains and the Rocky Mountains. There museum patrons see moose, mountain lions, and most impressive, American bison. A collection of badgers, beavers, bears, otters, ocelots, wolves, and wolverines, all gathered around an artificial lake, completes the scene. Even in an age of museum animatronics and modern video displays, the panorama is impressive.

Wonder does not translate into popularity, however. The Kansas Museum of Natural History looks exactly as an underfunded university museum should. Exhibits are dated, interactive models are broken, and each time I have visited the panorama, I was the only patron in the room. But it was not always so, for the panorama had a brilliant beginning. The display was first unveiled as the centerpiece of the Kansas State Pavilion at the 1893 Chicago World's Fair. The Kansas building was large—one of the biggest state pavilions of the fair—and the panorama dominated the structure. Eight railroad cars crammed with animals and accessories were required to ship the panorama from Lawrence, Kansas, and once these were in Chicago, five technicians worked for several hectic months to ready the display for viewing.[2] In an event dedicated to celebrating American progress and technological achievement, it was this motley collection of stuffed things that captured everyone's attention. Nearly fifteen thousand visitors saw the panorama on opening day, immediately establishing the animals as a World's Fair must-see. Hometown newspapers, such as the *Kansas City Star*, helped create an early buzz. The panorama is a "wonder of the world," the paper trumpeted, "for nothing in its line in Europe or America excels it."[3] This singular uniqueness was a common theme, and other news outlets repeated a similar commentary. F. D. Palmer in *Scientific American* described the panorama as "one of the most remarkable exhibits to be seen at the great Fair." "Professional men from all over the world," the author continued, "say this is the finest group of mounted animals they have seen, and that there is nothing like it in the world."[4] In *The Book of the Fair*, a commemorative guide to the Columbian Exposition, the historian Hubert H. Bancroft was equally effusive. The panorama was not just the highlight of the Kansas building; it was also "one of the features of the entire Exposition." The large exhibit, he concluded, contained the "best specimens of taxidermy . . . in the world."[5]

Applause for the quality of the taxidermy was everywhere, but a closer examination of these reports suggests that the display meant something more. Many fairgoers approached the panorama not as a curiosity but as art. Bancroft considered the display "an exhibit of animal sculpture," and the panorama, designed with an artistic sensibility, received the deference that all fine art engenders. The mounted animals drew comparisons to the famous paintings of Sir Edwin Landseer and his countryman Richard Ansdell.[6] But appreciation did not stop there, for local boosters saw in the panorama even greater significance. The display—a mélange of science, craftsmanship, and

Figure 3.2. Panorama of North American Plants and Animals at the Chicago World's Fair. Photo courtesy of University Archives, Spencer Research Library, University of Kansas.

nature—was evidence that Kansas had advanced in "natural history beyond Agassiz." In referencing Harvard's Louis Agassiz, perhaps the best-known natural scientist in America, panorama supporters elevated the scientific significance of the display. This was not a wax museum sideshow but rather an empirical examination of the physical world. The high praise continued with one more expansive claim: the panorama stood as proof "of Kansas culture and Kansas progress."[7]

If it seems odd that Kansas residents would find *cultural* validation in a mounted beaver, it is. But it was not the mechanics of the posed animals that drew so much attention; it was what the multifunctional panorama represented. Equal parts science, art, and Victorian "clutter," the panorama was a three-dimensional reflection of late nineteenth-century American culture.[8]

Finding a human context in stuffed animals places a large analytical burden on these displays, but taxidermy remains an intriguing tool for social investigation. In this essay I use taxidermy to engage questions about humans and nature in a modern age. The mounted animals of the Kansas panorama certainly look like unmediated first nature just as their transformation into mounts reveals the production values involved in the transition to second nature, but to understand the exhibit requires an awareness of how nature and natural science intersect with the changing place of the physical environment within human society. As a blend of natural science and environmental representation, taxidermy situates the natural world within a human context, and through these posed animals we can make connections between biological processes and our understanding of the human ideal. Taxidermy's critics see mounted animals as a sanitized view of the physical world or, worse, as a bizarre form of nature appreciation.[9] Yet to explore taxidermy seriously is to see the linkages between natural science, knowledge, and authority that reveal just how embedded our social practices are in the natural world. Before modern natural science split the observer from the observed, the spectacle of taxidermy put on display the kinds of connections we usually view as separate: human-animal, nature-culture, even alive-dead. The panorama embodied a particular historical moment of how we see nature, but more importantly it also offered clues to a bigger story: how our renderings of nature structure how we see ourselves.

Reality and Illusion

Taxidermy works for our purposes because it combines natural science, popular education, and natural appreciation. Taxidermists claimed that unlike nineteenth-century systematics that reduced animals to comparable specimens, their work invigorated environmental study. Taxonomists patiently examined hundreds, if not thousands, of specimens searching for small differences in animal forms. From the record of these slight variations came zoological classification schemes. But such work, however significant, was a celebration of sameness. Exhaustive species ordering drained the natural world of color. Displays such as the panorama, by contrast, were both popular and populist. The intent was to bring nature to a broad audience but more importantly to help viewers reconnect with the natural world. The sweeping panorama emphasized the animals within its environment creating an enlarged picture of the physical world. In Chicago, as visitors walked around the panorama, they saw impressive individual mounts, such as a large bull moose or an American bison, each with independent significance. When seen as part of the larger whole, however, these animals became part of an important collective drama. In the panorama the physical world was encapsulated in a single frame, allowing visitors to see nature as if it existed "all at once," but the stuffed animals of the panorama also created a visual narrative about how citizens understood the physical world. What they saw was nature's intricate design revealed by science to be rational and progressive.[10] Such work delivered a message about the value of community and the commitment to a greater good. Just as there existed a natural order, so too was there a proper American political order.[11]

Americans found the panorama intriguing because it engaged so many questions about late nineteenth-century life. The panorama was, for instance, a study in natural science. The exhibit presented proper ecological facts about adaptation and species interaction. The size and coloring of each specimen were rendered as accurately as possible. Exhibit materials emphasized the scientific fieldwork and biological collection techniques behind the display. It was precise, positivist, and ordered. The emphasis remained on order. American natural scientists believed that objects properly classified and displayed could convey scientific knowledge.[12]

In how the animals were presented, the display also provided insight into the social context of the age, and the range of viewer interpretations was impressive. Many of those same enthusiastic Kansas boosters saw in the display confirmation of their environmental stewardship. Preservation of exhibit animals became evidence of a broader political commitment to conservation in the wild; the mounting of a representative sample stood as an effective way to counter species loss.[13] More nostalgic visitors saw the display of iconic native animals as a celebration of national pride or better yet, because of an emphasis on large male specimens, as an affirmation of contemporary gender roles.

Still other messages were embedded in the display as the panorama reflected the ideology behind the fair. The Chicago World's Fair highlighted national achievement in commerce influenced by late nineteenth-century ideas about expansion and empire.[14] The Columbian Exposition showcased trade objects from distant markets, encouraging Americans to pursue the material possibilities of a global empire. With the world's goods on display in Chicago, contemporary discussions about progress and development became political debates about race and colonialism.[15] The panorama was not a commercial exhibit, but it was expansive in vision. Mounts were presented as "animals in full"—as healthy and robust as possible with thick fur, substantial bodies, and broad antlers. Special attention was devoted to each animal's carriage and stance. Many of the mounts were displayed with senses alert and muscles tight, emphasizing both strength and grace. Visitors to the panorama saw evolution in progress as they viewed idealized American specimens arranged in deliberate positions, each considered a perfect example of its "race."[16]

In the nineteenth century, nature displays frequently linked natural resources to national destiny. In Chicago preserving American animals, even in frozen form, was folded into discussions about protecting and exporting American values. Race, eugenics, and preservation became part of the same conversation.[17] When the foremost American zoologist of the day, the Smithsonian's William Temple Hornaday, traveled to Chicago to see the Kansas display, he came away impressed with the animals and the taxidermy. That the panorama spotlighted handsome species was important, but of equal significance to Hornaday were the feelings of pride stirred by the sight of American animals mounted by "all-wool-yard-wide American" scientists. Both the animals and the scientists, Hornaday emphasized, contained not "a foreign drop of blood." Creating animal displays required artistic skill and scientific precision, but the panorama also incorporated an environmental context into debates about cultural nationalism.[18]

Many of these ideas about nature and society were delivered through the unique physical form of the panorama. During this era panorama paintings, often of nature scenes, were very popular. Visitors flocked to metropolitan galleries to witness the latest pictures unveiled. By providing entrance into an idealized landscape, panoramas offered guests a new way of understanding the physical world. The aim, explained one scholar of the genre, "was to reproduce the real world so skillfully that spectators could believe what they were seeing was genuine."[19] To make this possible, panorama artists chose scenes that appeared "completely natural and true to scale," so viewers felt "transported to and situated within the outdoor site represented on the canvas."[20] Part of the attraction was simply the scale as these massive panoramas drew visitors into a unique and aesthetically powerful viewing experience. In popular panorama exhibits, the canvas and the display space were part of a shared created environment. That is, everything from the design of the hall, the placement of lights, the construction of the observation platform, and the wraparound effect of the canvas itself was constructed to "produce an unpre-

Figure 3.3. Panorama of North American Plants and Animals under construction. Photo courtesy of University Archives, Spencer Research Library, University of Kansas.

cedented level of verisimilitude." Critical to this dynamic, and to the power of the panoramic form, was its veracity, and since the viewer's eye rarely left the frame, the impact was significant.[21]

The Kansas panorama was engineered for similar effect. When guests leaned in at the Chicago exhibit, they saw the original animals (parts of the originals, but the originals all the same). The display process was complicated and involved a great deal of manipulation, but the real feathers, skins, and furs mounted against a backdrop of real sticks, plants, and rocks gave viewers the sensation that they were looking at the actual thing. In addition, despite the crush of people viewing the panorama, guests were not hurried through. They were permitted to move slowly around the exhibit, taking in the vivid still-life portrait of the natural environment. Special visitors could push the illusion even further and literally surround themselves with nature as they were allowed to enter the display and walk in and among the animal groups.[22]

Figure 3.4. Close-up of mounted moose. Photo courtesy of University Archives, Spencer Research Library, University of Kansas.

Such appeal is not unexpected as multidimensional displays are indeed engaging, but as museum professionals recognize, the danger in this kind of display is that dynamic objects are also easily bumped out of context. Pieces drawn from the distant past or from strange environments or from exotic cultures are often displayed without important supporting materials or context. The result is an "otherness" that sets these objects apart from their original utility and importance. That was not a problem in Chicago as the mounted animals of the panorama, like panoramic paintings, were part of an integrated and perfectly re-created environment. Visitors looking at a display lifted "straight from the wild" intuitively experienced the scene as "true."[23]

Of course, there was nothing "real" about the display even though accuracy was critical to claims of scientific authority. Craft labor produced such realism.[24] To highlight the obvious, everything in the panorama was dead.

Yet visitors were supposed to believe that they were gazing at life suspended, not life extinguished.[25] As the historian James Cook explains, this too was intentional. Displays such as the Kansas panorama "navigated a kind of middle course between complete illusion and self-conscious illusionism." Illusion is readily understood as false perception, but illusionism is more slippery. Illusionism, best explained by scholars of the visual arts, is a cultural practice, or aesthetic mode, by which viewers participate in the construction of an alternate version of reality.[26] The academic discussion about the blurry boundaries between interpretation and imitation is important here because viewers of the Kansas display were not unsophisticated dupes. The panorama was not a ruse to take in visitors; rather the display asked guests to engage in complex modes of interpretation. The panorama hinged not on the effort to convince visitors that the mounts were alive but rather on the cultural work accomplished by separating the deaths of animals from their ideal mounted forms.

The Columbian Exposition is a perfect place to consider the link between imitation and authority as the fair was awash in ersatz reality. Visitors to the Florida pavilion, for example, could stand in a re-created sixteenth-century Spanish fort. A short walk to the Pennsylvania building brought guests to a replica clock tower from Independence Hall. Irish castles, Japanese temples, Austrian beer gardens, and, floating on the fair's artificial lake, full-size copies of the Niña, the Pinta, and the Santa Maria were open each day for fairgoers. These re-creations permitted guests to witness reality in a contained form, but they were not mere theatricals; these objects also held clues to understanding American cultural perceptions.[27]

Late nineteenth-century Americans approached displayed objects, such as Portuguese sailing ships or midwestern stuffed animals, as material representations of ideas. Observed objects were metonyms by which the fragment represented a larger body of knowledge.[28] On one scale, then, illusion encouraged visitors to approach the Kansas display as a scientific model, and of course models are everywhere in science. Students learn chemistry by building compounds with wooden sticks and balls, engineers create detailed replicas of construction projects, and physicians display oversize organs to illustrate anatomical operations. In these examples the purpose is either to make visible the unseen or to render the complex understandable. But the panorama's animals do neither. They were not valued for their "analogical power, their manipulability, or their ability to render things on a human scale"; rather their importance lay in their authenticity.[29]

Within this wide-ranging discussion, taxidermy belongs to the expansive tradition of natural history. Defined as the systematic study of natural objects and organisms, natural history encompasses everything from the natural encyclopedias of ancient Greece to early modern royal butterfly collections. Centered on the close observation of origin and evolution, natural history engaged a range of fields from botany and geology to theology. As the field matured, natural history expanded to include anthropology, paleontology, astronomy, and biology, but the observational focus on nature remained critically important.[30] In nearly all forms of natural history, it was the effort to explain what the eye saw—what the historian and theorist Michel Foucault famously labeled "the nomination of the visible"—that mattered most.[31] Close and practiced observation of nature promised a nuanced understanding of divine operations just as it could deliver clues about natural order and evolutionary development. It was a particular way of knowing nature and the social world that surrounded it, and it dominated thinking about the natural world from the late eighteenth century forward.

In an American context, natural history entered national life through a variety of forms, including early national period lyceums and public lectures and nineteenth-century survey expeditions and museums. Practiced by amateurs and professionals alike, American natural history was part of a larger effort to explain the workings of the natural world. This initiative moved forward on two fronts, one practical and the other conceptual. As a practice, natural history involved the expected work behind public displays such as the Kansas panorama: collecting plants, cleaning bones, painting pictures, and stuffing skins. More significantly, as a concept natural history organized the physical world "into grand, fixed schemes." Natural history, as the curator Sue Ann Prince explains, was grounded in the faith that "humans [could] . . . attain dominion over nature by naming, labeling, organizing, and theorizing about its endless manifestations." Even before Charles Darwin, American natural historians accounted for nature's diversity by constructing an authoritative catalog of the natural environment. Believing that nature had a purposeful structure and that humans were capable of understanding that structure, natural historians "created elaborate . . . systems to make sense of what was . . . an untidy natural world."[32]

In the last decades of the nineteenth century, however, natural history began a slow decline as natural science grew in prominence. The early attempts to organize nature were intended to stimulate the senses, but soon laboratory experimentation replaced naked-eye observation as the preferred means

to understand the natural world. Perhaps because of the continuing emphasis on the visual, natural historians often approached specimens in isolation
rather than as parts of ecological systems. Natural historians accumulated
a massive amount of information about individual species—and developed
a complex taxonomic language in the process—but the result was only a
limited comprehension of the interconnected physical world.[33] With the pro-
fessionalization of natural science, however, a biological perspective that
emphasized community and complexity became the starting point for environmental investigation. The result was the creation of a more expansive (and
modern) understanding of the natural environment.

The shift from natural history to natural science is often portrayed as a
Whiggish tale of scientific development. The religious imperative lessened,
amateurs moved offstage, trained professionals arrived, and presto: advanced
natural science emerged. But it is important to recognize that natural science
was not simply a methodological advancement of natural history. These
modes of inquiry are in many ways different epistemologies. Despite our preference for contemporary means of investigation, each renders the historical
and sociological connections between knowledge of the physical world and
human communities in particular ways. It is all too easy to see the division
with one side armed with too much culture and the other too little as science anchors its claims to truth on the marginalization of the social variable.[34]
But if the transition in thought and practice suggests anything, it is that culture always remains in flux and in play. Natural science and natural history
offer different cultural lenses for mediating knowledge about nature.

Let us return to the panorama, for it is here that taxidermy—as a bridge
between these different ways of understanding nature and culture—becomes
significant. Taxidermists made the physical world accessible to a range of visitors, but they were also simultaneously producing new scientific knowledge.
They believed that this knowledge was democratic—the proper display of
nature could foster virtue.[35] Unlike the English example in which "natural
history was guided by cosmopolitan aristocrats" working within a framework of genteel society, American natural historians saw the field in more
nationalistic terms. If we can understand taxidermy in form and purpose as
civic biology, we can see how it engaged different constituencies in an effort
to aid an understanding of the social meaning of nature and natural science.
Natural scientists of the age supported a philosophy—what one scholar labeled a "biotechnological meaning of culture"—that connected questions
about biology and ecology to public life.[36] One of the standard historical

themes from this period is how well-known social changes caused by urbanization and industrialization prompted an embrace of the natural world. Nature was understood as a corrective to an overcivilized society. That is true enough, but the notion of civic biology expands this conception because how to organize nature provided clues that applied to society. The idea of a "modern nature" emerged at virtually the same moment as did the vision for a modern America. The mounted animals of the Kansas panorama were intended to illustrate an organism's place in a web of relationships within the natural world. In drawing meaning from natural representation, taxidermy became a key part of what we can now recognize as the "biological turn."[37]

The Kansas panorama may seem an unlikely participant in the national discussion of modernity, but exploring why the exhibit resonated with visitors in Chicago provides an important final context for the display. In the lead-up to the fair, the panorama had its share of local skeptics. One small-town newspaper editorial argued that no one in Kansas wanted "to be known to the world as the stuffed animal state." The complaint was not about the stuffed animals, of course, but what they represented. City officials wanted to showcase progress, not natural curiosities. Another paper, from Topeka, the state capital, was more direct; it reported that this "huge display of dead beasts" so dominated the fair building that visitors would leave knowing nothing of modern state advances in "horticulture, manufacturing [and] mining."[38] These voices of caution were largely silent by the end of the fair as popularity in Chicago translated into applause back in Kansas, but still, in their complaints these critics often missed the point as the display reflected the social changes of the era. The World's Fair was an urban venue frequented by middle-class spectators. To many of these viewers, the panorama was a pleasant reminder of America's preindustrial world. Fairgoers worn weary by the clang and clatter of city life could use displays like the panorama to reconnect to an agrarian past.

The panorama, however, invoked premodern ideas through thoroughly modern techniques. As we have seen, the realism of the display reflected contemporary interest in new modes of scientific inquiry. More substantially, to complete the massive panorama required assembly-line techniques, but the finished mounts, more machine than animal, bore no evidence that they were mass-produced—another hallmark of modernity. In addition, with no visible presence of the craftsman's hand, these animals were understood as objective. Along with Bell's telephone, Edison's phonograph, and Eastman's camera, the panorama's animals were representative of the modern age of re-production.[39] In visual culture of the period, abstraction and impressionism signaled the arrival of the modernist impulse. But in pushing viewers to re-vise their angle of vision, to consider input from other senses, the panorama was very much part of the modernization process.[40]

Animal Essence

The panorama was the creation of one individual, the naturalist Lewis Lind-say Dyche (1857–1915). At the time of the fair, Dyche was a busy man. Profes-sor of anatomy and physiology at the University of Kansas, Dyche would soon add professor of zoology, curator of mammals and birds, and chair of systematic biology to his titles. But it was his role as a taxidermist that trans-formed him into a minor celebrity in Chicago. The Kansas exhibit received high praise, but even more rained down on Dyche, a natural scientist com-plimented for achieving a "perfect mastery of his art."[41]

Although just thirty-six years old when the World's Fair opened, Dyche already had fifteen years of experience in the natural sciences. He arrived at the University of Kansas as a first-year student in 1877 and, like all entering freshmen, was offered a choice in program of study: "classical" or "scientific." Intending to study literature, Dyche picked classics and began a curriculum that emphasized languages, humanities, and literatures. But even classics stu-dents were required to take courses in botany and zoology, and it was there that Dyche, perhaps unexpectedly, found his focus.[42]

Dyche's decision to embrace the sciences no doubt reflected the influence of *how* natural science was taught at the University of Kansas. The school's small science faculty was composed of men of faith. They approached the study of nature as a search for evidence of creation and creator. They found it. At the university the earth and all on it were understood as unchanging elements of God's great plan. Such positions were not unexpected as even in a post-Darwinian age collegiate science faculty members across the nation held to similar articles of faith. Raised in a devout family, Dyche shared his professors' spiritual commitments, but it was their teaching, not their testi-monies, that he found most compelling.

In their natural science courses, University of Kansas professors empha-sized the direct study of nature. It was teaching through induction. Students were asked to observe first and construct generalizations later. Undergradu-ates in botany, for example, were required to "daily furnish themselves with

Figure 3.5. Lewis Lindsay Dyche and his Kansas undergraduate students. Photo courtesy of University Archives, Spencer Research Library, University of Kansas.

fresh plants from the forest and prairie for dissection, description, and classification." Nature took "precedence [over] the textbook in the apparatus of instruction." It did not matter whether classroom lectures were on fish or flowers, students were "to detect the peculiarities of the specimen in hand rather than to read . . . what some other observer has seen."[43] Such methods were popular with Kansas undergraduates. No longer would students hear long recitations about unseen natural forces. They now engaged in nature's firsthand study. Unusual in antebellum America, this approach became modern scientific practice by the 1870s.[44]

To support this means of investigation, members of the Kansas science faculty became passionate collectors of nature. Theory and advanced laboratory work now dominate the natural sciences, but in the nineteenth century, collecting was essential to the study of the physical world. Natural science is, at base, a work of categorization. In a world of infinite species, classification systems were required to make sense of natural variability. Without exacting categories, the physical world would remain an "unstructured blur"—difficult to study and impossible to understand.[45] Creating these categories required exhaustive evidence, and so museums, universities, and research institutes built large holdings of natural specimens. These collections became important learning tools in the classroom, but they were also part of nineteenth-century debates about animal adaptability. Advocates of permanency used collections that highlighted gaps between species just as other scientists looked for evidence in their holdings to illustrate the opposite principle of natural selection. Collecting, then, was never a simple matter of placing animals in their proper boxes but an "instrument of evolutionary theory."[46] Mid-century nature collecting was eclectic, even casual, but given its importance to the maturation of American natural science, it soon became systematic and standardized.[47]

When the University of Kansas opened in 1866, the natural history collection ("a few geological specimens collected by the faculty in their travels") was kept in a small museum on the cramped top floor of North College Hall, the university's first building. Growth was steady, and less than a decade later the natural history department filled an entire floor of the newly constructed anthropology building. "The cabinets of birds and insects, of every color, size, and shape," the university newspaper proclaimed, make for "fascinating study."[48] Expansion continued, and the university soon received funding from the state legislature to build a large hall dedicated to natural history. When the newly christened Snow Hall opened in 1886, it contained four different museums with updated laboratories and "commodious and well lighted" workrooms.[49]

It was left to university science faculty to fill these museums. Wealthy institutions built their natural history departments through purchase. Harvard, Yale, and Princeton, for example, each bought specimen collections from a New York–based commercial natural-history supplier.[50] The University of Kansas could not match resources with these universities; their collections had to be homegrown. The local newspaper tried to put a positive spin on the school's hand-built collections by noting the "feeling of pride, mixed with not a touch of wonderment" that accompanied the university's growing natural history catalog, but such achievement required considerable investment from faculty and students. Beginning in the 1870s, University of Kansas professors supported their near-constant local collecting with larger annual expeditions through the American Southwest. These trips required participants to acquire an intensive skill set. Some labors, such as the endless sorting of similar specimens, were hardly exciting, but advanced work in the field often was. In the field Kansas faculty routinely "endangered life and health" to collect "in regions infested by hostile Indians, by malarial diseases and by pernicious extremes of hot and cold."[51] But that was a large part of the attraction. Specimen collecting combined outdoor adventuring with a commitment to scientific precision. It was camping with an empirical purpose. As an added scientific bonus, local environmental knowledge gained while collecting was critical to understanding species development and behavior. One result of the emphasis on field expertise was that nineteenth-century natural scientists saw their work as just as rigorous and sophisticated as that of more established scientific fields.[52]

At the end of his sophomore year in 1878, Dyche was one of a handful of undergraduates invited to join these summer excursions. Student biologists tramped through New Mexico, Arizona, and Colorado securing cases of insects, plants, and fossils. These scouting parties returned to Lawrence with an array of skins and skeletons of deer, antelopes, bears, and mountain lions, all part of an expanding natural menagerie on campus. Dyche quickly became an accomplished collector, and in 1882 the onetime classics major was awarded a teaching position in the university's natural history department. Two years later his undergraduate career ended, but his collecting did not. As the university's natural holdings continued to grow, it became Dyche's primary responsibility to manage the school's important natural history collection. His rustic youth ensured that he knew how to hunt and skin animals, but even now, as a graduate student in anatomy and physiology, he knew little about the practical techniques of preservation and taxidermy. In 1887 Dyche traveled to the Smithsonian Institution to learn those skills.

In Washington, Dyche trained with William Temple Hornaday, the same naturalist who in a few short years would write approvingly of the full-blooded American character of the Kansas panorama. Hornaday, one of the most accomplished taxidermists in America, was a perfect tutor with a solid background in taxidermy. At eighteen, the Indiana-born Hornaday joined Henry Ward's Natural Science Establishment in Rochester, New York. Ward, the largest supplier of scientific specimens in the world, ran a natural-history warehouse stocked with skins, skeletons, minerals, and fossils from around the globe. He employed a skilled team of geologists, taxidermists, modelers, osteologists, and expert craftsmen to prepare displays for his company's many clients.[53] At Ward's request, the young Hornaday became an international collector obtaining specimens in Europe, Asia, India, Africa, South America, and Australia.[54] In 1882, the same year Dyche finished his undergraduate degree, Hornaday was appointed chief taxidermist at the National Museum of Natural History. Once in Washington, Hornaday built on his experience from Ward's Natural Science Establishment with a commitment to a new style of animal display: the habitat group. Instead of stuffing individual animals or mounting species in isolation, Hornaday displayed animal groups in their native habitats. The intent was to make American taxidermy as realistic, and scientific, as possible.

At the time of Dyche's visit to the National Museum, Hornaday was at work on what would become one of the most famous habitat displays, the "Buffalo Group." Alarmed by the rapid demise of the American bison, Hornaday wanted to acquire a specimen for the museum before the buffalo disappeared. In the fall of 1886 he made the long journey to eastern Montana, discovered one of the last remaining wild herds, and promptly shot twenty-four bison. Any feelings of guilt associated with hunting an endangered species were outweighed by Hornaday's belief that a mounted trophy would act as a "monument" to the majestic animal.[55] He insisted that stuffed bison could draw attention to the plight of "real" bison, perhaps saving the species from extinction. Killing in order to protect may seem strange, but it became central to the political function of American taxidermy.

Throughout their summer together, Hornaday introduced Dyche to the latest techniques of taxidermy as they prepared the Montana bison for display. Early nineteenth-century taxidermy was crude. Animal skeletons were wired together to create a basic frame, skins were then hung over the skeletal support, and straw or rags were stuffed inside to make the mount resemble the living animal. Even as taxidermists continued to refine their technique with more precise wooden cutouts to replace an animal's skeletal structure, the basic stuffing method continued. The resulting mounts, often poorly preserved and overstuffed, looked more like animal caricatures than actual specimens. Hornaday's innovation was to discard much of the original animal and begin with a hollow wooden model that replicated the animal's body as closely as possible. The model, or "manikin," was then covered in rope to add dimension and coated with modeling clay to provide muscular texture. Finally the animal's preserved skin was stretched over the completed form. The improved result, Hornaday claimed, were lifelike animals that looked as if they could "breathe."[56]

Hornaday's method was not just an improvement in technique but also a refinement in philosophy. He admitted that replacing the original animal with so many artificial parts created a species "counterfeit," but he did not see his mounts as mere imitations. Rather his animals were *ideal* representations,

Figure 3.6. Bison manikin. Photo courtesy of University Archives, Spencer Research Library, University of Kansas.

better than the original. "Animals of all kinds, even in a state of nature," he wrote, "assume attitudes that are highly ungraceful, unpleasing to the eye, and anything but fairly representative of the creature's form and habitats." Because nature too often produced "an ugly attitude," it was up to the taxidermist to create the archetypical specimen. Hornaday considered taxidermists magicians with animal forms. His goal was to produce an individual mount that reduced an entire species to its "essence." The target was a kind of elemental buffaloness. "We are aiming for perfection," he explained—not nature's perfection, of course, but the human perception of the consummate animal. If achieving this standard required a heavy hand, so be it. Intervention and manipulation were justified "for the sake of truth and justice." Hornaday put such an emphasis on the process because he believed that when museum patrons saw his mounts, they were receiving a moral education. When he spoke of truth and justice, he was serious. Taxidermy should not "startle and appall the beholder," he counseled, "but rather . . . interest and instruct him." Nature's observation was educational: it provided lessons in natural order.[57]

Dyche agreed, and once back in Kansas, he made good use of his Smithsonian lessons. Today's keen observer of the panorama will find evidence of its age. Mounts with exposed seams or discolored eyes or matted fur are, despite conservation efforts, part of the exhibit.[58] One consequence is that it can be difficult to remember how fresh this display once was. The panorama burst onto the national scene during a period when natural science and the arts, especially works dedicated to nature, achieved authenticity through very different means.[59] Science, of course, was all "facts" with little room for drama or flair. Scientific authority was built on generic description. The arts, by contrast, subsumed accuracy beneath aesthetic appeal. In replicating the natural world, artistic concern favored the consumptive experience. There is more here than the search for an appreciative audience as these two impulses help explain the place of nature and science within contemporary American society. Dyche's panorama, however, was a mixture of both efforts. He admitted to a professional colleague that he had artfully arranged the panorama "in a way which I thought would please the mass of the people," but he was foremost a scientist.[60] He held advanced degrees in natural science, he taught undergraduate courses in zoology and graduate studies in comparative anatomy and osteology, and the majority of his writing appeared in scientific journals.[61] Devotion to scientific method lay at the foundation of the panorama.

The particular ways that science was made manifest in the display also made the panorama a guidebook to nature's value. Dyche's mentors introduced him to leading nineteenth-century scientists such as the botanist Asa Gray, the mathematician Benjamin Peirce, and the physicist Joseph Henry. His training also included other influences, such as Ralph Waldo Emerson, the naturalist Paul Chadbourne, and the English author John Ruskin.[62] From these figures Dyche learned different environmental lessons about the power of observation and intuitive reasoning. Presented in their natural habitat, free of explanatory text and other distractions, the animals of the panorama *were* nature. Museum objects cannot represent an entire culture, but in the panorama the mounted animals embodied the whole of the physical world. Dyche created a stuffed animal composite portrait that came to define a real experience of natural interaction. The panorama was as much about how to "see" nature as it was about natural science.

Figure 3.7. Lewis Lindsay Dyche preparing a mounted moose. Photo courtesy of University Archives, Spencer Research Library, University of Kansas.

In 1910 Dyche took administrative leave from the university to become the Kansas state fish and game warden.[63] That he could or would do so illustrates the many facets of American nature study. He worked for decades killing and mounting animals and then shifted easily to working for their preservation. As different as these tasks may appear, both were anchored in management and both remained part of an active stewardship that began with animals, extended to the whole of the natural world, and eventually reached into society.[64] Respecting nature, Dyche believed, was respecting the community. As game warden he began animal-education programs for state residents and expanded scientific research opportunities in species management, but above all else, he used the power of the state to expand democratic access to nature. That goal was familiar to Dyche for it remained the primary objective of the panorama.

The panorama was supposed to be nature revealed, a site where natural history and natural science came together to understand the complex physical world. It was never quite that, in part because of an emphasis on the visual but also because of the shifting place of nature in American life. During my last visit to the panorama, the normally empty halls were filled with third graders from a local elementary school. That the Kansas Museum of Natural History serves a different audience than it did a century ago should not surprise anyone who has visited a similar institution in the past decade. While America's art museums attract a sober adult audience, science museums pull their core audiences from the nation's young. Children being in a museum is a good thing, but their presence also illustrates how ideas about science and nature are now delivered to American audiences.[65] What was interesting about this field trip was what the students came to see. It was not, as we might expect, to glimpse nature as it is. Rather, at the beginning of their tour, the teacher instructed her young charges to be on the lookout for how nature "used to be." Her instructions were closer to the mark than she realized. The animals of the panorama were crafted to represent their species. One animal stood for the whole. Now many of the mounts are individual examples of what remains. What was lost was exactly what Dyche hoped to create, a sense that nature's ordering could encourage an enhanced sense of belonging.

The narrative of loss built into the framing of nature "as it is" and "used to be" permeates much of the political dialogue about environmental change. Elevating an essentialized nature that existed before humans messed with the works does significant labor for environmental activists and natural enthusiasts alike. Yet this is neither what Dyche attempted nor what visitors demanded—nature without the taint of humans. The panorama reordered the animal form to make death mimic life, and as a result, the display tells us more about our understanding of nature than it does about what the physical world was *really* like more than a century ago. Guests to the Kansas panorama looked past the lifeless mounts and found exactly what the twentieth-century scientific perspective now makes less visible: connections between the natural and the human. These changes are as significant as they are ongoing. Perceptions of the panorama continue to evolve. Today when visitors come to the display, what they see, from multiple vantage points and definitions, is a lost world.

Chapter 4

Digit's Legacy: Reconsidering the Human-Nature Encounter in a Global World

Marguerite S. Shaffer

> We need the power of modern critical theories of how meanings and
> bodies get made, not in order to deny meanings and bodies, but in
> order to build meanings and bodies that have a chance for life.
> —Donna Haraway, "Situated Knowledges"

On the evening of February 3, 1978, Walter Cronkite led *CBS Evening News* with the story of a brutal murder in Africa. A gang of six men in the remote mountains of Rwanda had repeatedly stabbed their victim; the body was found decapitated and with both hands amputated. Despite the violent spectacle of this crime, it was rare, given the larger political and economic issues that had continually plagued Africa in the post-colonial era, for a single murder in tiny Rwanda to make national news in the United States, but this was no ordinary victim. He was a silverback mountain gorilla, one of only 250 left in the wild. More importantly, the victim was one of the renowned primatologist Dian Fossey's study subjects living near the Karisoke Research Centre in Parc Nationaux des Volcans, Rwanda. His name was Digit.[1]

Fossey, with the support of National Geographic, had spent the past decade conducting a field study of approximately ninety animals living in the

Figure 4.1. Portrait of Digit. Photo by Dian Fossey, c. 1974. Reproduced courtesy of Dian Fossey and National Geographic Creative.

Virunga Mountains of Rwanda and calling attention to the threat of extinction. At the time of Digit's murder, she had already gained international fame for her unparalleled work with the mountain gorillas. Digit too had achieved celebrity status for his role in the 1975 National Geographic film that documented Fossey's work. So on December 31, 1977, when poachers attacked him with spears and machetes, taking his head and hands to sell off as souvenirs—the hands as ashtrays, the head as a safari trophy—Digit became an international cause célèbre.[2] Looking back, one of Fossey's colleagues noted the impact of Digit's death: "Few in the listening audience knew anything about Rwanda or its people, but millions had seen Digit reach out to touch Dian Fossey in a recent National Geographic film special. For them this was almost like a death in their extended family."[3]

Digit's public obituary changed his status as well as the status of all mountain gorillas. The visibility of his death reflects the rising value of his species, a value that emerged in connection with Dian Fossey, National Geographic, and a western consumer public.[4] It also raises the question, how and why could western audiences mourn the death of a single mountain gorilla while the deaths of countless Rwandan and African people went unrecognized and remained invisible? The stories that rendered Digit's life and death visible and meaningful to a western public reveal the interconnections between western audiences, mass-mediated science, and the emergence of global popular environmentalism. In one version Digit's story became a global wildlife tragedy that affected scientists, conservationists, politicians, environmentalists, and nature lovers from the United States and Great Britain to Africa and beyond. But the events that led up to Digit's death and the ensuing battle to control his legacy go beyond wildlife tragedy. Rather they offer multiple versions of Digit rendered as savage beast, scientific subject, threatened species, safari trophy, fund-raising opportunity, and tourist attraction. These interspecies encounters with Digit reveal the fraught struggle to come to terms with nature in the culture of postcolonial global capitalism.

In this essay I argue that Digit's story challenges not only the timeless and transcendent ideal of the human-nature encounter but also the seemingly fixed boundaries that divide nature and culture.[5] Digit's life and legacy suggest that the human-nature encounter is neither timeless nor transcendent, despite our cultural proclivity to frame it that way. Rather the interspecies stories that coalesce around Digit are the products of colliding and deeply intertwined cultural and environmental histories; histories that bring together celebrity science, popular media, transnational wildlife conservation, and global capitalism; histories in which economic and environmental necessities—what Donna Haraway has called "a dialectic of love and money"—facilitated the commodification of desire for innocent, authentic, human-nature encounters.[6] Examining this cross-species connection between gorilla and woman demonstrates how, on the one hand, it rendered a complicated entanglement of nature and culture. On the other hand, it unmasked the social and environmental imperatives that underwrote the public vision of fundamentally separate worlds of ape and human that briefly, magically touched across the divide—a separation that has served not only powerful conceptions of humanness but also equally powerful ideals about nature.

Gorilla Taxonomies

If I were referring to Digit by his scientific name, *Gorilla beringei beringei*, I might begin this story in the late Pleistocene between four hundred thousand and eighty thousand years ago when climate change, specifically colder temperatures and a more arid climate, constricted and divided the extensive forest lands that stretched from the central Atlantic coast of Africa to what is now eastern Congo. Gorilla taxonomy locates the emergence of the gorilla as a distinct species some nine million years ago and currently recognizes two distinct species of gorilla: the western gorilla (*Gorilla gorilla*) and the eastern gorilla (*Gorilla beringei*).[7] Although primatologists argue that "the evolutionary history of gorillas in central Africa is inherently difficult to unravel," they believe that the ancestors of these two species of gorillas began to diverge in the lowland forests of west-central Africa.[8] As the population expanded, some migrated east along the north side of the Congo River. Since colder temperatures and drier conditions created isolated patches of the wet forest habitat that supported divergent gorilla populations, one eastern group split off and is believed to have moved into the highland area around Lake Albert, Lake Edward, and Lake Kivu on the borders of the present-day Democratic Republic of Congo (DRC), Uganda, and Rwanda. From there they crossed the lava fields of two active volcanoes to reach the forests of the Virunga massif now included in the Virunga National Park in DRC and Parc Nationaux des Volcans in Rwanda.[9]

This group evolved into the subspecies *Gorilla beringei beringei*, commonly known as the mountain gorilla. Scientists further divide the present-day population of mountain gorillas (*g. b. beringei*), numbering approximately 790, into two groups: those living among the Virunga Volcanoes found in

DRC, Rwanda, and Uganda; and those living in the Bwindi Impenetrable National Park, Uganda.[10] At one time the diverse montane forest habitat that supported these two groups had stretched continuously from the Virunga Volcanoes of present-day DRC and Rwanda to the Ruwensorie Mountains (Mountains of the Moon) of Uganda and on to the Bwindi Impenetrable Forest, the far western border of the mountain-gorilla range. However, as humans migrated to the region beginning around ten thousand years ago, they inhabited much of the lowland that connected these mountain ranges, thus isolating and dividing this population of mountain gorillas.[11] At present scientists disagree about whether the mountain gorillas located in the Bwindi Impenetrable Forest in Uganda might constitute a third subspecies distinct from *Gorilla beringei beringei*. This scientific debate not only highlights the interconnections between biological evolution and human history but also exposes a biological narrative under construction, raising questions about the objective materiality of nature.[12]

Following this evolutionary narrative, Digit's most immediate ancestors inhabited the mountain slopes and the saddle of land between Mounts Visoke, Karisimbi, and Mikeno, the three western-most Virunga Volcanoes straddling the border of DRC and Rwanda. The Virungas massif is defined by a chain of eight volcanic mountains running in a roughly east-west path along the present-day borders of Uganda, Rwanda, and DRC. These eight peaks connected by saddle zones at one time comprised a contiguous ecosystem dominated by moist, high-altitude forest.[13] Human migration into the region some ten thousand years ago, which brought both agriculture and pastoralism, resulted in the clearing of valleys and lowlands, permanently separating this extensive forest landscape by 1500.[14] Beyond human habitation, the remaining isolated montane rain-forest habitats maintained a diverse range of vegetation. Moss-draped Hagenia trees dominated the landscape, while dense foliage of nettles, wild celery, and vines created an entangled ground cover. The gorillas moved between various vegetation zones, traveling from the mountain slopes spotted by Veronia trees where they liked to make their nests, to selected bamboo zones that served as a seasonal source of food, to the brush zone lush with blackberry and other fruit shrubs, up into the higher altitudes containing brush and grass.[15] However, the pressures created by colonial and postcolonial economies centered on resource extraction resulted in increased land clearance, deforestation, and competition between herders and farmers. Consequently the valleys and mountain slopes were further transformed into pastureland and monocrop farmlands devoted to export crops such as coffee, tea, bananas, and pyrethrum, a flower used as a natural pesticide to replace DDT, which had been in decline in the western world following the publication of Rachel Carson's *Silent Spring* in 1962.[16] In response, the mountain gorillas adapted to higher altitudes, as their natural habitat was pushed higher and higher into the mountains.

Focusing on the human side of this history from a political and economic perspective, Digit's story might more appropriately begin in the late nineteenth century with the imperial race to discover, claim, and divide the vast natural resources of central and eastern Africa. Under colonial rule, the montane forest that comprised the mountain-gorilla habitat was carved into distinct and competing political territories. From the mid- to late nineteenth century, European powers scrambled to take control of the kingdoms of central and eastern Africa: Belgium under King Leopold II established a brutal rule over what would become the Democratic Republic of Congo (DRC); and Germany annexed Rwanda in 1897 and assumed control of the region until the end of World War I, when the territory was taken and then transferred to Belgium. Colonial rule not only established a hierarchical and racialized division between colonizer and colonized; it also capitalized on the ethnic divisions among the native Africans in order to more effectively control the labor force and efficiently extract natural resources.[17] Digit's taxonomic identity is wrapped up in this process of colonization. In 1902 a German officer, Captain Von Beringei, leading an expedition for the German East African Force across the Virunga Mountains, killed two gorillas and had their corpses sent back to the Humboldt University Zoological Museum in Berlin for documentation. Through this expeditionary killing he had "discovered" a new species. The taxonomist in Berlin marked and honored his colonial act of exploration, conquest, collection, and discovery in the scientific nomenclature by naming the new species *Gorilla beringei*.[18]

As the early twentieth century began to unfold, the newly identified species gained popular attention on a number of fronts, establishing a conservationist perspective that would also pave the way for Digit's rise to fame. In 1936 the Akeley African Hall opened at the American Museum of Natural History located in New York City's Central Park. Conceptualized and created during the 1920s by the noted naturalist, taxidermist, and artist Carl Akeley (1864–1926), the hall presents a panorama of twenty-eight dioramas depicting the distinct habitats and carefully crafted reproductions of charismatic African mammals. Representing the diversity of geographic areas that define the African continent, each diorama presents a small family group consisting of a large watchful male, one or two females, and a baby or two. A small herd of African elephants dominates the center of the hall. They are surrounded by habitat groups representing most of the major mammals of Africa: lions, water buffalo, zebras, okapis, warthogs, leopards, and cheetahs, among others. In the south corner, Akeley mounted the pride of the exhibit, a mountain-gorilla family of five set in the volcanic mountains of Lake Kivu and featuring "the Giant of Karisimbi," a standing silverback mountain gorilla pounding his chest. Likening the exhibition to a kind of cathedral to nature, Donna Haraway notes that the Akeley African Hall was Akeley's attempt to re-create and commemorate "nature at its moment of highest perfection."[19] The mountain gorilla, according to Haraway, was "the highest quarry of Akeley's life as artist, scientist, and hunter."[20] Not only did Akeley and his wife extensively document the expeditions they took to Africa to observe, kill, and collect the mountain-gorilla specimens mounted in the diorama, but in addition Akeley was buried on Mount Mikeno above Lake Kivu, the scene depicted in the diorama. Akeley's diorama dramatizes the mountain gorilla's precarious future and hints at the uncertainty of humanity's future: "The moment seems fragile, the animals about to disappear, the communion about to break," Haraway writes. "[T]he hall threatens to dissolve into the chaos of the Age of Man. But it does not. The gaze holds, and the wary animal heals those who will look. . . . The animal is frozen in a moment of supreme life, and man is transfixed. . . . This is a spiritual vision made possible only by their death and literal re-presentation. Only then could the essence of their life be present. Only then could the hygiene of nature cure the sick vision of civilized man."[21] In many ways Digit's story and his connection to the larger issues of species extinction and global wildlife conservation would reflect the same themes of threat and salvation.

From an even more popular perspective, Digit's story became increasingly intertwined with a series of iconic gorilla representations that captured public attention in the United States. In 1933 the RKO blockbuster *King Kong*, with its gigantic ape star, broke box office records and dazzled American film audiences. Although more sci-fi monster than real-life primate, Kong embodied a widespread fascination with jungle fantasies that reached back to Edgar Rice Burroughs's popular novels *Beasts in the Jungle* (1913), *The Land That Time Forgot* (1918), and *Tarzan of the Apes* (1918). The story of Kong's savage unrequited love for Ann Darrow, a modern-age blond beauty, and his tragic death by the forces of urban civilization and modern technology spoke to Depression-era fears and desires. But King Kong's story also channeled an

Figure 4.2. "Giant of Karisimbi," Mountain Gorilla Group Diorama, Akeley Memorial Hall of African Mammals, American Museum of Natural History, New York, NY. Reproduced courtesy of American Museum of Natural History Digital Special Collections.

ambivalent sympathy for the threat that civilization posed to primitive exotic "third world" nature—a sentiment that would help to create a sympathetic and receptive audience for Digit.[22]

These popular and scientific western accounts bore little relation to the local conflicts unfolding along the slopes of the Virunga Mountains. Those stories are more difficult to uncover and tell. Native folklore suggests that the original indigenous inhabitants, the Batwa, also known as Pygmies or forest people, who were nomadic hunter-gatherers, had coexisted with the mountain gorillas. Although the Batwa hunted bush meat—elephant, buffalo, antelope, gazelle, and even monkey—they avoided chimpanzee and gorilla because, as one informant explained, "they were formerly our peers (ngo n'abatwa bachu) and only with time have they degenerated and turned into animals (ngo zahinduts'inyamaswa)."[23] Migration of Bahutu agriculturalists and Batutsi pastoralists to the region constricted the habitat of mountain gorillas and marginalized the Batwa, ostracizing them as uncivilized and "impure" for eating wild game.[24] As European colonization put increased

pressure on local populations to cultivate and collect more exportable resources, herders, farmers, and forest inhabitants further encroached upon the
mountain gorillas, and interspecies relations became more strained.[25] Locals
killed gorillas for stealing their crops, straying into pastures, trespassing into
their communities, or accidentally activating snares or traps.[26] Poachers
killed and captured gorillas for more complicated economic and political reasons: to serve the western tourist trade; to supply western zoos; to threaten and
challenge western scientists; or to claim power and resources in the colonial
and postcolonial order.[27]

There is no history of gorilla poaching over the twentieth century.[28] There
are heroic accounts of western scientists and explorers killing the gorillas for
science and sport, and locals played a role in these interspecies conflicts.[29]
As mountain gorillas gained status in the western scientific and touristic
economy, they became valuable political and economic icons and prey for
locals seeking to gain power in the expanding global colonial and postcolonial network.[30] Increasingly the Batwa, who were denied access to their forest
homelands with the creation of national parks set aside to protect the mountain gorillas from the 1920s through the present and who, because of their
marginalized and displaced status, occupied the lowest rungs on the social
order in the region, were stereotyped as gorilla poachers.[31] From this perspective, the diverse and well-established local African communities that
bordered the montane forests inhabited by mountain gorillas were made
invisible; simultaneously stereotyped and marginalized African "savages" became villains in the story of mountain-gorilla survival and conservation.[32]
In this way Digit's diverse and complex habitat was transformed into an
African jungle, a pristine but savage wilderness beyond the boundaries of
civilization that would continue to exist only through western protection.

The political, environmental, and popular terrain of colonial Africa as
represented in scientific literature and popular imagery established the context for the stories that would coalesce around Digit in the postcolonial era.
Science framed the significance of the great apes, locating them as "man's"
closest ancestor and linking them in an evolutionary context to the genesis
of human culture. Apes, and mountain gorillas as the largest of the great apes,
walked a thin line between nature and culture, animal and human. From a
scientific perspective they offered some clue into "man's" origins. Even in the
post–World War II era, knowledge about them was sketchy. They are reclu-
sive animals living in a remote mountain habitat at the intersection of three
countries in central Africa struggling to overcome the legacies of colonialism,

racism, and poverty. Added to this was an extensive popular mythology and iconography of the mountain gorilla and primitive Africa steeped in stereotypical notions of civilization and savagery. From a scientific perspective the gorilla reflected nature as a source of knowledge—scientific data needing protection from the forces of history and culture. From a popular perspective the gorilla revealed the threatening savagery of nature—wilderness as a place apart demanding management and protection. From a political perspective, the unstable status of the countries of central Africa that were home to the gorillas reinforced these notions of savagery and the need for protection from the outside. Each of these complex and intertwined contexts reflects the heavy cultural baggage that we attach to mountain gorillas, animals, and nature; and each in turn supports narratives that legitimize an ideal of nature rendered as separate and outside of culture.

Nature as Celebrity Science

Digit, however, was not simply a representative of the mountain gorilla species reflecting a snapshot of scientific data. Rather he was rendered as an individual—an international celebrity—discovered by Dian Fossey, showcased on film, and embraced by wildlife advocates stretching from Rwanda to the United States. Digit embodied the drama and adventure of Dian Fossey's research and life commitment to wildlife conservation during the fraught decade of the 1970s, but more than that he represented the innocent mountain gorilla threatened with extinction by the encroaching forces of modern civilization, and his fate rested in the hands of humanity in a globally interconnected world. He captured public attention and sympathy because he embodied the possibilities of the human-nature encounter: the possibility that this interspecies exchange might lead to a better understanding of how to protect and conserve wildlife and realign the increasingly fragile balance between nature and culture.

Dian Fossey's story and Digit's rise to fame are deeply intertwined. As Fossey's story goes, in 1963 after a seven-week safari in East Africa during which Fossey, then an occupational therapist, sought out and met the acclaimed primatologist Louis Leakey, Fossey emerged as Leakey's second "primate girl," seeking to replicate Jane Goodall's field study of chimpanzees with a study of mountain gorillas.[33] From his archaeological work on the missing link between apes and humans, Leakey believed that the field of primate behavior studies might shed more light on the connections between

Figure 4.3. Dian Fossey, c. 1967. Photo by Alan Root. Reproduced courtesy of Alan Root and National Geographic Creative.

humans and apes. Goodall's field research in Gombe, Tanzania, had already yielded groundbreaking information about tool use, hunting, and meat consumption. Leakey was anxious to expand this research to include the other great apes. After three years of negotiation, Leakey selected Dian Fossey to conduct a field study of the mountain gorilla, despite the fact that she had little scientific training; scant knowledge of African history, politics, and culture; and absolutely no field research experience. By late 1966 Leakey had secured the necessary funding to support Fossey's work. She established her first base camp in the Kabara meadow of the Virunga Mountains of Zaire (now the Democratic Republic of Congo) in January 1967. The site had an iconic stature for those interested in the mountain gorilla. Not only was Karl Akeley buried there, but this was also the site of the noted University of Chicago biologist George Schaller's field study of mountain gorillas conducted in 1959–60. Civil war in Zaire forced Fossey to abandon her camp at Kabara after only seven months of fieldwork, despite its historic western stature. She reestablished her field study on the Rwandan side of the Virunga Mountains in the Parc Nationaux des Volcans approximately five miles as the crow flies from the Kabara meadow. It was there that she met, named, and befriended Digit.[34]

Fossey's relationship with Digit grew out of her particular, some would say controversial, approach to gorilla observation. By the 1960s the field of ethology (the science of animal behavior) called for detached, objective, empirical observation. Ethologists, in an attempt to distinguish their work from the observations of amateur naturalists and legitimate the scientific credibility of their observations, called for precise quantitative data: measurements, maps, charts, statistics, and hard empirical data. "Ethology was mainly concerned with discovering the 'mechanisms' underlying universal behaviors, not individual motives sculpting different responses."[35] The primary goal in field study was to try to have little to no impact on the behavior of the animals being observed. This posed a dilemma for scientists seeking to document the day-to-day behavior of animals in the wild. Objective observation seemed to require that the animal be unaware of the researcher, but the possibilities of humans remaining undetected in the wild were slim, especially with mountain gorillas. Because they inhabited a montane rain forest dominated by dense foliage and mountainous terrain, researchers had difficulty observing them on the ground from long distances. The accepted field research method, then, was to "habituate" the animals to one's presence by repeatedly and methodically visiting the group without threatening group members and thus systematically familiarizing them with a routine and predictable human presence. George Schaller, the reigning field expert on mountain gorillas at the time, maintained what he argued was an objectively determined distance of 120–150 feet. He claimed that anything closer altered the gorillas' *natural* behavior.[36]

Fossey hoped to go beyond Schaller's work. In her 1970 *National Geographic* cover story, she detailed her unique approach: "The textbook instructions for such studies are merely to sit and observe. I wasn't satisfied with this approach; I felt that the gorillas would be doubly suspicious of any alien object that only sat and stared. Instead, I tried to elicit their confidence and curiosity by acting like a gorilla. I imitated their feeding and grooming, and later, when I was surer what they meant, I copied their vocalizations, including some startling deep belching noises."[37] Describing her novel approach in a later *National Geographic* article, she explained, "Early in my research . . . I discovered that these powerful but shy and gentle animals accepted and responded to my attentions when I acted like a gorilla. So I learned to scratch and groom and beat my chest. I imitated my subjects' vocalizations (hoots, grunts, and belches), munched the foliage they ate, kept low to the ground and deliberate in movement—in short, showed that my curiosity about them matched theirs towards me."[38] Habituation for Fossey moved beyond the objective and detached stance practiced by Schaller. She questioned the separation between observer and observed, subject and object, human and animal. Instead she sought to habituate the gorillas by transcending the species divide and becoming a gorilla. In this way Fossey challenged the established fieldwork protocol, which rested on clearly established boundaries between the scientists and the subjects, the humans and the animals. She believed that her scientific observations could be legitimate only if she was, in effect, a virtual member of the gorilla group.[39]

Eventually Fossey pushed habituation beyond the boundaries of detached observation and into the realm of physical contact, which she interpreted as total acceptance by the gorillas. In early 1969 after over six months of observation of the various groups around Karisoke, she sent a telegram to Louis Leakey noting her success: "ALL 6 MEMBERS OF GROUP 8 APPROACHING ME FROM 5 TO 10 FEET. EXPECT PHYSICAL CONTACT WITHIN A WEEK. JUST HAD TO SHARE MY EXCITEMENT WITH YOU—DIAN."[40] As Donna Haraway has written, this physical contact between humans and apes in the wild, "the drama of touch across Difference," offered a kind of redemption to western audiences threatened by a history that pointed to nuclear annihilation and environmental catastrophe.[41] In addition to this promise of reconciliation between threatened nature and modern culture, Fossey unsettled gender norms at an auspicious moment for western women. By challenging accepted scientific protocols and rendering herself closer to nature through "aping" and intimate contact with the gorillas, she claimed her place in the masculine world of science while also asserting the power of her feminine proximity to nature.[42] As a literally liberated woman who had transcended gendered boundaries, both professional and geographical, her interspecies connection with the gorillas took on charged political meaning for western audiences caught up in the debate over feminism in the mid- to late 1970s. These themes and issues would underscore Dian's relationship with Digit and the stories she would tell about him.

Dian first saw the young gorilla she would name Digit right after she arrived in the fall of 1967 at what would become the Karisoke Research Centre. Estimating him to be about five years old, she described him as "a bright-eyed, inquisitive ball of fluff who came to be known as Digit because of a twisted middle finger that appeared once to have been broken."[43] He was a curious and rambunctious juvenile, and in her book she describes how Digit and his siblings played freely as she began to develop her observation techniques.[44] She attributed the special "friendship" she began to develop with Digit to the shift in relationships that unfolded over the course of her habituation of Group 4. Changes in group dynamics had a profound impact on Digit, according to Fossey. In the first half of 1971, three young females emigrated from Group 4 to other groups, leaving Digit without the peer group he had played with "during his transition from a juvenile to a blackback." She noted that at nine years old Digit was too old to play with the remaining juveniles in his group and too young to associate with the older females. She argued that because of his transitional status, he became "more strongly attracted to humans than did other young gorillas among the study groups who had siblings and peers."[45] She continued, "I received the impression that Digit really looked forward to the daily contacts with Karisoke's observers as a source of entertainment. . . . He was always the first member of Group 4 to come forward to see who had arrived on any particular day. . . . If I was alone, he often invited play by flopping over on to his back, waving stumpy legs in the air, and looking at me smilingly as if to say, 'How can you resist me?' At such times, I fear, my scientific detachment dissolved."[46]

Fossey's depiction of Digit tells the story of a sentient compassionate fellow being who welcomed her presence, sensed her joy and her pain, and cared for her in the same way he cared for his fellow group members. Giving this story a psychological twist, Sy Montgomery claims that Digit was the playmate, the sibling, the loyal family member Dian felt she never had.[47] One could easily conclude this from reading the stories Fossey lovingly recounted about her interactions with Digit. A selection of memorable exchanges illustrated the depth of their relationship: Digit welcoming her and touching her hair; Digit examining her thermos, notebook, gloves, and camera; Digit keeping watch over her and the group. In her book *Gorillas in the Mist* she describes a particularly moving encounter on a cold rainy day when Digit was standing sentry for Group 4. Although drawn to him, she writes, "I resisted the urge to join Digit, who was huddled against the downpour." Instead she left "him to his solitude" and "settled several yards from the group, a cluster of humped forms barely visible in the heavy mist." She continues, "After a few minutes, I felt an arm around my shoulders. I looked up into Digit's warm, gentle brown eyes. He stood pensively gazing down at me before patting my head and plopping down by my side. I lay my head on Digit's lap.[48] Another story recounts how Digit, sensing her sadness, came to her in the rain, peeled a stalk of wild celery, and dropped it in her lap.[49] In Fossey's story Digit was her "beloved" friend.[50] His story was the story of her complete acceptance by the gorillas, it was the story of her success as a scientist, but more importantly it revealed her completeness as a human being. In Fossey's telling, Digit's story reflected on her own accomplishments as a celebrity scientist and wildlife advocate; Digit's story validated her self-worth. But her relationship with Digit went beyond scientific study to become a platonic romance. With Digit, Fossey was able to transcend the species divide.

It is easy, given the drama of Fossey's life, to lose sight of Digit in these stories and see only the heroic woman and celebrity scientist devoting her life to protecting wildlife. This is a powerful story in western culture, perhaps even the dominant story that defines the relationship between nature and culture, positioning humans as guardians and protectors of wild animals and wild nature.[51] Too often the drama of environmental celebrity obscures the complexity of the relationship between nature and culture. In this particular version of the story, Dian's unique approach to habituation gave her insider status; she knew the nature of the gorillas like no other; she had gained the insight necessary to give them value and meaning. She became integral to their protection and survival. This is also a historically situated story. Dian's inspiring tale of independence, interspecies acceptance, and adventure in remote Africa helped to elevate her as a feminist icon in the mid-1970s, at the moment when feminism was gaining political and cultural ground in the United States. Her deeply personalized search for meaningful interspecies connection and environmental redemption reflects one of many responses to the larger cultural "crisis of confidence" that shaped the decade.[52]

Nature as Visual Spectacle

Digit's story is also a story about media and the constitutive power of representation in shaping our ideas and attitudes about nature. In photographs and film, Digit's story gained a popular meaning that extended beyond the needs and desires of Dian Fossey. Fossey was more than aware of the power of his image. In the early 1970s the Office Rwandais du Tourisme et des Parcs Nationaux (ORTPN), a newly formed institutional arm of the Rwandan government established to promote tourism and administer the country's national parks, asked Fossey for a photograph of one of the gorillas to use for publicity purposes. Fossey sent a portrait of Digit contemplating a stick of wood he had been chewing. "Shortly thereafter large color posters of Digit feeding on a piece of wood were scattered throughout Rwanda—in hotels, banks, the park office, the Kigali airport—and in travel bureaus throughout the world. In various languages the poster was captioned "Come and See Me in Rwanda!" Much to Fossey's regret, Digit had become the poster child for wildlife tourism in Rwanda. "I had very mixed feelings on first seeing the posters around Rwanda," she wrote. "Heretofore Digit had been an 'unknown,' only a young male maturing within his natal group. Suddenly his face was everywhere. I could not help feeling that our privacy was on the verge of being invaded. I certainly did not want the public flocking to Group 4."[53] Even if she dismissed the irony of her own role in introducing Digit to an adoring international public, Fossey adamantly opposed the development of gorilla tourism among her study groups at Karisoke. Not only did she question the impact of tourists on scientific field observation but she also worried about the spread of human diseases to the gorillas. She believed that conservation of the species depended on the preservation of wildlife habitat and protection from intruders—poachers and tourists alike. She had negotiated an arrangement with ORTPN to restrict tourists from viewing her research groups in the Parc des Volcans, but as media exposure brought Fossey's gorillas international fame, park guards established a lucrative illicit guide business. As more people came to know Fossey's habituated gorillas, more tourists arrived at Karisoke hoping they too could see the gorillas, and Fossey began to hate the tourists more and more.

Although Digit remained unnamed in the Rwandan park poster until Fossey revealed his identity, as the representative mountain gorilla he beckoned to western audiences, liquid eyes looking up into the camera, inviting viewers to meet him. George Schaller perhaps best summarized the alluring power of the gorilla's gaze in his popular account of his work with the mountain gorillas: "The gorillas talked to me at times with their expressive eyes, and I felt that we understood each other."[54] As Judith Butler has argued, recognition of the face, even the mediated face, evokes a sense of shared vulnerability and humanity, or in this case an interspecies connection.[55] A National Geographic film that aired in the United States in 1976 invited audiences to share vicariously this experience of interspecies understanding. The film marked a turning point for Fossey and for Digit. Where previously a select group who subscribed to *National Geographic* magazine had access to her work with the mountain gorillas, the film brought Fossey and Digit into the homes of millions of American television viewers.[56] *In Search of the Great*

Figure 4.4. Tourist poster featuring Digit distributed by Office Rwandais du Tourisme et des Parcs Nationaux, c. 1972. Reproduced courtesy of Houghton Mifflin Company.

Apes first aired on January 13, 1976, on PBS as a Gulf Oil National Geographic television special.[57] Part 2 of the film introduces Fossey in her remote mountain camp "as far away from human encroachment" as she could get. The opening scenes scan the mist-covered peaks of the Virunga Mountains and then close in on Fossey as she walks through a lush moss-draped landscape. As the narrator introduces Fossey, her work, and her world, scenes show her observing the gorillas, walking through an African village, hiking with porters to bring supplies up to camp, and working in her cabin. As the film tracks along a row of framed gorilla portraits hanging in Fossey's cabin, each labeled with the name of a gorilla, and ends on the image of Digit, the narrator explains that each gorilla displays unique behaviors and personality traits, suggesting, as Donna Haraway has argued, that "naming and portraiture" become "the signs of rational selfhood for the great apes."[58] The narrator notes that in the course of her research, Fossey has "photographed, cataloged, and even nicknamed" over ninety animals, detailing their personalities, habits, and how they communicate. Dramatizing the fine line between human and animal, Fossey remarks, "Sometimes it was difficult to know who was the observer and who was the observed." The ensuing interchange between Fossey and Digit—who is "the first gorilla to accept her," according to the film's narrator, and who "more than any other has revealed the mountain gorilla's world to Dian"—bears this out.

A lingering close-up on Digit's face introduces him to the audience. He stares into the camera, making eye contact with the viewer. The ensuing scenes show Digit up close smelling Dian's hand, examining her glove, lying next to her, and peering intently into her face. The narrator comments, "In the past we have brought these animals into our world caged for zoos and circuses. Now one human being has entered the world that is theirs." Close-ups of Digit's face invite the audience to imagine some mutual understanding. As Dian observes, taking notes and scratching herself in imitation of gorilla behavior, Digit responds by imitating her human behavior, carefully picking up, examining, and returning her notebook and pencil. The narrator reminds the audience of Dian's description of the first time she was touched by a mountain gorilla: "For that fleeting instant a bridge spanning a chasm of immeasurable time linked our two species." The viewer too is invited to imagine across time and space an intimate connection to Digit. Although Dian is the nominal star of this film, Digit is the real star. One cannot help but be drawn in by his pensive curiosity, his compassionate gaze, his gentle touch. Here is the unknowable wonder of nature at our fingertips, returning our gaze, responding knowingly to our longing to understand, to bridge the immeasurable chasm between animal and human, nature and culture.

The popular film *Gorillas in the Mist* enhanced and built on this image of Digit, drawing on a range of popular images to dramatize his character. In the film he is portrayed as the dominant silverback in the group. Produced in 1988 after Fossey's murder, the film hints at the more disturbing side of Fossey's story. Although the title of the film suggests that it is based on her book of the same title, a compromise script resulting from a legal agreement between Universal Studios and Warner Bros. included a more critical view of Fossey and her work based on a *Life* magazine story by Harold T. P. Hayes. Hayes's story portrayed Fossey as a vengeful paranoid alcoholic who sacrificed science and wildlife conservation to her own desires to have sole access to the gorillas and complete control over Karisoke. Blending Hayes's account with Dian's memoir, the film suggests that Digit's murder transformed Fossey from a committed scientist who had devoted her life to learning more about the mountain gorillas to an obsessed and possessive maniac who would resort to any means to protect the mountain gorillas and keep them to herself.

In many ways the film offers a reversed version of the King Kong story. Digit is not the savage jungle beast captured and put on display in an urban civilized western world; he is a loving, gentle giant protecting his family in the wilds of Africa, who welcomes the observation of the civilized western scientist. This is not a story of unrequited love between the primitive beast and the modern damsel in distress; it is a mutual love story, a "beloved" friendship between human and animal, scientist and subject, Africa and the West (the United States), a caring patriarch and an independent woman. But it is also a story of star-crossed lovers seeking to bridge the immeasurable chasm between them. As with Kong, Digit is murdered for transgressing the boundaries between nature and culture, which Digit does in his connection to Fossey. In the end, unlike Ann Darrow, Fossey is not rescued from the excesses of nature by the forces of civilization. Instead, following Joseph Conrad's Kurtz in *Heart of Darkness*, she goes mad in the African jungle, and after descending into a state of maniacal paranoia, she is murdered for her excessive and irrational desire to avenge Digit's death. Fossey too is murdered for crossing the boundaries between nature and culture, in her case boundaries about gender and a woman's *natural* place in society. The film fixes Digit's and Fossey's images as martyrs to the cause of global wildlife protection and conservation, suggesting that the fate of African wildlife and wilderness, one of the few remaining vestiges of untouched nature in the world, remains in the hands of western audiences.[59]

As the environmental historians Gregg Mitman and Finis Dunaway have shown, popular visual imagery—photographs and film—played an integral role in defining the development of a post–World War II environmental consciousness. Drawing on long-established references to the sublime and aesthetic wonder of wilderness, visual representations of nature in a post–World War II world threatened by nuclear war, pollution, rapid urbanization, and excessive resource use dramatized nature as romantic, threatened, vulnerable. Images of oil-covered birds, crying Indians, children in gas masks, atomic mushroom clouds, and Earth floating alone in space provoked emotional responses that transcended rational arguments for scientifically based environmental policy and wilderness preservation. Through these compelling images people forged an emotional bond that linked them to nature. Threatened wildlife, threatened habitats, and threatened wilderness translated into a threat to humanity. Digit's image invoked this shared bond and fear of this intertwined threat. In many ways the power of his story rests in these vulnerable images.[60]

The Value of Digit

The shared threat to wildlife and humanity became all too real when Digit was murdered in 1977. After his death Digit's story changed radically. Digit became a receptacle, a cause: his physical remains transformed into ashtrays collecting cigarette butts; his memory and his image a kind of investment accruing funds; his legacy a political battleground fought over by competing environmental organizations. Specifically, Digit the individual became the Digit Fund, a nonprofit wildlife organization established to raise money to protect living mountain gorillas and their habitats. Simultaneously, Digit's fellow gorillas became tourist attractions under the auspices of the Mountain Gorilla Project, which turned to ecotourism as a new integrated approach to community development and wildlife conservation.

In the aftermath of Digit's death Dian Fossey immediately began to consider a plan to publicize the atrocity of his murder to raise money for the protection of the gorillas. In an essay entitled "His Name Was Digit," written shortly after his death, Fossey explained that the purpose of the Digit Fund was to raise money "to maintain students, to train Rwandans in patrol of the park, and for additional census work" on the gorillas in Rwanda.[61] The Digit

Fund was legally incorporated in the fall of 1978 and linked to established conservation organizations including the African Wildlife Leadership Foundation and the International Primate Protection League.[62]

Simultaneously in Great Britain, Alexander A. P. "Sandy" Harcourt, a former Karisoke researcher and colleague of Fossey at Cambridge, worked with the British Fauna and Flora Preservation Society with support from the International Union for the Conservation of Nature and the World Wildlife Fund to establish the Mountain Gorilla Protection Fund.[63] Harcourt had also known Digit through his research at Karisoke. Although he was more of a rising academic than a celebrity scientist, he too was devoted to protecting the mountain gorillas and promoting his credentials as a top authority on mountain-gorilla behavior.[64] Like Fossey, Harcourt and his supporters believed that they could use Digit's murder to raise awareness and funds in support of mountain-gorilla conservation. Harcourt, however, approached the process with more political and diplomatic savvy. Appointed as director of the Mountain Gorilla Protection Fund by the Fauna and Flora Preservation Society, a leading conservation organization in Great Britain, in the summer of 1978, Harcourt worked with a range of individuals and organizations outlining a strategy to partner with Rwandan officials, specifically ORTPN, to develop a multitiered approach to gorilla conservation, which would include increased funds to train and support park guards for antipoaching efforts, an education program to familiarize the Rwandan population with the plight of gorillas, and a tourism program to provide for economic development.[65]

The biologist Amy Vedder and her husband the conservationist Bill Weber developed and implemented this "multidisciplinary approach to conservation—one that considered the needs of both people and wildlife" for the Mountain Gorilla Protection Fund.[66] Both had done research at Karisoke in early 1978 in the months following Digit's murder. Vedder focused on gorilla feeding ecology and habitat. Weber conducted a new gorilla census. Although their relationship with Fossey was strained, they built on their experiences at Karisoke to develop the Mountain Gorilla Project.

They began by conducting a nontraditional multidisciplinary study funded by the New York Zoological Society that focused on "the demographic, ecological, and socio-economic factors involved in the [mountain] gorilla's decline." A survey of the local population living around the Parc Nationaux des Volcans revealed that locals saw little value or relevance in the conservation mission of the park, and yet a vast majority agreed on the possible economic benefits of tourism development. Their survey also showed

that although the rest of the world knew a great deal about the mountain gorillas, Rwandans knew very little.[67] Building on this information, Vedder
and Weber proposed "attack[ing] the problem on three fronts: anti-poaching
to halt the killing, education to change people's perceptions and values, and
tightly controlled tourism to generate political support for the park and gorillas through foreign revenue and local employment."[68]

While Vedder was in the United States completing her master's degree at
the University of Wisconsin, Weber worked to identify and habituate (following Fossey's methods) selected gorilla groups around Mount Sabyinyo;
he also laid the groundwork for bringing in tourists. The process was not
without setbacks. In late 1979 Weber, while guiding a tourist group to see the
gorillas, was charged and bitten in the neck by a threatened silverback.[69] However, by 1980 Weber and his coworkers had established a viable gorilla tourism program. Tourists had to reserve their spots in advance through the
ORTPN to see the gorillas; groups were limited to six, not including guides
and porters; habituated gorilla groups could be visited only once a day for no
more than an hour; and a space of five yards between gorillas and tourists
had to be maintained during the visitation.[70] In following the "rule of six"
limitation and the other quality controls, they reasoned that "fewer people
would pay more money for an exclusive, high-quality experience."[71] Building
on the process of habituation made famous by Fossey, the Mountain Gorilla
Project transformed the gorilla encounter into a high-end commodity, a one-
of-a-kind tourist experience available to a limited and privileged few western
tourists interested in a transcendent encounter with real, live, wild nature—
almost the last of its kind in the world. Fossey's celebrity science popularized and legitimized by National Geographic combined with the support of
premiere wildlife conservation organizations, including the World Wildlife
Fund and the Fauna and Flora Preservation Society, added to the allure. Most
importantly, wealthy, white, western tourists could assuage any postcolonial
guilt in knowing that their tourist dollars were benefiting both community development and wildlife conservation in Rwanda, a country ravaged by
postcolonial instability.

In tandem with the tourism project, Weber also initiated an education
program. Targeting secondary schools and the 2 percent of school-age Rwandans "destined to be the government officials, teachers, businessmen, and
military leaders of the future," Weber gave film presentations using the National Geographic film showcasing Fossey and Digit, and he developed sup-
plementary curricular material focused on biology and environmental studies

to inform Rwandans about the gorillas.[72] Through education he hoped to change local people's attitudes about the gorillas and the national park set aside to protect them. He found that students "were surprised and proud to learn that Rwanda—their little country, so little known to the outside world—held the key to saving the mountain gorilla."[73] Through the education program, Weber and Vedder sought not only to educate local Rwandans about the value of gorillas but also to promote what they called "conservation nationalism" linking the gorillas to a sense of national identity and pride in the significance of Rwanda as an African nation.[74] Although the Digit Fund and the Mountain Gorilla Project embraced the same goal—to protect the gorillas—they vied for control of the funds raised in Digit's memory and the power those funds conveyed over transnational wildlife conservation practices.

By the summer of 1980 Fossey's reputation and health were in decline. In the meantime the Mountain Gorilla Project had racked up an impressive record of success through its multitiered approach to gorilla conservation. Over a thousand tourists had by that time visited the two gorilla groups habituated by the Mountain Gorilla Project. Foreign tourism increased and park revenues rose exponentially. Business expanded for hotels, restaurants, and other travel-related enterprises. Employment opportunities around the park expanded as service-sector jobs increased and the park hired more guards and guides. In addition poaching incidents decreased with the hiring, training, and supplying of twenty-six additional Parc des Volcans guards. Local and state support for the park and the gorillas grew.[75] In their memoir Weber and Vedder celebrate the accomplishments of this first year: "Overall, the gorilla conservation outlook was much more positive than when we began our work. Poaching was down, economic benefits were up, local attitudes were improving, and national support was strong. Gorilla numbers were uncertain, though we know of more births than deaths. A later census would confirm that the period after the MGP's inception was the turning point in the population's recovery."[76] Thus in a seemingly conflicting twist, by incorporating the mountain gorillas into a complex, postcolonial, global tourist economy that reached from Ruhengeri Province in Rwanda to the economic and political capitals of the West—London, New York, Washington, D.C., and beyond—and that depended on deeply layered, mass-mediated cultural images and experiences, mountain-gorilla habitats were protected and species numbers were increasing.[77]

This final installment of Digit's story dramatically conveys the limitations of thinking about the human-nature encounter as timeless and transcendent and the connected desire to pit nature against culture in an epic Sisyphean battle. Digit's stories depend on the complex intersections of science and popular culture, conservation and global capitalism, representations and real encounters. The mountain gorilla species, *Gorilla beringei beringei*, exists in and needs a unique, wild habitat to survive, and this habitat is increasingly threatened. But the rescue of the species on the verge of extinction has depended on habituation—the establishment of interrelationships between gorillas and humans. It has also depended on a complex interconnection between ecologies and economies as defined and preserved through gorilla-trekking tourism. The complications, connections, and contradictions are striking. The many stories that came together in Digit's life and death speak to the biological and cultural boundaries that divide nature and culture and the intertwined and layered narratives of wilderness, science, consumption, and desire that connect nature and culture. On the one hand, these are stories about scientific research and knowledge, ecologies and economies, communities and wildlife habitats, mass media and representation, wilderness and conservation policy, colonialism and tourism—the process of rendering nature meaningful in the culture of global capitalism. On the other hand, these are stories about how animals and humans—nature and culture in this particular historical moment defined by late global capitalism—coexist and are sustained. Together these intertwined and contested stories ask us to question and probe the established oppositional frameworks between nature and culture, animal and human, habitat and community. They suggest that the human-nature encounter in a global world might be better understood as the product of what Donna Haraway calls "naturecultures." As such, Digit's legacy defies the "binary dualisms" of nature/culture in favor of fluid, historically contingent, coconstituted relationships.[78]

Digit's Legacy

A link to a December 2011 YouTube video entitled "Touched by a Wild Mountain Gorilla" landed in my inbox as I was preparing to make a trip to Africa to go gorilla trekking. It depicts a spellbinding five-minute encounter between a camera-wielding tourist guide and a small group of mountain gorillas in southwestern Uganda. The video begins with a short introduction in which

Figure 4.5. Still from YouTube video "Touched by a Wild Mountain Gorilla" (December 2011). Reproduced courtesy of John J. King II and Jonathan Rossouw.

a white man with an American accent sets the stage. He explains that he and his tourist group on their last morning in the Bwindi National Park stepped out of their tent cabins and were met by the habituated Rushegura gorilla group. "The experience you are going to see next," he tells his anonymous YouTube viewers, including me, "just happened in a very natural way. There was no staging or choreographing. It was an innocent interaction with wild gorillas. And it was absolutely thrilling."[79]

The video, set on the concrete pathways that connect the eight tent cabins that compose the Sanctuary Gorilla Forest Camp in Bwindi Impenetrable Forest, shows eight mountain gorillas including a silverback and three babies walking along a stepped path edged with landscape lighting and encased by lush green foliage. Gustavo Santaolalla's strumming guitar soundtrack from the Che Guevara biopic *Motorcycle Diaries* begins to swell in the background.[80] The silverback, bringing up the rear of the group, pauses at an intersection, turns toward the camera, and then follows the group up the walkway. After a series of spliced shots depicting the gorillas from various perspectives cut short by a shaky, dark, out-of-focus shot that appears to be a gorilla up close, the video abruptly cuts to a new shot. A middle-aged white man is crouched by the side of the path surrounded by three or four gorillas. With his head down and gaze averted, he cradles a camera in both hands, hiding his face. A small gorilla stands next to the man, grasping his knee and then pressing close to the man's ear as if smelling him; the silverback stands to the left with two other gorillas close behind in the foliage and facing the camera. After a few seconds the silverback reaches over to the juvenile and pulls him away from the man, guiding him off the path. He pauses there for a few seconds, glances toward the camera, and then moves off the walkway and sits close by behind the man and the surrounding gorilla group. The other gorillas, as if on cue, then move in from behind and take turns grooming and exploring the man's graying hair and touching his black shirt, as the camera holder whispers in a British accent, "Oh, no way, John." A baby gorilla climbs onto the man's back, and then an adult gorilla moves in; the cameraman identifies the adult as a female. She strokes the man's head, places her lips on his ear as if kissing him, and then moves away. With that the silverback slowly gets up and leaves, moving back down the path with the rest of the gorillas following. The video ends with the crouched man laughing and gasping in wonder as he says repeatedly, "I am a gorilla." As of May 2012 the video had been downloaded over 1.8 million times. I probably account for at least fifty of those downloads. Of the eight thousand or so viewer comments, a number of them highlight the irony of this cross-species encounter. One example read, "Gorilla tour group coming to look at humans in their natural habitat . . . loved it."[81]

I flew over eight thousand miles from the midwestern United States to East Africa, read the prerequisite tourist literature, traveled the length of Uganda mostly on dirt roads, was educated and entertained by three Ugandan naturalists and guides, stayed at the same tent lodge and walked the very paths depicted in the video as I tried to figure out exactly where the man crouched and what paths the gorillas followed. I made two gorilla treks, one a strenuous nine-and-one-half-hour round trip hike and the other an equally difficult seven-hour round-trip hike to the very same Rushegura gorilla group shown in the video. There I made eye contact with a juvenile mountain gorilla named Tango and almost cried and then had heart palpitations watching the very same silverback from the video stand, vocalize, and rush at two cavorting juveniles less than ten feet away. I then flew the eight thousand miles back to the United States and downloaded over fifteen hundred photographs and an hour-long video of our own gorilla encounter with the Rushegura group. Considering all of this I am struck by the narrator's description of this gorilla encounter as "an innocent interaction with wild gorillas." Understanding the many stories that come together around Digit helps to make sense of this video, both the emotional pull and the claim that it represents "a *natural* and *innocent* interaction with *wild* gorillas." Thinking about the layer upon layer of complex economic, political, technological, ecological, to say nothing of the social, cultural, historical, and emotional relationships and narratives that undergird and frame this encounter calls into question every category of nature—natural, authentic, innocent, wild—invoked by the narrator. More importantly, it raises the question hinted at in the viewer comments: can we really separate where nature ends and culture begins?

In some ways this seemingly transcendent moment of interspecies contact breaks down the boundaries between humans and the wild. Dian Fossey and Digit transgressed the separation of scientist and subject and in the process spoke to a broad modern audience that hungered for the touch of the authentic that might be found in connection with wild nature. Yet in the dramatic crossing of a divide, the act reinforces that divide. For the moment of contact to appear so genuinely thrilling, it must be experienced as the ephemeral meeting of two fundamentally different worlds. This focus on the instant of encounter obscures the structures of economy, politics, ideology, and culture that both make that experience possible and render a series of complicated relationships between humans and gorillas. Underneath the "I am a gorilla" reaction in the YouTube video rests a logic of human exceptionalism. Yet if we follow the post-humanist turn, if we look at the world from the perspective of the Anthropocene, we can see that this momentary human-gorilla encounter evinces a complex network of relationships defined through history, biology, politics, technology, and power. These relationships define our shared future.

PART II

Bodies

Chapter 5

The Gulick Family and the Nature of Adolescence

Susan A. Miller

> Nothing is more certain than that each generation longs for a
> reassurance as to the value and charm of life and is secretly afraid
> lest it lose its sense of the youth of the earth.
> —Jane Addams, *The Spirit of Youth and the City Streets*

Jane Addams set the tone for *The Spirit of Youth* in the book's first sentence with the charming double meaning she invested in "the youth of the earth." Initially she uses the phrase to build her argument that humans have always yearned for a sense of authenticity; we must have faith that each and every dawn is the harbinger of a world, and a life, that can be made fresh. Humans inherently crave a young earth, she writes, a natural world that is receptive to their ministrations, pliant and impressionable, ready to receive an overlay of the culture we create. Yet before a reader turns the first page of the book, Addams has moved on to another meaning of "the youth of the earth." This definition does not refer to humanity's fascination with a freshly emergent natural world but rather invokes the redemptive innocence of America's youth. The average person, Addams avers, could not find resolution to existential quandaries through culture or nature alone—neither "literature" nor "glimpses of earth and sky" would serve. Instead adults should turn to the young, those beings who in their developmental essence combine culture and the natural world. Reassurance as to the value of life, she declares, "is never so unchallenged and so invincible as when embodied in youth itself."[1]

If more lyrical than most, Jane Addams was not at all alone among her contemporaries in this conception of youth as embodying the forces of nature and culture. In 1904, when G. Stanley Hall announced his discovery of a new life stage in his two-volume monograph, *Adolescence*, he firmly located youths' maturing bodies within a complex, and mutually constitutive, natural and social world.[2] For Hall, early childhood development was more an unfolding of innate inclinations; adolescence, however, was characterized by a virtual collision of cultural and biological forces, as his work's subtitle amply attests. Youth's rapidly maturing emotional and intellectual abilities, and especially their newly sexualized bodies, moved them away from a life in which they were merely individuals and placed them in a world in which they were part of the reproductive legacy of the "race." With their nature changing virtually by the minute and with those changes redounding to both personal development and the evolutionary potential of ensuing generations, adolescents were, Hall theorized, especially sensitive to environmental influences.[3] Hall's adolescents, buffeted by a maelstrom of evolutionary, psychological, and social forces, represented the fundamental entanglement of nature and culture that rendered humans human. If adolescence was a perilous developmental time, it was also one of great opportunity, serving as a unique window into the permeable relationship between the natural world and modern social conditions.

This view of the adolescent body as a porous entity that absorbed nature and transformed culture had a profound influence on Progressive Era reform, not least through the ideas of one family, the Gulicks. The siblings Frances Gulick Jewett, Luther Gulick, and Sidney Gulick used their own particular visions of adolescent nature, and a dynamic natural world, to frame what they viewed as the most pressing social problems of their generation.[4] All three Gulicks were major contributors to important Progressive Era conversations: Frances as a popularizer of hygiene and health; Luther as a YMCA leader, playground advocate, and founder of the Camp Fire Girls; and Sidney as a popular expert on Japanese culture and U.S.-Asian immigration policy. What united their work in these diverse fields was a belief that the continued positive evolution of the "race"—a term that was as ubiquitous as it was ill-defined at the turn of the twentieth century—was inextricably tied to the responsible stewardship of the American landscape and the proper development of American youths. Sharing Addams's optimistic belief in the spirit of youth and guided by Hall's theories about the newly defined developmental stage, the Gulicks sought ways to harness the power of adolescent bodies to promote social reform. In other words, not only did adolescents embody the complex ground between nature and culture, but in addition their liminal status rendered them enviable models for a nation that sought to harness its natural bounty in service of its rapidly modernizing social structures.

What would become an influential, and identifiably Gulickian, interpretation of youth began in the ideas of their uncle John Thomas Gulick, who had advanced a theory of evolution that depended on a unique interaction between environment and organisms. When the Reverend John Thomas Gulick, a missionary and naturalist who corresponded with Charles Darwin, published *Evolution, Racial and Habitudinal* in 1905, he advanced a theory of speciation that depended on a complex interaction between living creatures and their environment. Gulick could not believe in a theory of natural selection in which the "environment worked alone" but rather postulated that organisms helped to shape isolated environmental niches, which in turn influenced the development of diverse species. For John Thomas Gulick, entire families of *Achatinellae*, the Hawaiian land snails he studied throughout his life, were created thanks to this interaction. Although John was best known in scientific communities for his theory of isolation, his ideas about the interactivity of organisms and the environment were seized upon by the so-called "social Darwinists," the latest incarnation of pundits and policy makers who had long been interested in the relationship between human development and achievement, and social or environmental conditions. At the turn of the twentieth century—the dawn of the "Century of the Child," in the Swedish reformer Ellen Key's words—many paid particular attention to the first years of this interaction.

A positive, formative link between younger children and the environment is at least as old as the publication of Jean-Jacques Rousseau's *Emile* (1762). Enlightenment thinkers and early nineteenth-century romantics often cast young children as the embodiment of natural purity who needed only a wholesome environment and room to grow in order to develop properly. Education reformers, including Friedrich Froebel, enshrined this idea in the creation of the kindergarten—literally, the "children's garden"—a movement that linguistically tethered child development to physical space. By the close of the nineteenth century, this positive affinity between children and the

environment had expanded to include slightly older children, who increasingly became the targeted audience of the nature-study movement.[5] Proponents believed that youngsters were naturals at the study of nature; they
enjoyed plants and trees and were unabashed in their devotion to animals.
Their bodies thrived in the pursuit of nature study, even as their impressionable minds picked up wholesome lessons from the out-of-doors.[6] Moreover
the relationship was reciprocal: children's best nature could be coaxed to the
fore in the natural world, just as the health of the environment could be read
in the development of children's bodies. But sadly, as all Progressive reformers knew, not all children and not all environments were equally healthy.

At the first National Conservation Congress in 1909, Mrs. J. Ellen Foster
gave a speech on what she believed was the nation's most important natural
resource. In "The Conservation of Child Life," Foster exhorted her audience to
apply themselves to the protection and conservation of the raw material that
was the nation's youth population. A boy who was protected from factory
labor and raised in a wholesome environment would, in the fullness of time,
"make a better tree out of which to cut lumber" that could be used to build
social institutions, such as churches and schools, that would benefit all Americans.[7] Although Foster's figuring of the child not simply as a resource to be
conserved but one that could be cut up and used for construction was unusual,
the trope of the child as raw material to be saved and nurtured was widely deployed, from Children's Bureau publications to Theodore Roosevelt's procla-
mation that the "best crop is the crop of children."[8] Framing children as a
natural, and national, resource served as a powerful rhetorical device that
helped Progressive reformers argue that the care of children was not simply a
domestic matter best left to "natural parents" but was a legitimate concern of
the state. When combined with the scientific research that was emerging from
the nascent child-study movement, this vision of children nudged them away
from a simple natural innocence and toward a space that was shaped by politics and culture. If this was true for the youngest children, then how much
more applicable was this realization to those who were poised on a threshold
between a natural childhood and the cultural world of adults?

This particular connection between adolescence and an evolving environment permeated the thinking of multiple generations of a single family and
resonated beyond it. Through the writings, policies, and new institutions promoted by various members of the Gulick family, this interaction between
nature and culture was inscribed onto an entire generation of American
youths. For the Gulick siblings, these ideas undergirded their analyses of U.S.

immigration policy and child-labor laws, the development of public school curriculum and private summer camps, as well as the creation of a "new race of Americans." At the center of it all were adolescents, whose developing bodies, caught as they were between childhood and maturity, mirrored their unique position between natural forces and cultural imperatives. For the Gulicks, this social and biological location invested youths with a particular ability to shape both the physical world in which they lived and the culture they would soon inherit.

John Thomas Gulick: Isolation and Adaptation

Unlike his niece and nephews, John Thomas Gulick did not spare much thought for the nature of youths or the trials of puberty. He did, however, devote an extraordinary amount of time to snails, specifically *Achatinellae*, a genus of Hawaiian land snails that he studied off and on for more than sixty years and from which he developed the theories that culminated in his 1905 monograph, *Evolution, Racial and Habitudinal.*[9] His work with the snails, whose richly colored and diversely striated shells varied from one lush but remarkably similar Oahu valley to the next, led him to articulate a complex theory of speciation in which environmental isolation and the adaptive pro-clivities of organisms interacted to influence evolution. John, a missionary whose religious convictions did not stand in the way of his quick conversion to Darwinian theory—"all these *Achatinellae* never came from Noah's Ark," he wrote—also doubted that all those astonishingly diverse snails were gen-erated by the "environment acting alone," a phrase he employed to describe Darwinian natural selection.[10] In place of what John saw as a predominately mechanistic, if not fatalistic, view of the natural world and its inhabitants in which a particular environment virtually dictated the success of certain traits, John hypothesized a dynamic interaction between the physical environment and living beings in which each influenced the other. In his theory nature selected organisms' traits, but those traits then helped organisms shape the natural world. John's process was multivalent and symbiotic; organisms re-sponded to the natural world, but nature responded and changed in turn, creating a system in which influence flowed back and forth from landscape to living beings.

According to his son and biographer, Addison Gulick, John's penchant for assigning importance to isolation and his appreciation for the formative in-teraction between the physical environment and living things were virtually overdetermined by the circumstances of his childhood.[11] Born in 1832, John was the third son of Peter and Julia Gulick, Congregationalist missionaries who were among the first families posted to the Sandwich, now Hawaiian, Islands.[12] The remoteness of his birthplace, compounded by his parents' strict religiosity and their injunction to avoid all contact with the islands' native peoples, left the youngster quite alone. He was a shy and sickly little boy, plagued by a serious but undiagnosed eye infection that compelled his parents to quarantine him in a dark room for almost two years. John emerged from this physical deprivation not with a reactive affinity for a vigorous life, as his family had hoped, but rather with a deep appreciation for quiet observation and solitude as well as a tendency to view life as profoundly influenced by the environment in which it took root.

Once released from the darkness that did little to help his vision, John encountered an environment that he found lyrical and inspiring. "Life is an ocean wave," he observed as a youth while traveling the valleys and shores of Oahu in search of *Achatinellae*.[13] Although John was acutely attentive to physical minutiae, noting the slightest variation in shell hues and markings, he largely remarked on the world in terms of what he called the "lesser senses." For this visually impaired boy, the Hawaiian landscape was all birdsong and the crash of waves or the sensation of mist and dappled sunlight on his skin, and John reveled in the intimate bond he felt with the landscape. His strict upbringing, however, ensured that this intimacy was tinged with anxiety. As a young boy, John was troubled by his love of nature—it was, after all, a secular passion. He was also wary of the pride he felt in his growing ability to observe and interpret the natural world. Saved from self-recrimination by the assurances of his eldest brother, Halsey, and by his reading in natural theology, a doctrine that saw the endlessly inventive hand of God in nature's rich diversity, John allowed himself to marvel over the natural world and began to hope that he might offer a theory to explain how it came into being.[14]

In *The Voyage of the Beagle*, Charles Darwin noted the presence of different species in what appeared to be precisely identical environments, an observation that matched John's experience of the diversity of snails he encountered in strikingly similar Hawaiian valleys. In *The Origin of Species*, Darwin equivocated, for such data did not help the cause of natural selection, a theory that he well understood to be as incomplete as it was compelling. Darwin's champions mounted what came to be known, somewhat derisively, as the "ignorance hypothesis" to explain away this embarrassment of inexplicable diversity in virtually identical landscapes. In this theory organisms evolved in response to environmental conditions that were critical to their survival but whose presence eluded the observational powers of naturalists. John was not the only skeptic of this view that suggested that snails or finches were more attuned to fine gradations of nature than were humans. It was not hubris, however, that led him to seek an alternate hypothesis but rather a firm conviction that animate beings were endowed with vast powers of adaptation and that the natural world was somehow responsive to those adaptations. Neither organism nor environment alone drove evolution; each participated in the dynamic, and each was profoundly affected by the other. In analyzing John's contribution to evolutionary thought, the philosopher of science Ron Amundson rightly emphasizes the role of the "active organism" and stresses this "relational" worldview over the theory of isolation for which John was better known.[15] It is more difficult to know how to interpret John's understanding of a landscape that came tantalizingly close to being animate itself, or to theorize about what this meant for the human beings who lived in this dynamic world.

John Gulick did not frequently speculate on the ways in which evolution shaped humanity, and he was vigorous in his opposition to Herbert Spencer's ideology of social Darwinism. Still, he had lived and traveled in many an exotic locale in his youth, and mid-nineteenth-century men of science were intensely curious about all those magnificently "odd" peoples who lived in far-flung regions of the globe. In 1854 the Geographical Society and Ethnological Society of New York invited John and Halsey to give a talk on "the many species of the genus Homo" that the brothers had encountered during their travels in Micronesia.[16] John obliged. In a human analog to Darwin's finches, John believed that he had found slightly different peoples inhabiting each of the diverse, isolated South Pacific islands he visited, from the Marshall Islands to Pakin and Ponape in the Caroline Island chain. Each island, according to its particular nature, had encouraged the development of a natural and rightful type, and yet there were individuals who had the potential to transcend their environment and see beyond their home island's limited horizon. It was not coincidental that the islanders who were most savvy about other worlds were the younger members of the tribe.

As an example, John related the story of a king's shrewd son who, upon being asked if he would like to go to America, replied, presciently in John's opinion, "What's the use, I have no money to spend."[17] The young man understood perfectly the defining feature of the mainland's environment and knew that despite his royal blood, he could not thrive there. To John, a man's

individual character, to say nothing of his family's inheritance, was important, but men were also shaped by a "historical, a progressive life, with deep
current undisturbed by the waves of individual life that ripple upon its
surface." Different races were bound to the particular environments that had
first given rise to them, and only when races "subjected themselves to new
forms of selection" could their fundamental character be altered.[18] For John,
this bond between race and environment constituted not a limit on human
development but a social problem and even a potential opportunity. It was this
bond that was scrutinized by members of the next generation of the Gulick
family, who were in equal measure troubled and enthralled by what awaited
the next generation of Americans as they encountered a modern, evolving
American landscape.

The Next Generation of Gulicks

Human beings are, of course, buffeted by currents of cultural change, if not
perhaps in precisely the sense theorized by John Thomas Gulick. Historians of
nineteenth-century family life suggest that the great forces of modernization—
the maturation of industrial capital, social and physical mobility, the growth
of civil society, and access to education—served to complete the collapse of
primogeniture that had been in the works since the middle of the eighteenth
century. An eldest son who could no longer rely on inheriting the family
business or press his traditional claim as head of household once the father-
son dyad was eclipsed gained in other ways. Lost deference, historians argue, was replaced by affection and devotion among siblings who were bound
together as a generation in what the historian Leonore Davidoff has termed
"life's longest relationship."[19] This declining importance of birth order coincided with a predilection for sentiment as well as increased recognition of
women's talents, which served to cement sisters' positions within family units.
Concomitant to these changes was yet another. In the mid-nineteenth century there was increased sacralization of children as middle-class parents began to limit their family size and invest greater financial and emotional
resources in fewer offspring. Most scholarship in the history of youths examines the effects of these tighter emotional bonds on the parent-child relationship, but siblings too were affected and learned to value their brothers and
sisters as key constituents in middle-class family life.

This new emphasis on generational affections did not entirely replace vertical ties to ancestry, but it did create space not only for siblings but also for

cousins, aunts, and uncles to move to the center of a new configuration of family life. These strengthened horizontal webs of kinship were instrumental in the creation of familial-specific versions of habitus, a classical concept of human social structures most recently explicated by the sociologist Pierre Bourdieu. As siblings aged out of natal families, selected marriage partners, and raised children of their own, they remained enmeshed in the sensibilities of their youth. Although brothers and sisters often lived out their adult lives at great physical distances from each other, they were emotionally and intellectually connected in the "sibling archipelago."[20] This metaphor of connection between physically distant yet integrally related bodies is apt for the Gulicks, a family as proud of its extended ties as it was of its connections to the literal archipelago of the Hawaiian Islands. In fact the trope of generational linkage was instrumental in the lives of the Gulicks even beyond their blood kin. As the historian Joy Schulz notes, the children of missionaries formed the Hawaiian Mission Children's Society in 1853, called each other "cousins," and often relied on this "Cousins' Society" for support, both financial and emotional.[21] Thus the childhood ties between Gulick siblings depended on what they understood to be both "natural" and "cultural" affective generational bonds. Frances, Luther, and Sidney maintained these bonds into adulthood; they vacationed together, edited and commented on each other's work, and sustained a lifelong correspondence.[22] They were also influenced by intellectual ties to their uncle John, reaching back a generation as they each individually began to theorize about the future generations of American youths.

Frances Gulick Jewett and the Next Generation

"As we know, however, we cannot altogether separate physical inheritance from the power of the environment. The two have joined hands, and they travel together," wrote Frances Gulick Jewett in *The Next Generation: A Study in the Physiology of Inheritance*, the last work of her prolific publishing career.[23] Fanny, as she was known to friends and family, deployed this argument about the interconnectedness of biological heredity and the physical environment in order to create a transition between a chapter about the inheritance of feeblemindedness, featuring the infamously dysgenic Kallikak family, and one that detailed the oppressive working conditions of child laborers.[24] Although in these examples she lamented the effects of poor conditions and unfortunate parentage on children's development, Fanny was typically more interested in how a proper environment and sound heredity could work together to ensure healthy children. Interestingly, she also understood this symbiotic relationship between heredity and the natural world as a touchstone in her own family's narrative.

Decades before Addison Gulick wrote the biography of his father, John Thomas, Fanny memorialized her own father in *Luther Halsey Gulick: Missionary in Hawaii, Micronesia, Japan and China*.[25] Like her cousin Addison, she emphasized the stark power of an isolated environment and an individual's ability to adapt to the natural world as key components in the evolution of a young person's character. Halsey, as her father was known in his youth, was isolated not by the physical limitations that afflicted his brother John but also by the geographic and cultural isolation of the Hawaiian archipelago. The islands did not hold the same appeal for Halsey as they did for John; where his brother saw a diversity of bountiful life filling every valley, Halsey perceived the social deprivation caused by an absence of intimate friendship. His devout albeit progressive Congregationalism, however, led him to understand this fate as both a blessing and an opportunity.

After attending medical school and the seminary and marrying on the U.S. mainland, Halsey decided to complete his mission in an even more remote environment than the one chosen by his parents. In 1851 twenty-three-year-old Halsey and his new bride, Louisa, sailed for the island of Ponape. Micronesia was a frontier for the Congregational Church, and with only a handful of fellow missionaries scattered across the vast expanses of the Pacific Ocean, the sense of isolation Halsey felt in Hawaii was exponentially increased. Aside from the rough men who crewed the occasional whaler, the only other "whites" with whom the newlyweds had contact were on the bi-monthly mail boat. But when their mission board conceded that it could no longer afford to repair the aging vessel, the young couple was forced to rely on the charity of youngsters. Children from the mission board's home in Boston as well as both indigenous and white missionary children in Hawaii contributed their pennies to outfit the packet ship *Morning Star*.[26] "A highway opened by the hands of children bound Micronesia to the world again," Halsey wrote in his dairy; "it is easy now to forget all the loneliness of the past, when we think of the ten thousand little owners following her like guardian spirits."[27]

The childish philanthropists whom Halsey so admired were recent cultural creations. Proper middle-class Americans in the mid-nineteenth century had begun to remove their children from the workforce and ensconce them in the role of sentimental helpmeets, prized for their economic dependency, powers of moral suasion, and ability to inspire adults by acts of selfless sacrifice.[28] But economic dependency is not the same as economic disengagement, and the above profile fitted perfectly with many reform activities. From Civil War sanitary fairs to temperance campaigns and missionary societies, children played their part in the solicitation and collection of funds. Arguably, children's participation in charitable commerce broadened their reach beyond familial and local economies and gave them an economic identity that had national and even international implications. Halsey's "ten thousand little owners" were not separate from the modern world of commerce—he repeatedly referred to them as "stockholders"—but they could be born and thrive only in a "civilized" environment that both protected them and paid attention to the gifts that grew from their protected status.

"As in the hotbeds of American democracy, that latest development of modern civilization, there are no children, only infants and men, so on Ponape," Halsey observed. "The Ponapean passes from infantile dirt to the niceties of a dandy."[29] Significantly, albeit a bit cryptically, what Halsey lamented was the absence of the critical life stage of childhood, a life stage his daughter Fanny would know as adolescence. Although the precise meaning of his observation is difficult to discern, it is in keeping with a general understanding that many Europeans and Anglo-Americans had of "primitive" peoples: the harshness of climate and terrain, even the exotic nature of indigenous flora and fauna, created a crucible that sped up maturation, provoked precocious sexuality, and essentially bypassed the developmental stages when more "civilized" people experienced a slow awakening to vocation, romantic attachments, and religious calling. The tropics burned with too much heat, producing adults whose strengths were not well tempered, and whose dark exteriors belied an unfinished interior and hollowness of spirit. Natives leap from raw material to poorly realized final product: in Halsey's words, from "dirt" to "dandy." Although Fanny did not choose to elucidate what her father meant by "the hotbeds of American democracy" that he compared to the undesirable environment of Ponape, her own work reveals that she shared a concern that the land he enshrined as the "latest development of modern civilization" was not quite what it should be if it was going to nurture the next generation of civilized Americans properly.

Sarah Frances Gulick, born in the midst of Ponape's 1854 small pox epidemic, gained prominence in Progressive educational circles as the author of the popular Gulick hygiene series, published by Ginn of Boston from 1906 to 1916. Although the title of the series reflected the imprimatur of her younger brother, Luther, it was Fanny who wrote four of the five volumes, providing lessons in biology, nutrition, and physiology for young readers. The volumes were consistently well received by the *School Review*, whose editorials and reviews praised the books' combination of clearly presented, pragmatic science and valuable advice about posture, exercise, and abstinence. Considered an exemplary combination of theory and practice that was appropriately didactic while not condescending to its child audience, the series was frequently recommended as a platform for advanced elementary school and freshmen-level hygiene curricula. However, to understand Fanny's relationship to the environment, it is necessary to look beyond *Good Health* and *The Body at Work* and focus on two slightly quirkier titles that, when read in tandem, articulate her theory about how the natural world and cultural progress converged in the lives of individual children.

Although *Town and City* (1906) and *The Next Generation* (1914) each ostensibly had a single focus—environmental conditions and the physiology of inheritance, respectively—in truth their arguments were intertwined. Fanny, like many of her contemporaries in Progressive circles, believed that as powerful as Mendelian heredity was in guiding human evolution, the environment was an equally potent force in sculpting the human race.[30] Historians of science have tended to explain this pastiche of belief by invoking a lingering faith in a conveniently self-serving brand of Lamarckian evolution; the ability to pass down traits acquired during the course of a disciplined life held a powerful allure for ambitious Americans who fancied themselves self-made men. I would argue, however, that for Fanny Jewett, it was not Lamarckian traits acquired in a lifetime of struggle but rather the environmentally sensitive active organism of her Uncle John's theories that permitted her to combine the two.[31] Her books depended on an intricately reciprocal relationship between the world in which children lived and the ancestors from whom they descended. If adults would only facilitate it, children could use a properly constituted physical world to improve their innate endowments and then repay this investment back to the land—whether that environment be the town, the city, or "the wild."

"For years thoughtful people have noticed that, as a rule, children are good or bad, that they live or die, according to conditions about them," Fanny observed in *The Next Generation*. Children, she concluded, "are cursed or blessed by their environment."[32] Readers of *The Next Generation*, however, would have been well advised to consult her earlier work for a description of this blessed environment. *Town and City,* a Progressive treatise about municipal sanitation and public health, began with an interesting anachronism, far removed from debates about sewers and street cleaning. In the first sentence, Fanny invoked a kindhearted Indian, his wigwam, and the spacious American prairie. She did not, however, hold up this iconic scene as an idyllic landscape. She felt that natives were vigorous and content but not as productive, sociable, or efficient as they could have been had they enjoyed a more complex human society.

To Fanny, the environment and its inhabitants improved as population density increased, making both land and mankind serve both to the best of their ability. Of course, a tipping point was soon reached—she suggested that for New York City this occurred around 1800—when humans overwhelmed the environment and brought ruination instead of uplift. Children, unable to find even the smallest patch of grass, failed to thrive and, having been disinherited from their environmental birthright, lost the ability to improve the landscape. This spiral of degradation between man and nature, Fanny argued, could be arrested only by the nation's youths.

In *The Next Generation,* which Fanny dedicated to the boys and girls who were "guardians" of human heredity, she helped children understand their responsibility to control their health and heredity by carefully controlling their environment. To be sure, children needed to learn how the principles articulated by Mendel and Darwin linked each generation to its predecessors, but readers were not to assume blithely that ancestry equaled destiny. Their individual lives would flourish through the acquisition of healthy habits, but those habits had to be practiced in the proper place: a sufficiently pastoral landscape with enough human interaction for social development but with its natural endowments of flora and fauna intact. Fanny's lesson on the creation of a "new species through a changed environment" may have focused on beetles, but the implicit message permeating the text was that humans worked the same way. "Each of us carries his own ancestral standard through life. Each received this standard from men and women who are ranged back of us in endless rows," Fanny explained. This ghostly army of ancestors had been able to march through a landscape that was positively arrayed to ensure its progress. With this progress now in doubt, children needed not only the lessons available to them in the Gulick hygiene series but also adults who would help them to reshape the world. To examine the manifestation of Fanny's ideas, we must turn to the man who wrote the introduction to *Town and City,* who argued that this book "represents a new step in the evolution of young citizens,"and who believed that it was his life's work to shape that evolution.[33]

Luther Halsey Gulick and the Dynamics of Boyhood and Girlhood

Luther Halsey Gulick was born in Hawaii in 1865 and spent virtually his entire childhood abroad, accompanying his parents on a series of missions that took them to Europe and Japan. At fifteen he was sent to the U.S. mainland to complete his education, but a series of chronic health problems, including heart and digestive troubles as well as severe migraines, caused him to switch schools; he moved from Ohio to New Hampshire before landing at the Sargent School of Physical Training in Cambridge, Massachusetts.[34] The time Luther spent under the direction of Dudley Sargent, professor of physical training at Harvard and a gymnastics enthusiast, changed his life. Luther, like his acquaintance Theodore Roosevelt, believed that a redemptive experience of rigorous physical training had helped him overcome his sickly boyhood, and it converted him to an unwavering faith in the restorative powers of exercise. He embarked upon a professional career—including stints at the YMCA, the Playground Association, and the New York City schools' physical education department—that would allow him to advocate for, indeed proselytize on behalf of, the health benefits of a vigorous physical regime. Early in his life Luther had contemplated joining the family business—he became a doctor in order to serve as a medical missionary—but his commitment to exercise and the healing powers of the out-of-doors persuaded him to minister to a population who appeared to be in special need of these lessons. In the words of one biographer, Luther devoted himself to "the salvation of American adolescence."[35]

Like many of his peers, including Roosevelt and G. Stanley Hall, Luther was concerned about the changes that the modern world had wrought on human beings, especially on youths. What would happen to young people who were separated from the wholesome American landscape, raised in urban areas, and consigned to lives structured by mechanized work and commercial amusements? Children's malleability, the fact that they were, by definition, in a state of becoming, made them uniquely susceptible to the dynamics of cultural and environmental change. For teens on the cusp of sexual maturity, there was an added threat: their newly functional reproductive powers, along with their growing bodies, were vulnerable. Exposure to unhealthy environments, both social and natural, not only endangered the younger generation but also threatened generations yet to be born. This concern for pubescent youth was frequently expressed in terms of the risks associated with their sexual bodies and generated a pall of anxious obsession over questions of adolescent gender roles and sexuality. In this regard Luther was little different than his peers. However, he had a rather particular vision of the natural world that permitted him to propose novel solutions to youths' dilemma, even if the most popular ones emanated from men he greatly admired.

G. Stanley Hall's academic treatises and Teddy Roosevelt's public pronouncements on youth complemented each other, as both men advocated for a "strenuous life" born of the nineteenth-century philosophy "muscular Christianity." The historian Gail Bederman has argued that this emergent vision of manliness was honed by a sharper edge and trumpeted a virile masculinity rooted in physical prowess, competitive sport, and outdoor adventure.[36] Wilderness was natural man's proving ground; all things urban were suspect as they were artificially imbued with culture and its implied femininity. Although Luther deeply admired Hall and Roosevelt, he did not evince the same need for a rugged masculinity, nor was he willing to castigate urban life quite as easily. For Luther, any landscape or physical environment offered opportunities for a wide-awake young man to improve himself, provided that he attend carefully to the activities and exercises that naturally belonged to the place. Natural activities, what he often referred to as "primitive exercise," belonged in the out-of-doors. But urban nature too had something to offer young men, and it was specifically young men whom Luther addressed.

Luther was influenced by a strand of evolutionary thinking, popular in his time, that had murky roots in Darwinian theory.[37] How, proponents asked, could one account for a sexual dimorphism that resulted in the obvious inferiority of women? Although considered weaker, slower, and less intelligent than men, women somehow managed to thrive generation after generation even though they did not manifest the positive evolutionary changes that redounded to the benefit of men. In short, how could the men chosen by natural selection father such indifferent daughters? The answer lay in an evolutionary rupture that occurred at puberty. Since great men added to their stock of physical and mental abilities in their maturity, after they had passed through sexual maturation, those gains were available to their male offspring only after they too reached adolescence. Daughters did not reap these benefits, acquiring only the generic inheritance their fathers possessed in boyhood. For Luther, boys' differential inheritance meant that they need not fear an urban world. Their male ancestors had strived mightily to build this new environment, and boys who paid proper attention to its demands and complexities could also thrive there. Borrowing ideas from his uncle John's work, Luther wanted to help young men adapt to an environment that, while man-made, could help make them into better men.

Luther Gulick was enamored of the city—he made New York his home for two decades—and enmeshed in its institutions. He worked for the Playground Association, sponsored by the Russell Sage Foundation, and maintained his earlier ties to the YMCA. He was principal of the Pratt School in Brooklyn before serving as director of the public schools' department of physical education. In all of these positions Luther tried to re-create the urban landscape of New York so that it could better serve its youngest residents. Playgrounds, gymnasiums, recess yards, and public parks were integral pieces of a "natural city" to Luther, built by humans for their own enjoyment, and he saw no reason why youths could not adapt themselves to these environs. Older boys who were part of the workforce faced other challenges, he admitted, but through a carefully developed program of exercises and hygienic living they need not permit office work to jeopardize their health. Luther devised programs of exercises—for the mind, the voice, the body—that youths could practice in their apartments, on the streets while walking to work, in their Y's facilities, or even in their offices. For the adaptable boy who understood the demands and opportunities of city life, there was nothing inherently unhealthy in the urban environment.

In a wonderful series of eight still photos that introduce Luther's 1906 *Efficient Life*, a veritable handbook of good health and hygiene practices, he portrays a vigorous man moving through a series of dynamic poses. Arms raised in forceful emphasis, he strides purposefully across a stage; he leans, somehow aggressively, into an assembled audience to offer physical punctuation for his argument. There is little question that the reader is invited to see these eight stills as a fluid whole; to scan rapidly through the shots creates the dynamic, staccato action of early motion films. Luther dedicated *The Efficient Life* to the man in these images, Theodore Roosevelt. He honored Roosevelt not as a big-game hunter or a Rough Rider but as a man who was master of urban nature. This was an accomplishment to which Luther felt certain his young readers would aspire.[38]

If Luther could not quite believe that urban spaces were an unmitigated disaster for young men, he was equally reluctant to believe that girls could develop properly without recourse to a rather different experience of the natural world. Trapped in the rhythmic periodicity of their reproductive systems and denied the spark required of evolutionary change because they ran true to type as nature's conservators, girls required a world that reflected their own unique nature. Luther and his wife, Charlotte Vetter Gulick, founded the Camp Fire Girls to provide first their four daughters and later tens of thousands of young women with properly constructed experiences of nature. This nature was timeless, reflective of older, "primitive" truths about the origins of the human race. Girls had to seek out the "wilderness" of summer camp, enlivened by Camp Fire ritual, because they were slower to adapt to the changes wrought by human culture. Girls embodied the core inheritance of the race, its most primitive impulses, and so required time apart from the modern world and time spent in a primitive nature in order to remind themselves of important truths about their racial history.[39]

Despite the paeans to nature that were rife in Luther's writing on the purpose of Camp Fire, he did not wish to return girls to a natural world that was entirely unmarked by culture. Just as Camp Fire Girls practiced certain stylized rituals that were meant to be evocative of Native American tradition, so too the organization required a wilderness that had been shaped by humanity. In a chapter devoted to Luther's Camp Fire philosophy, Ethel Dorgan, Luther's first biographer, suggests that it took keen vision and an extraordinary connection to nature for modern man to conceive of a landscape's potential. Most would have seen only a "field of rocks" unsuitable for cultivation along the shores of Lake Sebago, she wrote, but Luther Gulick recognized the land's potential to nurture a new generation of girls. For Luther, the fertility inherent in the land derived not only from soil and sun but also from the literary giants who loved the land and lionized it in their work. "The region has been sung by Longfellow, Hawthorne and Whittier," Dorgan explained, and these poetic voices had saturated the landscape, changing it into a form of nature that was perfectly suited to the imaginative nature of adolescent girls.[40]

During Camp Fire rituals, "primitive maidens" dressed in ceremonial gowns were invited to write lines of verse in celebration of the contours of the camp environment. In a natural world imbued with the best of cultural traditions, girls could create a culture that would strengthen their own nature. It was in this mutually constitutive environment—isolated from an urbane modernity that did not quite suit them—that adolescent girls could flour-ish. By bringing girls into just the right landscape Luther hoped to raise a new race of future mothers who could transmit the best of the racial past to future generations.[41] Luther's vision was expansive, but its influence was fleet-ing. After his death in 1918, Camp Fire continued, but much of its "poetic" basis was supplanted by the pragmatism and popularity of other girls' orga-nizations.[42] The quest for the ideal physical and cultural environment (be it camp or city) in which to raise the next generation of American youths was taken up by his brother, Sidney, whose vision for the future brought him back to the siblings' childhood home.

Sidney Lewis Gulick and the "Pacific Paradise"

Sidney Lewis, the third child and eldest son of Louisa and Luther Halsey Gu-lick, devoted himself to the family business to a greater degree than any of his siblings did: "my missionary tendency is I suppose somewhat hereditary," he observed.[43] After graduating from Dartmouth College and the Union Theological Seminary, Sidney took up his mission in Kumamoto, Japan, on New Year's Day in 1888. It was a posting that initiated his lifelong interest in the landscape, culture, and peoples of Japan. Sidney's mission, however, quickly diverged from his Congregationalist brethren; he spent less time in-troducing Christ to Japan and rather more effort introducing the Japanese to Americans. Frequently lauded as the most influential Japanese mission-ary of his generation, Sidney wrote dozens of books and articles, some in Japanese, in which he analyzed the history and contemporary configurations of Japanese politics and social conventions, always returning to what he called "the evolution of Japanese culture."[44] He was particularly interested in Japan's future evolution as a nation and a "race" and attempted to predict what might happen when a culture he characterized as isolated, homogenous, and tradition-bound began to modernize and claim a place on the international stage. His work on the "American Japanese problem," presented during a se-ries of speaking tours that he organized while on furlough in the United States, met with a far larger audience than those that typically gathered for the pre-sentations of returned missionaries.

This was not surprising given that late nineteenth-century American cul-ture was captivated by orientalism. The fashionable classes, following the lead of Anglo and European trendsetters, decorated their homes with expen-sive porcelains and silks and flirted with both Eastern philosophy and opiates, while working-class audiences at the Philadelphia Centennial in 1876 and the 1893 Columbian Exposition in Chicago crowded exhibits devoted to all things Asian. Japanese exhibitors attempted to control the nation's image, and argued for Japan's inclusion among the world's Western powers, by juxtaposing narratives of a proud tradition with a decisive commitment to modernity.[45] Still, Americans' fascination with the Orient was steeped in racism. Scholars of race theory suggest that turn-of-the-century America provided a particularly rich environment for the construction of new forms of racial prejudice. Nineteenth-century models predicated on a hierarchy of European "races" were breaking down, allowing even the lowliest Caucasians to assert a claim to "whiteness."[46] If this had clear, albeit disastrous consequences for people considered "black," its legacy for Asians was more complex. Gretchen Murphy argues that Americans cast the Japanese and, significantly for understanding Sidney Gulick's work, the Hawaiians in a complex dual role.[47] Hawaiians were people who inhabited the most distant reaches of the exotic Orient, the very edges of the Far East, and thus embodied the highest degree of exoticism accorded the Asian "races." However, the islands could also be reached by traveling west across the American continent, following a path of frontier expansion, subjugation of native peoples, and eventually the path of American imperialism. The Pacific islands and their inhabitants therefore occupied a virtual international dateline of racism and nativism where empire met exoticism and where, as Sidney phrased it, the future of "Asiatic citizenship" met the latest manifestation of "American democracy."[48]

A staunch proponent of Christian internationalism, Sidney believed that a shrinking world and an expanding American empire necessitated new ways of thinking about race and immigration. "There is also a new America," he wrote. "Whether we like it or not, the United States is an international power; we can no longer live to ourselves."[49] Historically, "race-mixing" had been the result of military conquest, Sidney wrote, but now that the globe was "wonderfully accessible," peoples mixed voluntarily and more readily, although they still carried with them a racial "self-consciousness" that would have to be tempered if they wished genuinely to assimilate into a new culture. For Sidney, the path to a coherent immigration policy, and thus a successful blending of cultures, rested in the scientific assessment of racial traits. If Americans wished to transform the "Yellow Peril" into a "golden advantage," they needed to understand the evolutionary heritage of the Japanese.[50] In order to "throw some light on the vexed question" of "race-nature," he wrote *Evolution of the Japanese*, in which he relied on his uncle's theories.[51] Sidney

thanked John Thomas for the "invaluable criticisms and suggestions in regard to the general theory of social evolution" he presented, and in keeping
with his uncle's theory of biological evolution, Sidney constructed a theory
of social evolution on the twin precepts of adaptation and geographic isolation.[52] However, he added his own focus on the importance of youths.

Sidney presents the crux of his argument in the monograph's fifth chapter, "Japanese Sensitiveness to the Environment." He argues that the cultural
and racial evolution of the Japanese was driven by the physical isolation of
their island nation. This isolation—which according to his uncle's theory was
a force powerful enough to create new species—encouraged the development
of a culturally and racially homogenous population. Traits forged in the crucible of isolation melded with proclivities that were inherent to the race to
produce key Japanese characteristics, including "keen powers of attention to
detail and of exact imitation."[53] All of this imitation enacted by a homogenous people within a monolithic culture reflected back on itself—imagine an
endless hall of identical mirrors—until it threatened to grind the race's development to a halt. Ironically, this potentially immobilizing tendency also
held the key to the continued evolution of the Japanese. Isolated as their home
was, it was equally volatile. Buffeted by tidal waves and earthquakes, Japan's
physical geography demanded a people who had the capacity to adapt to a
dynamic environment. Here the race's keen powers of perception kept it alert
to the need for quick adaptation. (This adaptability distinguished the Japanese
from the Chinese, whom Sidney, along with a majority of Western ethnog-
raphers, viewed as rigidly inflexible and disinclined to adapt to modern life.)
Thus the physical landscape both produced and interacted with a race's
characteristics to help define its social and cultural evolution. For Sidney,
however, the real test of a race's prowess came when it left its ancestral home:
would the Japanese remain mired in a simplistic cycle of imitation and mim-
icry, or could they use their penchant for adaptation to a productive end?
His answer, unsurprisingly, depended on the new environment to which they
immigrated and the age at which they did so.

In a passage that showcases the condescension with which Sidney could
view a people whom he did genuinely admire, he describes why continental
Europe often proved to be an unfortunate home for young Japanese scholars. It is "amusing to see," he wrote, the transformations that happened when
students went abroad.[54] Frequently they returned to Japan having adopted
the dress, manners, and even national character of the Germans or the French.
Sometimes they took on the traits of both nations, but alas, they did not do

it well. Like children playing dress-up in their parents' clothes, Japanese students looked comical garbed in Western manners, the culture resting askew on their shoulders. They did not truly understand what knitted together the fabric of Western civilization, and so they borrowed pieces here and there, creating a vaguely embarrassing motley costume of national traits that by rights should have remained distinct. Although Sidney argued that the European environment had made a mockery of the Japanese students' skills in adaptation, he insisted that they were the right people to lead their nation's forays into the wider world.

In his final book, Sidney Gulick identified the ideal environment in which the youths of Japan could thrive as they left their homeland and attempted to help integrate their nation into the modern world of internationalism. *Mixing the Races in Hawaii*—dedicated to "all kindred spirits who seek interracial understanding, appreciation and goodwill"—argues that the Hawaiian Islands could serve as the perfect platform from which to launch both Japanese internationalism and a new "American race."[55] The islands' geographic isolation had protected the people from a multitude of cultural ills that plagued the U.S. mainland. Immorality, alcoholism, and poverty had not, Sidney believed, gained a firm foothold in Hawaii, and if youths remained stalwart, then these vices could be held in abeyance. Additionally the islands' location on the edge of so many cultures encouraged a refreshing lack of racial prejudice. This liminal space, which was neither American nor Japanese and was home to a hybrid race that was not quite white and not quite Asian, had the potential to become a "Paradise of the Pacific." Hawaii's malleability, its position betwixt and between, dictated that the people best suited to embody its unique characteristics were those who shared them. Adolescents, individuals who found themselves on the cusp of so many identities, were Hawaii's best ambassadors, its best hope for the realization of Edenic dreams. "The hope of the country is in you, its young people," proclaimed one leader, a position earnestly endorsed by Sidney Gulick.

Twenty-four years before the birth of America's first mixed-race president, *Mixing the Races* identified Barack Obama's alma mater, the Punahou School, as one of several locations for the education and training of the new race. In Sidney's book, class pictures of Punahou graduates share space with images of integrated Boy Scout troops, healthy broods of biracial siblings, and encomiums to the power of the YMCA to culturally and "psychologically unify" a population that had long been welded together by the salubrious effects of isolation. Although Sidney, writing in the wake of Margaret Mead's *Coming of Age in Samoa*, was perhaps more inclined than his siblings toward an anthropological explanation for adolescence, he was still clearly convinced that biological evolution and cultural evolution were inextricably bound together.

In this essay I have suggested that the Gulick siblings grappled with a pair of related questions that currently occupy historians of childhood and youth: what forces in turn-of-the-century American culture helped to create and define the developmental life stage we know as adolescence, and how in turn did this new category of people affect the culture that gave rise to it? Historians have pointed to habits of reading and writing as acts of adolescent self-creation in middle-class schoolgirls and found working-class youths assembling peer cultures steeped in the burgeoning consumer culture.[56] The enforcement of mandatory, age-graded classrooms; changing familial demographics; and the maturation of industrial capital that drove youngsters out of the job market have all been identified as components in the creation of adolescence. For the Gulick siblings, however, these forces were ancillary to youths' interactions with physical environments.

All three siblings held views about heredity and environmentalism that required careful balance. They were convinced of the pivotal role of inheritance and had sympathy for many ideologies that can fairly be categorized as "positive" eugenics, and yet all were equally disinterested in aligning themselves fully with the most doctrinal social Darwinists. Their shared belief in the importance of heredity was, however, thickly marbled with a profound faith in the formative powers of the physical environment. Each sibling was able to sculpt an intellectually coherent worldview, and make meaningful contributions to his or her chosen field, by focusing on youth and by employing a version of John Thomas's idea of the active organism. The hectic dynamism that many Americans experienced as a hallmark of the early twentieth century seemed to match up perfectly with the storm and stress of adolescence. The nation and its youths appeared to be in a convergent state of becoming. By honoring heredity and history and by embodying the ability to shape and be positively transformed by the environment, youths could fulfill their promise as the next generation.

Thus understood as a unique and uniquely important moment of biological, individual, and national change, adolescence embodies complex relationships between nature and culture. Despite a tendency on the part of scholars and popular commentators to privilege biology over culture—or vice versa—in explaining adolescent behavior, the rise of adolescence as an important social category cannot in fact be understood from the basis of either one alone.[57] The Gulicks' influential framing reminds us that the currently popular neurological models represent a cultural shift away from viewing adolescence as a key site where nature and culture are rendered in tandem as a combination with important consequences for individual, generation, and nation.

Chapter 6

Children of Light: The Nature and Culture of Suntanning

Catherine Cocks

"Race denotes what man *is*," the economist William Z. Ripley declared in 1899, whereas "all these other details of social life"—environment, ethnicity, nationality, and language—"represent what man *does*."[1] This distinction between what humans are and what they do, which gained influence over the course of the first half of the twentieth century, summarized a major shift in the understanding of human variation. Ripley's remark underscores the binary thinking that underlay the new understanding: opposing nature to nurture, bodily inheritance to environmental influences, and perhaps most contentiously, race against culture. This final opposition proposed that on the one hand, people have bodies bearing obvious physical differences; on the other, they have customs and traditions derived from historical and social connections. One is biological, the other a human invention. Neither determines the shape of the other. Before 1900, though, *is* and *does*—race and culture—appeared to most intellectuals and ordinary people to be tightly interwoven and mutually determining; notoriously, they determined a system of fixed racial hierarchies, among many other inequalities. Picking this fabric apart to render race and culture as opposites played a critical role in challenging the inequalities of the old order. Yet by obscuring the "relational ontologies" that join nature and culture, this opposition makes it difficult to formulate an ethical politics that encompasses the relationship between our embodied, encultured, and culture- and biology-producing selves and the biosphere to which we belong.[2]

Revisiting the moment at which race and culture were rendered as opposites opens a way to think about the ways that bodies and cultures mutually construct each other without being captured by oppressive determinism or antimaterial idealism. The phenomenon through which I propose to make this argument is the spread of suntanning among white North Americans after 1900. This fashion trend literally embodied a critical change in the way that whites thought about the relationship between their natures and the rest of nature. Though only a few sunbathers waxed philosophical about their practice, its meaning emerges from its interweaving with phenomena that did have explicit intellectual rationales, including the scientific acceptance of natural selection as the mechanism of evolution, the spread of eugenics, the rise of germ theory, and the discovery of vitamins.[3] Precisely because it was a popular practice that embodied a specific relationship between selfhood and environmental forces, suntanning illuminates the extent to which nature and culture are not opposites but fluid conditions of possibility.

Environmental Determinism

The popular assumption today is that before the general acceptance of the concept of culture in the mid-twentieth century, white people conceived of human nature as determined by biology. In their ignorance they subsumed things today considered cultural—ethnic identity, family form, and gender roles, for example—into the body and called the assemblage "race." Supposedly we know better now; we know that *race* marks physical differences that should have no social effects and that *culture* is a set of values and practices we learn from those around us. Looking back through the lens of contemporary beliefs, the earlier theory seems at best simplistic and unenlightened. But the situation in the past was far more complex than this formulation allows, and that complexity sheds light on the extent to which the two concepts are closely related ways of understanding the relationships among human bodies, human cultures, and the nonhuman world. For centuries North Americans and Europeans considered human nature the product of a larger nature, the world outside the human body. Theirs was not a narrowly biological determinism but a broad-based environmental one, a grandly geographic vision. The shift that occurred gradually around the turn of the twentieth century was not the recognition that upbringing (culture) is far more important in the shaping of human beings than biology (race), as histories of the culture concept usually argue. That binary is the *product* of this shift and the often violent struggles that forged it, not a description of past beliefs. Rather, what happened was the erosion of the complex, long-standing set of beliefs that cast human beings in their individual and collective differences as the products of the places of their nurture, particularly the geography and climate. The idea that biology (human nature) and customs and traditions (culture) are distinct realms whose precise relationship is a problem stemmed from the breakdown of this older framework for understanding human variation.

I began to recognize this shift—and its misrecognition in the usual history of the culture concept—in the course of exploring the transformation of North American whites' attitudes toward the tropics between 1880 and 1940. What changed was precisely how they understood the relationship between their bodies and the natural world, and suntanning was the most startling expression of the new understanding. European and North American whites had long prized their pale skin as the insignia of superior virtue and natural mastery, and in the Americas in particular, skin color was a major dynamic in producing and practicing social inequality. For much of the eighteenth and nineteenth centuries, most white people in North America and Europe feared that exposing themselves to heat and strong sunshine would lead to "racial degeneration"—the transformation of whites into nonwhites.[4]

Behind this fear lay a widely shared environmental determinism in which climate played a particularly large role in shaping people both individually and collectively. At the largest scale, warm climates produced dark-skinned people who were hot-blooded, emotional, and indolent, while temperate climates generated light-skinned people who were cool, rational, and hardworking. At the smallest scale, each person's health depended on the interplay of the body with a place's "temperature, atmospheric vicissitudes, prevailing winds, humidity, its elevation above the sea level, its proximity to the ocean or oceanic currents, its contiguity to mountains, lakes, rivers, arid areas, soil, drainage, vegetable productions, malaria, general sanitation and other factors."[5] In a sign of the epistemological distance between us and the late nineteenth century, the author of this passage used malaria in its original sense of "bad air," not as the name of a mosquito-borne parasitic disease. From this perspective, human beings were malleable creatures easily penetrated and transformed by the natural forces at work where they lived. Health required maintaining oneself in harmony with one's surroundings, while morality suggested the wisdom of living where nature fostered human virtue. Civilization—the ultimate expression of that virtue—was truly possible, in this way of thinking, only among the pale-skinned peoples of Western Europe and North America.

This understanding of the relationship between humanity and the natural world dogged Europeans and North Americans in all their imperial adventures in sunny, warm places. When whites entered the tropics, both their personal health and the integrity of the race were at stake, because under the influence of tropical climates, whites would inexorably become more like the nonwhites native to such places. "Can men and women of the white race immigrate in large numbers to the moist hot Tropics [sic] and live there on the same high plane of civilization as that characteristic of their former homes, retaining their physical health and vitality, their mental and moral standards, and reproducing their own kind?" Harvard professor Robert de C. Ward asked. "Further, can future generations of white people, born in the Tropics [sic], maintain, in the years to come, these same standards of civilization and of physical, mental, and moral vigor?"[6] Many experts echoed Ward's emphatically negative reply. If the environment made race, it could remake it too, as it notoriously had in Latin America: "[T]here can be no doubt that the Creole whites, as a class, showed increasing signs of degeneracy. Climate was a prime cause in the hotter regions."[7]

Among the many dangers of hot climates to whites was the intense sunshine: "'Beware of the sun' is a good rule for the Tropics. There is, in general, too much sunshine in the Tropics."[8] Eighteenth- and nineteenth-century physicians especially worried about the effects of the sun's rays on whites' heads and kidneys, advising them to wear hats and special underwear and avoid the noonday sun.[9] By the turn of the twentieth century, developments in the study of the electromagnetic spectrum imparted a modern sheen to this long-standing fear. In an influential study based on research in the United States–occupied Philippines, army doctor Charles Woodruff argued that the greater proportion of "actinic" (ultraviolet) rays in tropical sunshine penetrated the vulnerable pale skins of whites and overstimulated them, leading to nervous exhaustion or "tropical neurasthenia." They could survive—but probably never thrive—in the tropics only with the proper prophylaxis: "*Day clothing should be opaque,*" hats "must be of wide brim and thick enough to exclude all the rays [of the sun]," and houses, schools, and hospitals must be kept dark.[10] In short, whites had to shield their vulnerable bodies assiduously from tropical nature, especially its blazing sunlight, if they were to retain command of both their faculties and their racial integrity.

And yet after 1900, during an era of virulent white supremacy that legitimized the bloody expansion of European and U.S. empires in Asia, Africa, and the South Pacific, pale-skinned people began exposing themselves to the sun for the explicit purpose of darkening their skin. This was not a minor outbreak of eccentricity; nor was it a protest against racism or imperialism. Rather, it was one element in the transformation of whites' beliefs about and uses of the tropics: the region ceased to be a hellish pit of immorality and disease and became the ideal site for a beach vacation. Beginning in the 1880s and accelerating after 1900, hotel, railroad, and steamship companies began investing in hotels, tours, and cruises in southern California, Florida, Mexico, and the Caribbean, places popularly considered tropical even when they were not geographically so. The beach cultures that emerged in these places modeled a new relationship between white people and their environment, one that emphasized rejuvenation through physical exposure to sea, sand, and especially sunshine, in flagrant disregard for Woodruff's dire warnings against the dangers of tropical light. Though European beach-going dated at least to the late eighteenth century, the idea of lying on the sand in scanty clothing bathing in the sun was decidedly new. By the 1920s women wearing clinging, one-piece "California"-style bathing suits were violating municipal dress codes on beaches everywhere in the United States (including California), and men increasingly went bare-chested. Cruise ships in the Caribbean sprouted swimming pools and sun decks. Cosmetics companies began to sell rouge and lipstick in tints designed to enhance bronzed skin. Similar developments occurred in Europe, centered in southern France and the Mediterranean, and in Australia.[11]

Why, under circumstances in which race was a matter of life and death for both individuals and nations, would pale-skinned people deliberately darken their skin? White people's suntanning constituted a kind of "brownface," a playful experiment in becoming nonwhite. Tanning, in the eyes of its early twentieth-century practitioners, allowed white people to partake of the qualities long attributed to nonwhites in the discourse of civilization, especially sensuality and youthfulness, while remaining essentially white. Although "nobody sympathizes with a sunburned elderly bachelor," one writer declared with a wink, everyone would admire the new man who emerged from the peeling, blistering white skin: "What a husky dog he is, and quite young-looking! Brown as an Indian." Tanning participated in a broader "primitivist" movement in which European and North American whites faulted their urban-industrial civilization for making them jaded, repressed, and unhealthy and sought rejuvenation by regaining the intimacy with nature—both human and nonhuman—supposedly typical of less civilized (that is, nonwhite and lower-class) peoples. This renewed intimacy, many well-to-do whites believed, would liberate them from the sexual constraints and physical weakness caused by being too civilized. Too much culture could be cured with a dose of nature.[12]

This primitivist subtext is visible in the way that tanning advocates justified the novel practice. Most constructed a genealogy of the practice that began with ancient sun worship, sometimes among Egyptians and sometimes among indigenous Americans, and ended in some form of the plea that modern residents of the United States must "recover the full heritage of health, energy, and high spirits rightfully ours as 'children of light.'"[13] "The native Floridians called themselves 'Children of the Sun,'" the Florida Hotel Commission's state guide asserted, and they understood the "therapeutic value of the actinic [ultraviolet] rays of the sun . . . centuries before the advent of the white man." The foolish Spaniards, however, "failed to learn that the secret of health could be found in the beneficent sunshine" rather than in its waters or the mythical Fountain of Youth. The true realization of Florida's wealth arrived only with a new generation of children of the sun, the U.S. settlers who recognized the peninsula as "a gigantic amusement pier . . . , a natural year-round playground for the nation."[14]

Not surprisingly, given the long association between whites' exposure to the sun and racial degeneration, many self-appointed social arbiters criticized tanning in explicitly racial terms, blaming it for a decay in manners and maybe even morals. In 1907 the *Chicago Daily Tribune*'s anonymous beauty adviser pointed "the finger of scorn . . . at the score of reckless sun bathers who . . . cherish an ambition to acquire a certain bronze color on neck, arms, and face." Such people behaved like "bands of savages, their faces tanned to a deep mahogany, their collars turned in, and their sleeves rolled up; they are not unlike the natives of some tropical island."[15] "All spring and summer, practically every living woman of you has tried to sun-tan as black as your hat," one fashion maven remarked with some exasperation at the onset of autumn. "Now, suddenly, every woman wants to look as white and fragile as a lily," so she offered some tips in response to her readers' "sudden yearning for a new face, all innocent and fair."[16] Black hats and lily whites: the stakes of skin color could not be clearer.

But tanning was not simply an aspect of primitivism; nor was it perpetrated by the fashion and tourism industries, though they actively promoted it. White people's desire to darken their skins participated in the contemporaneous scientific reconceptualization of the relationship between nature and human bodies, a shift in which the natural world lost much of its ancient power to reshape human nature. It began with changing medical ideas about sunshine. A logical extension of the traditional belief that environmental factors shaped health, "phototherapy" had emerged as a field of research and application in the mid-nineteenth century. After a brief and quickly discredited fad for the use of blue light in healing in the 1860s and 1870s, the first respectable recommendations for the therapeutic use of light, including sunshine ("heliotherapy"), came from physicians in the 1880s and 1890s. By the late nineteenth century it had achieved a measure of respectability and was incorporated into medical education.[17]

But prescriptions for heliotherapy were far from an endorsement of casual sunbathing. The San Diego physician Peter Remondino cautioned that "sunshine is healthy, but basking in the sun whilst sitting against some strongly reflecting surface in a still air and being immersed in a cool but not chilly sunshiny air in a tolerable degree of motion are wholly different and have entirely different results." Lying "like a Strasbourg goose, broiling your liver in a 'sun bath,'" he continued, could only have negative effects.[18] Sunbathing for the purpose of getting a tan, Dr. W. A. Evans declared, was wasteful: "If a person has gained his tan by out of doors work or play he has acquired physical capital. The same cannot be said for tans acquired by lying quietly on the beach exposed to the sun or wind. That is the counterfeit article."[19] Whites who tanned on purpose, in Evans's view, deceived nature into giving them the appearance of health without doing the work necessary to build a strong body (a critique, in a small way, of the distinction between *is* and *does*).

Cautious physicians found themselves simultaneously bolstered and undermined by new scientific discoveries. After 1900 a growing body of clinical and experimental evidence confirmed that exposure to sunlight could kill bacteria, hasten healing, improve mood, and heighten disease resistance, especially among tuberculosis sufferers. Research into the medical uses of light encouraged physicians treating urban children to aggregate and extend the previously scattered, partial evidence on the relationship between sunshine and rickets, a crippling, sometimes fatal failure of the bones to harden properly during infancy and childhood. In 1923 scientists experimenting on animals demonstrated that sunshine was a sovereign cure for rickets and related adult diseases. Still uncertain of the mechanism of this miraculous cure, researchers classified the unknown substance that human skin produced when exposed to the sun as one of a new type of nutrients: vitamins. Vitamins A, B, and C had already been discovered, so this new substance was labeled D.[20] (Although it is still popularly known by its original name, scientists now consider it a steroid hormone—not a substance we get by incorporating external resources into our sealed bodies but one we produce by interacting with the world around us.[21] But I am getting ahead of myself.)

The discovery of vitamin D and its source in sunshine simultaneously gave new life to the old idea that humans had to live in harmony with nature to thrive and challenged the older way of thinking about the relationship between bodies and nature. The medical perspective derived from environmental determinism cast human beings as permeable entities constantly interpenetrated by a vast array of natural forces. People were capable of achieving good health only by managing their relationship with these forces through such practices as draining wetlands, ventilating their houses properly, or traveling to an environment better suited to their constitutions. In contrast, vitamins were tiny, discrete, hitherto unimagined substances whose absence or presence in the diet had vast power to affect human health. The idea of vitamins—and "nutrients" more broadly—mirrored the rethinking of disease that began in the late nineteenth century with the rise of the germ theory of disease. It proposed that creatures too small to see, not a person's poor adaptation to his or her environment, caused illness by breaching the body's defenses. Both germs and vitamins helped to reduce the complex, individualized system of checks and balances between bodies and environments typical of nineteenth-century medicine to a matter of ingesting or avoiding specific substances.[22] Few people then thought that humans could alter the climate, but science could, or at least claimed to be able to, seal bodies against their tiny foes and encapsulate their tiny allies in pills so that people would not have to rely on fickle nature to provide their necessities. The closed body had little to fear from climatic or other environmental forces—they could not alter its essential nature.

The discovery of vitamin D reinforced the existing practice of heliotherapy and gave scientific prestige to the growing movement to bring whites back into closer contact with nature—but now with the promise of rejuvenation rather than the threat of degeneration.[23] Lolling in the sun would give white people all the benefits that nonwhites gained from their natural habitats in the tropics, without losing the virtues endowed by growing up in the temperate zones. Regaining the bond with nature characteristic of primitives did not mean relinquishing the benefits of civilization: "To get all the ultraviolet radiation we need, we do not have to exist like savages, nor put on weird costumes, nor give up a single boon of civilized life."[24] The news that tanned skin blocks the ultraviolet rays that stimulate vitamin D production provided a scientific rationale for the idea of limiting the sun's power to transform. Too much sun was not healthy, and the white body had natural means of preventing excess. "Remember," the physician Walter H. Eddy wrote in his regular *Good Housekeeping* column, "a quickly acquired brown pigmentation is not proof of having used sunlight healthfully. . . . [A] too tanned skin may prevent sun benefits. The disease of rickets is far more prevalent in infants of the dark-skinned races."[25] The implication was that whites benefited from the sun *more* than people of color did because whereas people of color could never adjust their skin to admit more sun, whites could regulate theirs: "Darkening of the skin . . . is not considered a benefit, rather a detriment, as it undoubtedly makes it more difficult for the light to penetrate. . . . Therefore one tries for a light or golden-brown tone of the skin."[26] By moderating their skin darkening, whites avoided the danger into which people of color had heedlessly fallen—that of becoming so dark that the sun could not do its health-giving work.

In this sense tanning was precisely the opposite of the racial degeneration that an earlier generation of physicians and geographers had feared as a result of whites moving into the tropics. It embodied the new understanding of the relationship between human bodies and nonhuman nature that underlay the scientific concepts of vitamins and germs. Although bodies remained vulnerable in both theories—people had to eat carefully and live hygienically to achieve the blooming health promised by the new science—individuals lucky enough to have pale skin were now largely autonomous, closed beings with the cultural tools to master the forces of nature. By managing them properly, a white person could enjoy all the benefits of an intimate bond with nature without degenerating into a nonwhite person. Deliberate suntanning, like vaccinations, frequent handwashing, and vitamin pills, expressed a new confidence that whites could regulate nature's powers to their own benefit. What people *did* (culture) might change, but what they *were* (race) would not.

Natural Selection

The reconceptualization of the body as a largely sealed system defined by its own biology also stemmed from scientists' growing acceptance of natural selection as the mechanism of evolution. Environmental determinism rested to a considerable degree on the idea that acquired characteristics could be inherited. The process of racial degeneration, for example, entailed white parents passing the demoralizing effects of the tropics—such as alcoholism, promiscuity, and laziness—on to their children, and not merely by example. In contrast, the concept of natural selection posits that organisms can pass along via bodily reproduction only those traits with which they were born. The environment affects the ability of organisms to thrive and thus their opportunities to reproduce, but its direct effects on a creature's body live only as long as it does. Natural selection is a much narrower, specifically biological mechanism than the evolutionary processes that environmental determinists had envisioned.[27]

Although scientists disagreed vociferously about how heredity worked (and, as Susan Miller argues in this volume, some developed theories that emphasized the ability of living creatures to shape the environment that in turn shaped them), it increasingly could be, and was, experimentally defined from the late nineteenth century. The growing importance of genetics in explaining human variation undermined the idea that race could explain complex social phenomena in part because the relationship between genes and human behaviors remains uncertain and in part because it drastically curtailed the ground on which the concept of race rested. Understood as the expression of a collective response to the natural environment, race could summon a vast array of forces and conditions to its defense. In genetics there were only genes, transmitted via sexual reproduction.[28] (This state of affairs says little about the social power of race, which has never relied primarily on scientific proof.)

Even as biologists gained the ability to explain human variation, a wide array of people committed themselves to the concept of culture, the idea that what people *do* determines what they *are*, rather than the reverse. The concept emerged as biology's opposite amid the erosion of the old environmental

determinism. Everything that genes had trouble explaining, culture adopted
as its own, except that, crucially, its advocates often seized on the concept of
culture as a weapon against the hierarchies typical of the old system. However, they wielded it mainly against an emerging biological determinism
rather than using it to challenge the declining geographic one. As the white
supremacist Henry Fairfield Osborn sniffed, "The favorite defense of these
inferior classes is an unqualified denial of the existence of fixed inherited
qualities, either physical or spiritual, which cannot be obliterated or greatly
modified by a change of environment."[29] Equally influential were the burgeoning nationalisms of the era, which perpetuated older ideas about environmental influences by citing the power of landscapes, state institutions, religious
affiliations, mythic histories, and languages to create a transcendent psycho-
social unity among the members of a nation. From the interactions among
emergent nationalisms, reform movements, and efforts both secular and religious to determine just what humans owed to nature emerged the concept
of culture. In the hands of progressives, culture was an increasingly effective
weapon against the biological determinism that underwrote many of the
inequalities of this era. In many ways this idea reshaped the course of world
history in the twentieth century, eroding gender hierarchies, fueling decolo-
nization, and delegitimizing white supremacy.[30]

But the distinction between *is* and *does* also served the cause of racism—a
sign that it was part of a larger shift in thinking about the relationship between humans and the rest of the world. Although initially wary of the implications of genetics for the vast intellectual apparatus of race, the defenders
of white supremacy drew on experience in conservation to elaborate a biological notion of white supremacy in the early twentieth century. Insisting
that the *is* of human existence is more important than the *does*, they came to
believe, would protect the racial hierarchy against the inexorable pressure—
and unpredictable effects—of historical change. As Ripley put it in opening his
dense tome on distinguishing essential from superficial alterations in human
bodies and societies, "Race, properly speaking, is responsible only for those
peculiarities, mental or bodily, which are transmitted with constancy along the
lines of direct physical descent from father to son."[31] Whatever is constant
constitutes race; therefore we know that race persists unchanged through
generations. If humans could really change only by means of biological reproduction, not as a result of acclimatization as the environmental determinists
believed, then the existing racial hierarchy might survive the expansive im-

perialisms, massive migrations, emergent nationalisms, and rapidly shifting political boundaries typical of the decades on either side of 1900.

The best-known of the early twentieth-century efforts to integrate the implications of natural selection and the revolution in genetics into the concept of race with the overriding goal of defending white supremacy was Madison Grant's *The Passing of the Great Race*, first published in 1916 and revised and republished multiple times in the 1920s. The founder and leader of the earliest U.S. conservation organizations, Grant had ready access to the highest levels of government; President Theodore Roosevelt was a good friend. In his magnum opus he proclaimed, "Nature cares not for the individual nor how he may be modified by environment. She is concerned only with the perpetuation of the species or type and heredity alone is the medium through which she acts."[32] Because Grant was first and foremost a racist, rejecting the possibility of the inheritance of acquired characteristics and endorsing the idea of natural selection meant that he had to locate white supremacy in the body narrowly understood—the body as a fortress unaffected by its environment. As Henry Fairfield Osborn wrote in the preface to the second edition of *The Passing of the Great Race*, "The great lesson of the science of race is the immutability of somatological [*sic*] or bodily characters, with which is closely associated the immutability of psychical predispositions and impulses."[33] In Grant and Osborn's fondest hope, race would persist no matter what nature did because it persisted in the body.

Given this understanding of race, the chief danger to white supremacy was reproduction across the color line and the chief defense was eugenics, or the selective breeding of human beings. Among the most powerful organized expressions of scientific racism in the twentieth century, this movement entailed far more than urging the "right" (white, well-to-do, and Anglo-Saxon) people to have more children. U.S. eugenicists lobbied—successfully in many cases—for public policies discouraging the growth of populations they considered inferior, including involuntary sterilization and race-based immigration restriction. This story has been told many times, but the venerable racism at the heart of eugenics has largely obscured the fact that the movement's understanding of the relationship between human nature and the natural world was quite innovative: it relied on distinguishing *is* from *does*, race from culture, humans from the nonhuman world around them.[34]

As the passages I have quoted reveal, Grant and his fellow travelers simply asserted that the complex traits and institutions they regarded as evidence of white superiority were biological in origin, without much understanding of the ongoing experimental efforts to figure out just what genes do and do not do. When natural selection or genetics did not support their beliefs, the eugenicists papered over the logical inconsistencies or lack of evidence with ideology, often by drawing on the very environmental determinism that they claimed to have abandoned. But in their insistence that race was fundamentally biological and, absent reproduction across the color line, unchanging across the generations, they helped to transform the concept and the popular understanding of it.

I read *The Passing of the Great Race* and kindred works in the hope that their authors would have something to say—negative, I assumed—about the craze for suntanning that gripped white Americans after 1900. Aside from Grant's note that "continuous sunlight affects adversely the delicate nervous organization of the Nordics," tanning did not appear to concern them in the least (it certainly did not stop Grant from wintering in Florida).[35] Nevertheless the white supremacists' recasting of race as biology draws on the same distinction between *is* and *does* that tanning popularized; both contributed to the erosion of environmental determinism and the rearticulation of race and culture as opposites. In recognizing the kinship of tanning and eugenics, we can see that ideas about human nature, while consummately cultural, are also simultaneously and necessarily bodily practices, that is, interactions with nonhuman nature as well as other people. I return to sunbathing to provide one slight but telling example.

In the 1929 satire "Tarred and Weathered," the author Weare Holbrook portrayed tanning as a blurring of racial distinctions, by then a well-worn trope in commentary on the practice. When well-to-do vacationers returned from beach resorts to the city in the fall, he noted, "a tribe of swarthy foreigners seems to have taken possession of the banks and office buildings. Apparently the predictions of certain pessimistic sociologists have come true, and the rising tide of color is threatening Nordic supremacy." The pessimist in question was Lothrop Stoddard, one of Grant's acolytes and the author of *The Rising Tide of Color Against White World Supremacy* (1920), a polemic against the growing threat people of color posed to whites' rightful domination of the world. Holbrook was less concerned, for he knew that by mid-October the blondes would have lost their sunburns and the brunettes their tans, until at last "we are pale December shadows of our gay September selves"[36] and stand revealed as the rightful masters of those banks and office buildings.

Not everyone thought the reemergence of this essential whiteness was such a great idea, though; not one determined and creative Mr. Oddleigh. "When the Oddleighs returned from their vacation at Septic Beach last summer they were parboiled and proud of it," Holbrook reported, but as is always the fate of the naturally wan, "eventually their tan and sunburn faded." Invoking the importance of sunlight in preventing rickets, Mr. Oddleigh "refused to let his environment daunt him." Nature, in the guise of the seasonal cycle, would not govern his being; rather he would wrench health from it by determined self-management. The lack of beach and summer sun in the autumnal city were no obstacle, he told his wife. "We can go right up on the roof of this apartment house. It's the ideal place for a sun-bath." Mrs. Oddleigh said to give it a try and let her know how it went.[37]

Braving the incredulity of his neighbors, Oddleigh donned his bathing suit and robe and ascended to the roof. But it "was much more complicated than he had expected. . . . a hodge-podge of pipes, posts, tanks and turrets. . . . The unobstructed portions of the roof were covered with a tarry composition, and in every corner little eddies of soot danced and whirled about." Chasing newspapers stolen from his grasp by the wind, Mr. Oddleigh found himself "hemmed in by a veritable jungle of radio aerials. A confused tangle of wires surrounded him on all sides; their cold, coppery tentacles curled about his knees and elbows, and he felt like a fly caught in a great metallic web." But stubbornly overcoming these cultural snares, our hero worked his way back to an open spot and lay down to commune with nature. All was well: "There was a cool breeze, but the sun was bright, and the roof itself seemed to radiate heat." He fell contentedly to sleep.[38]

Awakened hours later by a "world-weary" Pekingese, our hero "attempted to sit up, but to his dismay he discovered that some unseen force was holding him down"—roof tar, warmed by the sun. By the time he wrenched himself free, "his color scheme resembled that of a penguin." But rapid retreat to his apartment to conceal this parti-colored splendor was not possible, for the appalled owner of the Pekingese had locked the door to the stairs behind her as she fled. Unable to attract the attention of passersby below, the beleaguered Mr. Oddleigh finally crammed himself into the shaft for the dumbwaiter and lowered himself to his apartment. "Well," remarked his unflappable better half, "you certainly acquired a wonderful coat of tan anyway. Why, you couldn't have got a deeper, richer color if you'd spent the entire winter at Palm Beach!" To top it all off, "it is the sort of color that lasts"—even repeated scrubbings could not get it off.[39]

This modest satire on the foolishness of modern man is hardly in the same league as the critically acclaimed and much-discussed *Passing of the Great Race*. Yet it reflects the same confidence in the integrity of whiteness against forces external to the body. However much whites might desire to get closer to nature, they were bound to civilization (their culture) like Br'er Rabbit to the Tar-Baby. The harder they tried to break away, the more foolishly they failed. But there is another way to read "Tarred and Weathered" and sun-tanning generally: as evidence of how permeable and permeated we, and the most baroque elaborations of our cultures, are by nature, human and otherwise. It was nature that made a fool of Mr. Oddleigh, after all, by melting the roof tar of civilization beneath him. The permeability of our skin is a synecdoche for the permeability of our cultures; light and lifeways both get under our skin and remake us as we manipulate them to our own ends.

When those of us with pale skin court the sun, we hope to make ourselves look younger and sexier, traits that the ideology of white supremacy attributes to people born with brown skin. But although deliberate skin-darkening is a bellwether of the twentieth century, we have been changing color in response to our environment for millennia, ever since we lost the body hair that protects our primate cousins. Today biologists regard pigmentation as an evolutionary adaptation that enables the skin to regulate the amount of ultraviolet light penetrating the body; dark skin blocks more, pale skin less. Because we need some ultraviolet exposure to stimulate the production of the hormone popularly called vitamin D but not so much that our store of folic acid is depleted or our DNA is damaged, skin color is a Goldilocks condition: how much is just right varies according to where we live. What an altered hue means to us may affect how quickly or slowly the change happens. In our own time, the pale-skinned have warded it off with sun bonnets and miscegenation laws and welcomed it with tanning parlors and waning racism. Cod liver oil and pickled herring enable pale- and dark-skinned alike to thrive where the sunlight is weak and inconstant. Whatever the historical circumstances, we exist because of the entanglement of nature and culture.[40]

The double meaning of tanning in the years when it became fashionable among whites, the simultaneous assertion of human mastery over nature and a desire to renew human intimacy with nature, demonstrates that race and culture are not opposites but two closely linked ways of imagining the relationship between humans and everything else. Whereas race invokes nature as an imperative and history as the hope for transcendence, culture invokes history as an imperative and nature as the hope for transcendence. Both express the conditions of our possibility. Recognizing this entanglement suggests that revisiting the environmental determinism of the past while striving to overcome the inequalities it legitimized might enable us to imagine a body politics free of constricting appeals to unchanging nature and a cultural politics free of the hubris that we are masters of the material world. As animals who evolved a facility for shaping nature—human and nonhuman—to suit our needs, we are not good candidates for any kind of determinism, natural or cultural; someone will figure out how to get around it and a good reason for doing so. But having the capacity to shape ourselves and our ecosystems does not remove us from them; nor does it mean that we understand, much less have the ability to manage, the consequences of our actions. We might learn a lot from the story of Br'er Rabbit and the Tar-Baby.

Dr. Spock Is Worried: Visual Media and the Emotional History of American Environmentalism

Finis Dunaway

Everything about him seems so serious: his stiff posture, his stern expression, and his three-piece suit, taut necktie, and collar pin (see Figure 7.1). With hands in pockets, his lips tightly pursed, he looks down at the child, who seems completely unaware of his presence. Below the photograph a brief sentence printed in bold letters summarizes the scene: "Dr. Spock is worried."[1]

Published as a full-page advertisement in the *New York Times* in 1962, reprinted in seven hundred newspapers and numerous magazines, and then appearing as a poster "in store windows, nurseries, doctors' offices, and even on baby carriages," the Dr. Spock ad became the most important visual text produced in the campaign against nuclear testing. As the nation's leading child expert and author of *Baby and Child Care*, the best-selling parenting manual ever published, Dr. Benjamin Spock exerted tremendous influence in postwar America. His legendary book began with these words of reassurance: "Trust yourself. . . . [W]hat good mothers and fathers instinctively feel like doing for their babies is usually best." Although his manual tried to inspire parental confidence, now Spock evinced concern, indeed outright worry, about the dangers of bomb testing and radioactive fallout. He urged parents

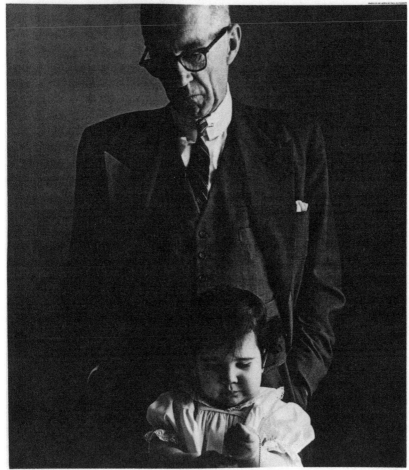

Figure 7.1. SANE, "Dr. Spock Is Worried," advertisement, 1962. Reproduced courtesy of SANE, Inc. Records, Swarthmore College Peace Collection.

to protest nuclear testing by writing to their elected officials and to contribute to SANE, the National Committee for a Sane Nuclear Policy.[2]

For SANE, the Dr. Spock ad marked the culmination of an extensive learning process, a five-year education in how to use media to communicate with the public about fallout. The significance of the ad can be gauged not only from its remarkable circulation and popular reception but also from its place within a longer history of representational politics—of how it departed from previous depictions of the bomb and nuclear testing and of how its visual and rhetorical style would recur in subsequent environmental campaigns. What did it mean, in the context of Cold War America, for a respected authority to express his anxiety about fallout and the future? What did it mean for the bomb, so often represented as a technological triumph and defender of U.S. democracy, to be seen as a sinister force that could threaten the nation's children?

Dr. Spock and other SANE ads challenged the sublime aesthetic of the mushroom cloud, the iconic rendering of the bomb blast that celebrated its technologically generated, awe-inspiring qualities. By moving beyond the mushroom cloud, leaving the spectacle of the blast to follow radioactivity as it contaminated the environment and entered people's bodies, SANE rejected the government and the media's aesthetic framing of the bomb to focus instead on its ominous afterlives. Combining empirical data with emotional concern, SANE sought to galvanize audiences through representations of vulnerable bodies. SANE used visual media to call for environmental citizenship, for the state to guarantee the safety of people's living conditions and the futurity of the nation's environment. In particular, the organization sought to picture Strontium-90 as posing a grave, long-term danger to innocent children.[3]

SANE ads and other environmental images demonstrate the constitutive role of the emotions in public life and offer revealing examples of the emotional history of American environmentalism. In contrast to the philosopher Jürgen Habermas, who famously defined the public sphere as a community based solely on the rational exchange of discourse, this essay builds on the work of scholars who have considered the emotionality of public culture and have explained how the public is constituted through acts of common spectatorship. As the theorist Michael Warner has observed, modern publics are often formed "in relation to texts and their circulation." By reaching strangers and bringing them into a shared world of discourse, a public is organized through the circulation of texts, including visual images that appeal to audiences' emotions. Similarly the communication scholars Robert Hariman and John Louis Lucaites have argued for the importance of emotional expression in understanding the politics of images. "By starting with a photo that evokes a strong association between visual imagery, emotion, and dissent," they write, "we can ask how a vibrant democratic public culture . . . is an emotional culture, how particular images communicate or constrain particular emotions, . . . and how disruptive emotions can be crucial for democratic citizenship."[4]

Likewise, I argue that environmental historians should think more about how public and private feelings have been mobilized in various environmental campaigns and about how the history of environmentalism could be understood, at least in part, as a history of the emotions in which images have played vital and complex roles. By examining the power of visual imagery to evoke emotion, we can reframe established concepts of nature and culture to consider how popular visual texts helped Americans to see themselves as part of a living, but also threatened, body politic.

In particular, I identify a recurring pattern in environmental imagery, one typified by the Dr. Spock ad: a focus on children as emotional emblems of the future. Throughout the history of popular environmentalism, the trope of the vulnerable child has evoked anxiety about the future to challenge environmental policies and practices in the present. This affective strategy, while sometimes dismissed as irrational, has in fact been closely connected to scientific studies and forecasts about particular environmental problems. In this way the analysis in this essay resonates with the claims of the philosopher Martha Nussbaum that emotions are "upheavals of thought" and of the political scientist George Marcus that "emotions enable rationality." By exploring the fusion of fact and feeling in environmental visual culture, I question the supposed separation between cognition and emotion and examine how images have fostered politically charged, scientifically informed feelings about the environmental future.[5]

What we see emerging in SANE ads and other texts from this period is a way to picture the temporality of the environmental crisis: a mode of risk based on the gradual accumulation of hazardous agents in the human body and the environment. Rather than the sudden, immediate destruction unleashed by nuclear war, the problems of the environmental crisis—such as air and water pollution, pesticide build-up in the food chain, and greenhouse gas emissions—suggest a long-term, slowly escalating sense of danger. The literary critic Rob Nixon terms this incremental form of ecological calamity "slow violence": "a violence that occurs gradually and out of sight, a violence of delayed destruction that is dispersed across time and space, an attritional violence that is typically not viewed as violence at all." Indeed the material realities of slow violence pose a representational challenge for environmentalists as they engage with the spectacle-driven dictates of the mass media and as they seek to move beyond the temporality of immediate catastrophe to warn of incremental crises-in-the-making. In the case of SANE, the focus on children rendered visible the invisible threat of fallout and provided an emotional emblem for the long-term danger represented by the accumulation of Strontium-90 in the environment and in human bodies.[6]

SANE ads, Rachel Carson's *Silent Spring*, and other texts helped produce ideas of environmental citizenship that placed new demands on the state to protect the citizenry from ecological harm. The materiality of environmental danger merged with the emotionality of environmental politics to popularize what I describe as an ecological lens: a way of seeing that placed human bodies and nonhuman nature in a shared, interlinked realm of escalating danger. This ecological lens—with its emphasis on the interweaving of humans and nature—differentiated modern environmentalism from wilderness preservation. Since wilderness groups tended to present nature as a pure, sacred space apart from human society, their campaigns narrowly defined environmental citizenship as the right of citizens (at least those who could afford to visit remote places) to experience wild beauty. In contrast, the ecological lens enveloped both humans and nature in a common geography of long-term, incremental danger. Rather than calling upon the state to protect distant realms of sublime nature, the new environmentalism worried about the survival of people and the nonhuman world in ecological systems increasingly threatened by pollution, toxicity, and other threats to futurity.[7]

The popular media sanctioning of environmental values depended on a shift in the emotional style of Cold War America. In the post–World War II period, governmental officials and scientific experts sought to discredit fear and anxiety as illegitimate emotions, especially in relation to technology, the environment, and human health. They denied the vulnerability of permeable, ecological bodies and urged the public not to be afraid of bomb testing and the proliferation of pesticides and other toxic chemicals. This discourse, though, came under attack, vigorously so during the early 1960s, as antinuclear activists and ecological critics such as Rachel Carson questioned the much-vaunted rationality of the experts and used scientific evidence to justify feelings of fear toward fallout and pesticides. Visual images played an active role in this struggle and ultimately helped to legitimate a new emotional style in American public culture. As fear and anxiety toward the environmental future became normalized, environmental citizenship rights could be more easily imagined, articulated, and realized. This change in emotional styles thus contributed to the emergence of popular environmentalism.

This essay seeks to reframe the historiography of environmentalism through consideration of broad conceptual issues often missing from the field: the emotions and public life; the links between science and spectacle; and the shifting boundaries between nature and culture. I draw on the methods of cultural history and American studies to examine how the emergence of the ecological lens intersected with important changes in U.S. public culture. The ecological lens abetted a transformation in popular thought, marking a shift in the idea of nature as a realm separate from human society to the notion of environment as an interconnected system that all beings—human and nonhuman—shared. SANE ads and other popular texts configured humans as part of nature by showing vulnerable bodies at risk and calling for an emotional response in viewing audiences. These texts fused fact and feeling to frame environmental danger as a slowly escalating crisis. In challenging the Cold War emotional style, popular environmentalism collapsed the boundaries between nature and culture to envision fragile bodies and ecosystems under siege.

By representing fear of fallout, SANE ads sought to counter iconic photographs of the Nevada Test Site, where the U.S. government detonated approximately one hundred nuclear weapons into the atmosphere during the 1950s and early 1960s. Often produced by the government and circulated through *Life* and other popular magazines, these photographs aestheticized the bomb and addressed Americans as spectators rather than participants in decisions that affected their lives. Media depictions of nuclear testing drew on the sublime tradition to generate a new category of representation: the atomic sublime, a way of seeing that emphasized the overwhelming power and beauty of the mushroom cloud. Rather than picturing vast mountains, towering waterfalls, and other monumental scenes of natural beauty, the atomic sublime naturalized the mushroom cloud to celebrate the spectacle of the blast. As government scientists downplayed the dangers of fallout, the iconic mushroom cloud provided spectators with sublime pictures of U.S. technological power. By encouraging audiences to see beauty but not destruction, to feel inspired but not terrified, to glimpse the mushroom cloud but not contemplate the lingering effects of fallout, the pictures excluded from the frame the threats that Strontium-90 and other radioactive elements posed to the environment and human health.[8]

This way of depicting the bomb denied human vulnerability to ecological risk and thus suggested that nature and culture remained separate, discrete realms. Government experts echoed this message, as they repeatedly claimed that the body was impervious to radioactive materials. One military film, screened for troops before a bomb test in Nevada, shows an animated cartoon of a human body being exposed to radioactive particles. The round objects simply bounce off the skin; unable to penetrate the flesh, they look like balls being thrown against a wall. Merging corporeal fortitude with emotional fortitude, the invincibility of the human body with the rejection of fear, Cold War imagery sought to control public feelings by disavowing environmental danger. Presenting themselves as the purveyors of fact and guardians of rationality, government experts sought to manage public fear by maintaining the boundaries between nature and culture and denying the reality of environmental risk.[9]

This dominant emotional style—and its dismissal of fallout fear—appeared across a diverse array of visual media. One episode of *The Big Picture*, an army-produced television show, presented to audiences the fears of American troops who worried that their proximity to nuclear tests and exposure to fallout might jeopardize their health. In one scene, supposedly filmed the night before a bomb test, two soldiers sit in the desert with a chaplain, who calmly tries to assuage their fears:

> "What seems to be the trouble, soldier?" the chaplain asks. "You look a little bit worried."
> "Well I am, Chaplain," the soldier replies, "just a little bit."
> "Actually, there's no need to be worried," the chaplain says, "as the army has taken all the necessary precautions to see that we're perfectly safe here."[10]

Having assured the soldiers that the army's scientific experts will protect them, the chaplain tells them that he has witnessed "a number of atomic tests" and then goes on to describe the aesthetic pleasure of the bomb blast. "First of all," he says, "one sees a very, very bright light. . . . And then you look up and you see the fireball as it ascends to the heavens. It contains all the rich colors of the rainbow. And then as it rises up into the atmosphere, it . . . assembles into the mushroom. It is a wonderful sight to behold."

In this nationally televised conversation, the chaplain instructed his soldiers to exorcise fear by putting their faith in the experts. He then mobilized the sublime aesthetic to glorify the bomb, by encouraging the troops to focus their attention on the awe-inspiring qualities of the explosion. Rather than succumbing to fear, they should instead surrender themselves to the intense feelings of awe and wonder summoned by the blast. Taking the chaplain's advice, they should become enraptured by the mushroom cloud. By showing the American public how the army addressed the fears of its troops, *The Big Picture* used TV as an instrument of emotional containment.

Similarly, *Life* magazine emphasized aesthetic wonder to quell public anxiety. In 1954, only a few weeks after a Japanese fishing boat (the *Lucky Dragon*) was showered with radioactive particles from a U.S. bomb test in the Pacific, *Life*'s photo-essay invited readers to stop worrying and marvel at how "Color Photographs Add Vivid Reality to Nation's Concept of H-Bomb." According to *Life*, the reality of bomb testing could be better grasped through the vividness of color photography, through a series of images that detached the bomb's visual properties from its destructive effects. To introduce the series, *Life* quoted President Eisenhower to explain how the photographs visually echoed his effort to dispel fear of radiation: "The greater any of these apprehensions, the greater is the need that we look at them clearly, face to face, without fear, like honest, straightforward Americans." From *Life* magazine to *The Big Picture* and beyond, government officials and the mass media masked environmental danger by celebrating the sublime spectacle of the bomb blast but concealed the accretive dangers of radioactivity.[11]

Founded in 1957, SANE sought to galvanize public concern over nuclear testing. The group announced its founding via a full-page advertisement in the *New York Times*, an ad that looked strikingly different from the Dr. Spock ad that followed five years later. The statement began, in large, bold print, with a warning: "We Are Facing a Danger Unlike Any Danger That Has Ever Existed"; it emphasized the ongoing "contamination of air and water and food, and the injury to man himself" caused by nuclear testing.[12]

Hoping to build a national movement but worried that this ad did not attract enough attention, SANE hired a communication consultant to evaluate the ad's effectiveness. He concluded that it was " 'too long' and . . . 'too wordy' "

Figure 7.2. SANE, "We Are Facing a Danger Unlike Any Danger That Has Ever Existed," advertisement, 1957. Reproduced courtesy of SANE, Inc. Records, Swarthmore College Peace Collection.

and argued "that a photo or graphic symbol would attract the attention of the general public." Indeed, SANE's first foray into the realm of mass communication was completely devoid of images, as lengthy text crowded the page. Even avid readers of the *Times*, the consultant explained, "had 'missed' the ad," had not even noticed it was there.[13]

SANE leaders soon followed the consultant's advice and began using images in its publicity program; eventually pictures would become even more prominent than texts in the group's most widely circulated ads. SANE's initial efforts to incorporate images, though, relied on familiar pictures of the mushroom cloud. The ads sought to recast dramatic scenes of the bomb blast by encouraging viewers to see the mushroom cloud as a harbinger of doom rather than as a sublime spectacle. The first advertisement to feature the mushroom cloud began with a warning above the picture: "Nuclear Bombs Can Destroy All Life in War." Below the image, another warning sought to connect the fear of nuclear apocalypse with the ongoing, gradually escalating risks associated with nuclear testing: "Nuclear Tests Are Endangering Our Health Right Now." Through this fusion of text and image, SANE hoped that readers would view the potential devastation of nuclear war and the actual threats of radioactive fallout as conjoined hazards. SANE merged these dual visions of apocalypse—the sudden, absolute catastrophe of nuclear warfare with the gradual accumulation of radioactive fallout in the atmosphere and food chain—to argue that both endangered the health of the citizenry.[14]

SANE continued to use mushroom-cloud imagery to critique bomb testing, but some activists urged the group to develop a different representational strategy, one that would focus on childhood vulnerability. Two weeks after the first mushroom-cloud ad appeared, one person wrote to SANE urging the group to place "[a]ds in popular newspapers that starkly present the problem," including, she suggested, "a picture of an engaging child with the caption: THIS CHILD WILL DIE OR BE DEFORMED BY CONTINUING NUCLEAR TESTS: WILL SHE BE YOURS?" This letter writer, along with others who wrote to SANE, believed that visual images, particularly pictures of young children, would align emotion with dissent to foster political activism. "Perhaps these . . . suggestions are too macabre," she concluded, "but I feel that public apathy must be met by the most dramatic presentation of this frightening subject."[15]

Even as the U.S. government used spectacle to pacify the public, these letter writers believed that visual images could also be used to engage and activate the citizenry in decisions that affected their lives and the health of their children. They suggested that a vibrant democratic culture, along with

Figure 7.3. SANE, "Nuclear Bombs Can Destroy All Life in War—Nuclear Tests Are Endangering Our Health Right Now," advertisement, 1958. Reproduced courtesy of SANE, Inc. Records, Swarthmore College Peace Collection.

the future health of Americans and their environment, depended on the infusion of the emotions into politics. Their letters provide us with a glimpse of spectacle emerging from below, produced in this case not by government elites seeking to discourage citizen participation but instead by people who believed that SANE could use visual imagery to galvanize the public.[16]

People who recommended that SANE deploy images of children suggested that environmental citizenship could best be imagined through a strategy that depicted the child as the nation's most treasured citizen. These pictures of futurity would ask the presumed audience of adults to worry not so much about the potential risks to their own bodies but rather to invest concern in the vulnerable bodies of children growing up in an increasingly degraded environment. This representational strategy can be compared with what the cultural critic Lauren Berlant has termed "infantile citizenship." Focusing on the 1980s, Berlant argues that public life and the image of citizenship became overwhelmingly fixated on future Americans, on "pictures . . . circulating in the public sphere" of children, "persons that, paradoxically, cannot yet act as citizens." Yet while infantile citizenship denies adult agency and shifts attention from pressing social problems, SANE's emphasis on vulnerable children contested the technocratic assumptions of government elites and visualized threats to permeable ecological bodies. By depicting bodies at risk, SANE tried to illustrate the long-term, incremental danger of fallout and to challenge the spectacle of the bomb blast through the counter-spectacle of innocent children.[17]

In 1962 SANE adopted the strategy recommended by letter writers by producing "Dr. Spock is worried" and other images that visualized the invisible danger of fallout. In the advertisement, the photograph of Spock and the toddler dominates the ad space (see Figure 7.1 above). Hovering over the girl, brooding over the dangers of fallout, Spock appears unsure how to protect the child. Below the image the text specifically addresses parents as the ad's intended audience: "If you've been raising a family on Dr. Spock's book, you know that he doesn't get worried easily." While his child-rearing manual sought to reassure anxious parents, the SANE ad expressed his fears. "I am worried," Spock explained. "Not so much about the effect of past tests but at the prospect of endless future ones. As the tests multiply, so will the damage to children."[18]

The design of the advertisement followed almost exactly the layout style developed by the ad agency that created it—Doyle, Dane, and Bernbach. Known for its distinctive and much-discussed campaigns, the firm created the memorable taglines "Think Small" and "Lemon" for the Volkswagen Beetle. In these and other ads Doyle, Dane, and Bernbach departed from the visual and verbal style of other agencies by using black and white photographs, minimalist design, and brief text, usually in the form of short, vertical columns at the bottom of the page. The Dr. Spock ad adopted this same approach but, unlike other ads by the firm, did not employ humor to make its point.[19]

Taken by Paul Elfenbein, the photograph of Spock can also be viewed in relation to larger developments in portrait photography, especially the work of Elfenbein's contemporary Arnold Newman, who pioneered the style of environmental portraiture. Seeking to capture the essence of a person's career through a photograph, Newman did not simply focus on the face before him but rather, in a carefully orchestrated manner, placed his subject in a meaningful context that helped define the individual. Just as Newman photographed the composer Igor Stravinsky near a grand piano and the painter Piet Mondrian in his studio, Elfenbein situated Spock, the nation's leading child expert, standing in a room with a young girl. Yet rather than gazing at her with confidence, assured in his knowledge of how to raise children, Spock looks unnerved and even uncomfortable in what should be a familiar environment, the domain in which he is the nation's preeminent authority.[20]

In response to the ad, many people wrote letters to praise SANE for adopting this strategy that appealed to the emotions. "The Dr. Spock advertisement is the greatest [SANE] has ever published," one writer announced. "It represents a sure-fire way of reaching people who would otherwise not be touched by even the most logical approach." Many believed that Spock's celebrity status and the respect that parents, especially mothers, accorded him would enable SANE to reach a larger public. "You know," one woman wrote, "the most faithful readers of advertisements are housewives looking for items for the home and family. For that reason, the Dr. Spock ad is by far the most effective ad SANE has ever sponsored." She also applauded the group for using a photograph and brief verbal appeal rather than relying too heavily on text. "The well-documented SANE ads with a couple of 1000 words of copy," she continued, "may be literary masterpieces—but the people who read ads as a rule aren't apt to read them!" Other writers described Spock as "practically a member of the family." "I was very moved by your statement," one explained. "Mothers have looked to you for advice regarding children for years. I sincerely hope they heed your voice at this time."[21]

As a man expressing his anxiety about fallout and his concern for children and futurity, Spock helped legitimate the role of the emotions in environmental politics. Jeanne Bagby, a cofounder of the antinuclear group Women Strike for Peace, wrote Spock to express her gratitude for the ad, which, she believed, would make an enormous difference in the campaign against nuclear testing. Breaking from dominant cultural notions of masculinity, Spock encouraged men to act as emotional beings and work together with women to protest the dangers of fallout. "I wish to join with thousands of other mothers in heartfelt thanks for your recent public statement," Bagby wrote. "For months and years, we have implored our doctors, scientists and government officials for the truth about radiation effects, for a more public discussion of the hazards of testing, for protection of our children. Our efforts have been largely dismissed as the rantings of hysterical women." According to Bagby, women protesters were too often ignored or ridiculed based on the misogynistic charge that they were overly emotional and thus unable to cope in a rational manner with the arms race and the debate over fallout. For this reason, she suggested that a man could more easily convey emotional concern and not be dismissed.[22]

In the photograph, Spock's facial expression seems to validate his ability to perform this emotive role in an acceptable manner. He does not, after all, appear excessively emotional. He offers solemn concern and informed judgment. Even as his anxieties are "written all over his kindly face," as *Time* magazine put it, Spock still maintains his composure, still enacts his masculine authority. In a culture of containment, he still seems contained, still possesses the capacity to impart his expertise.[23]

SANE continued to produce other images that warned of the long-term danger to children's bodies. An advertisement sponsored by a group called Dentists for SANE showed three youngsters, all sporting open-mouthed smiles and shiny white teeth. The text below, though, undercuts the carefree image. It warns, "*Your* Children's Teeth Contain Strontium-90." Delivered with scientific certitude and again directed at parents, the text explains that the teeth and bones of all children, even theirs, now contain potentially damaging amounts of "radioactive Strontium-90 from nuclear weapons tests." The image drew upon and popularized the findings of the Baby Teeth Survey conducted by the Committee for Nuclear Information (CNI), a group led by Barry Commoner and other scientists. The photograph of giddy children provided a visual counterpoint to the information presented in the text and offered a sentimental portrait of innocent children unaware of the danger lurking in their bodies. By presenting the children as living in no particular place, just anywhere in the United States, and by emphasizing that all young

Americans are vulnerable to the effects of Strontium-90, the ad conveys the idea of universal vulnerability. SANE used the same information gathered by CNI but packaged it in a more explicitly affective mode to mobilize parental anxieties about the radioactive threat to the nation's children.[24]

If readers bothered to scan the names of the more than two hundred dentists who signed the ad, they might have noticed that every one of them was a man—perhaps not surprising given that dentistry remained a male-dominated profession. Yet the signers' insistent maleness subtly underscored the gendered politics of SANE. Using their scientific knowledge to prop up their emotional selves, like Spock, all these male dentists expressed their anxiety about the future and concern about children's ecological bodies. "As dentists," they wrote, in language that upset the mode of detached expertise, "we deplore the buildup of radioactive Strontium-90 in children's teeth and bones. It is a measure of the sickness of our times." Scientific expertise, social responsibility, and smiling children converged in this ad to proclaim that every American, including every dad and every dentist, should demand an end to nuclear testing.[25]

SANE images presented white children as signs of the future and as emblems of universal vulnerability. Their whiteness, of course, went unremarked. Yet the repeated emphasis on white people together with the placelessness of the scenes represented—nobody in particular inhabiting nowhere in particular—worked to make the fallout danger seem even more generalized and all-encompassing. No place, the ads asserted, even the lily-white suburbs, those postwar bastions of prosperity and privilege, were immune to the risk of Strontium-90 and other radioactive agents. While Cold War culture often depicted suburban communities as hermetically sealed, blissfully insulated from the problems and perils of public life, these images of white vulnerability overturned dominant ideological assumptions about the human body, the environment, and public culture. SANE and other antinuclear groups mobilized scientific knowledge and joined fact with feeling to depict both men and women worried about children and voicing concern about the fate of vulnerable bodies in an atomic age. Their vision of the ecological body blurred the boundaries between nature and culture to depict humans as situated within threatened ecological systems.

In 1964 the Lyndon Baines Johnson presidential campaign produced TV commercials that appropriated SANE's visual motifs to express fear about fallout and the arms race. The iconic "Daisy Girl" shows a young girl pulling

Figure 7.4. SANE, "Your Children's Teeth Contain Strontium-90," advertisement, 1963. Reproduced courtesy of SANE, Inc. Records, Swarthmore College Peace Collection.

off the petals of a flower, counting each one in ascending order. Situated in nature—an icon of innocence, a child who makes a few mistakes as she recites her numbers—she seems, like the flower she clutches, to represent life and futurity. The commercial, prepared by Doyle, Dane, and Bernbach, the same firm that designed the Dr. Spock ad, again selected a white child to embody universal vulnerability. In contrast, an imposing, mechanical-sounding voice of a male narrator begins to count in descending order from 10 to 1. The camera moves in closer to the girl's face until images of the mushroom cloud appear on the screen. "Daisy Girl" turns the sublime spectacle of the bomb blast into an image of apocalyptic destruction; it does so by pairing the intimate with the frightening, the private with the public, the innocent with the overwhelming.[26]

Doyle, Dane, and Bernbach produced other commercials for the Johnson campaign, including one that showed a little girl licking an ice cream cone. A few seconds into the commercial, an unseen female narrator, presumably a mother figure, begins to speak: "Do you know what people used to do? They used to explode atomic bombs into the air. Now, children should have lots of vitamin A and calcium. But they should not have any Strontium-90 or Cesium-137. These things come from atomic bombs, and they're radioactive. They can make you die." After describing the long-term risks of radioactivity, she then explains how the 1963 Limited Test Ban Treaty, which put an end to aboveground nuclear testing, solved this problem: "Do you know what people finally did? They got together and signed a nuclear test ban treaty. And then the radioactive poisons started to go away. But now, there is a man who wants to be President of the United States, and he doesn't like this treaty. He fought against it. He even voted against it. He wants to go on testing more bombs. His name is Barry Goldwater, and if he's elected, they might start testing all over again." Viewed together, the two commercials—"Daisy Girl" and "Little Girl, Ice Cream Cone"—merged two ideas of apocalypse: the sudden, immediate horror of nuclear war with the gradual accumulation of fallout in the environment and in children's bodies.[27]

Airing about a year after the signing of the Limited Test Ban Treaty, the commercials visually codified the idea of environmental citizenship and confirmed the importance of continuing the ban. Eight years earlier, when the Democratic presidential nominee Adlai Stevenson argued that the United States should "take the lead in halting further test explosions," his claims were dismissed as being outside the mainstream. In 1964, though, Johnson would

Figure 7.5. "Daisy Girl," frame capture from TV commercial, 1964. Reproduced courtesy of the Lyndon Baines Johnson Library and Democratic National Committee.

Figure 7.6. "Little Girl, Ice Cream Cone," frame capture from TV commercial, 1964. Reproduced courtesy of the Lyndon Baines Johnson Library and Democratic National Committee.

laud the treaty for keeping American children protected from radioactive danger. "The deadly products of atomic explosions," he explained, "were poisoning our soil and our food and the milk our children drank and the air we all breathe. Radioactive deposits were being formed in increasing quantity in the teeth and bones of young Americans. Radioactive poisons . . . were a growing menace to the health of every unborn child." Johnson's comments revealed the popularization of key claims made by SANE and other antinuclear groups: that human beings inhabited vulnerable, ecological bodies; that Strontium-90 was becoming lodged, in frightening quantities, in the bones and teeth of young children; and that the protection of futurity demanded that nuclear tests no longer be performed aboveground.[28]

It is important to note that these two commercials offered different temporal framings of violence. While "Daisy Girl" adhered to notions of spectacular catastrophe and visualized the mushroom cloud as a sign of thermonuclear apocalypse, "Little Girl, Ice Cream Cone" warned of the delayed effects of radioactivity and other toxic elements. Even as "Daisy Girl" commented on these broader ecological concerns, the commercial most likely was understood by audiences at the time as a frightening portrayal of nuclear war—not as a depiction of the slow violence of environmental crisis. Still,

Doyle, Dane, and Bernbach's "Little Girl, Ice Cream Cone" reveals that the extensive time frame of fear—the temporality of environmental crisis—began to seep into American visual culture.

Even as the test ban put an end to the aboveground tests that spewed radioactive agents into the atmosphere, the arms race would continue, as the tests would descend to subterranean locales. The continued manufacture and testing of bombs would create a series of long-term risks—from uranium mining to weapons production and underground tests that contaminated workers' bodies and nearby environments—almost all of which remained invisible to the general public. Even though the arms race continued and the production of nuclear weapons created ongoing environmental problems, the sense of urgency about the testing issue soon faded from view. The generalized pictures of universal vulnerability circulated by SANE obscured the specificity of environmental risk by erasing locality, by offering viewers a counterspectacle of innocent children in no particular place and portraying everyone as equally vulnerable to fallout. While the test ban certainly reduced many children's exposure to Strontium-90, it also underwrote a broader pattern of inattention to the disparate spaces where radioactivity continued to enter the environment and people's bodies. The notion of universal victimhood—of every child in every place equally threatened by fallout—masked the ongoing presence of the bomb in the lives of many Americans.[29]

Published just a few months after the Dr. Spock ad appeared, Rachel Carson's *Silent Spring* also loosened the ideological grips of the Cold War technocracy. By injecting a long-term sense of fear into popular representations of DDT and other pesticides, Carson warned about escalating threats to futurity. Like Dr. Spock, she portrayed the home and the private realm as threatened by toxicity, by the assault of deadly chemicals on often-unsuspecting citizens. Her vision of environmental citizenship placed SANE's focus on the human body within a broader frame. Carson incorporated the buzzing, blooming world of nature into her sphere of ethical concern to argue that environmental citizenship included the rights of people to live in a healthy environment and to enjoy the scenic beauty of the natural world. In this way her book helped popularize the ecological lens and bring environmental values into the mainstream of American public culture.[30]

Carson's critique of the pesticide industry provoked a vicious counterattack, a misogynistic effort orchestrated by chemical companies to dismiss her claims, often by discrediting her credentials. Male scientists, especially those employed by the chemical industry, openly espoused sexism to charge that as a woman, Carson could not understand the complexity of science, and they claimed that she merely responded with her emotions rather than with reason to the pesticide issue. Chemical-industry journals published a barrage of negative reviews and scathing editorials; some of their sexist assertions would be trotted out by mainstream reviewers. *Time*, for example, belittled the book as an "emotional and inaccurate outburst" and chastised Carson for her "patently unsound" claims and "hysterically overemphatic" prose.[31]

While gendered condemnation shaped the book's reception, what is more striking and surprising is that many of Carson's ideas gained legitimacy within American public culture. She negotiated the media landscape and broader culture of images to challenge male proponents of reigning pesticide policy by presenting herself as a reliable, trustworthy source, a countermodel of expertise. It is beyond the scope of this essay to explore the various images associated with the circulation and reception of *Silent Spring* or to examine its curiously circumscribed effect on American agricultural and pesticide policy. Rather, I simply want to note that the representation of Carson's ideas in various media forms helped reveal the long-term, incremental threat that DDT and other pesticides posed to humans and nature.

During the late 1960s and early 1970s, Carson's time frame of fear became more widely understood and frequently depicted in the visual media. While *Life* and *National Geographic* had previously denied the hazards of DDT, these same magazines now visualized the threats to birds and the larger ecological systems that sustained them. Popular images depicted a crisis of reproduction, in which the severe thinning of eggshells prevented chicks from hatching, let alone developing into viable offspring. According to magazine articles and captions, as DDT became concentrated in the food chain, it weakened the ability of bald eagles, ospreys, and other species to reproduce. Striking visual evidence of pesticide poisoning could be seen in the widely circulated images of cracked, damaged, and deformed eggshells. *National Geographic*, for instance, featured a photograph of a dozen mallard eggs. "[T]hree eggs," the caption explained, "were cracked or crushed by the mother. Eight others failed to develop, and only one hatchling, rather than the usual 9 to 11, emerged alive." Similarly, *Life* showed a pair of ibis eggs, one cracked and crushed, and the other dented in the middle, resting on an abandoned nest, a site completely devoid of living ibises. "Their shells thin and easily crushed because of pesticides in the bird's food chain," the caption noted, "these ibis eggs never hatched."[32]

In response to the piece on ibis eggs, one letter writer articulated the ecological lens through which many readers likely viewed these heart-wrenching images of damaged eggshells. "Although the thought of a birdless world is a depressing one," she observed, "man's naïveté is even more frightening. From an ecological point of view man is just another species; the extinction of one species only brings closer the extinction of all species. When is man going to realize that the passing of a bird not only means a quiet, birdless sky but [also] is a harbinger of things to come: today the ibis, tomorrow man?"[33]

Meanwhile environmental groups sought to ban DDT and strategically deployed images as part of their campaign. In particular the Environmental Defense Fund produced advertisements that represented DDT as posing a severe and escalating risk to humans, nature, and their conjoined futurity. Published in the *New York Times*, one ad provocatively asked, "IS MOTHER'S MILK FIT FOR HUMAN CONSUMPTION?" Below these large, boldface words a photograph showed a white woman gently cradling a white infant. "Nobody knows," the text continued. "But if it were on the market it could be confiscated by the Food and Drug Administration. Why? Too much DDT." Another advertisement featured a photograph of a peregrine falcon and then asked, "Have YOU seen a peregrine falcon lately? Or a bald eagle, osprey, brown pelican . . . ? Chances are you haven't. Your grandchildren may NEVER see them." Together the advertisements framed environmental citizenship as a long-term, future-oriented vision that included the right of people, especially children, to be protected from environmental harm and the right of citizens, including those born in the future, to live in a world graced by peregrine falcons, bald eagles, and other charismatic bird species.[34]

The first celebration of Earth Day in 1970, the federal ban on DDT in 1972, and the emergence of the environmental regulatory state during this same period all demonstrated the profound shift in emotional styles in American public culture. Visual images played an active role in teaching Americans to see environmental risk as part of everyday reality. As tools of persuasion and vectors of emotion, images helped Americans reimagine their political world by revealing the long-term danger represented by the environmental crisis.

SANE advertisements and other images from this period would leave behind important legacies to the visual culture of environmentalism. Like so many images of environmental crisis that followed, these ads combined pictures with words, images with texts to convey scientific ideas to a larger public. SANE helped popularize notions of the ecological body by explaining the ways that Strontium-90 could enter the food chain and threaten human health. By calling attention to a material reality documented by science, these ads visualized the long-term, incremental danger of fallout. Like other environmental images, these ads also mobilized the private realm of home and family to represent ideas of citizenship and the nation. They called upon the state to protect the citizenry from harm and merged private and public concerns to imagine new concepts of environmental citizenship. While wilderness advocates had constructed nature as a pure, sacred realm set apart from the corrupting influence of culture, this vision of the ecological body portrayed culture—represented by the innocent white child—as an idealized domain, threatened by radioactivity and other toxic agents permeating the modern environment.

These ads also created a picture of universal victimhood, portraying all Americans, no matter where they lived and no matter their race or class, as equally vulnerable to environmental danger. This trope became central to popular framings of American environmentalism, as white bodies have frequently stood in for the nation to represent the notion of shared vulnerability. Even as media images have made the environmental crisis visible to a mass public, they have often obscured questions of race, class, and inequality. By presenting the archetypal American citizen as white and depicting white bodies as signs of universal vulnerability, this imagery has repeatedly masked the ways that structural inequities produce environmental injustice.[35]

For the most part, environmental historians have ignored the constitutive role of visual images and the emotions in the mainstreaming of environmental consciousness. By treating images as active producers of meaning and by analyzing the emotional history of environmentalism, we can reconsider larger interpretive issues in the field. For example, while consumption has long been emphasized in the historiography of environmentalism, we need to broaden our idea of consumption to include spectatorship and to examine the ways that practices of looking have, at different moments, been politicizing or disabling, sometimes fostering a sense of engagement and other times distancing spectators from decisions and environments that affect their lives. Likewise, while historians have shown how scientists and other intellectuals have participated in environmental politics, we need to consider how activists have relied not just on rational argument but also on the emotions to promote dissent and how they have used spectacle to communicate scientific knowledge. Furthermore, environmental historians have rarely engaged with media history and theories of the public. More effort could be made to situate environmentalism within public culture and demonstrate how, as Susan Douglas argues, "media history . . . allow[s] for the interplay between bottom-up and top-down history."[36]

From "Dr. Spock is worried" to Al Gore's *An Inconvenient Truth* (2006) and other recent depictions of global warming, images have not simply illustrated environmental politics but have also shaped the bounds of public debate by naturalizing particular meanings of environmentalism. This essay focuses on the emergence of a long-term, incremental sense of danger represented by fallout and pesticides. Yet the emotional history of environmentalism extends well beyond such manifestations of fear and anxiety. Other feelings, including environmental guilt, have played a central role in the making of modern environmentalism. Indeed media portrayals of universal vulnerability have often been paralleled by the notion of universal responsibility, the idea that all Americans are equally culpable for causing the environmental crisis. From the iconic "Crying Indian" commercial produced in 1971 through the familiar recitation of *50 Simple Things You Can Do to Save the Earth* (1990), the popular media have frequently mobilized feelings of guilt to instill a sense of personal responsibility for the environment. Likewise the media have often packaged a form of environmental hope that enshrines faith in the market to present a green consumerist vision of ecological salvation. Throughout the history of American environmentalism, images have given visible form to fear, guilt, hope, and other environmental feelings. In the process they have popularized the cause but also left crucial issues outside of the frame.[37]

PART III

Places

Chapter 8

Prototyping Natures: Technology, Labor, and Art on Atomic Frontiers

Andrew Kirk

The year 2011 marked the sixtieth anniversary of continental nuclear testing. In the year leading up to this milestone interest in the subject surged, journalists rediscovered atomic history, and scholars from a variety of backgrounds took a second look at the science, technology, cultural artifacts, and landscapes of the atomic Cold War.[1] Artists and photographers have long gravitated toward things atomic and the tainted landscapes of testing in particular. Those creative folks who spent their careers working on representations of atomic events and environments found new interest in and audiences for their work during the year of remembrance.[2] The Fukushima disaster on March 11, 2011, sparked even more global interest in atomic legacies and again raised basic questions about how we went so far down this road and how the testing of nuclear technologies affected the environments and peoples subject to this most spectacularly destructive science experiment.

Since the days following Hiroshima, regional atomic testing protagonists, atomic workers, protesters, and the Japanese Hibakusha have used visual representation to preserve their experiences and often to counter perceptions of their home regions as natural or cultural wastelands. For atomic workers who migrated across the globe during the Cold War to labor under bizarre and dangerous circumstances, art and visual representation of testing

Figure 8.1. Representing labor, nature, and technology during a time of secrecy. *Mojave Mountains Through the Test Tunnel Gates.* Dale Cox, oil on canvas. Courtesy of National Atomic Testing Museum Atomic Art Collections, Las Vegas, Nevada.

environments could make visible what was secret and serve as a medium for them to confront and possibly assuage their conflicted emotions about helping destroy places they came to understand and appreciate deeply.[3] Caches of atomic folk art and now unclassified oral testimony about history, culture, and environment available to researchers along with vast archives of declassified documentary environmental images recently made more accessible offer other ways to reread the landscapes of the Cold War.

For the purposes of this volume, the visual legacy of atomic testing offers an interesting way to think again about some of the most basic questions of environmental history: how should we define environmentalism? and whom should we categorize as environmentalists? for example.[4] We still need to ask these seemingly simple questions because of the contradictory behavior of even the most obvious lovers of nature and the convoluted interconnections between nature and culture that continue to shape environmental culture and politics. By looking closely at some of the most conflicted environmental advocates and the most compromised places, we can learn anew about how individuals and communities struggled in the past to conscientiously place themselves within the nature of their home places. Research on the landscapes where nature and culture most directly collide and on the people who live and work there has produced some of the most nuanced environmental scholarship of the past decades. Environmental histories of cities and farms, mines and fisheries, or industrial rivers and designed landscapes offer complicated case studies of the fluid complexity of the nature-culture interplay and call into question fixed notions of one or the other as essential categories.

If, as the editors of this volume suggest, one of the greatest challenges for environmental historians is to continue to transcend the notion that a more authentic world exists out there and to strive to explore how nature and culture have been rendered as separate and opposing realms, then a careful reconsideration of places perceived as irredeemable wastelands inhabited by marginal and morally compromised people offers opportunities to expand research into uncomfortable new frontiers and test our willingness as environmental historians to push the boundaries of what places, people, and topics are open for consideration.[5] There are few more challenging places to raise questions about who can claim to be an environmentalist and what we are to make of tainted landscapes than the vast cultural/natural global atomic proving grounds. These places were chosen as nuclear testing sites explicitly because of deeply entrenched cultural perceptions of nature and hierarchies of natural value.[6] Further, the atomic proving grounds were, in the words of the art historian Emily Scott, "landscapes where unresolved conflicts boiled at the surface and came into view."[7] In selecting sites for destruction in the atomic age, politicians, bureaucrats, generals, and citizens engaged many of the issues that fascinate environmental historians. Their introspection during this period reveals tenacious older patterns of thinking about nature along with emerging insights from experience with the global militarized landscapes of World War II. In revisiting the environmental history of atomic proving grounds, we can see again how cultural conceptions of nature have, in the words of our colleague Finis Dunaway, "created, shaped, and impacted ecological systems," and "observe the extent to which ecological systems resist even the most extreme efforts to remake them."[8] Along the way we can grapple with the contradictory relationships embedded in the work of the people who were simultaneously testing weapons of mass destruction while prototyping an environmental/ecological sensibility best represented through the wide array of visual culture artifacts they left behind. More than a decade ago the historian Richard White showed us how "it has often been the people most intimately connected to technological invention and building the human world who have come to understand our place in nature."[9] The artifacts of the atomic workers and peoples of the atomic regions offer another way to understand how people know nature through labor and experience.

Like many environmental historians, I have a long interest in the historic relationships between technology and environmental cultures and the interplay between technological systems and the natural environment. My focus is primarily in the postwar period and on the diverse groups of technologically enthusiastic "ecopragmatists" and "appropriate technologists" who struggled during this period to fashion an environmental ideology that fit the contradictions of their times and accommodated their desire for expressions of self through things and as tool-making creatures. These pragmatic greens were at odds with the wilderness-based movement of their day but on the leading edge of the do-it-yourself and market-friendly "sustainability" sensibility that emerged in the early years of the twenty-first century. They were the kind of hard-to-pigeonhole, environmentally aware people who do not easily fit standard definitions of environmentalist and who through their actions raised questions about who gets to speak for nature.

At first glance these ecopragmatists appear as children of their countercultural moment, but strip away the fashion, drugs, and music, and their questions and compromises appear less naive, more complicated, and more in keeping with a much deeper struggle that challenged all American environmental advocates. These were certainly not perfect people with all the answers but interesting people who at the very least raised important questions. The iconic pragmatist and technocrat Buckminster Fuller and his notion of a "Design Science-revolution" provided the intellectual foundation for these ecopragmatists and an emerging countercultural environmental ethos for the self-styled "tool freaks," "thing-makers," "prototypers," and "ecological designers" who became surprisingly successful and powerful environmental advocates at the end of the twentieth century.[10]

In the 1970s the anthropologist Claude Lévi-Strauss's notion of "savage bricoleurs" and rational engineers was turned upside down by the ecopragmatists and fellow traveling outlaw artists and ecological designers. For a new generation of green innovators, "bricolage," the creation "of a structure or structure of ideas achieved by using whatever comes to hand," was linked with lay participation, while formal modes of science and learning were criticized as too rigid. The ecological designers and ecopragmatists of the 1960s were messy bricoleurs working outside the mainstream of science and engineering and expressing their accomplishments through the "medium of things and images."[11] Like earlier environmentalists such as Thoreau and Muir, they were rendering their version of nature through art, prose, and technology alongside efforts simply to preserve more traditionally natural places such as wilderness areas and parks.

The countercultural ecopragmatists of the 1960s and 1970s joined a long line of human reconcilers that the historian Dan Flores traced all the way back to the Neolithic technological revolutionaries of six to ten thousand years ago. Surveying the *longue durée*, Flores wondered where "along the lengthy but connected trail that follows toolmaking out of the prehuman primate's rocks and sticks to our bulldozers . . . should we or could we have stopped?"[12] Flores recognized the danger inherent in looking for clear stopping points to a process so deeply connected with the evolution of our species. Identifying the moment when humans went off the rails and became "unnatural" too sharply divides nature and culture, leading to wistfulness about golden ages that never were.

For all that, some moments in the knotted history of nature and culture do appear so revolutionary and transformative that any reasonable observer would have to wonder if the scales had forever tipped and future compromise and balance were impossible. The decades following the Industrial Revolution were such a moment. The period following the bombing of Hiroshima was another. The building and testing of arsenals of ever more powerful atomic weapons on proving grounds around the globe created vast blasted and irradiated landscapes, dead places that seemed lost into the distant future. The specter of invisible radioactive isotopes floating around the globe and raining silently down on feed grasses before showing up in baby teeth terrified three generations of people all over the world. During the Cold War, the line between nature and culture never seemed blurrier and our ability to shatter natural systems never greater. But even on the ground zeros of the devastated proving grounds, nature persisted along with indigenous peoples and other transplanted residents of these most notorious abominations of modern technology. If, as Richard White suggests, "there is hope in hybrid landscapes," then is it even possible to find it here?[13] Can we learn a little more about the entanglement of nature and culture by looking at the most tainted places and the ways historical actors created and represented these atomic landscapes and then struggled to reconcile their destructive labors with their often-insightful appreciation of the desert, island, and steppe environments they inhabited?[14] In the visual legacy of testing we can at least find some intriguing evidence of Rebecca Solnit's haunting notion that "[o]ur morality is complicated by the fact that the sky above even the most demonic folly is often exquisitely colored, and its clouds as breathtakingly pure."[15]

The art historian Emily Scott suggests that it was no coincidence that communities of countercultural artists gravitated to the proving grounds of the Mojave Desert during the period of atomic testing. These artists joined amateurs who were already there exploring art as a means of recording otherwise secret working lives and landscapes. In the 1960s a range of artists from earthworks engineers such as Michael Heizer to painters such as Robert Beckmann and performance artists such as Jean Tinguely used western deserts as creative versions of the Atomic Energy Commission's "outdoor laboratory" to prototype art and culture and work to better represent misunderstood landscapes others saw only as wastelands.[16] These artists were fully aware of the atomic context of their work and explicitly addressed relationships between nature and culture in atomic environments.

Among those using visual culture to reveal the beauty and value of the desert while critiquing Cold War culture were the iconoclastic environmentalist Stewart Brand and his team of *Whole Earth Catalog* bricoleurs, who staged several "Productions in the Desert" to explore the connections between art, technology, and nature in the desert. The countercultural ecopragmatists who published *Whole Earth Catalog* might seem far removed from atomic test site workers, bureaucrats, and Atomic Energy Commission (AEC) scientists, but atomic testers were the ultimate "tool freaks," and some of their questions about the relationships between technology and nature were not so different from the technologically enthusiastic *Whole Earth* folks or the other artists scattered across the desert and grappling with the nature of the Cold War landscapes. As the anthropologist Mary Louise Pratt observed, "castaways and captives . . . realize the ideal of the participant observer." Laborers at the Nevada Testing Site (NTS) were like captives and castaways to a certain extent and they had little choice but to become participant observers.[17]

The historian Mark Fiege recently took a second look at the atomic West and the scientists who traveled there during World War II and stayed through the Cold War. He urges readers to listen carefully to the way atomic scientists talk about nature. Their "transit from delight to dread" and doubt and then sometimes action on behalf of nature, he argues, mirror the experiences of Aldo Leopold and the progressive conservationists who preceded them, linking the seemingly exceptional enterprise of nuclear weapons development to broader trends in environmental history and filling a critical gap in our understanding of environmental culture in the early Cold War period.[18] We know much about the scientists and their views on nature but much less about the hundreds of thousands who worked to turn science into reality and lived much more closely with the results of the experience than the visiting researchers who retreated to enclaves protected from their own creations. The vast corps of more regular folks who toiled to build a four-thousand-square-mile outdoor laboratory in the Mojave Desert and those outside the gates who worked to maintain their ways of life on the land while this craziness encompassed them also left a legacy of environmental culture worth exploring. How did Nevada become a magnet for testers and prototypers, and what is the visual legacy they left?

Environmental Containment

Beginning in 1951 the Nevada Proving Ground, just sixty-five miles north of downtown Las Vegas, replaced the Pacific Islands as the site where the United States perfected its nuclear arsenal. Mushroom clouds and dramatic atmospheric nuclear tests became visual spectacles that defined the modern history of the region. By 1957 the Nevada Test Site (NTS) was well established as an "outdoor laboratory" and "experimental landscape" central to U.S. Cold War weapons development and host to an array of remarkable and often reckless government-sponsored scientific activities.[19]

The NTS is both a bigger and a more complicated place than most would know from the kind of visual information supplied by those who controlled it for half a century. The federally controlled testing bioregion occupies a massive four-thousand-square-mile swath of mountains and valleys in southern Nevada established initially as a bombing range in 1941. The Western Shoshone claim the entire region under the 1863 Treaty of Ruby Valley. During two generations of protest, Western Shoshone tribal leaders steadfastly protested the confiscation of their ancestral homes both at the gates and in the courts.[20] They worked to counter AEC assertions that their homeland was devoid of life and value. On the east the bombing range borders the remarkably preserved 1.5-million-acre Desert National Wildlife Refuge (DNWR), established in 1936 in what was then "one of the least disturbed bighorn sheep ranges in the Southwest."[21] Wild horses and other charismatic megafauna roamed in abundance throughout the DNWR and the bombing range. In addition Mormon ranchers had lived and worked across the region for three generations by the time the military claimed the land as empty.[22]

The NTS was the atomic Comstock lode of the postwar West, and the cultural artifacts of these diggings and their engineers, miners, workers, cooks, prostitutes, barkeeps, sheriffs, and ranchers are every bit as interesting as those of the century-earlier silver lode communities that so captivated Mark Twain and other chroniclers of the nineteenth-century West. But like that earlier Comstock, the NTS was less a place of exceptional or exotic experience than one might assume. Even at its weirdest, the testing landscape was populated by diverse people with familiar motives for migration, work, home, and quality of life. It was a place of racial, religious, and ethnic tensions and reconciliations familiar to the West. Between 1963 and 1992 over 828 different underground complexes were excavated for 921 nuclear explosions. The only visible evidence of this extensive subterranean activity is the subsidence craters scattered across the playas in the deepest valleys visible only from the air. Below the ground one can visit the ruins of the secret working world of the Cold War and measure the economic costs in thousands of feet of million-dollar-a-foot cables, "line-of-sight" pipe, and giant millisecond-closing containment doors ordered by the dozens. However, the human and environmental costs are harder to quantify. The people who called this testing region home were often conflicted about issues of patriotism and secrecy in the face of atomic-era concerns about environmental health and safety, but like earlier migrants, they came to appreciate misunderstood environments in ways that gave them perspectives quite different from those created by government propaganda and fostered by broader cultural assumptions about desert wastelands.

Unlike their atomic counterparts in more familiar places such as Los Alamos and Livermore, the Nevada testing communities were not planned utopias or exclusive enclaves for science and scientists. NTS workers lived with equally intense secrecy, surveillance, and restrictions at work but ranged more freely across the region and surrounding towns without the benefits of the exclusive community. The hundred thousand men, women, and children who worked or lived in and around the NTS enjoyed little of the status or patriotic celebration that attended the elite scientists and the families of the lab cities around the West. Their primary home, Las Vegas, was tainted with cultural baggage before the creation of the NTS, and Nevada was a poorly understood blankness on the mental map of the West and the nation at best—a despised and disparaged backwater to many. But none of those more

Figure 8.2. Martha Bordoli Laird and the complicated issues of the testing region captured beautifully by the photographer Carole Gallagher for her landmark documentary history of the downwind zone, *American Ground Zero*. Photo courtesy of Carole Gallagher.

celebrated places of the atomic West could have existed without the NTS, where theories and technologies became frightening reality with the help of a vast corps of unheralded laborers, soldiers, and technicians. The atomic Athenians needed their Sparta—a place where the rubber could hit the road, the people and place were expendable, and things could get really ugly.

During the height of atmospheric nuclear testing between 1951 and 1958, the Federal Civil Defense Administration (FCDA) and the Atomic Energy Commission relied on visual imagery to shape public opinion about the testing region and to explain and justify continental nuclear testing. The graphic documentation of the tests, both by accident and by design, created misperceptions of the Nevada desert as an empty wasteland. Picturing the testing region as a place without nature or history had a lasting impact. Over the course of the twentieth century, this visual archive would facilitate the creation of the Yucca Mountain high-level radioactive waste facility, drive policies that would harm "Down-Winders" who were exposed to the blasts, and influence global debates about radiological health and ethics in the atomic age.[23]

Images of atomic detonations, frozen in time and divorced from place, became icons of the Cold War and the most recognized visual legacies of atomic testing. Published pictures of atomic tests typically focused on super-natural plasma balls floating in perfect darkness. These disturbing, yet entrancing, photographs created an enduring impression of atomic Armageddon and human vulnerability in the Cold War. Yet they left almost no image of the Mojave Desert, neither the natural environment nor the regional residents who called this atomic Cold War landscape home.[24]

Widely publicized "civil effects" tests between 1953 and 1957 are of particular importance for understanding the ways that atomic imagery shaped popular perceptions of the testing region's environment.[25] Publications such as *Newspictures* an FCDA flyer distributed to small media markets and rural communities, along with carefully selected film and still images, were often the public's only source of information about atomic testing and its possible effects on American citizens and environments. *Newspictures* used simple graphic images to educate the public about atomic science and nuclear testing effects and to assure Americans that testing was safe and under control. To communicate a sense of authority and competency, the masthead of *Newspictures*, for example, featured a line drawing that included a helmeted worker directing cars with an authoritative hand gesture, two workers building a test house or shelter, and another rescuing a boy after a blast.[26] Throughout the 1950s *Newspictures* and other AEC and Civil Defense pamphlets published photographs, such as *New Atomic Ghost Town: Odd Shapes Arise from the Nevada Desert*, that depicted bombs exploding, alongside short, breezy articles that described the construction of mock civilian targets and destruction of them at the Nevada Test Site. The publications nearly erased the five-thousand-square-mile continental atomic testing bioregion of the Mojave and Great Basin Deserts and its inhabitants from public view, referring to the area as "landscapes almost as barren as the moon," "wastelands," and "submarginal" places sparsely populated by politically "insignificant" people.

The notorious "Doom Town" series of civil effects tests conducted between 1953 and 1957 were some of the most striking published photo essays to shape public perceptions of atomic testing and to make the testing zone's environmental conditions seem "vacant" and "wasted."[27] For these events, CD designers and teams of local laborers constructed elaborate stage-set towns and domestic scenes that they populated with mannequin residents and farm animals. Then photographers and filmmakers documented their destruction to measure the blasts' effects on cultural landscapes and potential victims. The sociologist Joseph Masco aptly called images of these "atomic ghost towns" and the mushroom clouds that created them "detailed renderings of theatrically rehearsed mass violence."[28]

Thousands of soldiers famously participated in these Doom Town events. As burned or imploded structures and cars still smoldered, the soldiers left their trenches and marched toward ground zero. Films of the unprotected soldiers facing the blasts and sucking up radioactive dust are well-known reminders of the reckless spirit of the early Cold War. Less well remembered are the hundreds of live pigs, mice, and dogs placed nearby. Like the mannequins, the animals were proxies for citizens. As Brett Mizelle's essay in this volume shows, pigs have a special role in our cultural understandings of nature.[29] For atomic testers, pigs were favorite subjects because they share many anatomic characteristics with humans, making them excellent proxies for blast and radiation experiments. At NTS pigs were strapped to tables at various distances and carefully dressed in civilian clothes and military uniforms custom-made by the Department of Agriculture in a Maryland workshop. The gruesome mass killings of pigs and macabre ghost towns of the Doom Town series captured international media attention. Over time the entire testing region, including Las Vegas and the growing NTS town of Mercury, Nevada, were collectively remembered as Doom Towns—mysterious places where secret science-fiction scenarios played out deep in shattered desert valleys.

Perhaps the most interesting thing about the popular Doom Town stories and the historic artifacts that emerged from the early period of testing is the visibility of living people and actual nature before the iconic apocalyptic mushroom cloud images, which the art historian Peter Hales identified as the icons of the "atomic sublime," became the way most saw the place.[30] In early Doom Town coverage, workers and local residents were still at the center of the story. Press coverage and interviews of the time focused on the fantastic dummy residents of Doom Town but also highlighted their connection to the real place next door—Las Vegas—and included interviews from locals who remembered the ominous mushroom clouds rising from Doom Town as a "stairway to hell" clearly visible from their backyards. But fairly quickly the story of atomic testing's regional hosts faded. They faded in part because of the efforts of the FCDA and the AEC to use visual representation to craft a particular image of the Mojave and its people.

From a set of experiments called "Operation Doorstep," a photograph entitled *Wooden House* is typical of the visual style used in CD publications to communicate a particular message about the testing environment as an empty setting for important scientific work. In *Wooden House* two cars are parked near a newly constructed faux two-story suburban house typical of the era. Power poles and street signs replicate a familiar neighborhood scene. The house is situated in an expansive but ill-defined landscape. Another photograph captures a close-up of the female mannequin that sits in the passenger seat of one of the cars, with her head turned sharply behind.

Interior shots of the house show a family of mannequins posed amid common household items, such as lamps and tables. Without irony, photo captions explain that alert citizens who hope to survive an atomic attack should emulate the readiness of the mannequins. The workers who constructed the scenes are never visible in these images. The AEC published many photographs of scientists posed with reassuring authority in control centers but none of common laborers because showing actual living people in the picture frame of the target areas would counter the agency's assertions that the testing sites were "uninhabited." The ubiquitous wildlife of the desert region, such as bighorn sheep, desert tortoises, coyotes, birds, and rabbits, are also conspicuously absent in published images, reinforcing the implicit message that the testing bioregion was lifeless and expendable.

Unlike artists and photographers, who generally wait for the ideal light of breaking dawn or setting sun when long shadows best capture the variegated beauty of the desert, the Doom Town photographers shot during broad daylight or, as in the "Nancy" atomic test event, during the night.[31] Harsh glare and complete darkness voided out the natural background and made the desert appear as an empty stage devoid of life. In addition to special lighting techniques, remarkable new photographic technologies capable of freezing awesome atomic blasts in their otherworldly first milliseconds bolstered official efforts to portray the Mojave as a vacant landscape and created an "atomic sublime." Images from the still and the special high-speed gun-site movie cameras shooting one thousand feet of film per second that caught the famous Doom Town explosions are truly mesmerizing.[32]

The best-known sequence features the Doom Town house obliterated frame by frame in the wake of a nuclear blast. In the first frame, the blast lights up the house for a split second within the darkening desert. The second frame catches the front of the house combusting as the heat wave envelops it. The final frame freezes the house at the moment it explodes, as the blast wave slams into the structure, scattering debris across the desert. Those watching the event with the naked eye included six hundred CD representatives who were perched on the surrounding hillsides, and fifteen million people viewed segments of the Doom Town event live via new field broadcast television technology deployed en masse for the first time.[33] Official government press releases said that the images captured that day were "for the purpose of impressing Americans with the deadly seriousness of nuclear device detonations and the need for arousing a keener interest in civilian defense."[34] It worked. All those present remembered the use of civilian artifacts as eerie and disturbing, and the doom house images remain instantly recognizable icons of Cold War culture.

Some rarely seen photographs complicate the context for these events by illustrating the contrast between how the photographers and the spectators viewed the event at the site and how the scene was rendered in print form. For example in one set of images taken by AEC contract photographers capturing doom scenes, the desert landscape dotted with Joshua trees visually overpowers the distant thirty-thousand-foot mushroom cloud, which takes up just a small portion of the picture frame. These photographs makes visible the actual place and the people who lived and worked in it, in contrast to the more common CD publicity photographs of the atomic events that zoom in to the top of the mushroom cloud with no background whatsoever.

In addition unpublished official documentary photographs, such as *Six Vehicles*, *Cain Springs Cabin*, and hundreds of others, illustrate the broader environmental context for atomic testing that official publications omitted and that the more familiar atomic sublime concealed.[35] Unlike for the pictures of Doom Towns or of the bombs, for these unpublished landscape images photographers tended to work under better lighting conditions and included the testing region's variety of natural and historical features within the picture frames. *Cain Springs Cabin* captures an old lean-to that attests to the site's cultural history, and it along with *Six Vehicles* portray the Mojave's variegated topography: a remarkable diversity of trees, grasses, and shrubs, and the water sources that support them. These rarely seen declassified photographs raise questions about the photographers' intentions because the images

Figure 8.3. *Complete Destruction of House No. 1,* Nevada Test Site, Operation Upshot-Knothole, March 17, 1953. The time from top to bottom was 2.2 seconds. The camera was completely enclosed in a two-inch lead sheath as protection against radiation. As with most of these images, the bomb provided the only light. Photo courtesy of NSA–Nevada Site Office, Las Vegas, Nevada.

are so different from how the agencies wanted the public to perceive the test site. Were the government photographers who worked under strict secrecy and surveillance surreptitiously trying to capture a sense of history and place? Hundreds of unpublished images suggest that at least some individual photographers worked to capture a more complex and perhaps accurate documentary record of regional life and labor.

One practical rather than ideological reason that these lesser-known landscape images portray the diverse local environment is because they are often photos taken prior to the dropping of the bombs. The public generally saw only either the sanitized, cropped, and simplified images such as *Wooden House* or after-photos of seared landscapes—both of which confirmed perceptions of the testing regions as empty and devoid of life. Civil Defense publicity images, such as one simply titled *After*, focus on flat, dry lakebeds and seemingly lifeless desert playas and salt flats—that is, anomalous features in an otherwise mountainous region. *After* was the centerpiece of a popular testing publication distributed to all CD regions for use in public information programs. In this photograph fully suited technicians are shown retrieving a shelter door in a blasted lunarlike landscape near ground zero in the center of Yucca Flat. The monotone lighting conditions and low-contrast printing techniques make it appear as if the workers are on a two-dimensional sound stage rather than in an actual landscape. As with most of the popular testing images, the published picture frame zooms in closely on its subject and the wider setting is cropped out. In the final print version, the mountains and even the sky are completely replaced with solid black ink. The result is a picture of an anonymous place divorced from any familiar natural features, without any signs of previous human habitation, and without any sense of its use to anyone. Viewers looking at *After* would never guess that Cain Springs was nearby.

These selective visual interpretations of the testing grounds are significant not only because they misrepresent the natural environment but also because they obscure the region's deep and complicated history. The Western Shoshone occupied the area for centuries and controlled sites such as Cain Springs as part of seasonal resources networks across the region. During the years of testing, the tribe fought AEC claims that these areas were worthless and looked to the agency's own archaeological studies for proof.[36] Their concerns were pushed aside as Cold War public information campaigns simplified both nature and regional human history in service of atomic goals. The experiences of the Shoshone mirror those of other indigenous peoples affected

Figure 8.4. After. Workers retrieving samples after blast conducted during Operation Plumbbob, June 1957. Photo courtesy of NSA–Nevada Site Office, Las Vegas, Nevada.

by atomic testing across the globe. Global nuclear testing sites share environmental characteristics and were all, in the words of the atomic lexicologist Michon Mackedon, "hearts of darkness . . . with politically insignificant populations and, in conventional eyes, un-lovely landscape features."[37]

The British tested their weapons in Nevada and Australia. In both locations official government reports presented the testing regions as largely unoccupied and worthless. The Soviets shamelessly made similar arguments about the significantly populated Semipalatinsk region in Kazakhstan where over a million people lived and still live on and around their test site. The pattern was repeated in Algeria, Chili, China, India, Micronesia, and Pakistan where areas described as frontiers lightly inhabited by presumably irredeemable indigenous people were sacrificed, or according to some, finally made useful, in the name of national security programs.[38] In all of these places scientists, engineers, miners, and laborers regularly encountered the supposedly absent inhabitants. Government photographers had to work to craft images that erased these people.

Not unlike the American Indians and other global testing region inhabitants, NTS workers who migrated to Nevada to take advantage of Cold War

Figure 8.5. Cain Springs Cabin, c. 1955. Photo courtesy of National Atomic Testing Museum photo collections (PH:6).

employment opportunities came to know intimately the region's natural environment through their work and daily lives.[39] They often spoke of the region with great feeling, describing the NTS as a beautiful place: "It is, seriously. . . . Oh, my God, simply beautiful." Likewise protesters who spent long periods between 1951 and the 1990s camped outside the gates came to know and appreciate the complex character of the Mojave, describing it as "heartbreakingly beautiful" and "sublime." Indigenous peoples, workers, and protesters shared a common appreciation of this misunderstood place despite their very different motives for being there.[40] In their eyes this was a living landscape, not a wasteland.

Atomic Folk Art

The vast and subtle American testing bioregion revealed in declassified visual artifacts and the experiences and memories of the three hundred thousand people who labored in nature there are mostly absent from historical depictions of the NTS.[41] Instead two metanarratives generally frame the history and popular understandings of the region. The first focuses on atomic

Figure 8.6. Arthur Rothstein's iconic 1936 Dust Bowl photograph *Father and Sons Walking in the Face of a Dust Storm*," Cimarron County, Oklahoma, April 1936. Library of Congress, Prints & Photographs Division, FSA/OWI Collection, #LC-DIG-ppmsc-00241.

science and the troubled geniuses that created and tested the weapons. The second concentrates on the downwind effects of the tests and the protesters who steadfastly fought to reveal the human and environmental consequences of testing. By studying the wide range of declassified documentary photography of the testing regions, we can better place this history in the broader context of the postwar period. Historians are familiar with photographs such as Arthur Rothstein's iconic 1936 Dust Bowl image of a father and his sons walking past the ruins of their devastated farmstead, a hallowed symbol of American culture being swallowed up by the unforgiving forces of nature and human hubris. Likewise uncompromising films such as Pare Lorentz's *Plow That Broke the Plains* (1936) conditioned a generation of Americans to rethink our capacity to master the environment.

Working only fourteen years after the famous Farm Security Administration image makers, the documentary photographers of the NTS were spe-

Figure 8.7. *Generator Building.* Photo courtesy of NSA–Nevada Site Office, Las Vegas, Nevada.

cifically called on to erase any ambivalence about the government's ability to harness nature and, in turn, to picture atomic energy and atomic explosions as safe and containable. The AEC maps drew sharp borders between the testing zone and surrounding areas with thick black ink, and photographic images were carefully constructed to support assertions that the valleys of the NTS were somehow compartmentalized from their surrounding ecosystems and broader regional context. An image titled *Generator Building*, which shows figures standing before an abandoned building within an overwhelmingly devastated landscape, is hauntingly similar to the photographer Arthur Rothstein's famous image of a Depression–era father and sons fleeing a dust storm. Photos such as *Generator Building* remained classified throughout the testing period because, like the famous Rothstein photograph, they depict complexity, not stasis.

Hundreds of unpublished photographs such as these reveal the links between the NTS and the broader cultural and natural environment—for example, buried telephone lines and the swirling windblown clouds—neither of which was ultimately contained or controllable. Photographs, such as *Generator Building*, that depict the interplay between human activity and natural systems fill in gaps in the historical record skewed by decades of hypnotizing propaganda.

For Native Americans, downwinders, and Yucca Mountain opponents protesting the legacies of testing in the past two decades, perceptions of environmental containment have proven difficult to overturn. As the Doom Town stories became the stuff of legend and the atomic sublime became the official and accepted visual record of testing, 1950s-era assumptions about the nature of the Mojave environment hardened. The Doom Town photographs and films so powerfully shaped perceptions of the testing region that even into the twenty-first century the popular media depicts Nevada, the most mountainous state in the union, as flat and featureless, dead and lifeless. Yucca Mountain proponents likewise relied on the earlier atomic imagery to make their case in the 1980s that Nevada was the only appropriately desolate place for nuclear waste disposal.

The photos released during the Doom Town series represent only a fraction of the visual legacy of testing. Miles of film and archives of photos were generated during hundreds of atomic "shots." Combat artists documented the blasts in sketches and paintings. Tens of thousands of publicly invisible laborers left a remarkable cache of material and visual culture that has only recently been revealed. Regional protagonists, workers, and protesters in surprising numbers often turned to their own forms of visual representation as means to preserve their experiences and to capture an alternative view of their misunderstood desert home.[42] Despite a wealth of wonderful scholarship on atomic pop culture, little has been done with the nuclear combat art and craft created by those who worked or lived throughout the testing regions capturing their views of land, labor, science, technology, and historic events.[43]

After 1957 increased fears of espionage, an expanding protest movement, and widespread concerns about fallout shifted coverage of the events at the NTS. As the Doom Town stories became the stuff of legend, the history of the people and the environment of the Mojave region faded. Even those who witnessed the tests in person rarely remembered much about the place beyond the extraordinary atomic event. Frustrated testing protagonists, unable to explain their experiences in any other way, turned to a wide variety of forms of visual representation as a means to preserve their unique experi-

Figure 8.8. *Stokes—Operation Plumbbob, 1957.* Kristian Purcell, pen and ink, Courtesy of the artist.

ences and to capture the misunderstood desert environment they came to appreciate despite their destructive day jobs.

Atomic folk art created by those who worked or lived throughout the testing region captured environmental insights gleaned from years of working and living in this supposedly dead and worthless landscape. This art took many forms, from formal oil paintings and carefully composed photography to model making, drawings, sculpture, and stained glass. This atomic *art brut* forms a second visual record of nature and culture at the NTS. Miners and engineers who built the byzantine labyrinth underneath the desert learned the geology and landscape that existed above and below the ground. They captured the environment in photos but also in drawings and sculptural models that often surpassed their utilitarian purpose and became unintentional artworks. Protagonists with no formal artistic training or apparent prior natural

Figure 8.9. *House Number One.* Kristian Purcell, charcoal drawing. Courtesy of the artist.

inclination turned in surprising numbers to art. Living and laboring in an environment of strict secrecy forced workers to seek alternative modes of expressing their concerns about the dangers of the work, their sense of shared purpose and camaraderie, and their conflicted relationship with the land.

Following military tradition certificates, patches, stickers, and other insignia created by participants were issued at the NTS to key personnel involved in tests. These officially sanctioned folk art souvenirs served the dual purpose of fostering a sense of exclusive community and shared purpose while supporting a culture of secrecy and restriction. NTS officials encouraged this art as a means of creating an esprit de corps that bolstered off-site silence about everything from science and ecological effects to workplace safety and human health issues. Even in this sanctioned outsider/insider art darkly humorous code names, inside jokes, and visual ciphers provide clues to the ways participants chaffed at some of the strict controls of NTS life and work. Some of these artifacts show the unintended consequences of efforts to contain blasts and radiation and reveal concerns about the environmental consequences of testing.

Conflicts over who had the authority to speak for the nature of the desert also appear in this art. Power struggles between scientists, engineers, and laborers often centered on who knew how to read the landscape best in order to accomplish science and avoid environmental catastrophe. Likewise the characteristics of wild nature across the testing region are consistently featured illuminating the strange mix of preservation and destruction central to the history of the NTS. Endangered desert tortoises make frequent appearances, lovingly represented along with examples of on-site wildlife preservation, the iconic and beloved Joshua tree, and examples of the familiar road signs that cautioned, "Drive Safely—Protect Wildlife."

The power and authority to speak for the environment of their region was always an issue for those living throughout the testing region. Successive generations of regional artists and photographers interpreted official documents, people, nature, science, and atomic artifacts in their own productions and for their own reasons. Artists across the broader testing region naturally turned to the subject of atomic testing, as it was a defining factor of life and history for millions. The poorly understood dangers of lingering radiation throughout the region qualified everyone living around the NTS as a Cold War protagonist. Some of these art and craft works are on display at atomic museums and exhibits throughout the world. However, these are primarily museums of technology that dazzle and horrify but generally reveal less about human experience in place and time than they do about abstracted technological achievement. They do a good job of presenting atomic kitsch but rarely include examples of more serious efforts to represent this controversial history visually.

The legacy of atomic folk art and lesser-known observations about history and the environment now available to researchers along with vast archives of declassified documentary environmental images offer other ways to read the landscapes of the Cold War and think again about the Gordian knot of nature and culture. In intention and effect this visual evidence reveals the ways people perceived their environment during a frightening time of change. By looking closely at the most conflicted environmental advocates and the most compromised places, we learn anew about how individuals and communities conscientiously struggled in the past to understand *their* nature however disparaged and compromised that nature might be.

By grappling with the outrageous contradictions of those who genuinely worked to protect and appreciate the nature of the Mojave Desert while creating and testing atomic weapons, we might find it easier to comprehend how more ordinary folks reconciled technologically mediated cultural life and nature appreciation in more familiar surroundings. The extraordinary prototypers of the atomic proving grounds were demonstrating the extreme version of the routine creation "of a structure or structure of ideas achieved by using whatever comes to hand" that everyday environmentalists later used to make environmental compromises in the postwar period. Thinking of people as always deeply conflicted actors with the capacity to understand the complexity of their world, as active prototypers with agency, gives us a different way of theorizing the nature/culture relationship.

Official images of environmental containment, which celebrated the sublime power of humans to dominate the elemental forces of life and death, rendered the Mojave as a natural wasteland, in effect stripping it of life and people to justify and legitimize the human capacity to master nature. Atomic *art brut* sought to render a more ambiguous landscape, a living environment inhabited by living beings, which persevered despite the very real environmental destruction of atomic testing. Juxtaposing these conflicted images reveals the process by which nature and culture were parsed into distinct categories to serve both political and personal ends. Propaganda for atomic weapons relied on representations of empty places devoid of people, plants, and animals to keep the focus on the politics of human domination over nature at its most elemental level. These images depended on both the invisibility of the Mojave Desert and the silence of those who worked and lived there. Simultaneously they embraced the aesthetics of the sublime to invoke a sense of awe similar to the reverence of natural wonders. Insider/outsider art sought to reconcile the contradictions of living and working in a place devoted to the annihilation of life. These images drew on a long-established visual vocabulary of idealized nature to challenge the power of the atomic sublime. In depicting picturesque landscapes and documenting the beauty and uniqueness of indigenous species, they referenced well-worn tropes of nature set apart from civilization to validate their experience as inhabitants of these atomic landscapes. That these images have long been suppressed exposes yet another layer of invisibility, silence, and separation. In sorting through these layers of rendered nature one cannot help but be struck by the entanglement of nature and culture at every level. The imagery of environmental containment substituted elemental nature for environmental nature; atomic *art brut* sought to reconcile the two. These opposing environmental visions allow us to see the humanity behind the images. Perhaps more importantly they reveal humanity's fraught desire to come to terms with our role as a force of nature.

Chapter 9

River Rats in the Archive: The Colorado River and the Nature of Texts

Annie Gilbert Coleman

A tall, athletic young businessman showed up in Green River, Utah, at dinnertime on July 9, 1940. He was looking for a small group of strangers and the river. Starting in Wyoming, the Green flows through Utah on its way to meet the Colorado River and the Grand Canyon. There the river runs a mile below the Colorado Plateau and drops two thousand feet in less than three hundred miles. The man was joining the second ever commercial river trip through the Grand Canyon and was ready to go. He wrote in his journal that night, "Here I was starting out to do something that has held a fascination for me ever since I first heard of the Colorado—The Powells—The Dellenbaughs—the Kolbs and the other men who have tried their hands at running this strange river. . . . This same river on which their success and their failure came as often as this fickle river changed its course—Yes—here I was going to have my little whack at it—To get it done and out of my system then probably sit back on my haunch and wonder why."[1] The 1,440-mile-long Colorado drains water from seven states as well as Mexico. While its basin has a long history of human habitation predating European contact and the first Spanish explorer spied the Grand Canyon in 1540, the river as it flowed through that region remained largely a mystery until the one-armed Maj. John Wesley Powell completed his expedition in 1869. With his new companions, Barry

Goldwater would bring the documented number of people who had run the entire canyon to seventy-five.[2]

The river's history, iconic nature, and physical challenge all pulled Goldwater to the Colorado as it flowed through the Grand Canyon. Goldwater was then thirty-one years old, the father of three (the youngest a four-month-old infant), and the owner of Phoenix's largest department store, a business he had inherited from his father. His political career was still a decade away. He sought the river and wrote in his journal as ways to make sense of the world, broadly speaking, and he seemed to enjoy the trip. He took turns at the oars, hiked up side canyons, set piles of driftwood aflame, basked in the scenery, and wondered about its past. Earlier expeditions sometimes colored his observations of the moment at hand. On July 16 he wrote, "The excitement of fast water is overshadowed by the rugged beauty of the Cataract Canyon, named by Powell for the cataracts that pour over the cliffs in the rain."[3]

At first glance Goldwater's journal reads as one might expect. How many of us have experienced nature with his anticipation and awe? And the nature in this story seems clear: the cliffs; the fast water; the cataracts. We know that experiencing nature—especially modern recreational nature—is physical and sensual and emotional; it can be work or play or some of both, but either way we *feel* it. Indeed that is how we know it is real. Barry Goldwater made a point to get himself to Green River, Utah, that July and to experience the Colorado River as directly as possible—to have his "little whack at it—To get it done." It was important for him to see the canyons himself, to wrestle boats through rapids, and to hike until his knee gave out. Sun-burned skin and wrecked knees testify to the materiality of nature; they document the encounter between person and world, physical residue from the friction of rubbing up against the environment. Physical experience matters, and through it we recognize and interact with nature in its less adulterated forms. We get some traction. But there is something more at work here too. Goldwater did not just feel it through his skin, eyes, ears, and knees. Rather than merely "get it done," Goldwater wrote that he wanted to "get it done and out of my system." The canyon and the river were in him already.

How did they get there? The answer is, through books, photographs, maps—representations. John Wesley Powell, Frederick Dellenbaugh, and the Kolb brothers traversed all or parts of the Grand Canyon in 1869, 1872, and 1911, respectively, and published the first three and perhaps most influential popular accounts of Grand Canyon river adventure.[4] Goldwater singled them out as the sources of his fascination—the reasons why he ultimately had to do it himself. These texts, the places and experiences they recount, and the hold they had on Goldwater suggest that nature is not so easily identified by its physical touch. Words can get it into your system too.

If Powell and others who had been through the canyon in the past shaped Goldwater's experience of the Colorado—the way he rubbed up against that material world—so did the family he was leaving at home. He missed his wife and counted the days before he could reach a phone to call her, and when he saw her and their daughter at the end of the trip, "weeks of lonesomeness were wiped away in an instant."[5] He had been gone over seven weeks by then, a fact he noted a few days earlier in his journal and one that woke me from my reverie in the Huntington Library's Ahmanson reading room. That was how long I had been away from my family doing this research. We had both been exploring the Colorado River, noting its every canyon, rapid, and historic moment, for seven weeks. Sixty-six years after the fact, Goldwater was getting the river into my system and out of his at the same time.

I too had read John Wesley Powell and Ellsworth Kolb—that is partly how this New Hampshire girl wound up researching the Colorado River—but now Goldwater's river joined theirs in my head, a 1940 version to add to the earlier ones. Although we hardly think of Barry Goldwater as a nature writer, we can relate to his practice of keeping a journal. He wrote, as so many have, in response to the rapids and the rocks, the aches and pains, the beauty, and the surprises of rafting through the Grand Canyon. Running the river was the point, but setting his experience down on the page captured his particular experience and the river too—a river he recognized as fickle and ever changing. Moreover, Goldwater's journal enabled reflection, a way for him (and me, and anyone else who was interested) to "sit back on my haunch and wonder why." How his river-born musings would affect this man who profoundly influenced post–World War II politics his journal does not reveal. Reading Goldwater's entries produced a more immediate, physical experience than a historical one. It reduced sixty-six years into an instant, and I almost feared that his muddy rapids would inundate the Shakespearean scholars whispering two tables over. The Colorado River and the Grand Canyon take place and they take time, but at the Huntington Library I realized that they do not always stay put. They got into my system, as they did Goldwater's, and I am not sure they will ever leave.

Our mutual experiences with the Colorado suggest that "environment" and "nature" are not necessarily fixed in space, time, or substance. They exist as a fluid, shifting process, a set of relationships among people, physical spaces, and the cultural practices that give meaning to the world around us. Yet both scholarly discourse and public discourse embrace a philosophical separation between nature and culture that sometimes obscures the ways we "know" nature by blending the physical with the cultural.[6] Following a place where it goes geographically, textually, and historically makes visible the rendering process at work in creating what we understand as "the Colorado River" in all its manifestations.[7]

The river, the Grand Canyon, Goldwater's journal, and the larger archive of river texts compose a formative system, producing and exchanging meaning by guiding our sensory experience of that world, directing the ways we represent it culturally, and anchoring the material results of those acts in place. As the anthropologist Tim Ingold argues, "to move, to know, and to describe are not separate operations . . . but parallel facets of the same process—that of life itself." The sentient body, "irrevocably stitched into the fabric of the world" as both producer and perceiver, "traces the path of the world's becoming in the very course of contributing to its ongoing renewal."[8] As we inhabit nature with our imaginations as well as our bodies, places such as the Colorado River and the Grand Canyon become more than just settings or material things. They take their shape through motion and through cycles of experience and cultural production that cut across boundaries of time and space and challenge the division between material and representational modes. How we feel the river can be textual; how we read and write about it can be sensory. Tracing this path will eventually lead us out of the Grand Canyon and away from the Colorado River, but these connections show up even in the experiences and words of John Wesley Powell.

By the mid-nineteenth century the twin acts of exploring nature and writing about it had become practically inseparable, and John Wesley Powell understood this quite well. He wanted to map a river, but his group did much more than survey. Despite overturned boats, destroyed instruments, frequent dousing, and the loss of three members at Separation Canyon, his first expedition netted one surviving journal, belonging to hunter Jack Sumner, and a series of letters Powell had sent home along the way. From them along with information from his second expedition and two added sections on the region's physical features and zoology, Powell cobbled together *The Exploration of the Colorado River of the West and Its Tributaries* in 1875.[9] Part official report and part adventure tale, his volume became a classic and kicked off a long tradition of Colorado River stories featuring a mix of scientific observation, practical description, artful expression, and outdoor exploits—literally, river texts. A deeply crafted composite, Powell's *Exploration* highlighted his group's immediate and physical interactions with nature: broken boats, starving bodies, tense emotions, wet everything. It is almost a literary equivalent to Goldwater's sore knee—physical residue left over from the author bumping up against the environment—but published and thus accessible to a mass audience.

Less thrilling but more informative, Frederick S. Dellenbaugh's *A Canyon Voyage* (1908) became the established account of Powell's 1871–72 expedition. This second trip stopped at Kanab Creek, short of the first approximately one hundred miles above Separation Canyon, but gathered an extraordinary amount of data—hydrological, geographical, ethnographic, photographic, and pictorial. It elicited nine separate diaries and four sets of field notes, not to mention hundreds of photographs. Dellenbaugh, the appointed artist for the expedition, built his narrative from at least three diaries plus some of his letters home, and he talked extensively with Robert Brewster Stanton, an engineer who was in the second ever group to make it through the entire Grand Canyon in 1890.[10] Emery and Ellsworth Kolb were the twenty-sixth and twenty-seventh through in 1911. They ran a photography studio from their home at the head of the Bright Angel Trail and were extremely familiar with the local landscape. They considered Powell's book "a classic, literary and geological." Regarding Dellenbaugh they said, "[W]e could hardly hope to add anything of value to his wealth of detail." Yet with facts and figures borrowed from Dellenbaugh and other help from Julius Stone and Nathaniel Galloway, who recorded their own canyon trip in 1909, the Kolbs added Ellsworth's illustrated *Through the Grand Canyon from Wyoming to Mexico* to the collection in 1914.[11] According to the *San Francisco Argonaut,* "Mr. Kolb writes his book exactly as it should be written, with an admirable mixture of incident, adventure, reflection, and personality."[12]

These three books chronicle what it was like to be on the Colorado River in the Grand Canyon. They describe sweaty labor, soggy campgrounds, monumental scenery, and frightening rapids in intimate detail. They reflect, exclaim, and record nature, but they also reflect and record other writers. Between Powell's dependence on Sumner's journal and data from his second expedition, Dellenbaugh's access to multiple diaries and Stanton, and the Kolbs' use of Dellenbaugh, Galloway, and Stone, each author expressed his personal experience of nature in part through the eyes and observations of others. With such help Powell, Dellenbaugh, and Ellsworth Kolb built up the initial layers of Colorado River texts, which tourists, history buffs, and river runners still seek out and consult. Their books hold a place of honor among published writings on the Grand Canyon, which number now, according to one author, more than forty-two thousand.[13]

Powell, Dellenbaugh, and Kolb integrated a whole series of responses to the river and the canyon. They have continued to shape and inform the experiences of thousands more since. Moreover, these canonical texts and their rereadings have influenced the course and composition of the river itself. These texts evoke the river as an environmental palimpsest—a material rendering of place emerging from layers of authorial perspectives of and sensory relationships to the environment. Such river texts participate in a never-ending cycle of cultural production, but their most immediate messages convey their authors' own responses to the Colorado and its canyons. Nature courses through the culture of river writing.

Culture also permeates the nature of the Grand Canyon. We may consider the canyon itself as a river text with no visible author, a monumental nature that seems to transcend time itself. Reading this landscape is not so different from reading Powell and Kolb. Indeed, Powell described the land as a book throughout his writing on the canyon. "One might imagine that the [Grand Canyon] was intended for the library of the gods, and it was," he wrote. "The shelves are not for books, but form the stone leaves of one great book. He who would read the language of the universe may dig out letters here and there, and with them spell the words, and read in a slow and imperfect way (but still understand a little) the story of creation."[14] We still read the canyon, and we interpret the story of creation through a particular language suggesting the divine but anchored in science. The Vishnu Schist and Zoroaster Granite visible in the Inner Gorge date to over 1.5 billion years ago; the Grand Canyon Supergroup and rock layers above them tell the story of more recent geologic, climatic, and environmental changes. As straightforward and impressive as this sounds, our understanding of geology, and even of time itself, as Frieda Knobloch argues in this volume, emerged from a specific historical and cultural context. Similarly we have named canyons and labeled them by river mile, imposing not one but many symbolic practices to organize this natural world.

The notion of environmental palimpsest gives us new ways to conceptualize the ongoing relationship between nature and culture on the Colorado River. Beyond the construction of river texts and the Grand Canyon, we can use the term to examine how human practices continue to shape and define the river and its canyons. On its way to the Grand Canyon, the Colorado River once flowed through Cataract and Glen Canyons (now inundated by Lake Powell) before reaching Lee's Ferry, mile marker 0, and the northeast end of Grand Canyon National Park. These canyons and more, each unique in its physical features, record both environmental change and the Colorado River's ongoing history of exploration, economic development, and recreational use. Sometimes all you have to do is look on the walls to see the evidence.

Ancestral Puebloan ruins and pictographs document a long history of native habitation in the region. Their writings offer clues to an earlier palimpsest, alternate attempts to organize relationships to the river. Euro-Americans inscribed a different sort of textual structure on the Grand Canyon's nature: they wrote their names. "I was here," they said, asserting their own daring or loneliness but also defining nature in relationship to themselves and their endeavors.

D. Julien came through in 1836, carving his name twice along Cataract Canyon and twice above it in the Green River's Labyrinth and Hell Roaring Canyons. His name and the year are all he wrote; others later figured out that he was Denis Julien, a French-Canadian trader based in St. Louis and probably on a trapping expedition. Powell's second group of information gatherers left their mark near the mouth of White Canyon on the Green, and then the surveyors showed up. In 1889 the engineer Robert B. Stanton teamed up with Frank M. Brown, president of the Denver, Colorado Canyon, and Pacific Railroad Company, to try and get coal from western Colorado to Los Angeles. Their efforts to survey the canyons of the Colorado proved challenging, to say the least. The shortest version of the story appeared on Marble Canyon's walls at miles 12 and 25: memorials first to Brown and then for two other members of the expedition, all drowned and lost in the rapids.[15]

Hopes for the railroad fizzled, but the Stanton expedition launched other plans to mine along the Colorado's path. James Best led a group for the Grand Canyon Mining and Improvement Co. in 1891, which crashed one of their boats in Cataract Canyon and carved: "Hell to Pay No 1 Is Sunk and Down." They added their company's initials next to D. Julien's twenty miles farther along but disbanded at Lee's Ferry. Such meager marks and scratches left on the rocks might raise more questions than they answer, but they transformed the river and its canyons nonetheless. The act of writing on canyon walls recruited the river and its geologic forms into parallel processes of exploration and trapping, mining and railroad building; it defined the Colorado as an adventure, a potential source of wealth, and a burial ground.

Figure 9.1. Photographed in Glen Canyon during the Stanton expedition, these petroglyphs now reside beneath Lake Powell. *Picture Writing in Glen Canyon.* Photo by Raymond Cogswell, 1909. Reproduced courtesy of Julius Stone Collection, Cline Library, Northern Arizona University.

This practice of canyon nature writing continued well into the twentieth century, with help from the photographers the Kolb brothers in 1911; the 1923 U.S. Geological Survey (USGS) group in search of dam sites; Clyde Eddy's film-making trips in 1927 with cameramen, dogs, and a bear cub; and Norm Nevills's commercial tourist trips starting in 1938.[16] When this first tourist group came through the Grand Canyon to Elves Chasm at mile 116.5, they found a whole list of names on the wall. To Galloway from 1897, Frank Dodge from 1923, and Eddy's name (twice), Nevills added "Nevills Expedition '38.". He repeated this performance two years later on his next trip through. During this trip, which started higher up on the Green River, he began writing just after Ashley Falls. "[It] was quite a job to get names up," he recalled in his journal; "had to work from a sling. Saw a good many names, including those of the Stone party. Our names, written under NEVILLS

Figure 9.2. Here lies the last physical evidence of Frank Brown. *Name Inscriptions—F. M. Brown.* Used by permission, Utah State Historical Society, all rights reserved.

EXPEDITION 1940[,] are about 75' above the river, in white paint."[17] While Nevills certainly viewed the Colorado River as a source of wealth and opportunity, the cash and fame he sought came not from development exactly, but from paying clients. He took a botanist and her assistant down in 1938, and in 1940 Goldwater and an adventurous secretary from Buffalo each paid six hundred dollars for the privilege. Nevills's wife, who accompanied her husband, insisted that it was silly to write their names on the wall. They were tourists, not explorers, she pointed out, and anyone knowing a tiny bit of river-running history would see the Nevills inscriptions as incongruous. Yet the man continued to paint. Maybe he fancied himself an explorer; maybe not. Either way, Nevills realized that putting his clients' names on the wall would alter the meaning of the canyon, and he built from behaviors associated with exploration to promote his tourism business.

Nevills worked this angle in other contexts too, leading his 1940 group to "discover" and name a natural bridge, which they later found was already known.[18] With good reason but maybe a little too much drama, he led them carefully through rapids and emphasized their danger. Nevills was not a perfect river guide, but he understood that adding his clients' names to the list on the wall adjusted the context of their travels from mere recreation or tourism to something more exciting. The significance of his authorship reaffirmed the transformative muscle of earlier scribblers, for without them his act would not have worked.

River runners soon took to writing on paper rather than the canyon walls. A group of Boy Scouts organized a river register at Dark Canyon in 1957, pasting the notes people had left in a cairn there since 1946 into a little book, which then accumulated comments through 1962. A message from 1955 summarized the river's changing identity: "This country may be alright for river runners to explore," Rusty Mussleman and Raymond McCalister wrote, "but it's damn poor for prospectors."[19] Today the Grand Canyon derives most of its meaning through its status as a national park. Almost five million people visit the place annually, but the number of people seeing it from the Colorado River each year is closer to twenty-five thousand. Although the park service strictly regulates camping along the river and writing your name on the wall would probably get you arrested, commercial river trips continue to inscribe meaning on the landscape through a variety of performative cultural practices.[20] Outfitters offer excursions emphasizing the canyon's history or geology; they feature special opportunities to hike up side canyons, practice yoga, or even listen to a string quartet along the way. Such behaviors enlist nature for recreation and create a whole range of more specific meanings in the canyon, if only fleetingly. After the food, sleeping bags, and yoga mats are all packed away, someone else comes through and tries something else.

Of course the Colorado River as a tourist destination rests in large part on its function as a water and energy supply system. Its water flows through an arid region, and many have compared the Colorado's watershed to a giant plumbing system.[21] Dams had been proposed along the Grand Canyon as early as 1913, and the 1923 USGS expedition identified a series of potential sites there, first for irrigation and later for hydroelectricity. Such use developed in concert with tourism; surveyors, boatmen, and adventure tourists were often one and the same in the years before World War II. Like those before and after them, dam builders wrote on the canyon walls, but they did it with heavy equipment and dynamite. Dam-site residue at river miles 33.2 and 39.7, traces of an old tramway cable above Redwall Cavern, and Marble Canyon's more significant exploratory tunnels all suggest some of the plumbing that might have been. They document political struggles over proposed use of the river through the 1950s and 1960s (most notably dams associated with the Colorado River Storage and Central Arizona Projects) and suggest the river's importance as an economic resource after World War II. As texts, artifacts, and interpretive stops along the tourist's path, these sites continue to define the river and its canyons as a contested landscape.[22]

Outside the confines of Grand Canyon National Park, however, the Bureau of Reclamation's obvious successes tell a slightly different story. Hoover and Glen Canyon Dams (1935, 1963, respectively) represented the power of American engineering and the promise of hydroelectricity and irrigation for the twentieth-century West. Instead of adding words to the canyon palimpsest they added layers of concrete—simultaneously building new meaning on the river and covering up much of the past under Lakes Mead and Powell. These dams rendered the ancient canyon walls, not to mention the inscriptions on them, temporary and ephemeral. The last people to run Separation and Lava Cliff rapids went through in 1937. Lake Powell filled Glen Canyon and a few others by the summer of 1964. Reshaped to generate electricity and irrigation for urban populations, the Colorado and its canyons look different. Now energy demands in Tucson determine water flow below Glen Canyon Dam more than the weather does; beaches along the river slowly disappear while sediment builds below the houseboats in Lakes Mead and Powell. We know that what is left of Denis Julien and the Best mining expedition languishes sixty feet below the waterline in Cataract Canyon; the Dark Canyon Boy Scout register survives in a library basement. Some physical constructions serve to silence old texts, just as those old texts rendered prior inscriptions illegible. Places and artifacts sunk beneath the floods serve as reminders of how the broader political process of reengineering the river as a hydroelectric aqueduct rested on the loss of other possible Colorados. At the same time, it paved the way for the river to become understood and experienced as an integrated recreational, tourist, and symbolic landscape.

Powell, Dellenbaugh, the Kolbs, Nevills, Goldwater, and more recently yogis and classical music fans all participated in unique environments on their way through the Grand Canyon. Their interactions with place depended on their own perspectives, paths, sensory experiences, and symbolic practices; the canyon palimpsests they made and perceived changed with each layer of representation and experience. But more than that and on a more basic level, the world we inhabit moves. Dams, weather, technology, and erosion (not to mention the continual process of palimpsest-making) render the Colorado River *and* its canyons fluid. If Glen Canyon famously disappeared under Lake Powell, Crystal Rapid appeared out of nowhere. It formed in 1966 after a

debris flow entered the canyon and now represents one of the most challenging rapids on the river. Fluctuating water levels have often turned passable
rapids into death traps. Our scribbled responses to them record a momentary
experience for posterity. On the walls such messages become part of that
experience. On the page they capture only a snapshot—reactions to a fleeting
expression of environment—but in preserving that nature they sometimes
have a longer shelf life than the actual places they describe.

The environmental palimpsest that is the Colorado River begins to unfold
as a physical landscape layered with texts, marks on the land as well as the
more literary, published variety. But beneath these public layers lies a wealth
of private letters, journals, photos, film, and notes that never made it to press
or public view. By themselves these ephemera do not mean much or last
long; as records of individuals reenacting someone else's earlier adventures,
they might echo but not add meaning. But gathered together, organized, preserved, and examined, such texts take on new power.

A variety of scholars have examined how the meanings of objects change
once removed from their original contexts and reorganized in a collection
or archive. Collections function as their own systems of meaning or narrative,
helping us understand the nature of the world through material examples
and the collectors' perspectives.[23] Archives give collections an institutional
and official imprimatur. Archival collections are nothing new; including ones
focusing on nature or the environment. Like others, they typically reflect the
lives and interests of their collectors and the political concerns of their institutional homes. As Andrew Kirk has shown, for example, Denver Public Library's
Conservation Collection both emerged from and exemplifies the politics and
evolving philosophy of Arthur Carhart and America's grass-roots conservation movement.[24] Archives also create meaning through silences. In preserving
some things, others are buried, such as the inscriptions drowned underneath
the reservoirs.[25]

There is one collection of river texts, however, that makes sense of the Colorado in a surprisingly fluid and dynamic way. You could say that there is a
Colorado River lying in boxes at the Huntington Library, one arguably more
real than its avatar flowing through the Grand Canyon. In many ways this
archive of the Colorado organizes, interprets, and controls our experiences
on the river. What makes this river of texts so real, and how did it land in the
Huntington Library? The answer to both: professional river guides. More specifically, Otis R. "Dock" Marston.

Marston first went down the Colorado in 1942 as a client with Norm Nevills. He was working for the brokerage firm E. F. Hutton in the San Francisco Bay Area when a friend who was trying to organize a Grand Canyon trip told him, "I think you're just damn fool enough to go." So Marston read Dellenbaugh's *Canyon Voyage*, ignored his boss's warnings, and set off with Nevills. In following summers he joined Nevills again, first as a client and then as a boatman. Nevills's ignorance of the region's history drove Marston batty, and by 1946 Marston was buying books and researching fast-water navigation of the Colorado in earnest. A year later he left E. F. Hutton, determined instead to run rivers and write a little booklet on the first twenty-two successful trips through the Grand Canyon. Fragmentary and conflicting accounts sucked him in deeper and deeper. In a 1947 letter to river man Frank Dodge, he wrote, "I am not sure which is the muddiest—the river or the stuff written and said about the river."[26]

Marston contributed to this problem at the same time that he struggled against it. Regarding his nickname, he explained in another letter to Dodge,

> I am called Dock because of the vile crop of whiskers I grow on the River which make me look like an old fashioned pill roller. When we were on the Salmon River run, we stopped to visit an isolated rancher, who got me aside and said "I hear they call you doctor." "Yes, that's right." "Well, I'd like to talk to you about my prostate." I was so befuddled I didn't think of a comeback until that night. I have told the story saying that I replied "I'm sorry but I'm the wrong kind of doctor. I'm a Doctor of Divinity." I told the story that way when I talked before the Alameda Kiwanis Club since they had a minister as president. I told them that it was partly fiction. The newspaper came out with the headline "RETIRED MINISTER TELLS OF RIVER RUNNING HOBBY." So to many I am now PARSON.[27]

Happily confusing the Kiwanis, what Marston sought for himself, and I imagine for the river too, was the truth. He never met a source he did not question, and he had strong opinions about all of them. He called the Powell, Dellenbaugh, and Kolb accounts "fiction" and spent the rest of his life seeking the real story, a clear history of the Colorado and its navigation, from those who had lived it. If nature prompts many of us to document our experiences— on the page, on the canyon, in a letter, through a song, or even in a yoga

Figure 9.3. Neither M.D. nor doctor of divinity, Dock Marston blended the practices of river running and historical documentation with archival collecting. Photograph of Otis "Dock" Marston, 1950. Reproduced courtesy of P. T. Reilly Collection, Cline Library, Northern Arizona University.

pose—going down the river set Marston to research and reading. Rather than authoring prose himself he gathered it, from every person he could find who had run the Colorado, and from every anthropologist, historian, and archivist he considered an expert. He collected, and he corresponded, and he collected some more. Instead of a little booklet that was true, what he wound up with was a mass of thinly orchestrated chaos: a small history project gone awry in epic proportions; a monumental accumulation of data still not fully contained or understood; a river of texts to rival the Colorado itself.

When he died in 1979, Marston had been living in the Bohemian Club in San Francisco and was still at work. Legend among the curators at the Huntington has it that Marston had one room for himself and one to three more, filled with shelves and boxes, for his research.[28] Now processed and housed in the Huntington's archives, the Marston Collection includes 432 boxes, 54 microfilm rolls, 251 volumes, 162 motion picture reels, and 61 photo boxes. It contains approximately 250,000 pieces, about the same number as the square miles draining into the Colorado River Basin. "While the principal focus is the history of river-running," according to the catalog, "the collection also touches, often in depth and with original materials, on the geology of the entire region, the history of mining, water issues, hydroelectric power development, recreational use and policy issues, the history of transportation, the ecology of various riverine ecosystems, exploration, the film industry and promotion of the West, and indigenous cultures."[29] The finding aid alone runs to 238 pages.

This vision of Marston's avid and ultimately overwhelming collecting evokes the French theorist Jacques Derrida's framing of an archive. The collecting impulse, he argued, embodies the human struggle between what Freud called the death drive and the pleasure principle. The act of collecting, preserving, and honoring the artifacts of human life challenges the inevitable passage of time, in effect denying death by preserving the remnants of life. Simultaneously collecting and archiving celebrates the experience of the present and seeks to capture it as a promise of the future.[30] Marston sought to preserve the river both as archaic entity and as embodied experience, the piles of accumulated paper a bulwark against the shifting waters of the Colorado. The three decades of his collecting (1940s–1970s) spanned those years when the river underwent its most drastic changes, and Marston understood that old riverways were dying, to be replaced by new ones. In his archive the primordial river might still flow, and yet his collection was more than a eulogy. It supported an ongoing reinscription of the river as recreational experience, in part by serving as another place in which to run the river. If a palimpsest both preserves and overwrites older versions, then Marston's collection worked similarly to save the historical Colorado from death and also sustain it as a portal for unending sensory pleasures.

As the Colorado River runs through time and space, so does Marston's collection, albeit in slightly different ways. The actual river flows through ancient walls but manifests itself physically only in the present; Marston's texts portray a much older, deeper, and fuller version of the Colorado through multiple perspectives, at different times, and from a variety of vantage points. As the Colorado emerges from a system of smaller rivers and environmental palimpsests in place, so Marston's river emerges as a system of river texts. Its driving force? His unconventional organizing principles. A river runner and aspiring archivist, Marston sought scholarly recognition but knew his subject from the seat of a boat. As a result he organized his collection of written materials using multiple frameworks: alphabetical, chronological, and geographical.[31] This perhaps accounts for the sheer volume of paper he accumulated: he made copies galore and tried valiantly to keep up with his cross-referencing. Unsurprisingly, he lost that battle. In the end each section offers a separate and distinct view of the Colorado as nature and culture entwined. Taken together, these sections form a unique organizational structure that distinguishes Marston's collection from others at the Huntington and puts Marston's Colorado in motion.

The alphabetical section reinforces the idea that we know nature through other people as much as through our own senses. Here Marston represents the Colorado River as a set of individuals, neatly in order by last name, linked to the river and to one another by a strong and complex web of relationships. Explorers, boatmen, geologists, photographers, tourists, and guides all reside here. When you get to know them a little, you come to appreciate how the river could transform an individual's identity and how it created community among people sometimes fondly referred to as river rats. Frank Dodge, for example, first came to the Colorado to work for the 1923 U.S. Geological Survey. He got to know the chief topographical engineer named Birdseye in Hawaii, where Dodge grew up and had an amazing variety of jobs including measuring stream flow in the wilderness, ranching, being a forest ranger, and assisting a volcanologist. In the Grand Canyon with Birdseye he began as a lowly rodman but quickly established his skills with a boat. He would act as head boatman for three more trips through the Grand Canyon in 1927, 1935, and 1937 and become known as one of the best river men around. Marston collected Dodge's autobiography and put it in a box with correspondence between him and Dodge, Dodge and his passengers, and more. He documented Dodge's personal transformation into a river man, his integration into the river's history, and his participation in the history of Marston's collection.[32]

Through the alphabetical files I also met Elzada Clover, a botanist. She and her assistant Lois Jotter became the first women through the Grand Canyon in 1938 with Nevills. Mildred Baker, the secretary from Buffalo, went two years later with Barry Goldwater. Baker and Goldwater conspired to lag behind Nevills on one occasion so she could take the oars of their boat and run a rapid on the Grand Canyon by herself. She did this with grace, humor, and aplomb, happily declaring herself in her journal and to Goldwater the first female to successfully run a rapid on the Colorado. While highly encouraged to cook and wash dishes for the party along the way despite their status as paying clients, all of these women performed at least slightly transgressive expressions of gender as they rode, rowed, botanized, bird watched, hiked, and explored their way down the river.[33] Vacationing along the Colorado gave them room for such cultural expressions, and Marston gave these women voice too. He asked Clover and Jotter and Baker what they thought, gathered their journals and publications, and put these materials in the appropriate files. The history of Colorado River guiding and Marston's own masculinity helped craft a river of texts defined largely by men and for men. But because Marston sought comprehensive rather than selective documentation for his river history, he relinquished the authoritative control typically exercised by collectors and provided space for alternative narratives too. When those narratives gave him trouble, they fleshed out his river of texts further than ever by revealing the process of its creation.

Most alphabetical files contain diaries, journals, or other self-authored accounts of the river along with letters to and from Marston and other correspondents. Lorin Bell's file proved surprising. When the boatman and geologist Don Harris had to leave the 1938 Nevills expedition at Lee's Ferry, Nevills drove to the trading post in Tuba City looking for a replacement. He woke Bell up and asked if he wanted to go down a river. According to Clover, Bell replied sleepily, "Hell yes! What river?" By the end of the trip the relationship had soured, to put it mildly, and Bell told Nevills, "I wouldn't go anyplace with you; not even across the street." Bell's perspective of that trip emerges from Marston's limited interview notes and letters from others; Bell himself continually put off Marston's requests for a fuller written account in language that sounds either insane or brilliant, and sometimes like a rap-infused text message. On one card dated only "Too Early," Bell wrote, "Deer Doc—Shore Glad Yu Preciated That Ther Letter—Sory we run outa paper. Wil Rit yu sum mor—sur as we can git in and likwidat that ther popskull—AND git sum mor paper, AND lern how tu rit, AND git un tangl'd, AND git sum tim tu reed all o' yur questions, AND find sum Ansers." Once he wrote a letter to Marston on toilet paper, all about how he went to college but did not get a chance to learn to write, and told him, "we couldn't rit yu now eny way becuz we've run uf paper—As yu kin C." Such prose belied his intelligence. To his friend Bill Belknap in 1955, Bell made his point faster: "Tell Dock Marston to go to hell for me!" he said. Belknap wrote Marston, "I told him you couldn't finish your book without his account of the first Nevills trip," but, he concluded, "I'd hesitate to send his reply through the mail."[34]

Here we see a collection in the making and a set of relationships shaped by the river and by Marston. Both emerge only through Marston's efforts to piece together the whole story from 1938. In her published account of the trip

Clover called Bell a "true westerner, unafraid, courteous at all times, and a great favorite of us all." When Marston asked her to rate the boatmen on that trip, she put him first.[35] Letters from Frank Dodge too make an appearance in Clover's file, as he met her and her assistant briefly along their way and shared his impressions with a friend. Dodge found Clover uninteresting—a spinster. Her assistant Jotter made a much stronger impression: "Both her feet are on the ground. Has a good face, plenty smart, a swell scout. Make a fine mate for some explorer scientist; could shoot Indians!"[36] Marston's collection and the process by which he assembled it thus describe the river in human form: a strong, vibrant, and sometimes turbulent community of people united by river running, divided by gender and class, and all connected to Otis Marston. Gathered at the river as a material place, people whose identities were shaped by work and recreation joined together to form an entangled community of nature and culture that slowly expanded as texts inside Marston's apartment.

Most collections end when the materials reach the letter Z. Marston's certainly could have; his alphabetical section is huge. In addition to specific individuals, Marston included organizations both readerly and riverly (the *Utah Historical Quarterly*, Western River Guides Association, Grand Canyon Expeditions, Inc., National Academy of Sciences), subjects ranging from Mormons to dams (both existing and proposed), a huge section under the topic navigation with parts on the river gauge and specific boats, and still more individuals under topics such as trappers and traders. Marston remained dissatisfied with only this biographical organizational structure, however; he thought about the river in spatial and historical ways as well.[37]

The chronological section defines the river as a historical environment. It helps decipher the drama of the alphabetical section, lumping people together by year of their expedition and putting their respective journals next to one another. It widens our view of the river well beyond the path of its flow too, by chronicling the routes of explorers, traders, settlers, outfitters, developers, and locals to and from the Colorado. In 1857, for example, Brigham Young explored a route across the river to transport goods and immigrants; there was extended conflict between the federal government and Mormons culminating in the Mountain Meadows Massacre; Capt. R. B. Marcy led a military expedition along the Gunnison River; Edward F. Beale crossed the Colorado on his way from Texas to California; Antoine Leroux declared the Colorado navigable from the Virgin River down (as he had run it in 1837); and Joseph Christmas Ives proved it by taking a steamer up to the head of

Black Canyon, surveying and running some rapids along the way.[38] Each slice of time shows the Colorado River as part of a larger geography—of western exploration and settlement in this case, but in other years mining, hydroelectricity, and national tourism. In organizing the river across time, Marston gives it a geographically more expansive look.

At the same time, oddly enough, he gives us a closer look at particular things. John Wesley Powell, as you might imagine, takes up some space in the alphabetical section—seven boxes' worth to be exact. In the box for 1869 we see less about Powell the man (Marston thought him a bad planner and a poor leader, and called him "scared") and more about what he left behind. Here we see the river as represented in time by historical sources and material culture. Marston got hold of a typescript of Powell's diary made in 1975 from the original at the Smithsonian. He included a copy of the version printed by the *Utah Historical Quarterly* in 1947 and edited by the Powell scholar William Darrah and he noted the differences between the two (which seemed minimal to me). Another folder contains copies of the 1869 handwritten contract between Powell and the hunter-guides he hired, outlining their respective responsibilities. The next folder documents Marston's hunt for copies of Powell's original letters home, as published in the *Chicago Tribune* in May, June, and August 1869. Marston even went out of his way to find the life preserver used by Powell on that first trip. He convinced a friend who lived in Washington, D.C., to reach a Miss Brown of the Smithsonian's Historical Division in 1953. Together they found the preserver, and Marston wound up with photographs of it—front and back, as it was signed by Powell—for his collection.[39]

Such artifacts, even reproductions, flesh out the size, shape, and meaning of the actual Colorado River. Marston used them to try and figure out the real story of 1869—which rapids Powell ran in the Grand (Sockdolager), what level the river was at, and where primary accounts differ and why. Powell's brother Walter was not to be trusted, it turns out, as a stay in Andersonville Prison had rendered him "mentally deficient," and while Darrah knew much about Powell, he "did not know the river through direct observation."[40] Marston sought to re-create the historical river of 1869 by getting as close as possible to its historical leftovers, but these kept leading him astray. Every source recorded someone's particular impression of the river, and in its perspective and use, each one expressed a slightly different place. Looking for just one true river, Marston missed the point that he had collected at least three: the river as national adventure (Powell's letters to the newspaper); the river as work and responsibility (the contract); and the river as physical test and forger of celebrity (the preserver). Perhaps more significantly, Marston's focus on historical artifact and evidence in the chronological section effectively extended his river of texts to the Smithsonian and other archives across the country, not to mention to the human community of correspondents and helpers he engaged to collect his sources.

Marston would have disliked this conclusion, and he made perhaps the most inspired part of his collection in order to nail down the real river not just in time but also in place. Working through the geographical section, readers can run the Colorado from top to bottom, all in the air-conditioned chill of the Huntington's Ahmanson Reading Room. Starting at the headwaters, the materials in the folders and boxes progress downriver mile by mile until another river comes in. Then the collection jumps to the head of that river and follows it down to its mouth on the Colorado. In this fashion Marston incorporated the Colorado's side canyons and tributaries, and the collection builds momentum as the river gains volume and flows into the Grand Canyon. Here the look and feel of the river are the point, and Marston renders the river visible, tangible, and audible through the voices of those who have experienced it in person.

Marston's favorite writers and correspondents, the boatmen, knew how to observe a river. Paying attention was part of their job, and they knew the value of recording its size, shape, and form for the next ones through. Those who worked "real" jobs with the USGS, such as Harris, or as photographers, such as the Kolbs and Bill Belknap, brought complementary expertise to the river. Clients-turned-boatmen (Dodge, Marston), professional botanists (Clover, Jotter), and amateur ornithologists (Baker) similarly interpreted the river and its canyons with highly attuned senses. Flora, fauna, river level, historic sites, scenic views—they noticed it all. Their observations of the Colorado and its canyons appear in the geographical section like a stop-motion camera—giving clear pictures of individual moments, accumulated over time by Marston—perceiving and producing a nature constantly in flux.

At mile 179.5 below Lee's Ferry, Lava Falls (aka Vulcan) Rapid has gotten probably the most attention. Here basalt lava flows erupted above and within the canyon about seven hundred thousand years ago, damming the river, building giant reservoirs, and then causing huge flood events when those reservoirs failed. This geological history, and the rocky debris coming out of Prospect Canyon, formed a spot in the river with a thirteen-foot drop and studded with huge boulders. People called it "dreaded," "the most feared," and "the daddy of all the Grand Canyon rapids." One Frenchman watched entire logs disappear into the hole at the bottom and declared, "That is imponderable." So of course people pondered it. As one author explained, "[E]very river trip in the Grand Canyon is prelude and postlude to Lava Falls."[41] And in the folder for River Mile 179–80, Marston gathered about a century's worth of their thoughts, descriptions, and experiences.

Stanton, who went through in 1890, remembered Lava Falls dropping eighteen to twenty feet over a length of about three hundred feet. "It would have been impossible," he remembered. The Kolbs noted in 1912 a rock barrier extending across the top of the rapid, leaving an opening on the right only. The boatman Elwyn Blake's diary in 1923 similarly noted, "The south half of the river is literally studded with protruding boulders so close together as not to leave oar room." According to his boss Birdseye, "so many dangerous rocks here extend across the river that no one has attempted to run through."[42] He was only partly wrong—George Flavell ran it in 1896. Stanton believed Flavell, but decided that "it must have been at a higher stage of water than when we were there."[43] Indeed the look of Lava Falls changed from day to day and week to week depending on the stage of the river. The 1923 expedition happened to be above Lava Falls when the river flooded. Blake wrote in his diary that "the rapid has completely changed." Boatmen measure the Colorado's flow in cubic feet per second, or CFS, and on that day Frank Dodge estimated that the river went from 20,000 CFS to 100,000. Blake watched the river rise fifteen feet. "No rocks are showing at all," he wrote. "There are huge waves now, with one at the foot of the rapid which rises to a height of twenty or thirty feet and seems to imprison a quantity of air within itself. As the weight of the water compresses the air it is released with a booming sound, like a cannon shot."[44] More recent observers have called this, appropriately, an "explosion wave" and describe the experience of hearing Lava Falls well before arriving there. By the 1960s Marston had diagrams too, noting major holes and waves at 50,000 CFS in 1950, 101,300 CFS in 1958, and 37,600 CFS in 1962. He had a long and deep written account of the rapid in all its forms.[45]

To organize these images over time he integrated these journal entries and reports with others, fashioning a Lava Falls of notes and arriving at an abbreviated list of its navigation that went like this: portaged boats around it (Powell, 1869); lined boats down it (Stanton, 1890); ran it (Flavell, 1896); ran it? (Monett, 1908); lined it (Stanton, 1909); lined it (Kolbs, 1912); lined it (Birdseye,

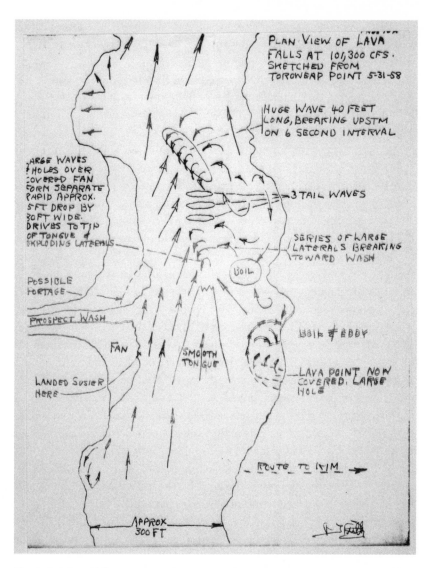

The text within the image reads:

PLAN VIEW OF LAVA FALLS AT 101,300 CFS. SKETCHED FROM TOROWEAP POINT 5-31-58

HUGE WAVE 40 FEET LONG, BREAKING UPSTM ON 6 SECOND INTERVAL

LARGE WAVES & HOLES OVER COVERED FAN FORM SEPARATE RAPID APPROX. 5 FT DROP BY 30 FT WIDE. DRIVES TO TIP OF TONGUE & EXPLODING LATERALS

3 TAIL WAVES

SERIES OF LARGE LATERALS BREAKING TOWARD WASH

BOIL

POSSIBLE PORTAGE

PROSPECT WASH

BOIL & EDDY

FAN

SMOOTH TONGUE

LAVA POINT NOW COVERED. LARGE HOLE

LANDED SUSIE R HERE

ROUTE TO RIM

APPROX 300 FT

Figure 9.4. Lava Falls as it ran on May 31, 1958, at 101,300 CFS, on paper. *Lava Falls*. Otis Marston Collection, box 341, folder 23, Huntington Library, San Marino California. Reproduced by permission of the Huntington Library, San Marino, California.

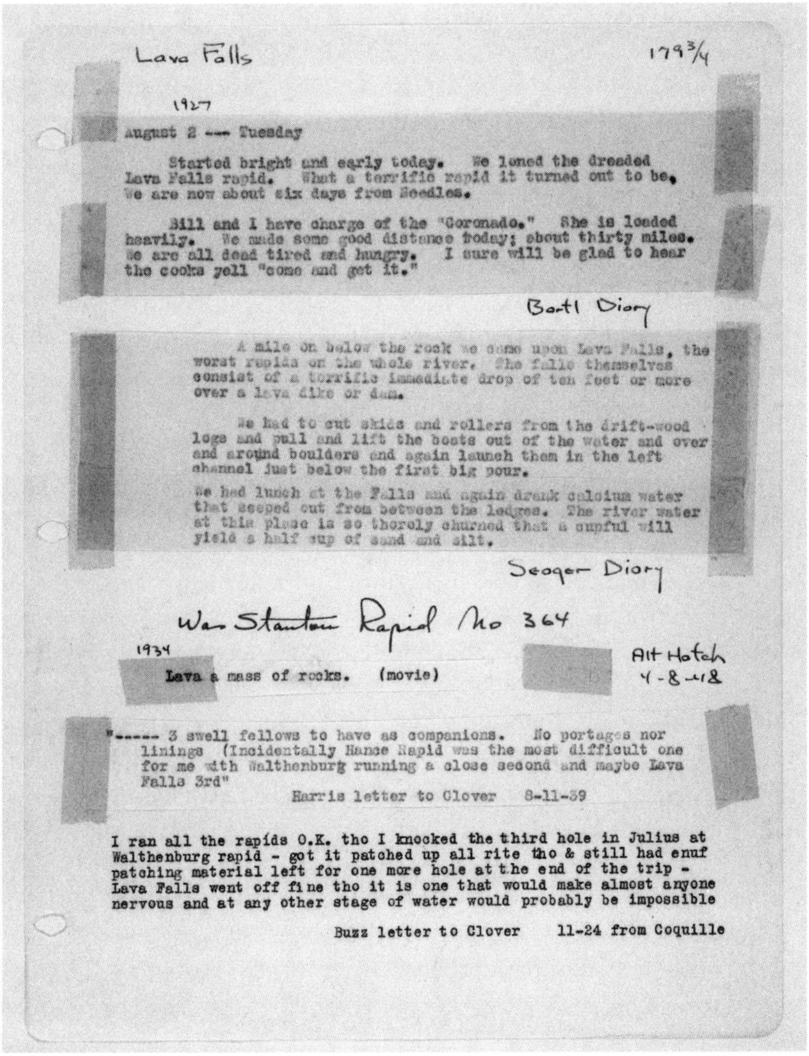

Lava Falls   179 3/4

1927

August 2 --- Tuesday

Started bright and early today. We loned the dreaded
Lava Falls rapid. What a terrific rapid it turned out to be.
We are now about six days from Needles.

Bill and I have charge of the "Coronado." She is loaded
heavily. We made some good distance today; about thirty miles.
We are all dead tired and hungry. I sure will be glad to hear
the cooks yell "come and get it."

Bartl Diary

A mile or below the rock we came upon Lava Falls, the
worst rapids on the whole river. The falls themselves
consist of a terrific immediate drop of ten feet or more
over a lava dike or dam.

We had to cut skids and rollers from the drift-wood
logs and pull and lift the boats out of the water and over
and around boulders and again launch them in the left
channel just below the first big pour.

We had lunch at the Falls and again drank calcium water
that seeped out from between the ledges. The river water
at this place is so thorely churned that a cupful will
yield a half cup of sand and silt.

Seager Diary

Was Stanton Rapid No 364

1934

Lava a mass of rocks.   (movie)   Alt Hotch
                                                   4-8-18

"----- 3 swell fellows to have as companions. No portages nor
linings (Incidentally Hance Rapid was the most difficult one
for me with Walthenburg running a close second and maybe Lava
Falls 3rd"

Harris letter to Clover   8-11-39

I ran all the rapids O.K. tho I knocked the third hole in Julius at
Walthenburg rapid - got it patched up all rite tho & still had enuf
patching material left for one more hole at the end of the trip -
Lava Falls went off fine tho it is one that would make almost anyone
nervous and at any other stage of water would probably be impossible

Buzz letter to Clover   11-24 from Coquille

Figure 9.5. Marston's Lava Falls in notes. *Lava Falls.* Otis Marston Collection,
box 341, folder 23, Huntington Library, San Marino, California. Reproduced by
permission of the Huntington Library, San Marino, California.

1923); lined it (Eddy, 1927); ran it but crashed (Frazier, 1934); lined it (Holmstrom, 1936); lined it (Caltech, 1937); lined it (Nevills, 1938); ran it (Loper, 1939); ran it (Nevills, 1940); lined it (Nevills, 1941, 1942), and so on through the 1950s. Such a view underlines the dynamism of the place. It also suggests that the environment's meaning derived not only from its physical form but also from boatmen's reactions to it.

To really know the rapid—not just how it looked but how it moved and how it felt—Marston collected people's physical and emotional responses in the geographical section and matched them to the course of the water. Russell Frazier started to run the left side in 1934 but got thrown off into a hole that he thought "would twist his legs off." In 1939 Bert Loper entered far to the right and then pulled hard left to avoid a rock projection and hole halfway down on the right. He thought Hance Rapid was worse. In 1940 Nevills described his route as "complicated tho possible," all hinging on "making the perfect moves at the exact correct time," but he took so long to scout his route that no one paid attention to where he went. By 1960 more people had been through, the rapid's reputation had grown, and so too had the river's stage: "Silently and with some awe we surveyed the scene below us," one of Dock Marston's passengers wrote. "The coffee-colored water poured fiercely down the tongue, forming a ridge off both sides of which the water peeled to drop into deep holes and to rise again in two huge curling waves. The hole and the wave on the right hand side were of terrifying dimensions. Beyond these was a boiling, heaving turmoil of white water." She watched from the side as Dock's twenty-four-foot boat went right, hit a corner of the wave, and was tossed into the air. The passenger aboard got so bounced around that he suffered a compound leg fracture.

Boatmen continued to make a variety of choices at Lava, from lining the boats loaded, to portaging supplies and running the boats empty, to running boats with the whole gang. They also chose different routes. Left-of-center worked for a kayaker in 1960, while the huge pontoon behind him blasted right down the middle twenty minutes later.[46] Lava Falls Rapid looks and feels unique every time someone goes through it, and that has been true since before Powell's time. We know this because Dock Marston collected their responses and put them all together. In his river of texts—alphabetical, chronological, and geological—we participate in material nature as dynamic process more fully than ever. Through these archived texts the material river is fixed in the past and the present, in the Grand Canyon and the Ahmanson reading room. The Colorado River, in other words, runs through the Huntington's archives.

Running Marston's Colorado River at the Huntington won't send you into the air or break anyone's leg. It smells strange, but it doesn't sound like a cannon. You can't hear its rapids around the corner, but the river waits for you nonetheless, and it can be frightening. It scared Marston, who put it into motion in 1949 and then struggled to stay afloat on the current. You could even say there were casualties: two librarians retired and Marston died before the collection got to San Marino. During his work on the collection, though, Marston corresponded with them—Leslie Bliss, the librarian, and Gertrude Ruhnka, his assistant—for eleven years. They copied and accepted the diaries, logs, and notes he found for them, and they became his guides to the archival world as he built his own collection. They gave him lessons on preserving things ("thumbs down on iron staples in manuscripts") and sent huge numbers of boxes and folders north to him—an act that Marston repeatedly described as saving his life. Meanwhile he paid for his mistakes. "I must have pulled out a million staples. That isn't too difficult but there are a million more to pull." By 1957 the man who had run Lava Falls and derided Powell for being scared was in deep. To Ruhnka he wrote, "This research is a terrifying thing."[47] In the end the river took over. Unlike other collections at the Huntington, which tend to document an individual's life, the Marston Collection grew so deep and wide that Marston acted ultimately not so much as the subject of the collection but as the mechanism for creating it. Interpretive power shifted from Marston to the collection itself, which created its own meaning and reveals it to researchers.[48]

Marston's collection also scared David Lavender, the first historian to use it. "Although the Marston Collection is unarguably the world's greatest treasury of Colorado River history," Lavender's colleague wrote, "Lavender found its peculiar organization, sheer magnitude, and ingrown biases made synopsis a formidable goal. Worse, the collection was riddled with mildew, and the technicians who fumigated it miscalculated the proportions of formaldehyde and other toxins." In all likelihood the CS or "tear gas" used to detect the odorless pesticide methyl bromide reacted with the chemicals in all of Marston's thermofax copies, rendering the collection unpleasant but not dangerous. Either way, the materiality of nature's culture—the physical practice of making environmental palimpsests—almost did Lavender in. Between the mass of (as yet unprocessed) material and the gas emanating from it, the writer could go about an hour before "he would stagger, eyes streaming, temples throbbing, head spinning, into the gardens to recuperate."[49]

Both men kept going because they wanted to get the story, and because they were river men. Dealing with this full, flowing, turbulent river of texts was not simply an academic exercise or an ego trip; it was useful. When the National Park superintendent wrote Marston in 1959 to tell him that the Cooper party had turned a boat in Lava, dumping most of their equipment but sustaining no injuries, he did not do it for Marston's book or his collection. He did it so that Marston wouldn't make the same mistake the next week.[50] Boatmen wrote scores of letters, submitted to interviews, and otherwise indulged Marston's research efforts and prickly personality because they were invested in the Colorado River. Ditto for Lavender. They made the Huntington's Colorado real by bringing the library and the river together, and they still do.

In the Marston Collection guide there is a little note saying, "unlike other collections in the Huntington, an advanced degree is not a prerequisite for access." Technically nonacademics have access to all collections in the Huntington, but the Marston Collection does have a different clientele than most. Of the 15,700 researchers who have used the library since 1980, only 40 listed the Marston Collection as their primary target. Most of them hailed from California, Arizona, Utah, and Colorado; only 4 (counting me) have academic faculty positions.[51] It is safe to conclude that river guides are visiting the Huntington to learn about the Colorado River.

They are going to a *library* to learn more about the real place they already know like the backs of their hands. And they are bringing this river of texts back to the one flowing through the Grand Canyon and sharing it with their clients. This happens in all sorts of ways. Roy Webb and Richard Quartaroli have both wrestled with Marston's river and its wetter partner. Boatmen, guides, and archivists, they make their research and Marston's available to public, academic, and river-running audiences.[52] Brad Dimock guided on the Colorado between 1971 and 1998, during which time he also started the Grand Canyon River Guides' *Boatman's Quarterly Review* (BQR), a newsletter full of river people, issues, and history that "will take you back to the river if you can't be there in person."[53] He may or may not have made the trip to the Huntington Library, but references to Marston and his collection show up frequently in the BQR. When a guide goes to a Grand Canyon River Guides (GCRG) annual Guide Training Seminar or looks one up on the organization's Web page, she will get some lessons from Dock Marston via P. T. Reilly (another boatman/historian), Webb, or Quartaroli. Many read David

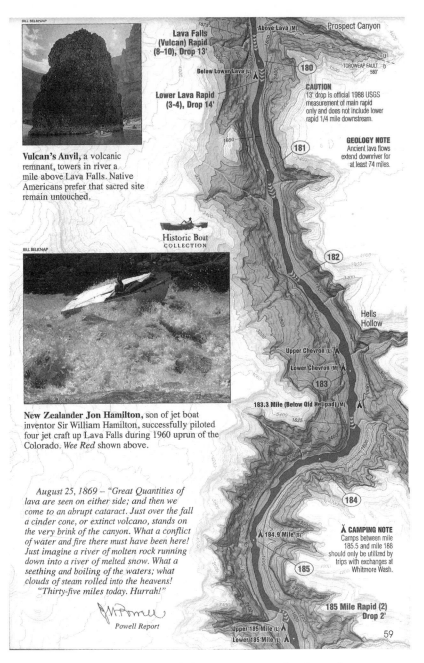

Vulcan's Anvil, a volcanic remnant, towers in river a mile above Lava Falls. Native Americans prefer that sacred site remain untouched.

Lava Falls (Vulcan) Rapid (8–10), Drop 13'

Above Lava (M)

Prospect Canyon

180

TOROWEAP FAULT 580'

Below Lower Lava (L)

Lower Lava Rapid (3-4), Drop 14'

CAUTION
13' drop is official 1988 USGS measurement of main rapid only and does not include lower rapid 1/4 mile downstream.

181

GEOLOGY NOTE
Ancient lava flows extend downriver for at least 74 miles.

Historic Boat
COLLECTION

182

Hells Hollow

Upper Chevron (L)

Lower Chevron (M)

183

183.3 Mile (Below Old Helipad) (M)

New Zealander Jon Hamilton, son of jet boat inventor Sir William Hamilton, successfully piloted four jet craft up Lava Falls during 1960 uprun of the Colorado. *Wee Red* shown above.

184

August 25, 1869 – *"Great Quantities of lava are seen on either side; and then we come to an abrupt cataract. Just over the fall a cinder cone, or extinct volcano, stands on the very brink of the canyon. What a conflict of water and fire there must have been here! Just imagine a river of molten rock running down into a river of melted snow. What a seething and boiling of the waters; what clouds of steam rolled into the heavens! "Thirty-five miles today. Hurrah!"*

184.9 Mile (S)

CAMPING NOTE
Camps between mile 185.5 and mile 188 should only be utilized by trips with exchanges at Whitmore Wash.

185

185 Mile Rapid (2) Drop 2'

Powell Report

59

Upper 185 Mile (L)

Lower 185 Mile (L)

Figure 9.6. Page from Belknap's guide layering current park policy and river characteristics with past use and history. Reproduced courtesy of *Belknap's Waterproof Grand Canyon River Guide,* all new ed. (Evergreen, Colo.: Westwater Books, 2011), 59.

Lavender's *River Runners of the Colorado*, "a bible for history-oriented guides."[54] And practically everybody reads *Belknap's Waterproof Grand Canyon River Guide*—even while they are on (or in) the Colorado. Boatman, guide, and photographer, Bill Belknap knew the river, he knew Marston, and he used Marston's research, too. Similar to Marston's collection but small, readable, and waterproof, his guide blends topical, historical, and geographical interpretations of the river in a beautiful layering of map, text, and images that moves forward with its readers not by page but by river mile.[55]

So the river of text still flows, spilling out from the Huntington through guide-training seminars, the *BQR*, Lavender's book, and Belknap's guide. Northern Arizona University's Cline Library, which has digitized over one hundred interviews that the GCRG conducted for the Colorado River Runners Oral History Project, participates in this riverine flow, as does Utah's Marriott Library Special Collections, which has a collection to rival Northern Arizona University's and the Huntington's. Guides and clients alike bring these texts to life and back to the Grand Canyon. When any of the approximately twenty-five thousand people who float through the Grand Canyon each year listen to their boatman guide, flip through Belknap's book, or join the GCRG, Marston's river gives the real one deeper shape and more tangible form. It makes the fleeting, momentary physical experience last longer and gives it meaning. Making abandoned dam sites, native ruins, famous rapids, and the historic path of the river visible can turn a boat into a time machine and a landscape of leisure into one of exploration or economic development. Recognizing the Colorado and its canyons as environmental palimpsests exposes the depth of culture lurking in our material world. Marston's collection puts those layered places in motion across space and time, joining text and water, past and present, researcher and guide.

Powell and Kolb and Dellenbaugh can still get the river into our systems, but so can the thousands of others who kept diaries or wrote letters so that they could "sit back" on their haunches "and wonder why." Barry Goldwater in particular stays with me. In 1976 Dock Marston declared that if you could choose only one book on the Colorado to read, it should be Goldwater's *Delightful Journey*. Even after he read Powell, ran the river, and published his own account of the 1940 trip, Goldwater stayed on the river and the river stayed in him. While outwardly supporting regional energy development in 1956, for instance, he confessed to river guide Harry Aleson "just between us river rats, I wish they would leave the Colorado alone." To the GCRG in 1996 he wrote, "I receive your publication every time you publish it, and read

Figure 9.7. River testing *Belknap's Waterproof Guide. Fran Belknap in Cataract Canyon*, August 1973. Photo reproduced courtesy of Bill Belknap Collection, Cline Library, Northern Arizona University.

every page before doing any of my other work." The *BRQ* editor replied, in a post that remains online still, "Thanks Barry, we do too."[56]

It is possible to see a powerful sense of nostalgia at work in these conversations among river rats. By tacking back and forth between the water and the words, they access the river that used to be. Given the tremendous physical changes to the river basin, they seek refuge in the palimpsest of texts—written on canyon walls, published and circulated in dog-eared copies, and collated in archives. But because the river is in their system still, most river rats engage with, think about, and try to protect the contemporary Colorado as well. They employ Powell and Marston and the *BRQ* to help them know and feel and interpret the river as it flows today, in all its layers. Goldwater might have read the *BRQ* to reminisce, but boatmen use it for their work. As an environmental palimpsest the Colorado flows and flickers, illuminated in a series of images and layers of text that move across space and time, while river rats create new natural landscapes on top of the canyons that came before. Text and water continue to swirl together as we keep on reading, running, and writing the Colorado.

Chapter 10

Rocks of Ages: The Decadent Desert and Sepulchral Time

Frieda Knobloch

Some geographical spaces have been visibly, many have said legibly, *engraved by time*, specifically deserts and canyons of the arid American West. These landscapes, including large areas such as the Mojave, Sonoran, Chihuahuan, and Great Basin Deserts (and smaller dry basins throughout the intermountain West), as well as canyons carved by rivers such as the Colorado and the Green, have always presented acute and life-threatening difficulties to travelers and produced ingenious approaches to habitation among ancient and contemporary indigenous communities. However the concern here is not the ecology or cultural or geological histories of arid landscapes, but something maybe harder to see: the cultural cast and historical specificity of that engraving hand of time. If we have learned to expect that ideas about "nature" or the environment vary significantly across times, places, and peoples, we have not yet come to terms with "time"—arguably a concept just as basic— in the same ways. Modern geologists—that is, geologists such as James Hutton or Charles Lyell, who by the 1830s had become untethered from a biblically based six-thousand-year Earth history—gave us the idea of "geologic time" as evidenced in observable and measurable landforms and processes, and it was this modern geology that accompanied John Wesley Powell and his scientific expedition down the Colorado River in 1869. Deserts have always been difficult or revelatory places, but they have not always been seen as marked primarily by the erosive hand of deep time as described by geologists. The eroding desert is a modern desert, and it is that desert that has attracted a distinctly modern love.

That Americans as such changed their minds about the desert by 1900 has been amply and succinctly demonstrated in Patricia Nelson Limerick's *Desert Passages*.[1] The short version is that a merely deadly desert became beautiful and newly valuable to many people, not for its uses but often for its absences (among other things), if still also deadly. Writers such as Dan Flores locate the same turn, at the same time and with the same results, in specific places, in his case in what he calls the horizontal yellow of the "Near Southwest."[2] The appreciative turn certainly corresponds with emergent appreciations of wilderness of all types in a modern, industrial mass society. Like other wild or undeveloped places, the desert is a site from which a critique of modern, industrial life is possible (if not guaranteed) or where nationalist ideals can be naturalized (if with some difficulty). Interestingly for our purposes here, geologic time and a preoccupation with erosion are nearly ubiquitous in desert letters accompanying and following the appreciative turn. It is that eroding desert, and the form of time it embodies, that is our concern here.

Geologic time has a cultural logic, one well suited to late nineteenth- and twentieth-century experiences of modernity, and it found exuberant expression in American desert letters, scientific and otherwise. The cultural logic of geologic time informs a specifically modern desert, a place of death, silence, beauty, natural magnificence, human insignificance, and above all *erosion* that for over a hundred years has been courted as the desert itself, confirmed over and over in spirited revelations of its powers by eye-witnesses from Clarence Dutton to Terry Tempest Williams, with healthy doses of John Van Dyke, Joseph Wood Krutch, Wallace Stegner, Edward Abbey, and many others in between. Throw explicitly personal experience into the teeth of geologic time, and you get a very specific manifestation of what Mikhail Bakhtin called a chronotope, a space specially charged and infused by time: a decadent desert suspended in what I call "sepulchral time," lest we confuse "geologic time" with time itself. One could die of exposure anywhere, but "the desert" provides the space to do so (or even want to do so) with edifying awareness of the depth of time, the deepest and the shallowest grave of all. In this context, modern geology as a science does not merely describe what may be true about any landscape but is instead part of a much larger and deeper set of cultural historical changes whose implications were felt before John Wesley

Powell went down the Colorado in 1869 and far away from the desert and canyon country he and his associates described in such vivid geological detail. So let us look at geologic time not as a contemporary and naturalized reality but as an emergent problem in the history of what came to be known as geologic science. Being sensitive to the modern quality of geologic time as a cultural—not just a scientific—artifact, we take a brief turn through European decadence before returning to American desert landscapes.

An understanding of "geologic time" marks the emergence of modern geology from biblically informed understandings of natural history, on the one hand, and classical assumptions of the (unmeasurable) vastness or eternity of time, on the other. Through the sixteenth century there was a standard list of formidable authorities on geology: Aristotle, Pliny, Strabo, Avicenna, Averroes, Albertus Magnus, Jean Buridan, and Albert of Saxony, among others.[3] This was a rich fund that included an understanding of the living earth as a formal macrocosm of all other life (shaped by cycles of generation and decay at various scales), that rocks and mountains were the earth's bones, and that earth, water, air, and fire were the fundamental elements of all things. It also included an understanding that the earth was subject to catastrophe on a large scale and was very old—for classical scholars, possibly eternal—though exactly how old would not become a problem until much later.

The "discovery" of geologic time has long been attributed to James Hutton, with *The System of the Earth* presented to the Royal Society of Edinburgh in 1785 and publication of *Theory of the Earth* through the same society in 1788. The discovery of geologic time, or its invention, hinges on the measurability of time, the perceived value of measuring it, and the paradoxical creation of an explicitly rational conception of time that nevertheless transcends human understanding and experience. Geologic time was not discovered until counting up the unfathomable ages had become a seemingly unavoidable task. That task began in earnest in the mid-seventeenth century with Archbishop James Ussher of the Church of Ireland, who wished to calculate the age of the earth based on Old Testament chronology. He put the year of creation at 4004 B.C.E. In 1654 Dr. James Lightfoot, vice chancellor of Cambridge University, refined this beginning to a time and a date: nine o'clock in the morning on October 26, 4004 B.C.E.[4] We will not follow countless commentators in guffawing at this point. Ussher and Lightfoot did what many had done before them: approach written authorities and the earth with an expectation that rational inquiry ought to carry the day in explaining what we see. They were not intellectual lightweights, and they did not believe in miracles as a means of explanation (neither did Leonardo da Vinci or Thomas Burnet, earlier explorers in geological questions). Answering why Ussher and Lightfoot and why exactly then is beyond our scope here.[5] In any case, it is only *after* these (rational) calculations had been made that people began to see the formidable trouble of reconciling the evident age of the earth with a time frame of about six thousand years.

It is one thing to accommodate classical understandings of vast quantities of time to the Mosaic chronicles as a narrative problem; it is entirely another to cram the history of every landform documented for millennia into a definite period of measured time.[6] James Hutton cracked this tight geologic schedule open in 1785. Unfortunately, Hutton was understood to be arguing that the earth was older than Ussher had claimed, as if this were a novel revelation. The celebrated geologist Charles Lyell did the same—and he clearly knew better.

As Lyell understood, from ancient India and Egypt to Greece and Rome writers were widely familiar with the idea that there had been "successive destructions and renovations of the world."[7] The prevailing classical sense of earth history was that "the agents of change now operating in Nature [are] capable of bringing about in the lapse of ages a complete revolution; and [Aristotle] even considers occasional catastrophes, happening at distant intervals of time, as part of the regular and ordinary course of nature."[8] Pythagoras introduced Egyptian ideas into Greece, among them "the doctrine of the gradual deterioration of the human race from an original state of happiness," on which Ovid relied in turn and which was analogous to geological decay.[9] The analogy became a relationship of cause and effect for medieval Judeo-Christian writers, for whom a singular flood punished the moral decay of people, creating a broken earth. The literary scholar Marjorie Nicolson has noted that there is "plenty of evidence [in the *Patrologia Latina*, a collection of church writings spanning a thousand years] for a theory that the original earth had been smooth and round and that mountains emerged for the first time after the Flood."[10] Like his predecessors, Lyell was acutely aware of a long past of geological thinking. His great innovation may be that he completed the first methodical and strategic excavation, one might say, of the orderly strata of geological thinking that came before him. His usable classical past includes the sort of repeated earth-shattering and erosive forces that he argued were still and always at work.

Establishing "geologic time" was part of the same rational project that had established the six-thousand-year-old earth; it simply held more generously open the calendar of the remote past, which contemporary dating technologies do not hesitate to fill. The rejection of the six-thousand-year limit may too easily strike readers as a triumph of rational thought. The price for its naturalist open-mindedness was a terrible distortion of time, a crisis of scale and representation resulting in a paradox: human experience is a mute, insignificant blip at the same time that human imagination pretends to understand periods of many thousands, millions, or billions of "years."

Lyell provides ample evidence of this crisis, though it comes to us in the language of ordinary, unremarkable, common sense throughout three elegantly argued volumes. The falls at Niagara, as we all know, are busily chewing their way upstream toward Lake Erie today as they did in 1830. "By the confirmed destruction of the rocks, the falls have, within the last forty years [since the 1790s] receded nearly fifty yards." Arguing, as he always does, by analogy and extrapolation, from effects visible and measurable in the present, Lyell calculates that "[s]hould the erosive action not be accelerated in [the] future, it will require upwards of thirty thousand years for the falls to reach Lake Erie (twenty-five miles distant), to which they seem destined to arrive in the course of time."[11] No one, not a person on the planet, assuming a person might remain on the planet with access to Lyell's lovely books, will know in thirty thousand years that Lyell made this careful estimate. No matter; human history is extravagantly not his point. "It would be as irrelevant to our present purpose," he writes of the role of earthquakes, as given to him primarily through ancient and more modern accounts of their destructive power, "to enter into a detailed account of such calamities as to follow the track of an invading army, to enumerate the cities burnt or rased [sic] to the ground, and reckon the number of individuals who perished by famine or sword."[12] The force of earthquakes, "so often the source of death and terror to the inhabitants of the globe, which visits, in succession, every zone, and fills the earth with monuments of ruin and disorder, is, nevertheless, a conservative principle in the highest degree, and, above all others, essential to the stability of the system."[13]

What edifying pleasure is there in imagining this sort of world? It could be a certain schadenfreude in taking "humans" down a peg—off the geologic calendar almost all together. But I do not think that was Lyell's pleasure. He wrote about his study (with disarming use of plural pronouns for himself) that "the charm of first discovery is our own, and as we explore this magnificent field of inquiry, the sentiment of a great historian of our times may continually be present to our minds, that 'he who calls what has vanished back again into being, enjoys a bliss like that of creating."[14] The "great historian" is Barthold Niebuhr, whose *History of Rome* was published in 1828. (Lyell surely had also read Edward Gibbon, whose three-volume *History of the Decline and Fall of the Roman Empire* was published between 1776 and 1789.) The scale of the analogy between Niebuhr's work and Lyell's (Rome for rocks) is literate human memory, which may well be measured in years (indeed about six thousand of them). But Lyell's vision is much grander than that. Still, what Lyell underscores is the creative and personal thrill of making a measurably remote past (and future) come to life. The vision of thirty thousand years on the Niagara River is a monument to Lyell's hard work right then in 1830, creating the place from which he could imagine himself and everyone else out of the picture. But of course he is not out of the picture; he made that version of it that is *Principles of Geology*.

The act of imaginative creation is pleasurable, but how one is supposed to live in the imagined world shaped by geologic time—the modern world, developed on a modern geological earth, especially once it has taken hold as the only rational world endowed with history—is not at all clear. This inhuman juggernaut of a clock was not ticking for Renaissance (or earlier) geologic speculators, but it was booming on the respectable mantelpiece of the mid-nineteenth century. The embrace of geologic time in the science of geology is part of the emergence of historical thinking ("history" itself as a development, not a chronicle) that Foucault locates so centrally in modern science in general; developmental time erupted into the sciences to explain, for example, the invisible functions and development of languages, economies, or organisms.[15] A decisive break in the experience of time marked even scientists' accounts of their own practices. By the 1840s modern sciences were busily setting their houses in order, distinguishing their methods of observation and calculation from armchair amateur speculation, the murky past from which "real" science emerged and could be distinguished. The rational pursuit of knowledge of the world had sent Darwin abroad on its oceans, with at least the first (and most historiographical) volume of Lyell's *Principles of Geology* in tow, and bringing back *The Origin of Species* by 1859. One plausible approach to living in such a world driven by time is to cultivate a decadent attitude and aesthetic, and court dissolution. I am not arguing that new science made aesthetic decadence possible. Modernity itself is the broader predicament, the eruption of measurable but staggering time in all the human and natural sciences, as well as aesthetics. Among all the ferment of artistic, intellectual, and political life in Europe by that time, I want to single out the emergence of self-conscious decadence, not to provide a complete account of that movement in relation to newly modern sciences,[16] but merely to remind us that people consumed with vice and artifice, and ostentatiously bored, who favored "art for art's sake" and reveled in the useless and the grotesque, were moderns too then grappling with modern time. They help us see better what sort of pleasure might accompany the willfully self-aggrandizing and paradoxically self-effacing posture of modern sciences. Walter Benjamin called the decadents "nonconformists."[17] Among all the voices I might choose to illustrate their embodiment of modern time and nature, the gloriously fetid (one would say "funky") imagination of Charles Baudelaire (1821–67) serves us well.

A stanza (lines 13–16) in "Hymne à la beauté" from *Les Fleurs du Mal* (1857) demonstrates a decadent appreciation of the beautiful that is typical of Baudelaire and that fully comprehends and invites mortality and threat; the sounds, rhythm, and rhyme seduce even as the jammed images startle:

Tu marches sur les morts, Beauté, dont tu te moques;
De tes bijoux l'Horreur n'est pas les moins charmant,
Et le Meurtre, parmi tes plus chères breloques,
Sur ton ventre orgueilleux danse amoureusement.[18]

He writes, "You walk over the dead, Beauty, pleased to mock them; / Horror isn't the least charming of your jewels, / And Murder, among your most lovely dangling charms, / Dances amorously on your proud belly." The proud belly is surely amorous too, ravenous in other poems, and Baudelaire repeatedly consumes himself in this odoriferous, voluptuous, sometimes tawdry feminine presence—including the real presence of his lover Jeanne Duval (a prostitute) but not reducible to her, and the city of Paris too, consuming, gusting, and disgusting, with all its buying and selling of food, sex, wine, and poems and leaving of corpses, all the simultaneously flowing goods of a mass modern city.

Beauty herself is both abstract and real in all these guises (masks, we might say, another of Baudelaire's many split images) and not in any simple way pleasurable. He is too split himself, too devoured by worms, too smitten, too hungry, too responsive to "the ideal" and a simultaneous "spleen" about its fate, and too keenly aware that his whole world works this way to feel anything as flat (or as unreachable) as "pleasure." How much can you get for a lyre in a pawnshop? He loses his halo in the mud of the streets, which is of no use to him as a modern poet dodging traffic.[19] Boredom is one of the hallmarks of his horrified oversaturation in a lavish world decaying around him. His *Fleurs du Mal* are evil or sick or both, but no less beautiful for that; if anything they are more lively, having taken their pallor and their fire from hell itself (the damned and the damning simultaneously), certainly more complicated than a pastoral respite in natural or conventionally beautiful things, or contemplations of an edifying past. That would be a self-deception. Nature and the past are not dead but are undead, which is worse. They stalk the present.

The teeming mess of modern Paris cannot be escaped, because there is nothing "out there" that is not also uncomfortably and ineluctably "in here." His nature includes "forests of symbols" (in "Correspondances") that look disarmingly and eerily at him, and crawl with such essential decomposers as worms eating (happy) corpses, along with wolves and crows and the awful carrion with which he steadfastly identifies. The food chain is lustily alive for Baudelaire, even within his own guts; he taunts his reader with intestinal parasites right up front in "Au Lecteur" (To the Reader), where he insists that the reader is his likeness, his brother, and a hypocrite, anticipating that (s)he resists this intimacy. He is not trying to convince anyone that his poetry is pretty or easily edifying. We are all food for worms, in our minds and hearts as well as in our bodies, in constant crackling and oozing decay.

What about regeneration? Birth? New beginnings? Enlightenment?[20] Decay is only part of the cycle, after all. Baudelaire might have had children (though that possibility seems grotesque, not hopeful, for him or his progeny). For Baudelaire, the "cycle" has been reduced to a simultaneity; there is only now. Its absurd juxtapositions as he experiences the present in Paris and in his own sensibility are dizzying and seductive. A lyric poet who cannot (even) pawn his lyre, he knows that the only thing that will sell is the new, the shocking, which depends for its effects on pointing to and not being "the old" explicitly. This is a modern problem, the mass nature and awareness of cycles infused with imperatives toward progress (and its discontents), the flicker of opposite states in an endless present bristling with "the new," spleen and the ideal entangled together, rather than slow seasonal or generational turns eulogized by the romantics. William Blake's rose may indeed be sick, but there is still some seemly distance (though it may be harrowingly small and about to collapse) between the beauty of the rose and its devouring worm, and for William Wordsworth, there is a distance, however tense, between the peeping botanist and his mother's grave. For Baudelaire, there is no distance. Why revel in decay specifically if the cycle is a package deal? Perhaps because Baudelaire is not yet exiled from the maelstrom, he is part of the modern world as it eats him alive; there is no elsewhere, and—unwilling to consign himself silently to the ooze—there is no comfort to be had at the same scale in uplifting visions of progress, or reassuring notions of cycles that transcend a single mesmerized, seduced, and even in some way paralyzed life. He feels as bad and as good as he does because he is paying attention to his world even as it dissolves him. Benjamin wrote of him, "He indicated the price for which the sensation of the modern age may be had: the disintegration of the aura [of the past, an ideal, a lyric voice] in the experience of shock. He paid dearly for this disintegration—but it is the law of his poetry, which shines in the sky of the Second Empire as a 'star without atmosphere.'"[21]

Baudelaire's honesty in this regard is remarkable to me both for its completeness and for its mid-nineteenth-century date, long before the excavation of an "active nature," a socially constructed nature, or the scientific pieties of complexity. He had the sense to moan and carry on. And lest we think he had too much time on his hands, he died at forty-six.

Modernity demands ruins and the definitive, nonnegotiable division of time between the past—any past, all pasts together, the staggering strata of pasts—and now. It is telling that among the first "modern" (developmental and analytical) histories were Gibbon's and Niebuhr's histories of an iconically ruined civilization. Fredric Jameson writes, "Decadence is clearly something which both resists modernity and comes after it, as a future destiny in which all the promises of the modern go slack and unravel," fantastic forms of the future "all borrowed from the misfits and eccentrics, the perverts and the Others, or aliens, of the present (modern) system."[22] The questions multiply and swarm, throughout the nineteenth century and energetically into our own. In this new modern world is nature a ruin (too)? Are non-Western societies ruins, remnants, or alternatives from wholly other worlds? How alive are they, all the "others"? Can they be "saved"? How alive and salvageable is anybody? And what is the status of the individual, that creative and visionary portal through which an obliterating eternity is glimpsed? If the decadent individual resists her dissolution this way (once she has so firmly internalized it), she is dissolved again and for good—buried, a stake through the heart—in sepulchral inhuman geologic time.

The modern desert—the geological desert—provided a space for exactly these questions, predicaments, insights, and frustrations. The decadent desert specifically courts dissolution, and geologic time becomes the moving frame of irresistible and lethal change, as well as superficially rational. Just two motifs of the decadent desert, erosion and nakedness, are offered here, and these only briefly. Many more are possible and all at great length. Tricks of lighting and perspective are ubiquitous too, as are isolation,[23] silence, the book and the pages of geologic time, and of course death and its tell-tale bones. Limerick wrote, acknowledging how variable American deserts were, "With all these variations in vegetation and topography, deserts are in other ways more alike than different. First, all these deserts have a high degree of exposed rock and soil—as if the desert revealed, in Tocqueville's phrasing, the 'skeleton' of the earth. Combined with the difficulty of sustaining life on uncertain water and food, this 'skeletal' impression of the naked—more precisely the flayed—earth gave deserts their almost universal associations with death."[24] Flaying demands some measure of time. Erosion, visible bones, and nakedness are related—the earth is denuded (geologically), and visitors and inhabitants may find themselves naked or wish to be naked in its explicitly geological, scouring embraces. It may well be that visible erosion, of all natural forces making landscapes, signifies "desert" (as opposed to "forest," for example, or other wilderness sites). Aridity is a condition; flaying and erosion embody time.

Erosion is an inherently historical process, and seeing "it" or its effects reveals problems of comprehending time. Clarence Dutton opens his *Tertiary History of the Grand Canyon District* with a clear statement of emphasis: "This work is devoted to a description of the methods and results of EROSION on a grand scale."[25] He writes, "If . . . we would know how great have been the quantities of material removed in any given geological age from the land by erosion, we have only to estimate the mass of strata deposited in that age. Constrained by this reasoning, the mind has no escape from the conclusion that the effects of erosion have indeed been vast. If then these operations have achieved such results, our wonder is transferred to the immensity of periods of time required to accomplish them; for the processes are so slow that the span of a life-time seems too small to render these results directly visible."[26]

Brushing aside all affinity between John Wesley Powell or Clarence Dutton with the romantics—"the extravagance, the gasping, the clutching of the overburdened heart"—Wallace Stegner likewise emphasizes the overwhelming truth of the Colorado Plateau as one of erosion, burying a panting romantic just because he can, in the pages of time, though the erosion and sedimentation take place at a scale "beyond human caring":

> Ten thousand feet of rock that still showed in the terraces stepping up to the lava-capped High Plateaus had once stretched away unbroken over the whole Plateau Province and had been swept away. The Grand Canyon itself was but one phase of a new denudation that would eventually sweep away the Marble Canyon Platform, and the Kaibab, Uinkaret, Kanab, Shivwits, the Cococino Plateau reaching southward, and level them down toward the ancient peneplain of dark Archaean schist that Powell's boatmen hated and feared. And at some immeasurably remote time beyond human caring the whole uneasy region might sink again beneath the sea and begin the cycle all over again by the slow deposition of marls, shales, limestones, sandstones, deltaic conglomerates, perhaps with a fossil poet pressed and silicified between the leaves of rock.[27]

Erosion, this monumental denudation, should not be mistaken for an image of human nakedness, of course. But it seems unavoidable when the body of the earth is laid bare. Desert and canyon privation ruins clothes, for one thing. If your fine city clothes are not mussed or gaping, you have not seen, or done, something truthful—something that signals your willingness to expose yourself, literally as well as metaphorically, to the bare facts and open body of a naked and generally hostile landscape. Powell's team on the Colorado River in the spring and summer of 1869 suffered all the calamities one might expect—rancid bacon and lost bedding, oars, boats, barometers, men— but as Donald Worster notes regarding their hardships, by August they understood that "the torrents of rain . . . illustrate[d] exactly how the canyons and rapids had been formed. Water cascaded over the rims, adding to the deafening noise of the river, water carrying mud and silt of various torrents."[28] Members of the expedition had by that time whittled their food supply, by loss and spoilage and consumption, to flour, some apples, and coffee. "They were feeling incarcerated in an endless and worsening privation. The rain resumed, and now they had no protection from the cold, drenching nights— no canvas or ponchos left, few hats or blankets, not enough clothing to cover their bodies."[29] That the state of an explorer's wardrobe (as well as provisions more generally) matters is suggested by Worster's attention to the clothing of the explorer Clarence King. King plays the part of a pretentious if brilliant upstart foil to Powell's earnest hard work and hard-won nakedness. King "knew what it was to traipse across rough country, but he always needed his lavender gloves, his comfortable bed, and his supply of good wine."[30] The lavender gloves say it all. King is a dandy, and Powell is allegedly something else. But Powell's willing, driven exposure is where the lavender gloves belong, an existential, experiential decadence, pointedly in a desert chasm, practically swallowed by geologic time. Neither Powell nor Stegner nor Worster would see it that way, because "lavender gloves" belong to libertines of the city. But decadence is not (just) about absinthe-soaked and syphilitic poets and fancy men on the trail; it entails a wholesale, conscious giving over of oneself to visible, inescapable forces, figured in space and time in the desert as eroding desert landscapes that would just as soon kill and bury you.[31]

Edward Abbey understood a basic nakedness about the desert, and like Stegner and Worster, he knew that seeing it as anything but what it "is" constitutes some sort of error. The desert's nakedness is a necessity unexplained by metaphor, one might say, the very absence of metaphor as untruthful excess. "When we think of rock we usually think of stones, broken rock, buried under soil and plant life, but here all is exposed and naked, dominated by the monolithic formations of sandstone which stand above the surface of the ground and extend for miles, sometimes level, sometimes tilted or warped by pressures from below, carved by erosion and weathering into an intricate maze of glens, grottoes, fissures, passageways, and deep narrow canyons," all made by a "fantastic order and perseverance."[32] But one nakedness in geologic time begets another. "Standing there, gaping at this monstrous and inhuman spectacle of rock and cloud and sky and space, I feel a ridiculous greed and obsessiveness come over me. I want to know it all, possess it all, embrace the entire scene intimately, deeply, totally, as a man desires a beautiful woman."[33] He not only cannot help himself but also ostentatiously refuses to help himself: "The personification of the natural is exactly the tendency I want to suppress in myself," he writes, but "I dream of a hard and brutal mysticism in which the naked self merges with a non-human world and yet somehow survives intact, individual, separate. Paradox and bedrock."[34]

There is, also, a dead man in a black bag in Abbey's desert season. He died on the edge of things—the geography is almost clear enough but not quite clear enough to say where—"not far from Grandview Point," where the view is "spectacular." Part of Abbey's eulogy reads as follows:

Looking out on this panorama of light, space, rock, and silence I am inclined to congratulate the dead man on his choice of jumping-off place; he had good taste. [The smell of decay is rich and sickening.] He had good luck [A large stain discolors the crotch of his trousers]— I envy him the manner of his going: to die alone, on a rock under sun at the brink of the unknown. . . . To die in the open under the sky, far from the indolent interference of leech and priest, before this desert vastness opening like a window onto eternity—that surely was an overwhelming stroke of rare good luck.[35]

Abbey's ashes were scattered in the desert, never mind the bar in New Jersey (and its greasy alley) that provides the true beginning and ending of *Desert Solitaire*. That may be one way to gauge a person's dedication to desert dissolution. But Terry Tempest Williams complicates everything by writing the desert, its sandstone and canyons, as "home."

Perhaps the most confused achievement of contemporary desert decadence belongs to Williams. Abbey was aware of a paradox—a problem—in linking the large-scale processes of erosion with an impossible self-realization. Williams is not. Williams attempts to transform erosion into an image of individual birth rather than decay and death. Williams does not want to repulse anyone, but she does want to shock, in an edifying and remedial way. Erosion is also associated with genocide for her, providing a caution against overeager certainty in any eroding landscape.[36]

For Williams, the area around the Birthing Rock in her home ground of Utah—a rock marked by fingerprints in sandstone, and petroglyphs, as an ancient place of giving birth—is "a theater-in-the-round choreographed on Navajo sandstone, reminding us of dunes that once swirled and swayed with the wind in another geologic time."[37] In this piece Williams is carried downriver by a terrifying flash flood that becomes a performance of deliberately birthing herself. Its power lies, however, not in any recombination, no generation except sui generis, not even some hybridizing contact except with debris and water through the immersion and forceful expulsion of birth itself (a difficult breech birth at that, given the position of her feet), under the sign of erosion:

Erosion. Perhaps this is what we need, an erosion of all we have held secure. A rupture of all we believed sacred, sacrosanct. A psychic scouring of our extended ideals such as individual property rights in the name of economic gain and the expense of ecological health. . . . Waves turn me upside down and sideways as I am carried downriver, tumbling in the current, dizzy. . . . There are others around me, our silt-covered bodies navigating downriver, feet pointing downriver, in boats of our own skin. . . . Erosion. I look up. Canyon walls crack and break from the mother rock, slide into the river, now red with the desert. I am red with the desert. My body churns in the current. . . . We can witness the power of erosion as a re-creation of the world we live in and stand upright in the truth of our own decisions.[38]

She emerges, serendipitously, at the Birthing Rock, where we began.

The lines of Williams's questioning sound eerily like the brittle corpus of Nietzsche, though hers spring whole from rocks and erosion in a real landscape where a person can presumably see clearly and act sensibly to re-create the world, deciding to do so. A great many people have subjected themselves, or felt subjected, to this sort of scouring, and it is not clear that its imperatives are in any way native to environmental or desert grounding, or more pertinent here, how erosion as an artifact of geologic time can lead to seemingly rational decision in human or humane time.

Nakedness, of course, is part of the desert wardrobe of honesty in an honest landscape, and for Williams it is through naked vulnerability that a true and intact self is forged rather than abandoned. In "The Bowl," a woman takes off her apron and leaves her family to "return to the place of her childhood, the place of her true nature," where she "shed her clothing, took out her hairpins, and squeezed the last lemon she had over her body." Williams writes, "For days, the woman wandered in and out of the slickrock maze" and struggled in the debris and water of a flash flood. "Finally, letting go of her struggle, . . . she wallowed" in the wet red clay, which felt "delicious."[39] The story is also a creation and flood story; the woman fashions her family and animals in clay before the flood and arranges them satisfactorily before she emerges from the silt, bathes, and returns to her family.

The tenacity and triumphant emergence of Williams's self and protagonists in the face of fundamental dissolution appear to evade what fundamental dissolution means in a modern era, in which the triumphant individual and its death in geologic time are both "natural" and mutually impossible. She invokes desert dissolution, but it has become "delicious" in a mildly and safely eroticized encounter. What Williams appears to claim, ambivalently, is simply pleasure, though the scale of erosion crucial to her settings threatens something else entirely. The self remains unshaken in a landscape where any "self" is an absurdity, where she acknowledges that some fundamental scouring takes place. This apparent confusion suggests how difficult it is to face, much less embrace, the absurd predicament of having to live in a perpetual present moment awash in the scientifically scripted depth of time. We all lie down amid leaves of one kind or another, stone or paper—a combination of tantalizing and horrifying effects that Baudelaire (and others) could have seen in the 1840s.

The cultural specificity of any approach to the desert should go without saying. That many Americans as such have learned to "love the desert" would suggest as much; that others never stopped loving it suggests the same thing. The decadent desert is also historically specific; its emergence can be dated to roughly the end of the nineteenth century. It is modern in that sense, even as it purports to be timeless or so full of time as to be eternal. Bernard De-Voto seems to have been aware that the desire to encounter visible geologic time—horrifying and beautiful simultaneously, and most certainly a danger to any rational "self"—was a puzzling phenomenon that might demand some explanation. "The enchantment that the desert works on many people seems to be very difficult to explain," he wrote:

> No one has explained it convincingly to me, and I do not understand it. Certainly all the hideousness I have mentioned, and I could itemize it for many additional pages, can be counterbalanced by as much beauty, majesty, and sublimity. The rock deserts, those chromatic ecstasies, have been painted with comet's hair. The great chasms not only produce awe which I think the saints and mystics feel but overwhelm one with magnificence of color and light and change. Death Valley is only one of many areas where time has been frozen in geology, where mesas and mountains have been scattered as if, señor, God were a child petulant with his building blocks, and where consciousness angles down a very strange dimension.[40]

To see the desert "as itself" has no critical value; what is "itself" about it has to contrast with something else to be seen at all *as desert*. Otherwise it is merely home. To inhabit the desert as home has no critical value either, unless "home" becomes visible at the touch of something alienating and destabilizing, throwing the securities of home at once into the past and endangered pockets of remnant home places. An important contemporary assessment of the desert hinges on the value of a place and a time *away*—from the East, from humid regions, from society, from urban life, from secular life, from the modern present, often from all of these things together—but it is importantly an *explicitly historical* place from which the banality or absurdity or corruption of present society can be seen more clearly, even contested or opposed, on the basis of having seen its sepulchral end. The earth is laid bare in a process of laying bare in geologic time, in which everything one knows is sure to dissolve, taking the self with it, even as it is an individual's capacity for perception that reveals this end. The visible sepulchral time of the desert, not its "beauty," is what distinguishes the desert in contemporary modern life. In these ways a modern desert lesson is distinct from a forest lesson or a high-peaks lesson (among all "wilderness" lessons more broadly), though it may well depend on the loneliness or isolation of an individual and that individual's capacity to either succumb to unfamiliar hardship or see and feel something new.

The desert is not simply a "place," though, as if arid lands were ecological stages ready-made for human (or geological) dramas. We need to keep that caution in mind lest we return too easily to the notion that saguaros, slick-rock, sagebrush, sandstone, silt, and silence are only so much stage dressing that we may "love" or "dislike." Place and time are created simultaneously everywhere, a point well demonstrated by the work of Henri LeFebvre or Edward Soja.[41] The peculiar feature of modern desert time is that it is seen right there on the land and in it, all of natural history released in a minimalist if staggering performance space whose attendant rules of dramatic action, or inaction, with a lot of special optic effects, lead unto abject death. The desert represents a horizontal and excavated sublime of time, free of the drapery of ephemeral soil and foliage. Unlike the forest or the mountain, the desert is where a specific form of time is revealed in the soul and the body, and in the body of the earth.

Of all the cultural and historical sources we might look for to understand what any desert is or means, we should take care in selecting them so that we do not tell stories about the "development" of desert understandings as a thoughtlessly natural process "over time." When our understanding of time is at stake in understanding landscapes, as it is in understanding an important trend in understanding deserts, it should be a component of our analyses. It would be a mistake, for example, to assume that there is some simple continuity between the deserts of the Bible and contemporary desert encounters. Biblical deserts are not historical—they do not display developmental time; they do not erode. We cannot merely add a decadent desert (or any other time-saturated desert) to catalogs of culturally specific deserts either. Catrin Gersdorf's excellent account of contemporary cultural deserts certainly displays how malleable deserts are culturally.[42] But their simultaneity again begs a question about time: time itself is central to the whole idea that different versions of the desert could emerge and remain suspended together at all.

An account of American deserts sensitive to problems of time would not begin with the bedrock, because finding that "beginning" down below is precisely what needs to be explained in any question about geologic time. This is a common gesture in approaches to arid places, though, and Walter Prescott Webb's *The Great Plains* certainly started there: "In the geological formation of the Great Plains is found the first contrast between the arid West and the humid East."[43] We did not start here with the Red Desert of Wyoming either, though if the speculative geologic science holds up, this comparatively little basin had a major part to play in a very large-scale desert drama, including the formation of the Grand Canyon.[44] Such an approach would offer the illusion that "actual" landscapes—and not place and time together—are the only real subjects. A decadent desert blooms robustly in the light of sepulchral time, but we will not see it, much less any other forms of time and place (however much we might need them), if we naturalize austerity and awe as effects of erosion in unexamined geologic time.

PART IV

Politics

Chapter 11

Winning the War at Manzanar: Environmental Patriotism and the Japanese American Incarceration

Connie Y. Chiang

World War II has been remembered as a popular conflict that rallied millions of Americans behind the United States' effort to defeat the Axis powers and defend President Franklin Delano Roosevelt's "Four Freedoms": freedom of speech, freedom of worship, freedom from want, and freedom from fear. To win popular support, the federal government, in cooperation with private industry, developed a savvy propaganda campaign of posters, films, and advertisements that encouraged Americans to do their part to win the war. When they opened their newspapers, went to movie theaters, or walked down streets, they were bombarded with these government appeals. Many Americans responded to the calls to action and contributed to the war effort in myriad ways, from working in the defense plants and donating blood to buying war bonds and saving scarce materials. Indeed conservation messages figured prominently in the propaganda campaigns.[1] Illustrated with bright colors and bold graphics, war-time posters implored Americans to "Save Scrap to Beat the Jap" or to participate in car-sharing clubs because "When You Ride ALONE You Ride with Hitler."[2] The message was clear: save materials—metal, rubber,

Figure 11.1. Weimer Pursell, "When You Ride ALONE You Ride with Hitler!" (1943). Reproduced courtesy of the National Archives and Records Administration, Washington, D.C.

paper, kitchen fats—to ensure Allied victory. Failure to comply was the equivalent of providing direct aid to the Axis.

Not surprisingly, conservation-themed posters often presented racialized imagery, as did most war-time propaganda. For instance, the Wartime Forest Fire Prevention Program, in conjunction with the Wartime Advertising Council, created a campaign that used familiar anti-Japanese visual tropes. One poster with the slogan "Fire: Forest's Public Enemy No. 1" featured an "Asian Fire Devil" with slanted eyes and sinister smile. In another poster, with an orange fire ablaze in the background, the slogan "Careless Matches Aid the Axis" was accompanied by a dark caricature of a Japanese soldier holding a lit match that illuminated his large buckteeth. Thus not only did a racialized enemy endanger the nation's forests but inattentive Americans could inadvertently help this ominous, nonwhite threat as well.[3]

As the federal government implored Americans to both conserve and safeguard vital natural resources, it was also transforming the landscape of the nation's interior to confine Japanese Americans. In the wake of Japan's attack on Pearl Harbor on December 7, 1941, many Americans came to view all people of Japanese ancestry with suspicion. Of the roughly 127,000 Japanese Americans living in the United States in 1940, about 112,000 congregated on the Pacific Coast.[4] The federal government thus targeted this regional population for removal. Despite the fact that two-thirds were United States citizens by birth, federal officials uprooted them from their homes, forced them to pack their belongings and liquidate their property in short order, and eventually sent them to one of ten "relocation centers" in remote locales in the inland West and Arkansas. Army crews hastily built barracks, mess halls, lavatories, and sewage treatment plants; laid water pipelines; and dug irrigation ditches to isolate people of Japanese ancestry. Meanwhile, Roosevelt established the War Relocation Authority (WRA), a civilian agency, to administer these camps.

Government initiatives to encourage conservation and to incarcerate Japanese Americans may appear to have nothing in common, the former encouraging frugality and sacrifice and the latter banishing a potentially dangerous group. Indeed most narratives of the World War II home front make no connection between the two. Yet both programs were part of a broader war-time environmental history in which harnessing the nation's natural resources figured prominently in mobilization efforts.[5] In addition to calls for conservation, the federal government encouraged and facilitated the rapid environmental exploitation of resources deemed necessary to fight the war,

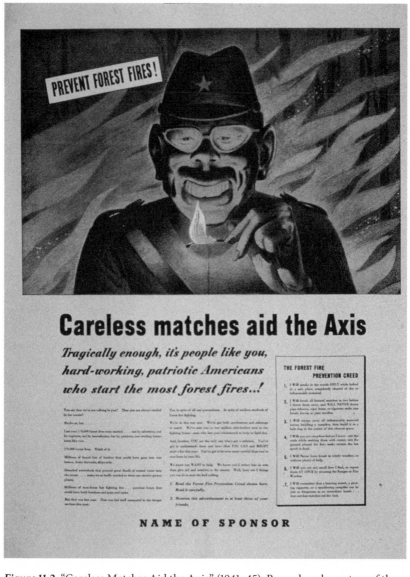

Figure 11.2. "Careless Matches Aid the Axis" (1941–45). Reproduced courtesy of the National Archives and Records Administration, Washington, D.C.

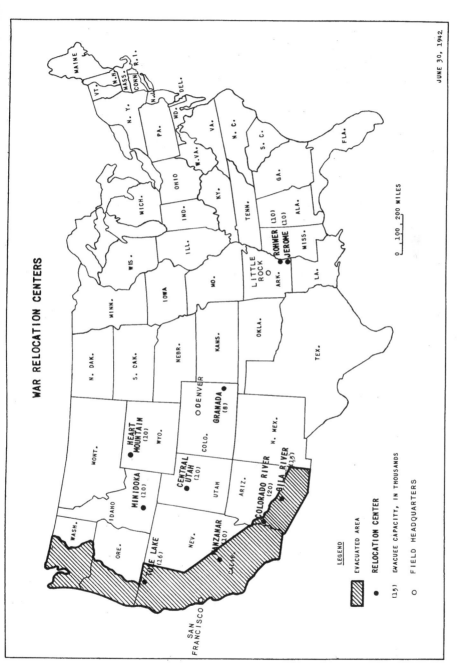

WAR RELOCATION CENTERS

JUNE 30, 1942

LEGEND

EVACUATED AREA

● RELOCATION CENTER

(15) EVACUEE CAPACITY, IN THOUSANDS

○ FIELD HEADQUARTERS

0 100 200 MILES

Figure II.3. Map of war relocation centers, *Relocation Communities for Wartime Evacuees* (Washington, D.C.: War Relocation Authority, 1942).

often at the expense of previous environmental regulations and policies.[6] For instance in Olympic National Park, National Park Service director Newton Drury permitted logging for Sitka spruce trees, which were needed for airplanes, in corridors intended for scenic parkways just outside the park's boundaries.[7] In Los Angeles oil executives pressured city officials to relax drilling regulations that had previously prohibited wells in residential areas so that they could fuel the navy's Pacific fleet.[8] In Hanford, Washington, federal officials took advantage of abundant water and electric power from the Columbia River and built plutonium production facilities as part of the Manhattan Project.[9] All across the nation, natural resources were militarized and turned into emblems of patriotism and weapons for victory.[10]

The ideological transformation of natural resources was part of Roosevelt's larger effort to create one front, "one line of unity which extends from the hearts of the people at home to the men of our attacking forces in our farthest outposts."[11] As James T. Sparrow argues, Roosevelt wanted to reinforce "the direct moral obligation that bound ordinary citizens to the heroic soldiers who gave their lives for their country." Forging this connection between home front and war front helped to legitimize the dramatic expansion of federal authority and the creation of a "warfare state" in which government officials compelled civilians and soldiers alike to "reorient their productive energies toward reworking the nation."[12] There was varied enthusiasm for the war-time calls for sacrifice, as federal officials "commonly despaired of the difficulties of transforming 'willingness into action.'"[13] Nonetheless many citizens accepted the expanded scope and power of the federal government and contributed eagerly to making their homes and workplaces "warminded." In the process, their claims on the government were "evaluated by way of comparison to the absolute sacrifice of the soldier who gave his life to the country."[14]

Complying with government mandates that dictated natural resource use was one way to express a broader commitment to the war effort—and the nation. Whether saving rubber tires or exploiting minerals, various environmental activities were infused with patriotism and deemed vital to winning the war. Government officials and industry executives did not push for these activities in order to protect the integrity of American nature or to increase private profits, although some groups may have been driven by economic gain; rather they embraced conservation and exploitation under the guise of patriotism. In other words, they deployed the rhetoric of environmental patriotism.[15] Environmental patriotism gained traction because of a widespread expectation that all American resources, human and nonhuman, should be put toward the defense of American ideals and the destruction of fascism. Those who failed to participate in or questioned the necessity of these endeavors could be easily branded unpatriotic.

In this way war-time Americans came to understand nature through nation. As federal officials marshaled natural resources for specific uses, they also shaped how Americans understood the relationship between the environment and the state. Narratives of nationhood—and of what it meant to be an American—thus influenced how they came to view nature. Environmental historians have often demonstrated the inverse—how Americans understood nation through nature. National park and tourism boosters, for instance, had long made the case that the nation's most awe-inspiring landscapes were evidence of American exceptionalism and could help forge an American identity.[16] During World War II, however, it was the high ideals of a nation fighting a global war that affected conceptions of nature and dictated its best uses. In the process, natural resources became, according to Jake Kosek, "symbol[s] of the nation itself," and physical changes to the land became markers of patriotic sentiments.[17]

How did environmental patriotism apply to the Japanese American incarceration, a program that seemed so far removed from war-time mobilization efforts? Despite physical and cultural isolation from mainstream propaganda campaigns, the rhetoric of environmental patriotism proved useful to multiple groups involved in the program. Municipal and federal officials used this language to both justify and challenge the importance of incarceration, obscuring some of their anti-Japanese sentiments. To expose the hypocrisy of the incarceration and improve their social status, Japanese Americans and their sympathizers called attention to how detainees, undeterred by the barbed wire fences, transformed nature to help defeat tyranny. Thus, rather than unifying Americans around a common cause, environmental patriotism served contradictory purposes and exposed entrenched social divisions— divisions that the war both created and exacerbated.[18]

The Manzanar Relocation Center in the Owens Valley of California illuminates this process. There the WRA, Japanese Americans and their supporters, and the Los Angeles Department of Water and Power embraced environmental patriotism to give their activities more symbolic resonance. While they often had competing claims to the camp's natural resources, they understood that it was necessary to frame their plans for land and water as crucial to the war effort. Given the constant calls for Americans to do their part to win the war, this rhetorical strategy was necessary. Ultimately the landscape of Manzanar—a place that violated the civil liberties of hundreds of Japanese Americans—became, ironically, a reflection of war-time patriotism. As they cultivated the land, detainees distanced themselves from the menacing Japanese caricatures of war-time propaganda and appeared as devoted, albeit nonwhite, Americans. In the process they assumed their place in the same nation that had banished them.

"The Most Illogical Place": The Manzanar Relocation Center and the Owens Valley

About 250 miles north of Los Angeles and bounded by the Sierra Nevada Mountains to the west and the Inyo Mountains to the east, the Owens Valley is perhaps best known as the site for early twentieth-century water battles involving the Los Angeles Department of Water and Power (LADWP). After purchasing land and water rights from local ranchers and farmers, the LADWP, under the command of William Mulholland, began constructing the Los Angeles Aqueduct, which was completed in 1913. Despite protests from local residents, the aqueduct siphoned water from the Owens River and the Owens Lake, channeling it south to fuel metropolitan growth in Los Angeles and its suburbs.[19]

The Owens Valley's role in Southern California's urban growth has been well documented by many historians, but few scholars have explored the area's role in the incarceration of Japanese Americans in World War II. After Roosevelt issued Executive Order 9066 on February 19, 1942, authorizing the establishment of military zones from which people could be excluded, the Owens Valley emerged as a possible detention site. E. Manchester Boddy, publisher of the *Los Angeles Daily News* and an Owens Valley booster, advocated the idea as a way to strengthen the local economy. He met with officials from the LADWP and Inyo-Mono Associates, a group that promoted the region's economic development, and introduced them to the Department of Justice's Alien Enemy Control Program coordinator Tom C. Clark (later a U.S. Supreme Court justice), who worked under Lt. Gen. John L. DeWitt. As commanding general of the Western Defense Command, DeWitt was in charge of the evacuation.[20]

Clark established a committee of local leaders so he could sell the project to Owens Valley residents, but his efforts fell apart when the U.S Army Engineers contacted H. A. (Harvey Arthur) Van Norman, chief engineer and general manager of LADWP, and demanded a lease of land in the area.[21] Van Norman immediately objected, pointing to the threat of sabotage posed by Japanese Americans living at the headworks of the city's water supply. If the very Japanese Americans who were being removed from Los Angeles were relocated next to the city's water supply, the supposed Japanese threat was not really leaving city limits. As an alternative, he suggested the use of Colorado River Indians' land in Parker, Arizona, about 250 miles from Los Angeles and on the eastern side of the Colorado River. It was isolated from "any water works, power plants, or other utilities," and Japanese Americans could clear and cultivate land, which would result "in a permanent improvement that could be settled by return soldiers at the expiration of the War."[22] Los Angeles mayor Fletcher Bowron concurred.[23] In a February 1942 radio address, he explained that the Parker site would allow Japanese Americans to be self-supporting while observing "nothing of military importance." They could also provide fresh produce to Los Angeles markets.[24]

While General DeWitt expressed some interest in Arizona—indeed the Colorado River Relocation Center (or Poston) was later established on Indian land near Parker—he still insisted on the Owens Valley. According to Milton Silverman, a *San Francisco Chronicle* journalist, the area was desirable because of its distance from defense projects, inaccessibility, ease with which it could be policed, and "its general geography." Van Norman realized that the use of LADWP land was inevitable, but he feared that DeWitt would take even more acreage from the city. In addition to his concerns about water purity, he was worried that the facility would take so much water that the hydropower plants at the San Francisquito Canyon would be compromised and that the city would have to build trunk-line connections to provide water for both the camp and the city.[25] The federal government tried to allay his concerns. When the Western Defense Command issued a press release in March 1942 to announce the acquisition of fifty-eight hundred acres of Los Angeles land in a former apple orchard known as Manzanar, it quoted a letter from DeWitt, who explained that the project would provide "adequate provision" to protect the water from injury and pollution and would bear in mind "the needs of the City of Los Angeles for such water."[26]

Angelenos also voiced objections to the Manzanar detention facility with racially charged rhetoric; the language of environmental patriotism was absent at this point. In a letter to Van Norman, Los Angeles resident T. Blevans explained that "it will take a great many thousand people to keep one or more of the 50,000 Japanese from crawling on their belly [*sic*] to get to the aqueduct and there infect the water. If 80,000 Englishmen could not hold them back in Singapore I do not see how a few guards will be able to protect our water supply." As was common during the war, Blevans equated Japanese Americans living in the United States, the majority of whom were citizens by birth, to the Japanese enemy. He concluded, "[M]any of our population are very much disturbed about planting the Japanese in the most illogical place that could be selected anywhere in the State of California."[27] Although Japanese Americans on the Pacific Coast were being targeted for removal in part because of fears of another sea-based attack, Blevans believed that they posed an even greater threat in the state's interior.

H. L. Ford echoed some of these concerns. He wrote, "It may be true that the Japanese could not dump enough poison in our aqueduct to kill many of us, but we do know that if they are put anywhere near the water sheds and supplies they will manage to plant Typhoid Cultures, Amebia [sic], Bubonic Plague, and Leprosy, and possibly other oriental diseases. We know they are capable of doing this very thing and I haven't the slightest doubt but what they will." A possible epidemic was "worse than machine guns," and Ford would rather the Japanese remain along the coast than "have them planted anywhere within 500 miles of our water supply, and if we permit them to be located in that vicinity we might just as well begin to look for an army of grave [diggers] and a new supply of boxes."[28] Ford assumed that Japanese ancestry conferred disease and dangerous character traits onto Japanese bodies and that therefore no Japanese could be trusted, especially in such close proximity to the aqueduct. These concerns over water resources, of course, could not be disentangled from war-time attitudes toward people of Japanese ancestry. Like Blevans, Ford linked Japanese Americans' racial inferiority with their potential to bring physical harm to Los Angeles residents vis-à-vis the water flowing in the aqueduct.

Concerns over protecting municipal watersheds from contamination were hardly new in Los Angeles or other American cities. Beginning with the construction of Boston's and New York's water systems in the 1830s and 1840s, city and state officials erected barriers, enacted laws, and delivered sanctions to ensure the purity of municipally owned and delivered water.[29] Earlier miasmic theories, which attributed disease transmission to "bad airs" or noxious vapors, propelled such efforts, and the advent of germ theory in the late nineteenth century only gave sanitarians more powerful medical and scientific justification to protect water supplies. But just as racialized ideas of disease transmission and contagion undergirded miasmic theories, they also shaped newer ideas in medical and popular discourses about germs as carriers of disease. This "gospel of germs" carried virulent and enduring ideas of racial purity and contamination.[30]

Indeed the rhetoric connecting public health to racial and ethnic difference was likely familiar to some Angelenos. Beginning in the late nineteenth century, as Natalia Molina has argued, Los Angeles public health officials developed a discourse that attributed the health problems of the city's Mexican, Chinese, and Japanese populations to "purported deficiencies in the groups' biological capacities and cultural practices." When a 1924 plague outbreak was confined mostly to neighborhoods inhabited by Mexicans, the association between filth, disease, and ethnicity was reinforced, as phalanxes of city sanitarians fumigated buildings and torched homes in these areas. According to Molina, health officers used health and hygiene norms to define "Americanness," which ultimately helped them "determine who was considered part of the body politic."[31] Such strategies seemed to endure into the war years. Despite their forced removal, Japanese Americans still constituted a health threat that continued to define them as a racial other, unfit to be living in the city or its connected hinterlands.

Despite this climate of racial hygiene, the *Los Angeles Times* editorial board supported the Owens Valley camp. Because the U.S. Army had promised "sufficient guards" to patrol and protect the aqueduct, "Southern California residents should, as a patriotic duty, accept the Army's decision and immediately cooperate in the main objective—that of restraining the aliens from any possible acts of sabotage against our military installations, plane plants, power stations and other essential wartime key centers."[32] The *Times* editorial board asked readers to set their priorities straight. The Japanese American population was a far greater threat dispersed in the midst of many war-related facilities than it was guarded closely in a camp in the Owens Valley. In this way the editorial board invoked the rhetoric of environmental patriotism, imploring residents to support the use of LADWP land for the relocation center as a way to show their commitment to the war effort.

LADWP officials remained firmly opposed to the camp, but they were also resigned to the fact that its construction could not be stopped. When Van Norman replied to Ford about his fears of diseased water, he explained that LADWP would "insist upon complete guarding of our properties against any sort of sabotage, including pollution of the water." He assured Ford that water samples would be taken on a regular basis, and he also explained that water from the Owens River took several months to reach Los Angeles, passing through many reservoirs along the way. He concluded, "With the intelligent sampling and bacteriological investigations . . . I think that we will be safe."[33] R. F. Goudey, LADWP sanitary engineer, tried to codify these efforts by creating rules to keep the water clean. Like others, he feared exposure to "Oriental carriers of cholera, dysentery, and typhoid."[34] He also worried about runoff washing surface pollution into the aqueduct. As a result he recommended that no more than ten thousand people live at Manzanar unless the sewage treatment plant facilities were enlarged. He wanted to prohibit fishing, wading, swimming, and the disposal of liquid waste in the aqueduct and its tributaries. All garbage should be hauled below the aqueduct for disposal, and no fecal matter or fertilizer made from sewage should be used on crops draining into the aqueduct. In addition corrals and animals should be located where they would not contaminate the aqueduct.[35]

Concerns about water cleanliness quickly morphed into environmental patriotism when Van Norman forwarded these recommendations to DeWitt. He reminded DeWitt that adopting these protective measures was important because the aqueduct supplied water to "over a million civilians, a large number of defense industries, and many war service units."[36] Van Norman likely recognized that the incarceration camp was a necessary war-time project, but he did not want DeWitt to forget that the LADWP too was performing an important war-time service by supplying clean water to factories and military facilities. The integrity of its land and water needed to be protected for the war effort as well.

By this point construction was already under way, and the first detainees arrived on March 21, 1942.[37] Originally a temporary reception center, Manzanar was turned over to the WRA on June 1 to be administered as a relocation center where Japanese Americans would live indefinitely. Not surprisingly, Mayor Bowron balked at this change in a May 1943 radio address and urged Manzanar's closure as soon as possible, but he did not want people of Japanese ancestry, whether American citizens or not, to return to Los Angeles.[38] For Bowron, Manzanar had displaced the Japanese threat rather than eliminated it. Public utilities connected hinterland and city, and people of Japanese ancestry belonged in neither. Nonetheless he visited the camp with Van Norman two months later. After his trip, Manzanar project director Ralph Merritt wrote to Bowron, noting, "It is my hope that you . . . carried away the impression that the Center is well guarded by adequate troops and that the approximate 9,000 present evacuees . . . are living peacefully."[39] Despite such assurances that Japanese Americans at Manzanar posed no threat to Los

Angeles, the brokered peace between the WRA and LADWP proved to be short-lived.

"Waving a Red Herring": The Los Angeles Aqueduct and the Manzanar Hog Farm

These early responses to Manzanar suggested the difficulty of separating possible water contamination or aqueduct sabotage from the perceived racial inferiority of Japanese Americans. They were seen as either essentially diseased or they were essentially subversive. In either case they were a threat to the health and safety of Los Angeles citizens. While Los Angeles officials occasionally used the rhetoric of environmental patriotism to bolster their pleas for adequate protection of their water supply, the racialized rhetoric was more common. However, when Manzanar was up and running and water-quality issues emerged, appeals to environmental patriotism became more pronounced. Officials from the LADWP and the WRA accused each other of being uncooperative, but they also emphasized their own contributions to the war effort. The problem was that they had different ideas of how to prioritize war-time demands on Owens Valley's natural resources and believed that their respective uses were more important to winning the war.

Manzanar's hog farm sparked the conflict. In November 1943 the Board of Water and Power Commissioners of the City of Los Angeles wrote to Manzanar project director Ralph Merritt alleging that the farm would threaten "the purity of our water supply" because of its location about one and one-half miles west and above the aqueduct. All of the camps had extensive agricultural and livestock operations so that they would be self-supporting and not be a drain on federal funds. However, the board reminded Merritt that the hog farm was "contrary to the letter and spirit of the correspondence between General DeWitt and ourselves," in which DeWitt pledged his commitment to protect the water supply. The board asked that the operation of the hog farm cease and be moved below the aqueduct: "While we are heartily in favor of enabling the inhabitants of Manzanar to supply food for themselves . . . we must, in the interest of the people of Los Angeles, endeavor to prevent any pollution of our water supply."[40] In other words, the needs of one war-time population came before those of another. WRA director Dillon Myer immediately wired Merritt and asked him to "make every effort to come to an agreement with Los Angeles Representative, so that hog feeding operations at [the] center may continue."[41]

Figure 11.4. Hog farm at Manzanar, 1943. Photo by Ansel Adams. Reproduced courtesy of the Library of Congress.

Both Merritt and the LADWP responded by soliciting input from other parties. Merritt enlisted C. G. Gillespie, chief of the Bureau of Sanitary Engineering of the California State Board of Health, who maintained that it was feasible to drain seepage to drying beds and build secured levies around them to protect the water supply.[42] Meanwhile, R. F. Goudey, LADWP sanitary engineer, appealed directly to the U.S. Public Health Service. He explained that the hog farm "would constitute a serious sanitary defect on our water collection system" because it was located upstream from the Owens River intake to the LADWP's Haiwee Reservoir. After reiterating the agency's support of Manzanar and its cooperation with developing water supplies for the camp, he recommended that the hog farm be located below the aqueduct.[43] Skeptical, Myer asked Merritt to investigate the alleged pollution; if the U.S. Public Health Service recommended the farm's removal, he would comply.[44] Merritt, however, wanted to move the hog farm below the aqueduct immediately in exchange for "an agreement of good will" and a reduction in rent and water charges. Improving relations with the LADWP was important, given "the devious, undetectable, but potent forces that can be brought into play by the City of Los Angeles in a case of this kind."[45]

Merritt's pleas seemed to be ignored, as the LADWP intensified its campaign against the hog farm. Van Norman wrote to Myer at the end of January 1944, incensed that the hog feeding grounds above the aqueduct had been enlarged and that the farm had added 300 hogs to the 175 that were placed there in November. He requested "immediate measures" to remove the "menace" to the city's water supply: "The Department desires to avoid unnecessary friction with the local Manzanar authorities, but, unless the hog nuisance above the City aqueduct is removed forthwith, it is our intention to seek civil and criminal remedies against the individuals in charge of the Manzanar Relocation Area."[46] Merritt responded that he was committed to protecting L.A.'s water supply, but he also noted that several other hog farms were within the city's watershed. Manzanar therefore was not the only threat to the water supply.[47]

Van Norman countered that the LADWP had been cooperating wholeheartedly with the government in "its problem relative to the Japanese evacuees" but that the WRA had failed to fulfill its promises. Despite General DeWitt's assurances that "adequate safeguards would be taken to prevent pollution of our water supply," the WRA showed an "utter disregard" for the LADWP's objections.[48] Van Norman concluded by calling attention to his agency's environmental patriotism, emphasizing that the responsibility to provide clean water to army and navy installations and L.A. residents "should not be secondary to the Manzanar Japanese Relocation Project."[49] For Van Norman, the calculus likely seemed simple. The water system serviced people who were directly engaged in the war effort, so their needs should come before those of Japanese Americans who were a possible threat to it.

Merritt quickly repudiated the LADWP's accusations: "In my estimation this outburst is merely another attempt to discredit the Federal Government's administration of one of our most difficult domestic wartime problems." He concluded, "[Members of the Board of Water and Power Commissioners] have taken the publicity method of waving a red herring across the trail of the real issue. The red herring in this case is a little pig."[50] Merritt implied that the uproar about the hog farm dismissed the importance of the war-time relocation project, an equally if not more pressing problem than Manzanar's questionable threats to the purity of the Los Angeles water supply.[51] Like Van Norman, he invoked environmental patriotism, suggesting that the Owens Valley landscape was central to discharging the WRA's war-time duties. Confining ten thousand people behind barbed wire at Manzanar—and protecting the nation from sabotage—justified and necessitated the WRA's transformations of the natural world.

Unmoved, the Los Angeles City Council adopted a resolution requesting that the L.A. City Health Department, the California State Health Department, and the United States Public Health Service investigate and work with the LADWP to "correct any condition deemed to be against the health and safety of the people of Los Angeles and our armed forces."[52] Charles Senn, director of the Sanitation Section of the Los Angeles City Health Department, and Councilman Carl Rasmussen, chairman of the Health and Welfare Committee, then traveled to Manzanar to inspect the hog farm. They looked over the concrete feeding platforms, the feeding pens, and the surrounding gutters that were flushed with water daily. They inspected various devices that prevented hog excrement from flowing into the aqueduct.[53] They also spoke with Ralph Merritt and his assistants, who explained why it was impractical to move the hog farm below the aqueduct. First, relocation would require transporting hogs and garbage over a narrow bridge that crossed the aqueduct, both of which could contaminate the water. Second, because the area below the aqueduct was outside the center, military regulations required that guards accompany Japanese Americans who worked there at a cost of at least six hundred dollars per month.[54] Thus the move would create a costly policing problem. War-time frugality and war-time security were at odds.

Given the protective measures in place, the hog farm's distance from the water supply, the large reservoirs that provided natural purification between Manzanar and Los Angeles, and the few water-borne diseases that could be caused by hog excrement, Senn concluded that the hog ranch was not a public health problem.[55] Satisfied with these measures, Van Norman recommended that no further action be taken, adding that his employees would "keep constant watch to see that nothing objectionable develops."[56] The Los Angeles City Council and the Los Angeles Health Department asked that the number of hogs not be increased and requested that the farm "be kept as clean and sanitary at all times as it was on the day of the inspection." Manzanar officials agreed.[57] By the time Manzanar closed in 1945, Japanese Americans had slaughtered over two thousand hogs, which yielded over 395,000 pounds of pork worth over sixty-seven thousand dollars.[58]

"Further Proof of Their Loyalty": Growing Rubber in the Desert

WRA and LADWP officials were not alone in their deployment of environmental patriotism. Japanese Americans too saw their use of the natural world as a way to express their support of the war effort. One project that occupied their attention was rubber. Because the Japanese military had gained control of areas in the Pacific and Southeast Asia that supplied much of the world's rubber, scientists identified guayule—a small, woody, drought-resistant shrub native to the southwestern United States and northern Mexico—as a possible domestic source. On February 28, 1942, Congress passed a bill that created the Emergency Rubber Project (ERP) to focus on domestic rubber crops and authorized the planting of seventy-five thousand acres of guayule and the purchase of all United States assets of the Intercontinental Rubber Company, which had conducted extensive guayule experiments in Salinas, California, before the war.[59]

With the creation of ERP, previous contracts between Intercontinental Rubber and scientists at the California Institute of Technology (Caltech) became "null and void." Nonetheless, Caltech scientists, led by Robert Emerson, decided to launch their own project. A Quaker and pacifist who was against the incarceration, Emerson recognized the talents of many Japanese Americans—some of whom were formerly employed as chemists, botanists, and nursery men—and believed that they could help to determine the potential of guayule. One of Emerson's colleagues, Robert Millikan, president of Caltech and the 1923 Nobel Prize winner in physics, added that he did not want to see these talented scientists "locked up" at Manzanar with "nothing to do but wash dishes." Emerson also believed that their work on the guayule project could prove that they were "more than willing" to serve their country.[60]

Like Emerson, Grace Nichols, a journalist and Quaker activist, promoted Japanese Americans as ideal participants in the guayule experiments. She wrote in an unpublished manuscript, "Superior skill in growing plants whose requirements are exacting has long been recognized as one of the native gifts of the Japanese." She went on to explain that those who worked on the guayule project "welcomed it as an opportunity to demonstrate in humble ways that a man's loyalty and patriotism, his love and devotion to his country and its ideals and principles, are elements which can never be measured by the narrow bounds of race or lineage or ancestral origin, - nor can the privilege of striving and sacrificing for those things in which one believes most deeply be limited to any one race or group." Although they had been "deprived of" their homes and businesses, she added, "their first thought is still to be of service to the country which has denied them the rights of free men." To corroborate this point, she quoted a "statement of policy" that hung on a Manzanar bulletin board: "Day after day, through wind and dust storms, we work with willingness and without complaint - not for individual profit, but for the success of the project as a whole. . . . we are hoping that the day may come when we are able proudly to place our accomplishments before the people." Nichols clearly understood and wanted to expose the hypocrisy of the Japanese Americans' active participation in war-related work behind the confines of barbed wire.[61]

After securing ERP assistance and receiving permission from the WRA, Emerson had to convince Japanese Americans to participate.[62] This was not an easy sell for all potential workers. Homer Kimura was reluctant because rubber was a military material, and he did not want to help produce something that would prolong the war. Two other Japanese American scientists eventually convinced Kimura to join the project. As Emerson noted, "They explained to Mr. Kimura that my principal purpose in developing the guayule program was to help some Japanese families to re-establish themselves in American society, and to contribute something toward the re-building of good-will in Americans toward other Americans of Japanese ancestry."[63] Japanese Americans could apply their knowledge to assert their rightful place in the American polity.

Guayule work at Manzanar began in earnest in April 1942 when Emerson hauled fourteen gunnysacks full of guayule cuttings to the camp. Immediately, Japanese American scientists faced challenges. Strong winds destroyed one lath house, a structure with narrow wooden slats on the roof that allowed in air and light. Jackrabbits ate the plants. Tending to thousands of guayule seedlings was challenging in the extreme climate of the Owens Valley. Nonetheless, Japanese American participants persevered. By June 1942 they had planted 169,000 guayule plants grown from cuttings, and the first yellow flowers began to bloom on the plants in the lath house. By the end of June, four plots with different types of soil, drainage, and location were set aside for guayule experiments, and three chemists, one statistician, two plant propagators, and sixteen nurserymen worked on the project.[64]

Soon the work of the Manzanar team became newsworthy. In September 1942 the journalist Neil Naiden wrote an article for the *Washington Post* focusing on Walter Watanabe and Shimpe Nishimura, both experts in plant propagation. They intended to cross-pollinate different strains of guayule in order to increase the rubber content of the plant. Suggesting innate if positive racial traits, Naiden explained that "the inborn horticultural talent of the Japanese may be what all the previous experiments lacked." He also singled out Nishimura for his "unbelievable patience. He will stand rooted by an experiment for hours at a stretch in order to place a drop of water or seemingly magic compound on a plant at the proper moment." While these men had "extra incentive" to work hard and prove their loyalty to the country, Naiden believed that the guayule project would be "encouraging" to the average American citizen. Even as the government responded to the dictates of military necessity, it had "given the evacuated Japanese an experimental task which will keep them active and curious."[65] Thus the camps had enabled Japanese Americans to prove their devotion to the United States.

The *Manzanar Free Press* reinforced this rhetoric of environmental patriotism. One article noted, "If the experiment at Manzanar proves successful, it would mean that the Japanese will have contributed a substantial share toward national defense and the Japanese residents are happy to receive their opportunity to give further proof of their loyalty."[66] Another article explained that Japanese American contributions to meet the rubber shortage would produce "something more valuable than a product for cash sale. They will have contributed toward the building of good will between the Japanese in America and their Caucasian friends and fellow citizens." Because this goodwill would benefit the entire Japanese American community, the writer concluded,

Figure 11.5. Robert Emerson and Japanese Americans inspecting guayule plantings at Manzanar, 1942. Photo by Dorothea Lange. Reproduced courtesy of the National Archives and Records Administration, Washington, D.C.

"their efforts merit your interest and appreciation, and, whenever possible, your cooperation."[67] This language of war-time unity is not surprising given that the WRA exerted editorial control over the content of the newspaper.[68] Nonetheless it demonstrates that journalists understood how to deploy ideas of loyalty and patriotism to frame the guayule project and potentially help to unite those incarcerated.

But the Manzanar guayule project was not just a front for patriotic rhetoric. Japanese Americans conducted experiments that yielded important

Figure 11.6. Walter T. Watanabe and George J. Yokomize tending to guayule plants at Manzanar, 1942. Photo by Dorothea Lange. Reproduced courtesy of the National Archives and Records Administration, Washington, D.C.

data. In February 1943 Emerson submitted a report to the United States Forest Service and the Bureau of Plant Industry. According to Emerson, the Manzanar researchers conducted experiments in three areas: propagation of guayule from cuttings; suitability of different guayule strains to the Manzanar climate; and extraction of rubber. Between August and November 1942 they made over ninety thousand guayule cuttings that were taken from different parts of stems, treated with different chemicals, and put in different grades of sand and gravel to root. They tried different methods for quick rubber extraction, with the hope that these techniques might have potential value for commercial extraction.[69] All of these experiments yielded tangible results. Japanese Americans succeeded in getting cuttings to grow by applying plant-rooting hormones; they developed hybrids that could survive in the harsh Owens Valley environment; and they came up with "an innovative, effective, and energy-efficient method of milling the guayule that yielded a low-fiber rubber extract" that had the potential to "revolutionize and modernize" this process.[70]

But the fact that Japanese American researchers were able to accomplish so much with such limited resources proved embarrassing for the ERP scientists, who received large federal appropriations. After the *Washington Post* article was published, Fred McCarger, secretary of the Salinas Chamber of Commerce, wrote a letter to Federal Bureau of Investigation director J. Edgar Hoover expressing doubts that the Manzanar researchers could have accomplished as much as the hundreds of ERP workers in Salinas. This sort of pressure led to declining support for guayule research at Manzanar. WRA officials shut off the water that irrigated the guayule plants and told Grace Nichols not to publish her article.[71] But given Japanese Americans' important contributions, this moment of contraction was brief and was followed by a period of expansion by spring 1943. Millikan secured grant money and other funding, while ERP director Paul Roberts promoted government monies. The pace of research at Manzanar accelerated.[72]

Ralph Merritt affirmed the contributions of Japanese Americans when he wrote to WRA director Dillon Myer in August 1943. He explained that Japanese American horticulturists, chemists, and engineers at Manzanar had confirmed that rubber could be produced from guayule and had developed the proper methods for rubber extraction. "Who are these men who are pioneering the way toward heavy duty rubber production in the United States," Merritt asked. "Their leaders are highly skilled and educated in our schools and universities. They give the answer to the question, 'what do the Japanese bring to our culture that is important?' It denies the assertion that the Japanese are purely imitative. It proves that the Japanese trained in our schools are of the most creative type . . . I could preach a sermon from the text: 'The stone that the builders rejected has become the head of the corner.'"[73] Merritt singled out those American-educated Japanese Americans for praise because they had distanced themselves from Japanese culture and proven their assimilation and devotion to the United States. Their exile at Manzanar had not precluded them from using their expertise to make essential contributions to the war effort.

Merritt's praise, however, served a specific purpose: he wanted to save researchers from banishment. In February 1943 the federal government asked Japanese Americans over the age of seventeen to fill out loyalty questionnaires in order to determine their eligibility to serve in a racially segregated unit of the U.S. Army. Question 28 asked, "Will you swear unqualified allegiance to the United States of America and faithfully defend the United States from any or all attack by foreign or domestic forces, and forswear any form of allegiance or obedience to the Japanese emperor, or any other foreign government, power, or organization?" Masuo Kodani, a Kibei born in the United States and educated in Japan, answered "no" to question 28, which could have resulted in his transfer to the Tule Lake Relocation Center, the camp that segregated "disloyal" detainees. Moreover, Shimpe Nishimura, who had received glowing praise in the *Washington Post* article, and Takashi Furuya applied for repatriation to Japan.[74]

Merritt pleaded with Myer to make exceptions "where men are engaged in work necessary to the war effort." He argued that requests for repatriation and answering "no" to question 28 "may not be in any way a reflection of an anti-American view or a pro-Japanese political view." Kodani, who had determined how to select seeds that produced plants with more rubber content, married a Japanese immigrant student who was sent to a detention camp after Pearl Harbor. Their baby was born there. Because Kodani thought his wife would be sent back to Japan, he answered "no" so he could be with her and their child. According to Merritt, his "no" answer should not detract from his "thoroughly American" point of view. He concluded, "If the United States is to produce heavy duty rubber from the only known source and the only known method, the men I have mentioned must be kept together and allowed to continue their work undisturbed by the regulations that are applied to others."[75] It is unclear if Myer intervened to prevent these men's transfer to Tule Lake. Nonetheless, Merritt's pleas demonstrated how Japanese Americans' knowledge of nature and their ability to produce a potentially valuable war-time crop were supposed to negate what could be construed as seditious, disloyal actions. They may have been unpatriotic in one context, but their efforts to produce guayule proved overwhelmingly otherwise.

Merritt seemed intent on publicizing the important work of Japanese American scientists. Toward the end of the war, he wrote an essay—his intended audience is unclear—once again extolling the environmental patriotism of Manzanar's guayule researchers. He began by noting that scientific research had flourished in an unexpected place: "behind barbed-wire fences in a soldier-guarded, wartime barrack settlement located on the desert in the shadow of our highest mountains." He thanked the various agencies and universities that had supported the research, and then he concluded that "the highest tribute goes to the large group of loyal men of Japanese ancestry who, after an evacuation that took them from their homes and former fields of productive activity, worked without hope of reward or regard to long hours, under many hardships and despite an antagonistic public press[,] that they might make their wartime contribution to the economic up-building of America." Merritt suggested in no uncertain terms that Japanese Americans had transcended their unfavorable circumstances to help the war effort. He concluded that their research served "as evidence that science has no limitations of racial intolerance and that those of Japanese blood may offer cultural and creative values to American life."[76]

At first glance, Merritt's writing may seem like a rousing defense of Japanese Americans and a refutation of the WRA's incarceration program. Indeed he was known to be sympathetic to the plight of Japanese Americans. However, he also displayed a paternalism that was consistent with Dillon Myer's attitude toward the detainees. Unlike Emerson, he did not oppose incarceration. One WRA staff member, Solon T. Kimball, recalled how Merritt viewed himself as the "father of Manzanar," committed to helping "his children to see the right way." For Merritt, the "right way" included speaking English and learning "American ways."[77] His effusive praise and defense of the guayule researchers indicated that they were the sort of "children" he was more than willing and enthusiastic to protect as a father. Despite their confinement, they had displayed, at least in his mind, a steadfast commitment to the war and, by extension, the American way of life. In this way detention at Manzanar had not undermined the principles of American citizenship. On the contrary, it had provided numerous outlets—such as guayule research— for Japanese Americans to express their patriotism and loyalty to the United States.[78] The government's betrayal of the ideals of freedom and equality were simply not part of Merritt's understanding of the incarceration, and he chose to emphasize how the camps facilitated the creation of devoted Americans.[79]

While Emerson, Merritt, and others clearly invoked environmental patriotism to describe the guayule project and to both defend and challenge the incarceration of Japanese Americans, it is not clear to what extent men such as Kodani and Nishimura pursued this work in an effort to prove their loyalty. The record is open to interpretation. Perhaps they were driven by a simple desire to advance scientific knowledge. Perhaps their work gave them some purpose and autonomy, filling what would have otherwise been somewhat monotonous, regimented days. Whether their discoveries improved their position in American society may not have been a paramount consideration when they chose to participate in the guayule project.

But the fact that Emerson and Merritt believed that Japanese Americans had valuable environmental knowledge to impart and that this knowledge could both undermine anti-Japanese sentiment and affirm their American identities is noteworthy. Japanese Americans could plant and tend guayule seedlings in the desert, conduct experiments, and make scientific discoveries that might be crucial for the war-time state. For Merritt, this work proved their assimilation and the success of the WRA's mission. For Emerson, Nichols, and others, this work weakened arguments for their incarceration and reinforced the dissonance between the war-time rhetoric of democracy and freedom and the oppressive nature of the camps. Emerson and Merritt worked from within the accepted patriotic framework of war-time America to advance their opposing claims.

Conclusion

Various Manzanar parties used the rhetoric of environmental patriotism to affirm widely different agendas. During the debate over the water supply, the rhetoric of environmental patriotism sometimes obscured the racial implications of LADWP's protests. LADWP officials and other Angelenos clearly saw Japanese Americans' presence near the aqueduct as a racialized threat, but emphasizing the need to provide clean water to military installations and defense plants allowed them to reframe their position as one largely motivated by a commitment to the war effort. For its part, the WRA viewed the control of over 110,000 Japanese Americans as a significant war-time problem and critical to the national defense. Its officials, therefore, believed that they were more than justified in making use of natural resources to keep Japanese Americans contained while promoting their assimilation. Given the patriotic war-time climate, both agencies defended their claims by pointing out that their uses of nature were crucial to winning the war.

With guayule, the rhetoric of environmental patriotism once again served different purposes. For Ralph Merritt, who oversaw Manzanar for much of its existence, this project confirmed the argument that the confinement of Japanese Americans actually helped to assimilate them, thereby validating the WRA's overall program. For Japanese American sympathizers such as Robert Emerson and Grace Nichols, who were adamantly opposed to the camps, the guayule project reinforced that Japanese Americans deserved inclusion in American society and highlighted the irony that these scientists were performing vital war-time work behind barbed wire. Both groups emphasized Japanese Americans' dedication to discovering guayule's potential and solving a serious war-time problem, but their use of environmental patriotism met opposing goals.

In invoking environmental patriotism, these groups demonstrated the intimate connections between nature and nation. They tried to shape conceptions of the natural world and promote certain environmental activities by drawing on patriotism and tapping into people's abiding devotion to the country fighting a principled global war. In the process, natural resources—from Owens Valley water to guayule shrubs—became much more than simple material commodities. They also had cultural value and gained civic meaning, which ultimately influenced who was included and who was excluded from the American polity. In the end the rhetoric of environmental patriotism was not unifying. Instead it was malleable enough that opposing groups could use it to simultaneously justify and challenge the incarceration program in a way that affirmed government pleas for Americans to contribute to victory. Environmental transformations in fundamentally undemocratic places—barbed-wire enclosed camps such as Manzanar—thus received a patriotic spin, but they came to represent Japanese American oppression and government hypocrisy as well.

Chapter 12

Unthinkable Visibility: Pigs, Pork, and the Spectacle of Killing and Meat

Brett Mizelle

Back in 2007 I attended the Pork Industry Forum in Anaheim, California. I had told the organizers at the National Pork Board that I was writing a book[1] on the relationship between humans and pigs and wanted to make sure I was getting the industry's perspective on the major relationship Americans have with pigs: eating them. I attended two days of talks and seminars, a highlight of which was the announcement by Dennis Treacy, the vice president for environmental and corporate affairs at Smithfield Foods, that his company was going to require its producers to phase out the use of gestation crates within a decade. Smithfield Foods is the largest single producer of pork in the United States (its Tar Heel packing plant in North Carolina can slaughter and process up to thirty-two thousand hogs per day), so their decision to move away from this industry-standard method of confining pregnant sows in metal-barred and concrete-floored cages that prevent them from turning around was truly newsworthy, receiving praise from groups such as the Humane Society of the United States and Farm Sanctuary. Smithfield's initiative came after voters in Arizona in November 2006 approved Proposition 204, the Humane Treatment of Farm Animals Act, which banned gestation crates and veal stalls, by a wide margin, despite an industry campaign that argued, "Proposition 204 is Hogwash."[2]

That evening I got to look at all the items up for bid at the members' auction. Many of them were images of individual pigs or of family farms. Many of them were patriotic in nature, and almost everything, whether a painting or a quilt, stood in stark contrast to the reality of the industry that I had heard about all day. These auction items conjured up a time when farmers knew their pigs as individuals, but in talking to producers (the word that has largely replaced "farmers" these days), they spoke of having hundreds if not thousands of pigs, most kept in confinement systems and often raised under contracting arrangements; in other words, many of these farmers did not actually own the pigs they were raising, much less know them. It seemed appropriate that the National Pork Board and the National Pork Producers Council held their business meetings adjacent to Disneyland, for this self-presentation of themselves evinced a powerful manufactured nostalgia for the rural past, one at odds with the reality of the modern pig and pork industry.[3] After all, who would want to make, much less bid on, a handmade quilt featuring stitched squares of large heated barns where visitors must wear protective clothing to maintain biosecurity, or a painting of a porcine genetics lab, or a sculpture of a sow and her piglets in a farrowing crate?

This contrast between the reality of pork production in the twenty-first century and the traditional imagery to which pork producers and, for that matter, much of the public still cling proved a key moment for me in thinking through the ideas and material that would become my book *Pig*. Much of that project is dedicated to what I call our "pigs of the imagination": to the cultural pigs we consume along with the material animal and that, I contend, often occlude the reality and experiences of living pigs. For example, in both literature and life we are drawn toward "saved from slaughter" stories that tend to focus on the salvation of individual, often named animals, enabling us largely to forget the rest, those millions of anonymous hogs and pigs measured in the aggregate and by the herd. Some of these narratives are well known, such as E. B. White's *Charlotte's Web* (written in part to save in literature the pig he could not save in real life on his farm, an occurrence chronicled in his 1948 essay "Death of a Pig") or Dick King-Smith's *The Sheep-Pig* (known to most of us through Chris Noonan's 1995 film *Babe*, which begins with a brief recognition of factory farming before Farmer Hoggett sees the potential in an animal otherwise destined for the dinner table). However, stories of special individual animals are equally central to the operation of farm animal sanctuaries and rescues that similarly focus on the exceptions, albeit as a way to critique the industrial farming rule.

Figure 12.1. Jennie Cell, *Butchering Day* (c. 1955). Oil on fiberboard. Reproduced courtesy of Smithsonian American Art Museum, gift of Mr. and Mrs. James M. Mundis.

This focus on individual animals is understandable given both the difficulty of wrapping our minds around the scale of contemporary animal agriculture and the long, entangled history of human and nonhuman animals in meat eating. Our human ancestors began eating meat millions of years ago, a development central to the very creation of humanness that remained crucial for both biological survival and the production of cultural identities.[4] Although the full scope of that history is impossible to tell in a single volume, the relationships between humans, animals, and the environment have been profoundly transformed over time. Through domestication, a process best seen as "a treaty between consenting intelligent parties who entered into the agreement in a spirit of mutual self interest,"[5] wild boars were transformed into pigs, developing longer bodies, shorter legs, large floppy ears, and curly tails while losing the spots and stripes necessary for camouflage in the wild. Eventually a wide variety of pigs existed throughout the globe, adapted to local conditions and suitable for household and small-scale farming. In the eighteenth century, efforts to create "improved" animals began and were so successful in creating modern breeds of pig (such as the Berkshire and Land-race) for new modes of meat production that much of the biological diversity of pigs has been lost.[6] Modernization and standardization of the pig along with new scientific processes and technologies used to raise, kill, and process pigs into pork have in effect "emancipated the hog industry from the demands of nature." However, as Nathanael Johnson noted in a perceptive summary of recent developments, "each freedom comes at a price. Each new liberty for pork producers depends on further control, further domination of the pig."[7]

Humans' power over nature in general and pigs in particular is made possible in part by our belief in the separation of nature and culture. Seeing nature as outside of human culture and therefore subject to human control creates instrumental attitudes toward animals, bolsters human exceptionalism, and makes it hard to see the many ways in which humans and animals are deeply entangled. We often think of the natural world as essential, elemental, and outside of human culture, but the very act of eating and the history of our modification of both plants and animals for human use should remind us that we are complicatedly enmeshed with an always already encultured nature, even if we cannot see or do not choose to see that connection.[8]

Questions of visibility and invisibility and the broader politics of transparency are the focus of this essay, which looks at selected aspects of the human-pig and human-meat relationship in American culture. Our control over nonhuman animals, of course, is both material and symbolic: it depends on our power and technology as well as the stories we tell and the cultural frames we apply to the human-animal relationship. Domination also depends on what we see or, more appropriately, what we wish to and/or are allowed to see as what is visible or invisible shapes both our knowledge of and practices toward nonhuman nature. However, there is no single or clear relation between the politics of sight and the status of animals in modern America. Although the invisibility and marginalization of animals involved in meat production are the norm and the stories and representations essential to the functioning of industrial agriculture are almost uniformly nostalgic and traditional, that has not always been the case. Farmers and meat processors have often sought greater visibility to demonstrate how modern and progressive their means of production were. Spectacles of meat production and consumption have also marked moments of transformation and have helped sell meat in an increasingly consumer-centered culture.

Many of these contemporary images and stories about animals and meat work to enable us to imagine that the connection between pigs and people is not as distant and alienated as it actually is.[9] Few Americans today have any direct encounters or experiences with living pigs, given how developments in the way pigs are raised and pork is produced have severed many of the historical connections between humans and pigs. This distancing, combined with the multiple ways in which we consume the "cultural" pig or the "idea of the pig," obscures the lives and the deaths of actual pigs and reinscribes the separation of nature and culture.

Perhaps the best place to see this is in southern California, a center of American image making, where in the industrial city of Vernon one can find happy and healthy pigs frolicking in an idyllic setting. Some are lazing on the grass in the sun. Others are drinking from a stream or eating at a trough. A buxom country girl, bursting out of her clothes, leads one on a rope. Calling to mind the oft-used phrase "when pigs fly," another pig is decked out in sunglasses and a baseball cap and is piloting a small plane towing a banner featuring the logo of the Farmer John Brand, "family owned since 1931." These pigs are the stars of the murals, painted by Les Grimes between 1957 and 1968 (when Grimes fell to his death while working on a portion of the sky in one artwork), that decorate the walls of the Clougherty Meat Packing Company plant in Vernon, California.[10]

The contradiction between the murals, with their nostalgic representations of individual pigs in the countryside, and the mass killing of pigs that takes place inside this labor-intensive factory in the industrial urban landscape should come as no surprise. In fact the activist artist Sue Coe has brought this tension to the surface in several of her paintings and drawings, which focus on the intertwined suffering of the immigrant human laborers and nonhuman animals at Farmer John's.[11] Coe had trouble accessing Farmer John's for her project, and today access to the site is made more difficult by the complete prohibition of parking around the plant and in the lot of the McDonald's across the street, where, if one visits at the right time, one can order the McRib sandwich, another simulation, this time of the actual ribs of a pig, manufactured out of pressed pork shoulder meat and drenched in barbeque sauce.[12]

Les Grimes's murals of these contented pigs on the walls of the Farmer John slaughterhouse mark our complicated and ambivalent human attitudes about and practices toward pigs. They remind us of a human-pig relationship

Figure 12.2. Les Grimes, "Farmer John" mural (detail), Clougherty Meat Packing Company, Vernon, California. Photo by Brett Mizelle.

that was perhaps not so distanced or as alienated as it is in the industrialized world today, even though that relationship has almost always been framed by and centered on the killing of pigs by humans. Today this killing for meat and other products derived from animals' bodies takes place on an almost unimaginable scale: hundreds of millions of pigs are killed yearly throughout the globe for food. On a single day in the United States—Friday, March 1, 2013—423,000 hogs were slaughtered from a national market herd of over 60 million pigs.[13] Coincidentally, since 1972 March 1 has been National Pig Day, a pseudoholiday originally intended "to accord the pig its rightful, though generally unrecognized, place as one of man's most intellectual and domesticated animals" that has now become an opportunity to celebrate eating them.[14]

This raising and killing of pigs is invisible to most Americans. In fact this invisibility is crucial to the functioning of the industrial agriculture system that produces the vast majority of the meat that Americans consume and to the maintenance and naturalization of our power over nonhuman animals and nature. Although the relationship between visibility and power can be tracked in a number of realms of American life, it may perhaps be seen most clearly in the largely unacknowledged lives and deaths of food animals: more than nine billion land animals are raised and killed for food annually in the United States. The production of meat is accordingly an aspect of the human-animal relationship in which, as Anat Pick notes, "relations of power operate in their exemplary purity (that is, operate with the fewest moral or material obstacles)."[15]

This essay examines a few of the many ways in which "distance and concealment operate as mechanisms of power in modern society," as Timothy Pachirat has succinctly put it in the introduction to *Every Twelve Seconds*, his important ethnographic study of the modern industrial cattle slaughterhouse.[16] It also focuses on several moments in which spectacles of meat consumption have worked to normalize transitions in food production, including the emergence of industrial agriculture. The human-pig relationship sheds light on the entanglements of nature and culture in America, a complexity that is often hard to see given how our tendency to think in binary terms— nature/culture, human/animal—contributes to the politics of invisibility that has been central to the development of a meat-industrial complex that profoundly affects humans, animals, and the environment.

From Living Animals to Representations: Pigs in the City

Although pigs were once ubiquitous in American urban spaces, central to subsistence economies, the environment, and everyday life, they were increasingly seen as nuisances that generated tons of waste and injured people and property when loose. The removal of pigs from urban spaces had profound consequences for humans, animals, and the urban environment. Today we are likely to see pigs in our cities only as meat in shops and restaurants and as representations, often as nostalgic, cute life-sized images of pigs in paint, fiberglass, and bronze that ultimately obscure the killing and consumption of millions of animals.

In the nineteenth century, foreign travelers noted that American cities were remarkable for the presence of living nonhuman animals, especially hogs and pigs. Visiting New York in 1842, the novelist Charles Dickens wrote of pigs in New York "roaming towards bed by scores" in the evening, "eating their way to the last" along Broadway. He urged his readers to "take care of the pigs," noting that these "gentlemen hogs" were "mingling with the best society, on an equal, if not superior footing, for every one makes way when he appears, and the haughtiest give him the wall, if he prefer it."[17]

Pigs were easy to keep in towns and cities because they did not require much space, could be turned out to wander (and be counted on to find their way home), and most importantly, would find their own food in the large amounts of human-generated garbage, thereby helping to clean the streets. Pigs efficiently converted garbage to meat, making them important animals in the lives of working-class and immigrant city dwellers, and each family often kept a pig or two for domestic consumption or for sale. Yet these pigs, kept in piggeries at night and turned out into the streets during the day by both individual owners and butchers, proved an incredible public nuisance. New York City passed its first law prohibiting hogs from running in the streets in 1648, inaugurating what John Duffy called a long "losing war with the pigs" that continued until 1860.[18]

The nineteenth-century effort to control the pig population in New York was deeply entangled with the politics of class and race amid urbanization and modernization. In a precursor to contemporary interest in multispecies justice and urban ecologies, working-class New Yorkers vigorously protested the city's efforts to confiscate their pigs, both in the courts and in popular demonstrations and riots against the hog carts in the 1820s and 1830s.[19] The press seldom came to the defense of these marginal New Yorkers, instead blaming the hogs for the poor condition of the city's streets and for the spread of disease. In the wake of a cholera epidemic in 1849 the city began a more effective crackdown, which culminated in an attack on piggeries in the area known as Hog Town (between 50th and 59th Streets from Fifth to Eighth Avenues) in 1859. Over three thousand hogs were captured in this raid and many hog pens were destroyed, with the paradoxical effect that the city had to spend much more money on the removal of offal and garbage than before. By 1860 pigs were removed to north of 86th Street and the era of free-ranging hogs in New York City, at least, was over.[20]

By the turn of the twentieth century, pigs had largely (if unevenly) vanished from most U.S. towns and cities, as the killing of pigs and the production of meat moved farther and farther away from the point of pork consumption. Other than as meat, as representations on signs for restaurants

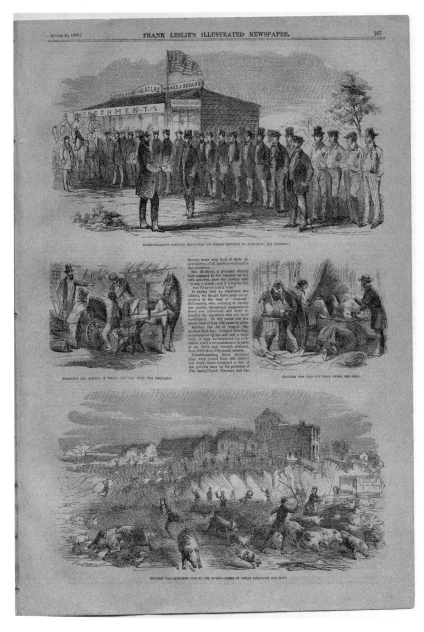

Figure 12.3. "Driving the Captured Hogs to the Pound—Scene of Great Confusion and Riot," from "The Great War on the New York Piggeries," *Frank Leslie's Illustrated Newspaper,* August 13, 1859. Author's collection.

and grocery stores, or as pets (Vietnamese potbellied pigs were first imported as pets in the late 1980s), pigs are now absent from American urban spaces. Urban residents can increasingly find representations of pigs in sculptures that mark the sites of markets and shopping districts, including Eric Berg's "Philbert," the mascot of Philadelphia's Reading Terminal Market, and "Rachel," who plays the same role at Seattle's Pike Place Market. These life-sized bronze piggy banks (donations go to local food-oriented charities) are celebrity animals, appearing in thousands of tourist photographs. While reminding us of the real animals behind the meat, they reflect the ambivalence in our relationships with nonhuman animals and are situated away from the actual butchers' counters. In contrast, the bicycle rack (1996) created by Louis Molina outside Los Angeles's Grand Central Market features a pair of pig heads cast in steel from ones originally purchased in the market. These pig heads refuse to be cute, serving as a rare and surly reminder of the once living animals' conversion into meat.

Molina's sculpture contrasts with the recent explosion of decorated fiberglass pigs. The use of decorated animals as public art and civic boosterism began with a fiberglass cow exhibit in Zurich in 1998 and a similar CowParade™ staged in Chicago in 1999. While the painted cows have appeared in over fifty cities, residents of Cincinnati pioneered the "pig parade" with its "Big Pig Gig" in the summer of 2000. Sponsors and artists collaborated on the design and the naming of the almost four hundred pigs that appeared on the streets of the city formerly known as "Porkopolis," attracting locals and tourists alike. The Pike Place Market mascot "Rachel" inspired Seattle's "Pigs on Parade" events in 2001 and 2007, while the St. Clair-Superior neighborhood of Cleveland saw the installation of forty pigs in its "Year of the Pig" public art campaign.[21]

While these charitable projects are undeniably popular with the public, the decorated fiberglass animals also reflect our tremendous distance from actual living pigs, which are for the most part raised in horrifying conditions in concentrated animal feeding operations. We are attracted to the symbolic pig but seldom think about (or consciously forget) the millions of hogs that are slaughtered in the United States each year.[22] That industry depends, of course, on our unwillingness to confront the contradictions in our relationships with pigs, taking advantage of the distance between humans and most nonhuman animals (pets being a significant exception). This partial replacement of the living animal with its representation marks both the repression of the complicated history of human-pig interactions and our radical distance from most nonhuman animals in late modernity.

Meat Spectacular: Celebrating Butchers and the Slaughterhouse

In the early nineteenth century, when urban Americans had a closer, yet still instrumental relationship to their food animals, a public spectacle marked new ways of raising and butchering livestock and selling meat. The "Grand Procession of the Victuallers" that took place in Philadelphia on March 15, 1821, along with subsequent efforts to promote modern methods of producing meat highlight changes to the complicated relationship between farmers, butchers, and consumers.

In December 1820 residents of Philadelphia started noticing advertisements in the papers calling their attention to a "Cattle Show" to be held in the new year and feature animals "of the finest breed" fattened by farmers in the regions around Philadelphia.[23] By early March 1821 William White, a prominent butcher and civic booster, was advertising an exhibition of these "superior bred animals" outside of his slaughterhouse on Front Street. According to the press, "thousands of spectators" witnessed this display of the successful efforts of progressive farmers to improve livestock breeds.[24] Given the contemporary vogue for the "improvement" of farm animals in Europe and the United States, this exhibition was not particularly remarkable.[25] What made the Philadelphia event stand out, however, was the killing of all of these animals by William White and his "Brother Victuallers" to make possible a two-mile procession of 86,731 pounds of meat from sixty-three cattle, forty-two oxen, four bears, three deer, ten goats, eight giant hogs, and numerous sheep. This meat parade included more than two hundred "Butchers mounted on fine horses, dressed in white frocks and Sashes," separated from the product of their labor, which was loaded onto carts and "driven by boys with white frocks ornamented with artificial flowers and gay ribbons." This spectacular procession drew a crowd of tens of thousands and was praised in the press and commemorated in popular prints based on a watercolor by John Lewis Krimmel.[26]

As the art historian Alexander Nemerov has noted, the meat parade and the prints of it that circulated through the 1860s served "to dramatize, and even create, the respectable professional identity of the city's victuallers,"[27]

Figure 12.4. John Lewis Krimmel, artist, *Procession of Victuallers of Philadelphia, on the 15th of March, 1821* ([Philadelphia]: Engraved by J. Yeager, printed by Charles Woodward Jr., [1821]). Reproduced courtesy of American Antiquarian Society, Worcester, Massachusetts.

helping to legitimize butchers and celebrate the men responsible for creating improved animals and the abundant meat that came from them, all of which sold in just fourteen hours on the day following the procession. A key moment in the killing of animals in American history, this meat parade perhaps marks the beginning of the disconnection between the people and their meat, as thousands of Philadelphians clearly reveled in this spectacle of killing and consumption on a grand scale, done for them by newly legitimate professionals heralding a new era of food processing. In Philadelphia, as urban, middle-class Americans stopped raising and killing their own meat, the bodies of both animals and human laborers became, briefly, hypervisible.

This effort to legitimize the butcher was a transnational project in the early nineteenth century, seen in texts such as *The Experienced Butcher*, published in 1816 and intended to show "the respectability and usefulness of his calling."[28] It can also be seen in material culture, in a series of model butcher shops that have been subject to debate over their intended audience. Are they, as the historian Robert Culff argues, children's toys from an era when young people would have had a closer relationship to the sources of their meat, or were they instead created as advertisements to be displayed in the butcher shop's window? Culff suggests that these were popular toys, as children enjoyed "taking down and wrapping Sunday joints for one's brothers and sisters, and presumably a certain amount about the prime cuts of meat was learned painlessly in the doing of it."[29]

These models reflected the emergence of the retail butcher shop as an urban sight and site, and like the victuallers' parade, they exemplify how "making meat visible" is connected to structural changes surrounding the production and consumption of meat. The creation of new public perceptions of livestock, butchers, and butcher shops through these models and spectacles that seem unusual today were, in the nineteenth century, both a reminder and a prediction of the victuallers' ability to provide plentiful meat to the American public through improvements in agriculture and meat processing. These improvements continued throughout the nineteenth century, both to animals' bodies and to the production and distribution of meat. After all, the nineteenth century also saw the rise of the slaughterhouse, a centralized system for turning animals into meat that was seen as the epitome of the "civilized" and "modern."[30]

Developments in Cincinnati, Ohio, in the first half of the nineteenth century heralded the modern pork industry, as entrepreneurs pioneered the use of mass-production techniques in their famous "disassembly line" that turned

Figure 12.5. Model of a butcher's shop made in England about 1850. Carved wood, painted; in a walnut veneered case. Reproduced courtesy of the Victoria and Albert Museum, London.

pigs into pork.[31] Visitors to Cincinnati—soon nicknamed "Porkopolis" for the hundreds of thousands of pigs that were driven to and processed in the city—marveled at this new world of animal industry. As Frederick Law Olmsted, the journalist and landscape architect, remarked in an 1857 account of what I like to call "meat tourism,"

> We entered an immense low-ceiled room and followed a vista of dead swine, upon their backs, their paws stretching mutely toward heaven. Walking down to the vanishing point, we found there a sort of human chopping-machine where the hogs were converted into commercial pork. A plank table, two men to lift and turn, two to wield the cleavers, were its component parts. No iron cog-wheels could work with more regular motion. Plump falls the hog upon the table, chop, chop; chop, chop; chop, chop, fall the cleavers. All is over. But, before you can say so, plump, chop, chop; chop, chop; chop, chop, sounds again.

There is no pause for admiration. By a skilled sleight of hand, hams, shoulders, clear, mess, and prime fly off, each squarely cut to its own place, where attendants, aided by trucks and dumb-waiters, dispatch each to its separate destiny—the ham for Mexico, its loin for Bordeaux. Amazed beyond all expectation at the celerity, we took out our watches and counted thirty-five seconds, from the moment when one hog touched the table until the next occupied its place. The number of blows required I regret we did not count. The vast slaughter-yards we took occasion not to visit, satisfied at seeing the rivers of blood that flowed from them.[32]

Thanks to the railroads, the technology of ice packing, and the centralizing forces unleashed by the Civil War, Chicago became the nation's pork-producing center, serving as "hog butcher for the world." Unlike in Cincinnati, where processors were scattered throughout the city, the postwar meat-processing industry in Chicago was centralized on the south side at the famous Union Stockyards, separating the production of meat from urban life.[33] While residents of and visitors to Cincinnati were shocked at the number of hogs in the city (Frances Trollope famously remarked, "I am sure I would have liked Cincinnati much better if the people had not dealt so very largely in hogs!"[34]), in Chicago the stockyards and processing plants became tourist destinations.

An indication of the appeal of a visit to the slaughterhouse can be found in a folder produced in 1903 by Swift & Company. This *Visitors' Reference Book* served as "a Souvenir of a visit to the plant of Swift & Company at Chicago, Ill., U.S.A., and as a reminder of the modern methods and activities of the American Meat Packing Industry."[35] This illustrated pamphlet provided facts about the size of Swift's operations, including the amount of meat produced, and emphasized the "close scrutiny" by both Swift and government inspectors of both the animals in the stockyards and the meat produced from their bodies for the public. The tour of the plant and the depictions of it included in this souvenir enabled the public to observe the conversion of animals into meat, from the visitors' entrance ("where the real sight seeing begins") to the loading platform where dressed meat was shipped "to every part of the known world."

Of particular note are the images of the transformation of living pigs into pork, remarkable in their depiction of a well-dressed family observing the hog pens and witnessing the killing of the pigs, deaths enabled by "the skilled

Station 2

Beginning Hog Dressing

AFTER a rest and a shower
bath the hogs are driven, a
dozen or more at a time, into a
pen at the base of the automatic hoisting wheel.
Each one is then shackled to the moving wheel
which raises the hog steadily until the shackle
hook is dropped to a sliding rail. On this rail
the animals pass the skilled dispatcher who starts
eight hundred an hour on the journey through
the dressing and cleaning rooms to the vast coolers.

Figure 12.6. "Beginning Hog Dressing," from Swift & Company, *Visitors' Reference Book* (1903). Reproduced courtesy of Advertising Ephemera Collection Database #A0340, Emergence of Advertising On-Line Project, John W. Hartman Center for Sales, Advertising & Marketing History, David M. Rubenstein Rare Book & Manuscript Library, Duke University, Durham, North Carolina.

dispatcher who starts eight hundred an hour on the journey through the dressing and cleaning rooms to the vast coolers." To today's viewer, the drawing of a little girl playing on the railing as the pigs behind her are being killed seems remarkable, for it is virtually impossible to imagine that level of interest in, much less access to, today's processing plants. As far as I can tell, no contemporary slaughterhouse offers public tours. In fact much of what we know about the meat industrial complex comes from journalists and activists who have successfully and often surreptitiously infiltrated these operations.[36]

The question that remains, of course, is how to account for this transformation. When did the killing of animals and processing of meat become largely invisible? As we have seen, slaughterhouses were to some degree publicly accessible and promoted themselves as such for much of the nineteenth and twentieth centuries, marking the pride that meat-processing firms took in their modern technologies that put food on Americans' tables. Producers turned the production of meat into a marketing opportunity, and through factory tours and product advertising they encouraged Americans to consume both meat and the spectacle of its production at a moment marked by the expansion of industrial capitalism and increased competition for urban consumers. Through at least the early part of the twentieth century, production and consumption were intertwined as what would become known as "factory farming" initially meant something positive: the triumph of agricultural engineering and the concomitant glorification of new and more efficient means of production that reduced prices and increased availability for consumers.[37]

While farmers and meat processors still take pride in their efficiency and their ability to feed more and more people, their means of production are much harder to see given the changes to the relationship between consumers and their food. Shifting public sensibilities, linked in part to transformations during the postwar period that saw the growth of animal welfare and animal rights movements, concerns about the environment and sustainability, and the passage of laws such as the Humane Slaughter Act of 1958, have made "factory farming" today a term that raises consumer concern, just as a century of food literature has gone from Upton Sinclair's factory- (and labor-) centered *The Jungle* (1906) to Eric Schlosser's consumer-centered *Fast Food Nation: The Dark Side of the All-American Meal* (2002). Interestingly, increasing environmental consciousness and consumer concern about the ethics and implications of food production in the post–World War II era have coincided with a steady decrease in public access to food production, a concomitant distancing between animals and meat, and the complete disappearance of these living animals from our everyday lives.

The Cultural Work of Bacon Mania

Consumer concern about animal welfare, labor, food safety, health, and the environmental costs of factory farming has been much on display in recent years, found in what seems like an endless number of books that diagnose what is wrong with our contemporary food system and suggest ways forward that range from "conscious carnivorism" to veganism. Many Americans have realized that eating is perhaps their most significant daily interaction with the environment and, through their food choices, are seeking to have a different and perhaps more authentic and ethical relationship to their food.

The meat industry is well aware of the challenges posed by new consumption patterns, as consumers who have always preferred convenience and low prices increasingly seem worried about food quality and safety and the welfare of the animals in modern systems of food production.[38] The pork industry, always attentive to consumer trends (think of the 1987 rebranding of pork as "the other white meat" in response to the surge in poultry consumption), has been forced to respond to a counterrevolution (actually, a return to tradition) that has followed in the wake of its success. Consumer interest in both better-tasting pork and animal welfare has led to the growth of niche pork producers. These producers, the most well known of which is the Niman Ranch Company, are "trying to adapt to who the pig is," rather than forcing the pig into an efficiency-based system. Niman Ranch pigs graze in pastures and root at the earth. They are produced naturally, meaning no artificial insemination, no growth-producing hormones or antibiotics, and no reconstituted pig leftovers for food; they are fed a vegetarian diet. Even though Niman Ranch pork costs more, the company is often unable to find enough producers to raise pigs according to its protocols to meet consumer demand.[39]

Much of the recent interest in niche pork is tied to the slow-food movement and the rediscovery of traditional foodways in Europe and America. American food critics and aficionados celebrate the Ibérico pig from southwestern Spain. These pigs, fed on acorns in the wooded meadowlands known as the *dehesa*, produce meat that is dark, red, and finely striated with fat. Even better, this fat is monounsaturated, the kind that is more healthful and produces complex flavors and aromas. *Jamón ibérico de bellota*, produced from pigs fed exclusively on acorns and herbs, is said to literally melt in your mouth. Ibérico hams are treated like fine wines and are expensive (hams imported to the United States can cost as much as one thousand dollars each), confirming the criticism that consuming food that is both tastier and better for humans and animals is a class privilege.[40]

Americans' hopes for their own Ibérico are placed on the Ossabaw Island pig, a descendent of the pigs the Spanish let loose on the islands of the southeast coast of North America. The pigs that survived on this Georgia coastal island are rare, and their pork is heavily marbled, making them a delicacy. While some small-scale farmers are raising Ossabaws and other heritage breeds for individuals and for restaurant use (for example, Emile DeFelice's Caw Caw Creek farm for twenty years raised "heirloom pastured pork" in the woods outside Columbia, South Carolina), other households are moving toward self-sufficiency by keeping livestock, including pigs. While chickens dominate the "urban farming" movement, pigs can be kept provided one has enough space (experts recommend a yard at least thirty feet by thirty feet), tolerant neighbors, and the proper permits. The Tamworth breed is often recommended for backyard farmers, for a feeder pig purchased at a weight of forty pounds will reach full growth and a butchering weight of two hundred pounds in about five months. However, both backyard and small farmers in the United States currently face a shortage of slaughterhouses to process their meat, as local, family-owned operations closed in the face of stricter health controls and the consolidation of the pork industry.[41]

Although relatively few people are raising their own pigs and restoring nearly extinct breeds, some are working to re-create artisanal pork traditions in the United States. In downtown Seattle, Armandino Batali makes, sells, and serves culatello, prosciutto, salami, and soppressata at his restaurant Salumi. Batali produces twenty-five hundred pounds of cured meat per month, with the pork coming from white-hoofed Berkshire hogs raised in Kansas, where they are free to root and range on a fifteen-hundred-acre spread. The meat, free of hormones, additives, and water injections and marked by large amounts of marbled, intramuscular fat, has attained mythic status among American foodies.[42] This effort to produce a more natural pig depends on the contrasting industrial pig to make it more palatable—culturally and gastronomically—to the higher-end consumer.

The popularity of Salumi and similar restaurants that can be found throughout the United States is part of a renewed interest in pigs and pork in the American culinary community, one in which pigs appear to be the foodie animal of choice. Numerous Web sites (including that for the Bacon of the Month Club) and blogs promote artisanal varieties of bacon and ham; several restaurants specialize in pigs and pork (including Donald Link's Cochon in New Orleans); and several pork-based cookbooks, including Stephane Reynaud's *Pork and Sons* (which won the Grand Prix de la Gastronomie Française in 2005) and Martin Picard's *Au Pied de Cochon—The Album* (drawn from his Montreal restaurant), have become best sellers. Pork has been so newsworthy in recent years that one writer has called this a "porcine renaissance," one marked by chocolate-bacon candy bars, pork cocktails, and chefs with pig- and pork-related tattoos.[43]

In addition to this fetish for naturally raised pork, which suggests that it is more appropriate for our human nature to eat more authentic natural pork, the current interest in all things bacon-related also reflects a new way to rebel against an increasingly health-conscious society. Fast-food products such as Wendy's Baconator (six strips of bacon atop a half-pound cheeseburger) and backyard inventions such as the Bacon Explosion (two pounds of bacon wrapped around two pounds of sausage and grilled, created by Jason Day and Aaron Chronister of Kansas City and publicized on their BBQ Addicts blog) are responses to elite foodie snobbery and claims to democratic eating pleasures. As Sarah Hepola writes in a summary of this bacon mania, for many, "loving bacon is like shoving a middle finger in the face of all that is healthy and holy while an unfiltered cigarette smolders between your lips"[44]—a way of demonstrating that one is not politically correct, not a vegan or a vegetarian, and not particularly concerned about the lives and deaths of delicious pigs.

Unbeknownst to most, however, the celebration of bacon in modern America has historical roots. In the United States today pork ranks third in per capita consumption behind chicken and beef, but in the nineteenth century pork consumption was so prevalent that Dr. John S. Wilson of Columbus, Georgia, wrote, "[T]he United States of America might properly be called the great Hog-Eating Confederacy, or the Republic of Porkdom." He noted that "so far as meat is concerned, it is fat bacon and pork, fat bacon and pork only, and that continually morning, noon, and night, for all classes, sexes, ages and conditions."[45] As Thomas Andrews notes earlier in this volume, this held true even among enslaved peoples, as bacon sat at the top of their list of longed-for meats. Connections between Americans and pork were made visible in *The Porcineograph*, an 1875 map of the United States in the shape of a pig, commissioned by William Emerson Baker as a souvenir for guests at the opening of his "sanitary piggery" in Needham, Massachusetts, and in an 1884 map titled *Nicknames of the States*, produced by H. W. Hill & Co. of Decatur, Illinois.[46]

The food-service industry helped fuel the recent bacon craze by adding the product to dishes and meals in which it had not been eaten before (most bacon has been typically consumed at breakfast, as strips). Retail innovations followed, especially the development and marketing of precooked bacon and flavored bacon. While at the high end there is interest in artisanal bacon that is slow-cured in traditional ways, for the most part the bacon being celebrated and consumed is the industrial product that can be produced in a modern pork-processing plant in a matter of hours (with wet-curing and vein pumping long ago replacing dry-curing of hams and bacon). Much of this obsession with bacon, however, does not involve pigs or pork at all, for there are countless bacon-themed products in consumer culture, including adhesive bandages, gift wrap, iPhone cases, and a seemingly endless variety of t-shirts. Bacon increasingly appears in places where one does not expect it, exceeding the boundaries of food while being literally disembodied.

Figure 12.7. Nicknames of the States, c. 1884. H. W. Hill & Co., Decatur, Illinois. Reproduced courtesy of Library of Congress Prints and Photographs Division, Washington, D.C., LC-DIG-pga-03942.

Figure 12.8. Chromolithographed trade card (interior), 1893, for Nelson Morris & Co., Chicago. The card is in the shape of a ham that opens to illustrate the meat production process. See Figure 12.9 for the exterior of the card. Reproduced courtesy of American Antiquarian Society, Worcester, Massachusetts.

Even many of the bacon-flavored products on the market are distanced from the lives and deaths of pigs thanks to the ability to synthesize the flavor of bacon chemically. These products seem to be everywhere, largely thanks to Justin and Dave's Down Home Enterprises, a company whose motto is "Everything Should Taste Like Bacon." They sell a range of bacon-flavored salts and a bacon mayonnaise called, unsurprisingly, "Baconnaise" that the comedian Jon Stewart described as the perfect product "for people who want heart disease but are too lazy to actually make the bacon."[47] However, these products are kosher and in the case of the salts vegetarian, for there is no actual pork in these food items. Artificial bacon flavoring has detached bacon from actual pigs, perhaps most obviously in bacon mouthwash and in the develop-

Figure 12.9. Chromolithographed trade card, 1893, for Nelson Morris & Co., Chicago. The card is in the shape of a ham that opens to illustrate the meat production process. Pictured is the exterior of the card; see Figure 12.8 for the interior. Reproduced courtesy of American Antiquarian Society, Worcester, Massachusetts.

ment (by Justin and Dave, of course) of bacon-flavored personal lubricant that one can use with latex condoms colored to look like strips of bacon.[48]

This extension of bacon beyond a food item into unrelated consumer products tells us a lot about viral marketing and our desire to celebrate the marginal and kitschy. It also tells us about our relationship to pigs. The hypervisibility of bacon, however cleverly presented, turns the lives of pigs and the production and consumption of meat into a joke (bacon-flavored lube literally began as an April Fools' joke before enough people wanted the product to justify producing it). Within the joke, however, lies a promiscuous connection between hypervisibility and invisibility. Whether as foodie fetish, fast-food anachronism, or novelty item, the more bacon appears in American

life, the more it seems to distance humans from pigs. Tracing these connections begins to illuminate the political structures that sustain the investment in
separating nature and culture.

The bacon meme in contemporary American culture also runs in uncanny parallel with the promotion of anti-whistle-blower laws in many states
that have come to be known as "ag-gag" laws. These bills seek to criminalize
efforts to expose the conditions on factory farms and are promoted and supported by agribusiness interests and groups such as the American Legislative
Exchange Council, which produces model legislation for state legislatures.
These laws are designed to make it difficult for employees to expose the mis-
treatment of animals, violations of labor laws, or environmental problems
and often seek to criminalize undercover work and the taking of photographs
or videos at factory farms. Thankfully most of these laws have failed to
pass thanks to outcry from animal activists, the general public, and journalists, although the lack of transparency in our food system remains a major
problem. As Mark Bittman put it after all of his requests to visit food producers
in Iowa were ignored or rejected, "When a journalist can't see how the food
we eat is produced, you don't need ag-gag laws. The system's already gagged."[49]

Industry efforts to promote these "ag-gag" laws share the same belief in
the politics of transparency that motivates activists, reminding us that "the
impulse to link sight and political transformation is strong."[50] While making
visible what we are doing to pigs and other farm animals may promote a more
humane and sustainable relationship to animals and nature, many people
still do not want to know how farm animals are raised and meat is produced,
or if they do know, they manage to compartmentalize this information to
keep on consuming inexpensive and abundant meat. Moreover some forms of
visibility preserve as much as they critique the capacity to separate pig from
pork—or pigs from humans. Artisanal pork and bacon mania obscure the long
history of interconnections between our two species, relationships that have
together produced both humanness and pigness on multiple levels. The issue is
not just what pigs mean to us and our culture, but how we are all deeply
enmeshed with animals economically, politically, technologically, culturally,
biologically, and historically. The story of humans and pigs complicates how
we codify, categorize, and connect life forms. These stories suggest that
thinking in binary and essentialist terms—pigs/humans, nature/culture—
helps to produce a politics of invisibility that obscures those connections
and underwrites the meat-industrial complex. It appears that when it comes
to animals, our contradictory attitudes and practices are the norm.[51]

Chapter 13

"Bring Tent": The Occupy Movement and the Politics of Public Nature

Phoebe S. K. Young

In the initial poster campaign that served as a catalyst for the Occupy Wall Street movement (OWS) in 2011, the central objective remained an open question: What is our one demand? Those drawn to participate shared a sense of outrage with economic inequality and alienation from the political process but generated little initial consensus on a list of specific reforms for which to agitate. The form of protest, however, was precise; instructions indicated a date, a place, and a single instruction: "Bring Tent." The tactic took off in ways that surprised both organizers and observers. At the height of its initial wave that fall, Occupy encampments sprouted in hundreds of cities in the United States and beyond, with at least fifty substantial and lasting tent protests in major urban areas from the original location in Lower Manhattan to Oakland, California.[1] The ultimate impact of the movement continues to be a matter of debate, and yet from the moment Occupiers made camp, they activated a series of potent cultural associations. For protesters, the tent might have promised nothing more than basic practical protection from the elements and simple visual testimony to their intent to stay. In the months that followed, however, their chosen shelter became a more complicated symbol than they may have anticipated. It kindled deep and often contradictory historical references that altered the course of the movement. In the end the tent became both medium and message, and the cause came to focus on the right to occupy.

It is possible to read this as a shift from substance to form, as a diminishment or distraction, as if the tent diverted attention from Occupy's substantive political challenge. Examples of this interpretation abounded. Some wished that Occupiers would abandon their disordered camps and articulate a more legible message, as more traditional marches or media events might do. The tent also served as a vehicle to deride the protesters as a bunch of white, wealthy tree huggers left over from the Battle of Seattle (the 1999 demonstrations against the World Trade Organization) with nothing better to do with their North Face gear. For others, tents associated Occupiers with handout-seeking homeless people and thus an urban nuisance rather than a legitimate assembly. Yet to dismiss the tent as merely a superficial manifestation of more authentic underlying causes and demands would miss much of the history of OWS. The tent was not a superfluous oddity. It sat at the heart of the movement's political approach, what it did and did not do, why it worked, why people reacted, and why it eventually got shut down.

To focus on the tent entails thinking about the entanglement of nature and culture it evokes, even though few observers explicitly placed it in meaningful relation to any traditional setting in nature. The tent cities of OWS appeared worlds apart from the idealized vision of woods and wilderness that camping out usually connotes.[2] The tent, together with its association with nature and the outdoors, is key to understanding the scope of the movement's resonance in American political culture. We have to ask why, in this particular social movement, the tent appeared simultaneously obvious, audacious, and natural. Why did it capture public attention and the movement's focus? This essay argues that it was precisely because the tent evoked ways that the outdoors has served historically as critical space for negotiating civic belonging and national identity.

There are three modes in which the tent has historically made meaning: political, functional, and recreational. Whether deployed as political pressure device, functional means of travel and habitation, or base for nature-oriented recreation, a tent lays claim to public space and identity. The multiple frameworks, however, tend to overlap, collide, and create ambiguity. If leisure camping appears wholesome and innocent, homeless camping might suggest danger and disorder. Camping out for a political cause might slip all too easily into reminders of one or the other, depending on the type of gear displayed. In any frame of reference, camping tacitly draws on historical narratives about individualism, freedom, and America as "nature's nation." The preeminent example is the National Park System, which exemplifies the use of natural spaces for establishing national identity. When Americans camp in Yosemite or Yellowstone, they render places of wild nature as national culture, as civic spaces for seeing and performing Americanness.[3]

The converse can also be true. If tents make the natural into the civic, they can also make the civic seem a part of nature. Camping renders space we might regard as private, unnatural, and controlled—in the case of Occupy city streets, government plazas, and bank facades—as a form of *public nature*. More than greening pockets of urban space, practices that render a place as part of the natural world can make it newly available to claim and define the public good. Tents come with a well-established set of narratives about nature and its uses. How do you transform Wall Street, a place of ownership and private property, into a place that reminds us of shared destinies and public commitments? The answer is, make it seem like a national park campground. More than a tree or a park bench, the tent made it possible to envision the concrete Zuccotti Park in Lower Manhattan as shared nature (rather than high finance) and thus made Occupy's arguments about equity and democracy more legible on the landscape.

How can a tent do this narrative work of political culture? As an example of the evidence for this process, briefly consider Figure 13.1, a poster designed by the staff at the Vancouver-based radical magazine *Adbusters* in the summer of 2011 as part of the initial call to action.[4] An early example of Occupy's visual style of internal and external communication, "Yes We Camp" uses a hip language of poster art that combines bold graphics, catchy phrases, and glossy satire.[5] What you might first notice is the cheeky play on the "Yes We Can" message of Barack Obama's 2008 presidential campaign. Recurring on handwritten signs, printed buttons, and graphic images, the "Yes We Camp" slogan could sound derisive, disappointed, hopeful, or merely ironic. In any case, invoking this well-known phrase attempted to tap into the power that had mobilized new political energy. Moreover it explicitly invoked the political mode of camping and envisioned an outside-the-booth strategy to achieve change through tent occupation.

Now look at the tent symbol in the poster. Not just any drawing of a tent, this displays the standard icon used by the National Park Service (NPS) on roadside signage directing drivers to designated campgrounds. As such, it tapped into a thick history that evoked the promise of the national parks to link nature and nation, camping and citizenship. The logo identifies camping

Figure 13.1. Making camp on political culture. "#OCCUPYWALLSTREET: Yes We Camp," *Adbusters*, August 16, 2011.

as a state-sponsored and subsidized activity, a wholesome and patriotic form of recreation and all-around social and civic good. Immersed in a political action, would these recreational associations occlude the seriousness of the protest? Some Occupiers would later disavow mere recreation, insisting, "We are not happy campers." To be an unhappy camper implied less savory associations and risked running afoul of the recreational privileges of camping. Many cities followed this reasoning and treated Occupy as they would homeless encampments, where functional camping represented a misuse of public space and campers people without rights to it. Although the NPS clearly has a mandate to control space and regulate practices—camp here and not there, this way and not that—it became one of the few public agencies defending Occupy as a political action rather than (functional or recreational) camping. Park Service director Jonathan Jarvis noted that the Washington, D.C., public spaces that protesters occupied were "First Amendment sites"—although, in a dispute played out in a televised hearing, some members of Congress did not share the same interpretations of the relationships between protesting, camping, sleeping, and exercising free-speech rights on a taxpayer-funded lawn.[6]

If national park land in the nation's capital brought up complicated negotiations, then what would happen at Wall Street, to which this poster instructed you to "Bring Tent"? The site of the first OWS protest, Zuccotti Park in Lower Manhattan, is a form of "privatized public space" that, as Hal Rothman observed, is the result of longer trends reducing shared urban space and replacing it with "private space [that] masquerades as public." Occupy's own battles, occurring as they did in this blurred terrain of public and private, shared and commercial, open and restricted, thus engaged core tensions in modern American life. By using narratives of nature in these complicated spaces, Occupiers chose a provocative mode by which to claim some ground for the public.[7] As material object, the tent implies the natural setting that typically surrounds it. The NPS recreational tent logo, set against the columns of the New York Stock Exchange rather than a scene of nature, simultaneously invoked and inverted those expectations. It provoked audiences to think about Wall Street in the same way they might think of a national park: as a public regulated space, as a national treasure, as a promise for future generations. The poster, and Occupy more broadly, explicitly drew upon layers of historical meaning invested in tents, camping, and national parks as part of its implicit political message. These forms of public nature became vehicles to assert voice, access, and a sense of commonwealth and shared future.

The tents of Occupy sat at the margins of politics and in between environmental history and cultural studies. The phenomenon resists obvious inclusion in a materialist-oriented environmental history, but without the environmental lens we might miss how outdoor space served as the fulcrum for the movement. Thus to figure out what the tent came to mean in this moment draws us into thinking about the entanglement of social practices, material products, cultural narratives, visual representations, historical memories, outdoor spaces, and natural elements. The sections that follow offer different readings of the tent as public object: 1) as part of a legacy of explicit, visible means for political protest; 2) as the fulcrum for considerations of transience and permanence, home and homeless; 3) as part of a tacit dialogue about access to nature and citizenship; and 4) as a meme for the expression of an aesthetic sensibility and a kind of rugged innocence. These episodes do not map neatly onto the contexts of political, functional, or recreational camping, each of which exists as a mode of practice and framework of discourse, all latent in any particular use. Rather each section treats a different point of convergence and conflict—where Occupiers and observers reckoned with the multiple meanings of their tents and made claims for civic belonging in terms of public nature.

Tent Army

Occupy blossomed as a unique feature on the twenty-first-century political scene, in part because of the tents. What motivated the organizers of this improbable movement to adopt camping in public spaces as its essential tactic? In an immediate sense, Occupy leaders envisioned themselves as the inheritors (and hopeful translators) of the energy of 2011's Arab Spring—as well as the tent-based protests by youth movements in Spain and Israel that followed. In a July 2011 public blog post that initiated the call to Occupy Wall Street on September 17, the editors of *Adbusters* explicitly invoked the memory of Tahrir Square. Their hope was to echo the form of the "Mubarak must go" chant by "incessantly repeating" an uncomplicated demand "in a plurality of voices." Camping offered a platform on which to sustain this drumbeat of protest. "If we can hang in there, 20,000 strong, week after week against every police and National Guard that tries to expel us," the editors reasoned, the nation would have to pay attention. The post ended with a call to "screw up our courage [and] pack our tents."[8]

Images of protesters defending their camps against attempts to dislodge them galvanized media attention in the early weeks of the protest. Occupiers noted how these clashes over place were making an impact, even as they encountered difficulty identifying the "one demand" among a diverse set of constituents with multiple causes and needs. Thus, in the face of public pressure to identify what Occupy was all about, members of the New York City General Assembly, the consensus-oriented representative body for the Wall Street occupation and proxy voice of the national movement, began to veer away from the language of "demands." Instead "they opted to make their demand the occupation itself—and the direct democracy taking place there," hoping that even a small, "somewhat rowdy occupation" would generate greater leverage than a traditional march.[9] Theorists looking back on this shift have argued that by refusing to comply with "proper" forms of politics that submit an enumerated list of "satisfiable demands" to accepted authorities, Occupy called attention to "the enormity of the problem" and modeled an impossible reimagining of society that exposed the very "illegitimacy of those authorities."[10] This apt, but post hoc, description does not quite capture the reasons why an initial focus on demands shifted toward the practice of camping in Occupy's evolving strategy of absurdist political theater. Nor does it explain why the public responded to the tent in such a way as to steer the answer to the initial question, "what is our one demand?, toward this deceptively simple object of public nature.

Occupy's commitment to a narrative about its impromptu origins and leaderless philosophy, and its desire to share in contemporary transnational protest energies, has obscured the reasoning process behind the decision to camp. Whether intuitive or deliberate, the decision to pitch tents was not random, historically speaking. Key precedents from the nineteenth and twentieth centuries suggest that its tactics were not as odd as one might think; they also suggest why the public took notice. Focus on the tent—as medium and then message—was newly explicit, but protesters who camp out for a cause are not new.

In the 1980s college campuses became primary sites for anti-Apartheid demonstrators, who set up "shantytowns" to pressure university administrators toward South African divestment. The particular appearance of these shacks, which symbolized the living conditions of South African blacks, differed from tents but shared similar purposes as tent-based protest. Evolving from the typical spectrum of activist tactics, anti-Apartheid activists decided that "sit-outs," camp-outs, and the shantytown attracted more media attention than rallies or sit-ins did in part because they disrupted the tidy campus landscape. Moreover organizers came to realize that the outdoor protests created a greater sense of inclusion and community among protesters.[11] In the 1960s and 1970s protests occasionally evolved into longer occupations in a similar fashion, perhaps most notably in May and June 1968 when the Washington Mall hosted what became known as Resurrection City, the culmination of Martin Luther King, Jr.'s Poor People's Campaign. With an eye to capturing the kind of public attention that the 1963 March on Washington had, the campaign highlighted multiracial poverty and urban issues. The thousands who marched to D.C. in the wake of King's assassination decided to stay; for six weeks twenty-six hundred people camped out on the National Mall in sheet-plastic frame tents.[12]

None of these protests was new either. The most commonly identified predecessor of Occupy was the 1932 Bonus Army. That year unemployed World War I veterans descended on Washington to pressure Congress to speed up the payment of bonuses they had been promised in recognition for overseas service. While the bonuses were not due to be paid until 1945, struggling and unemployed veterans took up the cause in the depths of the Depression to demand early payment as a form of relief. The Bonus Expeditionary Force came to include tens of thousands of recruits, many of whom camped out on the banks of the Anacostia River for two months in the summer of 1932. The group organized in military fashion, hoping to appear orderly and respectable rather than a rag-tag bunch of bums, despite close spatial proximity and the setting's visual resemblance to a Hooverville. Various public relations tactics—posing for and then peddling photographs of themselves maintaining neat, ordered families within canvas households—earned support and sustained pressure on Congress and the Hoover administration.[13]

When the proposed bill to grant the early payment was defeated, President Hoover decided to disperse the camp and its unsightly reminder of the nation's struggles. In late July he ordered the army to clear out the campers. Led by Gen. Douglas MacArthur, soldiers employed tanks and tear gas and then "applied the torch to the shacks in which the veterans lived." Though veterans defended their positions with weapons improvised from the grounds, "the disordered camp," the *New York Times* reported, quickly became "a mass of flames as the bonus seeking veterans set fire to their own miserable shacks." Two veterans were killed, and dozens were injured.[14] Because of both its presence and its violent destruction by the army, the camp made the veterans' protest more visible. The bonus marchers failed to achieve their central demand, but historians typically interpret the incident as undermining Hoover's reelection chances and shifting the political conversation around the federal government's role in addressing the economic crisis.

Less than a month after Occupy began the encampment at Wall Street, dozens of radio, television, and newspaper stories connected it to the Bonus Army, to different ends. A radio story likened the staying power and impromptu communities and speculated on Occupy's long-term prospects for success as compared to the effect that the Bonus Army may have had in fostering subsequent support for more substantive veterans' benefits, such as the G.I. Bill. Other reports in the newspaper and on television paralleled the forceful evictions of the Bonus Army and the Occupy camps, specifically in Oakland, California, as a cautionary tale of how such heavy hands can come back to haunt those who wield them. Historical comparisons to both the Bonus Army and Resurrection City suggested for others why the protests were unlikely to be effective, arguing that while public sympathy might reject police violence, it was difficult to sustain public support for countercultural groups that make mud-filled shantytowns of public places.[15]

A few others found the 1894 demonstration known as Coxey's Army, perhaps the original "March on Washington," to be even more amenable to historical lesson making. Jacob Coxey, a former iron-mill worker and a Populist, rallied several thousand men, many of them from the West and all of them reeling from the severe 1893 financial panic, who hopped trains, walked, and camped their way toward the Capitol with the aim to make a major claim for federal investment in infrastructure, public utilities, and unemployment relief. Their "petition in boots" struggled against a perception that they were idle tramps. They tried to represent themselves as citizens in search of democratic access, commanded national media attention (if not always sympathy) for weeks, and declared the Capitol grounds the rightful "property of the people." While some marchers were tolerated, others were arrested, and a force of hundreds of police barred Coxey from mounting the Capitol steps on May 1 to make a speech. Followers camped out in protest for three months, but as media interest waned, they began to disperse with no concrete results to claim other than establishing this precedent for future public protests. As one commentator noted in 2011, despite the immediate crackdown on Coxey's protest, his proposal for public investment eventually became accepted as a standard federal response to financial crisis; the implication was that "Occupy Wall Street should be so lucky" as to be a harbinger of future reforms. OWS had the chance to "influence the debate for decades ahead. It just needs some ideas."[16] Predicting success or failure, the common denominator among these searches for historically comparable tent armies was less the content of protest than the way the act of camping made protest visible.

These camping episodes, if understood broadly as ways to claim public identity and visibility, were not altogether new. In the post–Civil War era camping was crucial to the creation of the identity of the veteran as the emblematic U.S. citizen. Organizations such as the Grand Army of the Republic

(GAR), as the historian Stuart McConnell has suggested, worked out the "story about the place of the Union veteran in the newly restored Union and, at a deeper level, a story about the new Union itself."[17] The success of this veteran identity had much to do with its focus around the social rituals and remembrance of camp. What veterans recalled with fondness from camp life—the male camaraderie, the domestic haven from battle, the small comforts—typically omitted difficulties such as lice, dysentery, and dying friends. But more than nostalgia was at work. The GAR organized its local outposts as "Camps" and labeled its annual reunions "encampments," which frequently included tents and group camps in urban parks. In 1892 the GAR convened its national encampment at Washington, D.C., and the image of white, peaked tents in the shadow of the recently completed Washington Monument made a powerful visual connection between camping and national identity. As Union veterans became the embodiment of U.S. citizens of the restored union, their practices became embedded in the national reunification, along the way solidifying a link between camping, citizenship, and the nation. At this early moment, then, making camp was becoming a method of making certain claims on public life, inhabiting public space in a way that connected the nation and the outdoors.

In this way tents were not always symbols of the displaced or a kind of last-resort action. Tent armies could be literal, and the image of the veteran in his tent was a powerful one (in part what both Coxey's Army and the Bonus Army had been attempting to reference). But tents were also tools of state occupation, used more often to colonize than to resist. In the late nineteenth century not just veterans but also active troops in an expanding U.S. Army intent on clearing Indian title to western lands pursued conquest in part by making camp. The tent was thus not as inherently rebellious or as innocent as Occupiers may have wanted it to appear. It was symbolic of both the obligations and the freedoms of individual citizenship (veteran, protester) and the power and responsibility of the nation-state (to secure access to public lands as well as colonize and displace Indian people). To view tents only as weapons of the weak, symbols of how marginalized the protesters feel, does not account for these layers of history. In part tents make protest visible because they rest on a history of power in camping—in the ability to displace others and make other claims less visible while literally occupying space.

OWS displaced and obscured some claims even as it made others more visible, as the "Take Back Wall Street" poster shown in Figure 13.2 suggests.[18]

The message references the European takeover of Indian land as a prior form of occupation to turn the usual message on its head. First, the twist of taking back land already occupied suggests a long historical view. Wall Street's origins lie in the wall erected by Dutch settlers in the 1640s. Built by both white colonists and African slave labor, the wall was meant to protect the northern boundary of New Amsterdam from indigenous people inhabiting the rest of the island of Manhattan as well as from potential incursions by English colonists. By 1699, when it was taken down to allow urban expansion, the wall had become a twelve-foot-high fortification of substantial strength. The new residents kept the name Wall Street and its echo of early European occupation as well as its functionality as a meeting point for commercial traders.[19] In this sense the poster seems to be calling attention to the hidden ironies of reoccupying Wall Street, to liberate it back from seventeenth-century colonizers and twenty-first-century financiers (perhaps still in cahoots). And yet the quaintly styled font and an old-time, tinted photograph of a Lenape woman (cropped from an original taken around 1915) in traditional dress shaped the message as a historical remnant. She appears less as a person with a claim to make than as historic guilty conscience, the ghost of "occupy" past. Instead of using Occupy to bolster native land claims, the "Take Back Wall Street" poster uses an image of an indigenous woman to strengthen the claims of Occupy.[20] As a tool to "take back" Wall Street, Occupy's reading of history collapses context and creates invisibility. On whose behalf does Occupy claim to retake Wall Street? The answer is, more likely "the 99 percent" than the woman in the image. The implication is that Indian people (who composed almost exactly 1 percent of the U.S. population in 2010) are historic evidence of, or mascot for, the oppressed 99 percent rather than part of it.[21] The legacy of appropriation here—vanished Indian as metaphor for the subjugation of non-Indian people—serves to make Occupy visible at the continued expense of Indian political claims.

Other than the image of the tent or the word "Occupy," the 99 percent to 1 percent framing was the most resonant cultural artifact to come out of the first season of Occupy. On the one hand, 99 percent communicates inclusivity—almost all of us sharing an interest in reducing inequalities of wealth, grounds for common cause between seemingly countercultural protesters and "mainstream" Americans. Yet, on the other hand, within such a wide swath it is perhaps not surprising that participants jostled for voice and identity. Tents became part of this bid to define one's relationship to the

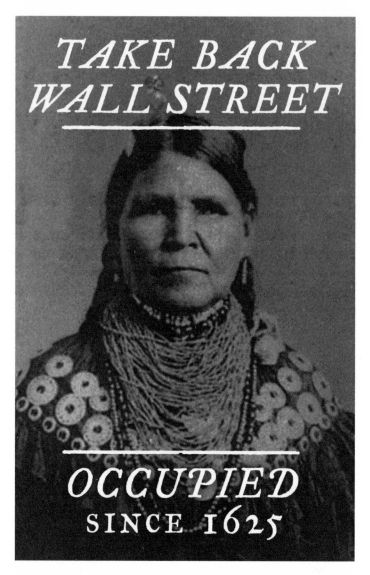

Figure 13.2. Occupy seventeenth-century-style. John Emerson, "Take Back Wall Street," October 7, 2011. The woman in the image is Jennie Bobb (Lenape), cropped from a photograph taken of her with her daughter in Oklahoma, c. 1915. John Emerson, "Take Back Wall Street," October 7, 2011, 56928, National Anthropological Archives, Smithsonian Institution, Washington, D.C. Reproduced courtesy of John Emerson.

99 percent. Sometimes the use of expensive branded camping equipment could draw the critique that protesters were simply rich kids playing at protest. At other times tents became markers of identity and inclusion, staking a claim to visibility within the movement.

An early struggle in New York over the influence of anti-Semitism in Occupy is a case in point. For some protesters, including *Adbusters* editor in chief and Occupy provocateur Kalle Lasn, the new criticisms against wealth, bankers, and power reanimated older anti-Jewish refrains and hinted at an insidious hidden reading of the 1 percent.[22] Sizable numbers of American Jews in Zuccotti Park responded with a visible display of identity and participation. The autumn acceleration of Occupy coincided with important Jewish holidays, and the encampment hosted well-attended services for Rosh Hashanah and Yom Kippur. In early October 2011 the celebration of Sukkot, an eight-day festival that commemorates the post-Exodus generation of Jews who traveled without a permanent home by the ceremonial building and dwelling in a temporary booth or structure (the "sukkah"), took on central importance in the Wall Street camp. By inhabiting tents as religious structures (with an ancient historical provenance), some stenciled with the label "pop-up sukkah," not only did Jews make claims to a rightful place in Occupy, but they also played a timely role in extending the protest. Local police were less than eager to draw strict distinctions between what was a religious structure and what was just a tent and chose for a time to let them all stand.[23] Thus the tent as a modern-day sukkah celebrated the inclusiveness of Occupy while seeding a message about the search for a just homeland.

What this layered history reveals is that whether representative of religious or national identity, of participation or protest, of citizenship or colonization, tents are neither empty nor permanent. They simultaneously connote power and marginality; they display and they hide. In Occupy, and before, tents were tools for creating public identities and space, both by inhabiting outdoor places in a physical sense and by drawing upon the imagined space of the nation.

Tent Life

Tent protests have often made visible impacts because they seem to offer a more forceful demonstration of the sentiment of "we will not be moved" than day-long marches that dissipate at the end of the day. Yet tents are fundamentally mobile and temporary dwellings. The Toronto tent emblazoned with its occupants' scrawled note "I am not moving!!" hides the inevitable in plain sight.[24] Tents are designed to be mobile, and eventually this one too will be packed up and moved elsewhere. Part of the tactic of "living in public space" was to evoke the precariousness and unsustainability of living in a world of increasing inequalities. In a way the tent offered a well-positioned symbol to exemplify both staying power and social precarity.[25]

The temporary nature of camp reinforces assumptions about the permanence of home, a formula that both defines recreational camping and sits at the heart of worries about transience. From concerns about tramps in the late nineteenth century and Depression-era migrants to contemporary homelessness, functional camping has aroused suspicion. In the 1930s vacationing campers cautioned each other to employ methods and equipment that would avoid the appearance of "hoboism," just as newly established state-run campgrounds instituted rules about maximum stays and regulated size and behavior of camping groups. At times local Occupy groups were careful to differentiate their camping as political praxis from the seemingly depoliticized camps of the homeless. At other times individual Occupy protesters adopted homelessness as an issue related to their signature claims about wealth inequality, lack of access, and the foreclosure crisis. The relationship was tense, with conflicts over turf and tactics. Protesters occasionally blamed homeless people for freeloading donated food and causing problems in the encampments. Elsewhere homeless residents expressed resentment that Occupy monopolized their usual camping areas and received laxer enforcement of trespass and anticamping laws.[26] Why should protesting campers receive special treatment? Why was camping tolerated as a temporary pursuit in specified areas of nature yet drew suspicion if it was a regular need in seemingly less natural public spaces?

From a standpoint of physical necessity, the tent speaks to two basic human needs: shelter and sleep. When it comes to articulating legal doctrines, these two needs operate as separate levers by which to restrict nonrecreational camping. On the one-hand, municipal anticamping ordinances usually identify the building of structures and the taking of shelter as the key difference between sleeping outside and camping. On the other hand, the act of sleeping can render a tent protest as unlawful trespass. Yet both defining and breaking these rules demonstrate the ways that, whether overtly political or not, camping has been a potent mode for negotiating access to public space and voice. The evolution of Occupy in a place such as Boulder, Colorado, engaged issues of shelter and sleep along with narratives of adventure and transience. Occupy arrived in Boulder, a city whose identity is tightly bound to outdoor recreation, just at the moment when its unresolved local debate over homeless camping was heating up. With camps in two locations, one near the municipal building, bordering a creekside park, and a smaller group in front of the old County Courthouse near a popular pedestrian mall, Boulder's Occupiers initially struggled with whether to pursue solidarity with homeless advocates contesting the city's anticamping ordinance. In the end, while Occupy drew more attention to this volatile local issue, the efforts to shut down Occupy encampments led to new closure ordinances and stricter enforcement for all.

As was the case in many larger cities, in the 1980s the Boulder City Council enacted a ban on camping in public areas, though initially the concern there had less to do with homeless people than with wandering hippies straying out of designated campsites in surrounding areas and onto city streets. In the intervening years, Boulder grew to be a stylish base camp for affluent outdoor adventurers bent on sleeping outside in the foothills of the Rockies, even as the reaction against homeless campers intensified. Revised in 2001, the ordinance prohibited camping "with a shelter" within any city park, open space, or other city property in order to "conduct activities of daily living, such as eating or sleeping." Shelter was defined as "any cover or protection from the elements other than clothing"; under this definition, sleeping bags were considered shelter. Local specialty outfitters certainly marketed sleeping bags as state-of-the-art forms of shelter to growing numbers of backcountry enthusiasts who came to Boulder to shop for the latest in outdoor gear. Napping during the day and picnicking were exempt, as were instances during disaster and local emergency, but other violations each incurred a one-hundred-dollar fine.[27] The terms of this law, using camping for shelter as a way of controlling how citizens use space, are not unique. Homelessness is not a crime, and U.S. courts have established that criminalizing an individual's residence status is unconstitutional. Nor has the Supreme Court been willing to allow municipalities to ban the act of merely sleeping in public. As such, urban "camping" has been at the center of legal tactics to make cities less hospitable to homeless settlements.[28]

Efforts to control uses of public space served to restrict access to the public itself. In 2011 the Boulder City Council rejected calls to replace fines for camping violations with a permit system, reasoning that legalizing camping would not alleviate the underlying problems of homelessness. Local legal aid groups responded, arguing that ticketing violators more regularly, as the police began to do, de facto criminalized the status of being homeless, since the city's shelter had beds for less than one quarter of the local homeless population and those sleeping outside were without other options. The American Civil Liberties Union (ACLU) filed one case on behalf of a man who, after being turned away from the local shelter, was ticketed for using a sleeping bag outdoors on a night when the temperature dropped to eleven degrees Fahrenheit. The ACLU argued that this constituted a violation of Eighth Amendment protections—that asking this man to sleep without shelter was cruel and unusual and went against the basic human drive to live.[29] But these and other cases were unsuccessful, and the city's law was eventually upheld when the Colorado Supreme Court declined to hear the case.

Legal advocates then pursued a different tactic that attempted to use the restricted access to public outdoor space as means to a public forum. While most homeless people previously pleaded guilty to the misdemeanor to be sentenced to community service in lieu of a fine, legal volunteers aided some defendants in pleading not guilty and pressing for jury trials. The dilemma of urban camping became a way of gaining access to a potent public platform and of claiming one of the most fundamental rights of citizenship, a jury trial. This tactic highlighted the way in which anticamping laws like Boulder's marginalized those whose use of public space comes from a basis of need and privileged the leisured citizen who participates in public space through enjoyment or consumption. This implicitly undermines the ability of homeless people to function as citizens and in some cases impinges upon their physical needs.

OWS, even when not making common cause with homeless advocacy, drew attention to this tension between leisure and necessity. On the one hand, performing basic human needs such as taking shelter and sleeping in highly visible public places rendered the movement a platform for political claims and demands to be heard. On the other hand, the encampments could also hint at a sense of enjoyment through the very incongruity of a downtown campout. Occupy groups and homeless people alike could experience hardship and show tenacity in sleeping outside; each could also be understood as making a rational choice within limited options—for access either to participation or bed space. Yet Occupy's differential access to public discourse derived in part from the fact that the protesters were not primarily camping from a basis of need. Most possessed the ability to return to a home, the sine qua non of recreational camping. Still, ticketed Boulder Occupiers followed

Figure 13.3. Camping in public. Ilan Sherman, "3 Occupiers on a Frigid Snowy Night at the Occupy Boulder Tent Camp in Front of the Boulder County Courthouse on Pearl Street, Boulder CO," December 7, 2011. Reproduced courtesy of Ilan Sherman.

the lead of homeless campers in the efforts to gain a public platform by demanding jury trials and retained the services of the same local lawyer.[30]

Because Occupy inhabited this gray area between political, functional, and recreational camping, it raised the stakes of these legal forums. When a Boulder police detail opened Occupiers' tent flaps to check for illegal activities, protesters encountered a new set of issues. Do campers have an expectation of privacy in their tents, and are they thus entitled to Fourth Amendment protections against unreasonable search? Does it matter where they camp—state campground, city park, or courthouse lawn? Colorado, given its large stake in outdoor recreation and the business of camping, is an interesting state to consider this, as it gives the tent some explicit protections. In a 1997 opinion, Colorado Supreme Court justice Gregory Hobbs argued that those camping on public or private land that is not clearly marked against camping or trespass had reasonable expectations of privacy and protection against unreasonable search. Hobbs's decision served as a reminder that the Fourth Amendment protects people rather than places, including travelers staying in hotel rooms, cabins, or tents, whether their belongings suggest leisured mobility or functional transience.

In part, Hobbs argued, this derived from the physical, metaphorical, and historical elements of the tent. "Whether pitched on vacant open land or in a crowded campground, a tent screens the inhabitant therein from public view. Though it cannot be secured by a deadbolt, . . . the thin walls of a tent nonetheless are notice of its occupant's claim to privacy unless consent to enter be asked and given." Setting up a tent suggested the desire and means to create privacy, as opposed to making camp in, say, a purely natural feature such as a cave. The court also took notice of the long history of the tent in Colorado and the West. Hobbs recounted past instances of tent usage in the region, such as the buffalo-skin, "Indian stile" tents described by Lewis and Clark in their journals, which Hobbs quoted, and the canvas versions used by the U.S. Army and surveying expeditions. He told of coal miners camping in tents during the 1914 strike and having their "tent colony burned to the ground" in the Ludlow Massacre. A Boy Scout handbook and state promotional material showcasing the Rocky Mountain outdoor lifestyle highlighted recreational camps where "wilderness trekkers, families car-camping for the weekend, and many travelers passing through Colorado, make tents their home away from home." Given the variable mountain weather, the tent was the "typical and prudent outdoor habitation in Colorado for overnight or extended stay."[31] Though the decision did not grant protection to trespassing tenters, it contained a comprehensive argument for the theory that pitching a tent conveyed logical intentionality to shelter oneself and thus entailed the expectation of privacy within public nature.

In Boulder the local courts struggled with these issues as they applied to Occupy. The city's camping resolution focused more on the site and the tent than on the protection of individual rights; in January 2012 the city decided to close all local parks and public squares to any activity between 11:00 P.M. and 5:00 A.M., essentially trying to sidestep the camping issue altogether. Other cities in the aftermath of the first autumn of Occupy made similar moves to tighten regulations on "urban camping" and close off public space to long-term and night-time actions.[32] While Occupy's tents highlighted the complications and ironies around transient camping, the material consequences of changed regulations fell more on homeless people than on protesters. From one angle, Occupy provided municipalities such as Boulder an expedient catalyst for further restricting homeless campers who compromised the image of the city as an elite consumer venue for outdoor recreation.

Tent Rights

What Occupiers were doing at night in their tents emerged as the crux of the debate in Washington, D.C., where two major Occupy camps sat on federal ground. One had obtained a permit to use the concrete Freedom Plaza near the National Mall; the other occupied McPherson Square, a 1.66-acre green space five blocks north, in apparent breach of a no-camping regulation. This ambiguity would eventually summon Jonathan Jarvis, the director of the NPS, to testify before Congress. In January 2012, sixteen weeks after Occupy protesters had pitched their tents in McPherson Square, the committee that oversees the District of Columbia convened a hearing with a title query of "Who Made the Decision to Allow Indefinite Camping in the Park?" Darrel Issa (R-Calif.), chair of the committee, and Trey Gowdy (R-S.C.), a member of that committee and the chair of the hearing, wanted to get to the bottom of what they saw as a clear conflict between the official ban on camping and seemingly clear evidence "that sleeping, cooking and camping are taking place"—which, they charged, was wasting "thousands of dollars in taxpayer money" by degrading the park grounds and incurring costs for police protection.[33] This framing invoked a series of conundrums to resolve: what were the differences between camping and a vigil, between recreational and political acts, between the privileges and the rights of citizens, and between outdoor space as an asset of nature and that space as a forum for public voice.

Jarvis took on the first of these questions and explained the agency's approach to Occupy as a vigil, in relation to a broader history of protest in national historic sites, including tent-style ones such as 1968's Resurrection City. The NPS regarded federal ground and national parks as uniquely important places for citizens to come not only for "reflection, commemoration, recreation" but also "to make their voices heard through public assembly and political demonstration." Accordingly, unlike city authorities, the NPS and the U.S. Park Police assumed a special responsibility for safeguarding citizens' rights to protest as much as for enforcing regulations on public space. This Occupy encampment was not technically required to obtain a permit in any case because it involved fewer than 500 people, at its height hosting about 350 residents. Jarvis then honed in on a key distinction: while "NPS regulations do not allow for camping within McPherson Square . . . temporary structures, including tents, are permissible as part of a demonstration to further their symbolic message or to meet logistical needs." He expressed confidence that protesters were engaged in "round-the-clock demonstration vigils," which were not uncommon in national park spaces. Legal precedent and latitude in regard to the First Amendment, he assured, protected exactly the kinds of "expressive activities" taking place in the square. As such, barring an emergency or imminent threat to public health or safety, he believed that the Occupy "demonstrators in McPherson Square and elsewhere in the city are allowed to continue their vigil."[34]

That a vigil might employ tents for symbolic and logistical means but somehow not signify "camping" drew skepticism from Issa and Gowdy, who had opened the proceedings with doubt that there might be a legitimate "difference between camping and a 24-hour vigil, especially when that 24-hour vigil lasts several months." Together they drove the questioning from a standpoint of recreational camping as the only possible use for tents. Issa's definition drew directly upon his personal experience. He knew what camping was supposed to look like because, he stated, "I'm an avid camper, both RV and tent over the years, and a very old Boy Scout."[35] The RV and Boy Scout camp invoked a quite different historical reference than did Jarvis's links to late 1960s protesters and recalled precisely the kinds of cultural rifts that had animated those earlier moments. That a rag-tag group of antiestablishment protesters might be allowed to camp but Boy Scouts would not seemed to bewilder Issa's colleague Gowdy, who put Jarvis on the spot: "I need a definition of camping. Because I need to go back to South Carolina and tell everyone who wants to spend the summer in one of our parks what camping is and what it is not. So define camping for me, juxtaposed with a 24-hour vigil, because you seem inclined to draw a distinction and I can't draw a distinction. What is the definition of camping?"[36]

That there might be several types of tent use or a gray area between protest vigils and camping made little sense to Gowdy, who called himself an "old country prosecutor" with no patience for the NPS's "measured and reasoned approach." How could the NPS prevent people from setting up camp anywhere in the United States and doing whatever they please as long as "they say they're in protest of something"? Why would the NPS discriminate against tourists "camping for fun"? William and Mary professor of law Timothy Zick testified that "there is a world of difference between a recreational camper and somebody who camps as part of a protest." This exacerbated rather than resolved the problem for Gowdy and Issa, for whom the quintessential, rightful campers were in fact those who pitched their tents in pursuit of outdoor recreation rather than political disruption. Issa's lament that innocent tourists could not "pitch a tent in McPherson square if they're camping for fun" while Occupy dared to go "camping in protest of fun" charged Occupy with both violating park regulations and perverting camping's wholesome character and, in the process, minimized OWS's grievances.[37]

Scrambling to address Issa's demand for a fixed definition of camping, Jarvis drew a distinction that at a vigil protesters are awake at all times and available to distribute information to passersby, whereas camping is "defined as sleeping or preparing to sleep at the site." Even if, Jarvis admitted, "we do believe that there is some camping going on at McPherson Square associated with their vigil," he identified the vigil as the primary purpose and the sleeping a secondary concern that could be brought into compliance. Protesters were not allowed to do whatever they pleased; the U.S. Park Police prevented them from building any semipermanent structures, such as wooden frames or shanties. But they were loath to disallow tents, which remained a central expression of the protest message. Seizing on a weakness in Jarvis's reasoning, Gowdy turned away from tents to focus instead on the sleeping; if the "linchpin of the definition of camping" is sleeping, could sleeping be a legitimate form of protest? Was there a difference between "First Amendment sleeping versus recreational sleeping"? Jarvis, in a rare display of frustration, threw up his hands and said, "I don't really understand that question."[38] It is difficult not to empathize with Jarvis. The question sounds absurd—recreational versus political sleeping. But the curious framing highlights a division between the rights and the privileges of inhabiting the outdoors.

That the state could dictate where citizens could and could not camp was not always a matter of general assent. Until the 1920s campers pitched their tents in an ad hoc way, assuming that whether on public or private ground they had tacit permission for temporary lodging. With greater popularity of recreational and automobile camping, regulations increased, with specific spaces set aside for camping and limitations set on length of stays and accepted behavior. Camping became an activity performed on public ground with permission of some public agency (or, as in homeless camping, in violation of those rules).[39] The default from which Gowdy and Issa operated was that sleeping outside was a privilege fundamentally regulated by the state; one could not assume any tacit permission or right.

Issa derived his mind-set from experience with recreational camping as a state-run enterprise, relating his firsthand knowledge of how rangers "check to see if somebody is allowed to be a camper," and if in violation or not "within lawfully designated areas," then "they're ushered out . . . if necessary at gunpoint." Here, Jarvis countered Issa's assumptions by asserting citizens' *right* to be in national parks, most of which were open 24 hours a day, 365 days a year. Issa sought instead to separate and privilege different forms of camping and protest. Campers could camp by permission only and protesters could "come with candles and stand" and then "get hotel rooms." Indoors or out, appropriate lodging required permission and fees, thus embedding Issa's definitions of recreational camping and protest with implicit class assumptions. He questioned why Occupy did not conform to these standard protest expectations, exemplified at a recent antiabortion rally: "They came, they protested, they left."[40] By parsing appropriate political action and conjuring the image of privatized public space where citizens are controlled (by their ability to pay for hotel rooms or by a park ranger's firearm), the debate over how we access nature and why it matters for political access persists. The proffered formula—they came, they stood with candles, they left—posits a circumscribed vision of citizen participation, precisely what Occupy sought to resist.

A central aim of Occupy was in fact to break out of this expectation of retreat, which can contain and defuse the impact of protest. Occupy D.C. campers amplified Jarvis's logic that the camping was ancillary to their vigil. McPherson Square tents bore signs that announced, in large block letters printed over a background of the Bill of Rights, "WE ARE NOT CAMPING. We are assembling peaceably to petition the Government for a redress of grievances." Red ink circled the First Amendment and insisted, "THIS IS OUR PERMIT."[41] Occupy D.C.'s written statement submitted to the hearing appealed to nonrecreational frames, arguing that members were "maintaining a site of protest, a physical presence that gives visibility and voice to our dissent." They did not choose temporary tent life as a middle-class vacation in nature as reward for their urban toil and accomplishments; nor did they "relish being in uncomfortable conditions that humans without housing have endured for millennia." Instead they saw camping as "a necessary tactic to express our concern for the country's direction in a way that will maintain public attention," and they asked the government not to suppress free speech and "evict patriots from their tents."[42]

Yet as strongly as Occupiers disavowed recreational camping, they also depended on iconic images from recreational camping, the long historical link between national parks and the rights of citizenship, and the even longer legacy of America as "nature's nation." A poster declaring "USING A

TENT ≠ CAMPING" placed the tent at the middle of a Venn diagram that held on the one side recreational icons for swimming, hiking, canoeing, picnicking, and fishing, and on the other objects associated with protest such as a pencil, a protest sign, a fist, and a megaphone, among others. This image, which attempts to separate camping from "petitioning government for redress of grievances," simultaneously links the two activities. The tent moves into one circle with all the associated background of the other. Occupy relied on implicit "back to nature" impressions that its protesters' camps conveyed—for example, that their organic communal kitchens related to the "organic" bottom-up nature of the protest. Here they invoked social necessities of camping, where, whether in wilderness or on Wall Street, people had to cooperate to meet group needs. As any camping manual will detail, collaboration is key for providing food, sanitation, and medical necessities. In that sense the meaning and practice of Occupy camping converged more than they diverged.

The material needs and impact of this form of camping in public became matters of some contention in the hearing, beyond the ideological debates over the definition of camping. The National Park Service had recently completed a rehabilitation of McPherson Square with spruced up benches, repaired drinking fountains, fresh paint, new fences, streetlights, trash cans, and an acre of sod. An estimated two-hundred-thousand-dollar lawn quickly began to show wear and tear as Occupiers expanded their footprint to up to three-quarters of the square. Occupy was attempting to minimize its impact, rotating tent placements in an effort to preserve the turf because, as one resident suggested, "This is our home too."[43] But House committee leaders saw it differently. In Issa's formula, individuals choosing to sleep in tents, whether part of a demonstration or not, were "basically using somebody else's asset, the American people's asset, in a way not prescribed or allowed within the regulations set about for all citizens." A similar concern arose in Los Angeles, where Occupy had encamped in front of City Hall, with explicit permission and even support from the L.A. City Council. But after a while the lush lawn, fringed by palm and fig trees, had deteriorated from "verdant green to yellow-brown, trampled by tents, bare feet and the regular arrival of heavy DJ equipment." Critiques emerged: "it's time to move on from *our* lawn at City Hall. It is everybody's lawn, not just those with their tents right now."[44] Los Angeles joined other cities in tightening anticamping ordinances, partially to ensure that the restoration of the lawn (as opposed to installing a more water-wise garden, as some advocated) would not be in vain. The physical nature of the lawn seemed to come in direct opposition to its symbolic

USING A TENT
≠
CAMPING

CAMPING

**PETITIONING
GOVERNMENT FOR
REDRESS OF GRIEVANCES**

OCCUPY

Occupy° Posters owsposters.tumblr.com

Figure 13.4. This is not camping. Stephen Ewen, "'USING A TENT ≠ CAMPING,'" owsposters.tumblr.com, 2012. Reproduced courtesy of Stephen Ewen.

purposes. Declaring that people "still have the right to sleep on sidewalks," the council asserted that they did not want to undermine citizens' ability to protest, but protesters had to keep off the grass.[45]

This distinction was meaningful; like preventing sleeping, limiting the use of public lawns further constricts public action and participation. Moreover in the case of federal squares and city hall grounds, it furthers the constraint of a compelling and historic purpose of those spaces to provide public ground for debate. Continuing the Olmstedian legacy, protecting the lawn preserves a landscape of refinement that favors the ideals and practices of a middle-class public ahead of those of rowdy protesters and the poor.[46] Rep. Elijah Cummings (D-Md.) suggested to the House committee that it should not allow "concerns over grass seeds [to] outweigh grassroots efforts to seek improvements and help for our most vulnerable citizens." The sacrifice of a lawn, he suggested, was a small price to pay to maintain space for public protest and conversation. The converse is also suggestive. Issa viewed the foreclosure of "somebody else's" protest a small sacrifice for preserving the lawn as a financial and physical asset of "the American people." Who had the right to use nature and the outdoors sat at the heart of what Occupy's struggle was all about—how the language of "assets" constricted access to public voice at the same time that it rendered successful middle-class consumption and well-behaved recreation as ideal practices of citizenship.

Tent Style

In its locations at the center of American cities large and small, Occupy quickly became more than a protest; in the words of one observer of McPherson Square, it was an "aesthetic and cultural phenomenon." Appearing in the "Style" section of the *Washington Post*, this commentary drew a different set of urban inspirations from Occupy. The maze of tents and tarps pointed to not only "the iconic symbol of the displaced" but also to how Occupy improvised "a vibrant urbanism" in a way that planners and architects try but usually fail to achieve. Occupy inherited its sensibility not only from the long line of tent protests but also from situationists and DIY urbanism and went about busily reclaiming public (and natural) space—and for more than political purposes.[47] Simultaneously verb and noun, "Occupy" became 2011's word of the year on the strength of its political advocacy and on its connotation of a certain hip, ironic urban meme. It came in at number 2 among *New York* magazine's "Reasons to Love New York" in 2011. The snippet accompanying a photograph of a messy conglomeration of tents expressed civic pride that "it started here," an amazement that an "obscure park" occupied in "squalor" could have instigated this raw excitement that spread across the country and a tidy, nearly sardonic, postmortem: "The drum circle may now be silent, but Zuccotti Park's boom was heard round the world."[48]

The tent became a symbol for making camp not just on a physical space but also on an idea and a way of being seen. This proved a powerful metaphor, and the infinitive verb "to occupy," with its notion of "making camp upon," through persistent radical reinterpretation came to modify not just urban spaces but also many nouns: occupy your heart, occupy racism, occupy the vote, occupy everything. The further the metaphor moved from the physical connection with the ground, the less the tents worked as a medium for protest and the more they became objects unto themselves. The image in Figure 13.5, from Occupy Denver, illustrates this transformation. The tent provides a large canvas on which to inscribe and broadcast certain sentiments, in this case referencing several issues about corporations, money, and politics. Occupiers often used their tents as billboards, broadcasting multiple messages from within their encampments. But this tent is more mobile than most, and whatever the message, in some ways it subverts the whole point of a tent, which is to provide shelter. Why in this instance use a tent at all? If a sign might have been a more practical choice for publicizing the message, the uncanny sight of a wearable tent provoked attention even if it privileged the form of the tent over the message. University of California, Berkeley, students took this even further. Instructed to strike their camp, Occupiers instead affixed helium balloons to several empty tents and floated them above their space, where they hung improbably a dozen feet in midair.[49]

These symbolic tents hint at the ways Occupy demonstrated the presence of "precarity" in modern life. Precarity has become a shorthand term for increasing factors of instability in individuals' work and living conditions in postindustrial, neoliberal economies. The tent, especially as a representation of transience, connotes precariousness in a material form, both in terms of physical occupation of disputed spaces—one definition of "precarious" is "your tenancy on your land is in someone else's hands"—and through the sanitation issues engendered by group-living outdoors.[50] Another definition of "precarity" might be that you have to think about where to pee. The more performative uses of tents, however, capture Occupy as a shared symbol for the common experience of precarity and the protest against it. Walking, floating tents participate in the same genre of Occupy actions as the October 2011 zombie march, where protesters costumed themselves as white-faced living-dead financiers and roamed about Lower Manhattan munching on Monopoly money and dramatizing the soulless nature of capitalism. Wandering on the edge between life and death, home and homelessness, zombies embody precarity as evocatively as tents house it.[51]

The many attempts to move, restrict, and dismantle camps called attention to this sense of precarity. In McPherson Square protesters were finally evicted ostensibly for worries over public health in February 2012,[52] and they responded by replacing their many personal tents with one extremely large

Figure 13.5. The wearable tent. Eric Verlo, "Occupy Denver, Protest Tent, We the People," notmytribe.com, October 19, 2011. Reproduced courtesy of Eric Verlo.

tent over a portion of the square. They draped a bright blue, star-spangled tarp over the top of the tall statue of Gen. James "Birdseye" McPherson, which stood at the center of the square, and rallied under what they called the "Tent of Dreams." Claiming the Civil War general as mascot, Occupy D.C. implicitly invoked the public claims of veteran identity and those claims' permanence as suggested in bronze and marble. The Tent of Dreams, as dramatic as it was, lasted just a few days, as compared to the 125 days of the McPherson Square occupation, and it was a tent in name only, instigating less debate over the meaning of tents and public access and more marveling at the form.[53] In Boulder, with an 11:00 P.M. closing of public space approaching, Occupiers called a dance party for 11:01 P.M. and took down all but one tent, which they left in symbolic protest. Ironically, while now not in violation of sheltering sleeping campers, the tent still ran afoul of the law and was seized as abandoned property.[54]

Because abandoned tents undermine both the performance and the protest, determining whether tents were occupied or not became a significant activity. Police forces of cities from Providence, Rhode Island, to Sacramento, California, and London, England, employed thermal imaging to ascertain whether protesters were in fact occupying their tents at night; the resulting images enhanced the sense of spectacle as much as they provided material evidence.[55] Occupy groups worried that being exposed as day campers might suggest a fickle commitment, and they resisted attempts to map the human geography of their encampments, preferring that the tents themselves represent the strength of numbers and staying power. Yet whether looking for campers to evict or hypocrisy to expose, the infrared cameras captured another kind of tent theater; whether simulating military or hunting techniques, the night vision makes suspicious targets of citizens engaged in some kind of public act amid these ghostly tents.

The theatrical tent was part of Kalle Lasn's plan to "wage a meme war," in which the tent as icon rather than shelter might change the national conversation. If Lasn did not invent the frustration that fueled Occupy, one interviewer wrote, he did "brand it." The sentiment of "Occupy" and the tent as its vehicle were, in Lasn hands, "tools to begin remodeling the 'mental environment,' to create a new 'meme,' the term coined by the evolutionary biologist Richard Dawkins for a kind of transcendent cultural message." *Adbusters*, which was subtitled *Journal of the Mental Environment*, had pursued such strategies before, a kind of "semiotic interventionism" the editors called "culture jamming." Its pages featured cutting parodies of corporations, consumerism, and conventional political discourse. In previous years it had sponsored events such as an anticonsumerist "Buy Nothing Day" and a "Carnivalesque Rebellion"—neither of which had as much success tapping into American cultural consciousness as Occupy did. Underneath all lay an attempt to find a cultural medium through which to shift political dialogue. Hitting on the tent, with its long history in American public nature, worked in a way that the unfamiliar, upside-down world of the Carnivalesque Rebellion did not. *Adbusters* promoted all these events on the premise that in the attempt to change discourse, "one of the most powerful things of all is aesthetics."[56]

Occupy clearly had an aesthetic. Camping gear and apparel have long displayed a kind of outdoor style beyond providing practical support for sleeping outside.[57] This rugged, modern, camping aesthetic invoked the meme of nature as much as it did politics—and recombined them in compelling ways. For example, Occupiers referenced their posteviction winter plans as part of a natural cycle of "hibernation" and reemergence in the spring. They framed going outdoors as a symbolic enactment of their desires literally to get outside dysfunctional structures of politics. As such, Occupiers tapped into

Figure 13.6. Occupy memory. Grégoire Vion, "Occupy Tent," grgwr.com, 2011. Reproduced courtesy of Grégoire Vion.

long-established ideas about wilderness and wilderness experiences (such as camping) as the antidote to the ills of modern society.[58] Graphic images typically featured not the high-tech dome tent types seen in photographs of Occupy encampments but older models, pup tents and canvas-and-frame styles that suggested an iconic, nostalgic form of camping—perhaps ones that communicated less stratification between types of campers. Branded camping equipment from expensive adventure outfitters might send the wrong message—less precarity, more one percent. In that sense, the tent as meme worked just as well as the actual tents did in forming the nature of Occupy's protest and performing precarity for a national audience.

The practices and public response to Occupy continue to evolve.[59] Although active camping and consistent media coverage have disappeared, the memory of the movement and the mobilization of the tent as political logo have left significant cultural traces. With its framing of the 1 percent to 99 percent divide, it brought the issue of wealth inequality to the forefront for a while. Whether it succeeded in making this a lasting issue for debate is unclear; the visible public protests of 2011 have not reemerged. Among their efforts at regrouping since then, Occupy advocates and intellectuals have launched a magazine devoted to *Occupy Theory, Occupy Strategy.* The eclectic print and Web journal contains academic essays, global connections, history lessons, political theory, and poetry. A goal of the journal is to contextualize what Occupy accomplished and where it might go, and in this it retrospectively confirms the significance of the tent. The journal's mission statement retells the movement's origins on a mythic scale: "On September 17th, 2011, Occupy Wall Street was born. A hundred people occupied Zuccotti Park . . . and opened a space for imagination. We began to share food, clothing and shelter. We sought refuge in the shell of a concrete jungle and found community." Judith Butler looked forward. Instead of mourning "the loss of Zuccotti Park or other public spaces where Occupy was dwelling," she urged Occupy to continue targeting sites of inequality, exposing their "public face" and "interrupting those processes by which inequality and increased precarity are being reproduced." In this strategy she highlighted camping: "Perhaps the task is to undertake squatting as a form of public protest, even if it is only episodic and targeted."[60]

The meme through which Occupy acted and captured attention thus continues to be key to its meaning. Its tents reveal a great deal about the ways in which nature and culture are powerfully intertwined. The tent housed new material uses, cultural forms, and political language at the same time. Moreover the outdoor space served as an important fulcrum for the movement. By bringing the issues of finance, wealth, and inequality outdoors, Occupy highlighted the ways in which Americans have often occupied nature to make public identity. In some ways we might look at Occupy not only as the NPS did—as one in a series of First Amendment protests with tents—but also as an engagement with a longer history of camping as part of defining the public. It dramatized a crucial connection between access to public spaces and the ability to participate in public life.

Camping is not just a way out, a way back to an unoccupied nature; it can also be a way in to a long-standing conversation about who has rightful access to nature both occupied and unoccupied, and thus to the public realm. Whether camping serves as a mode of nature-seeking recreation, as functional travel and transience, or as a means of political protest, the ways we sleep outside matter. To camp is to participate in the evolving debates about how we might conceptualize and control public nature. Tents have historically housed a search for connectedness and belonging at the same time that they have set in motion a process of social disconnection and exclusion. The tents of Occupy drew this debate into shared outdoor spaces and thus demonstrated how camping remains a potent mode of rendering a distinctly American public through nature. Among its chaos and contradictions, Occupy employed the tent and the long memory of camps past to evoke shared public connections between citizens and nature and to suggest new ways of understanding the entangled products of nature and culture.

Notes

Chapter 1. The Nature-Culture Paradox

1. Andrew C. Revkin, "Confronting the 'Anthropocene,'" Dot Earth Blog, *New York Times*, May 11, 2011, http://dotearth.blogs.nytimes.com/2011/05/11/confronting-the-anthropocene/ (accessed November 20, 2013).

2. Will Steffen, Paul J. Crutzen, and John R. McNeill, "The Anthropocene: Are Humans Now Overwhelming the Great Forces of Nature?," *Ambio* 36, no. 8 (December 2007): 614–21, quote from 614; published by Springer on behalf of the Royal Swedish Academy of Sciences, http://www.jstor.org/stable/25547826 (accessed November 20, 2013). See also "A Man-Made World," *Economist*, May 26, 2011, http://www.economist.com/node/18741749 (accessed November 20, 2013).

3. Steffen et al., "The Anthropocene: Are Humans Now Overwhelming the Great Forces of Nature," 615.

4. Ibid.

5. Will Steffen, Jacques Grinevald, Paul Crutzen, and John McNeill, "The Anthropocene: Conceptual and Historical Perspectives," *Philosophical Transactions of the Royal Society* 369, no. 1938 (2011): 842–67, http://www.rsta.royalsocietypublishing.org (accessed November 20, 2013). The Anthropocene encapsulates an expanding debate in the natural sciences, most notably in connection to the field of conservation biology, concerning the interconnection between nature and culture. The details of this debate extend beyond the scope of Chapter 1. However, the central issues revolve around how to conceptualize nature and assess its value in the context and practice of sustaining Earth systems. The debate between Michael Soulé's articulation of the principles of conservation biology and Peter Kareiva's articulation of the new conservation provide an entrée into the scientific parameters and cultural politics of how this debate is unfolding in the natural sciences. See Michael Soulé, "What Is Conservation Biology?," *BioScience* 35, no. 11 (December 1985): 727–34; and Michele Marvior, Robert Lalasz, and Peter Kareiva, "Conservation in the Anthropocene: Beyond Solitude and Fragility," *Breakthrough Journal* (Winter 2012), http://thebreakthrough.org/index.php/journal/past-issues/issue-2/conservation-in-the-anthropocene (accessed March 19, 2014).

6. Raymond Williams, "The Idea of Nature," in Raymond Williams, *Problems in Materialism and Culture* (London: Verso, 1980), 80.

7. Ibid., 83.

8. Donna Haraway, *The Companion Species Manifesto: Dogs, People, and Significant Otherness* (Chicago: Prickly Paradigm Press, 2003), 6, 8, 7.

9. Gregg Mitman, "Living in a Material World," *Journal of American History* 100, no. 1 (June 2013): 129. Mitman's conception of "relational ontology" extends from Donna Haraway's work.

10. Regarding the connections between American studies and environmental history, see Kendra D. Smith, "American Studies and Environmental History: Provoking Thought and Practice," *American Studies* 46, no.1 (Spring 2005): 5–22; and Hal Rothman, "Conceptualizing the Real: Environmental History and American Studies," *American Quarterly* 54, no. 3 (September 2002): 485–97.

11. Richard White, "American Environmental History: The Development of a New Historical Field," *Pacific Historical Review* 54, no. 3 (August 1985): 304. See the special issue of *American Studies* titled *American Studies: From Culture Concept to Cultural Studies* 38, no. 2 (Summer 1997), with essays by Jay Mechling, De Witt Douglas Kilgore, James Farrell, Richard P. Horowitz, Doris Friedensohn, Steven Watts, Barry Shank, Mark Hulsether, and Albert E. Stone. For the classic overviews of the field, see Gene Wise, "'Paradigm Dramas' in American Studies: A Cultural and Institutional History of the Movement," *American Quarterly* 31, no. 3 (September 1979): 293–337; and Gene Wise, "From 'American Studies' to 'American Culture' Studies: A Dialogue Across Generations," *Prospects* 8 (October 1983): 1–10. See also Paul Lauter, *From Walden Pond to Jurassic Park: Activism, Culture, & American Studies* (Durham, N.C.: Duke University Press, 2001); and George Lipsitz, *American Studies in a Moment of Danger* (Minneapolis: University of Minnesota Press, 2001). For recent anthologies of the field, see Lucy Maddox, *Locating American Studies: The Evolution of a Discipline* (Baltimore: Johns Hopkins University Press, 1999); Donald E. Pease and Robyn Wiegman, eds., *The Futures of American Studies* (Durham, N.C.: Duke University Press, 2002); and Janice Radway, Kevin Gaines, Barry Shank, and Penny Von Eschen, eds., *American Studies: An Anthology* (Chichester, U.K.; Malden, MA: Wiley-Blackwell, 2009). For the notable scholars whose work falls in this vein, see Annette Kolodny, *The Lay of the Land: Metaphor as Experience and History in American Life and Letters* (Chapel Hill: University of North Carolina Press, 1975); Annette Kolodny, *The Land Before Her: Fantasy and Experience of the American Frontiers, 1630–1860* (Chapel Hill: University of North Carolina Press, 1984); Elizabeth R. McKinsey, *Niagara Falls: Icon of the American Sublime* (Cambridge [Cambridgeshire]: Cambridge University Press, 1985); Leo Marx, *The Machine in the Garden: Technology and the Pastoral Ideal in America* (New York: Oxford University Press, 1967); Perry Miller, *Errand into the Wilderness* (Cambridge, Mass.: Belknap Press of Harvard University Press, 1956); Perry Miller, *Nature's Nation* (Cambridge, Mass.: Belknap Press of Harvard University Press, 1967); Barbara Novak, *Nature and Culture: American Landscape and Painting, 1825–1875* (New York: Oxford University Press, 2007); Richard Slotkin, *Regeneration Through Violence: The Mythology of the American Frontier, 1600–1860* (Middletown, Conn.: Wesleyan University Press, 1973); Richard Slotkin, *The Fatal Environment: The Myth of the Frontier in the Age of Industrialization, 1800–1890* (New York: Atheneum, 1985); Richard Slotkin, *Gunfighter Nation: The Myth of the Frontier in Twentieth-Century America* (New York: Atheneum, 1992); Henry Nash Smith, *Virgin Land: The American West as Symbol and Myth* (New York: Vintage Books, 1957); and John R. Stilgoe, *Common Landscape of America, 1580 to 1845* (New Haven, Conn.: Yale University Press, 1982).

12. Early on, environmental historians generally defined nature in opposition to culture as the "nonhuman world" or that which exists beyond human control. Most notably, see Donald Worster, "Seeing Beyond Culture," *Journal of American History* 76, no. 4 (March 1990): 1142–47.

13. Ellen Stroud, "Does Nature Always Matter? Following Dirt Through History," *History and Theory* 24, no. 4 (December 2003): 75–81, quote on 80.

14. Linda Nash, "Furthering the Environmental Turn," *Journal of American History* 100, no. 1 (June 2013): 133.

15. Worster, "Seeing Beyond Culture," 1144.

16. White, "American Environmental History," 299.

17. Donald Worster, "Transformations of the Earth: Toward an Agroecological Perspective in History," *Journal of American History* 76, no. 4 (March 1990): 1087–106, quote on 1089. For precedents, see Fernand Braudel, *The Mediterranean and the Mediterranean World in the Age of Philip II* (New York: Harper & Row, 1972); Hans Huth, *Nature and the American: Three Centuries of Changing Attitudes* (Lincoln: University of Nebraska Press, 1972); Donald Fleming, "Roots of the New Conservation Movement," *Perspectives in American History* 6 (January 1972): 7–91; Samuel P. Hays, *Conservation and the Gospel of Efficiency: The Progressive Conservation Movement, 1890–1920* (New York: Atheneum, 1969); James Claude Malin, *The Grassland of North America: Prolegomena to Its History, with Addenda and Postscript* (Gloucester, Mass.: P. Smith, 1967); Roderick Nash, *Wilderness and the American Mind* (New Haven, Conn.: Yale University Press, 1967); Carl Ortwin Sauer, *Sixteenth-Century North America: The Land and the People as Seen by the Europeans* (Berkeley: University of California Press, 1971); and Walter Prescott Webb, *The Great Plains* (Waltham, Mass.: Blaisdell, 1959).

18. William Cronon, "Modes of Prophecy and Production: Placing Nature in History," *Journal of American History* 76, no. 4 (March 1990): 1122–31, quote on 1123. Donald Worster summarized the three: "The first involves the discovery of the structure and distribution of natural environments in the past"; the second focuses on "the various ways people have tried to make nature over into a system that produces resources for their consumption"; and the third "is that more intangible, purely mental type of encounter in which perceptions, ideologies, ethics, laws, and myths have become part of an individual's or group's dialogue with nature" (Worster, "Transformations of the Earth," quote on 1090–91).

19. Ted Steinberg, "Down to Earth: Nature, Agency, and Power in History," *American Historical Review* 107, no. 3 (June 2002): 798–820, quote on 802. This is quoted from Roy A. Rappaport, *The Flow of Energy in an Agricultural Society* (San Francisco: W. H. Freeman, 1971), 80. The essays in this volume call into question Rappaport's and Steinberg's point suggesting that we need both nature and culture to survive.

20. Paul Sutter, "The World with Us: The State of American Environmental History," *Journal of American History* 100, no. 1 (June 2013): 94–119.

21. For recent environmental history that specifically addresses labor, class, race, and gender, see Thomas G. Andrews, *Killing for Coal: America's Deadliest Labor War* (Cambridge, Mass.: Harvard University Press, 2008); Dianne D. Glave, *Rooted in the Earth: Reclaiming the African American Environmental Heritage* (Chicago: Lawrence Hill Books, 2010); Andrew Hurley, *Environmental Inequalities: Class, Race, and Industrial Pollution in Gary, Indiana, 1945–1980* (Chapel Hill: University of North Carolina Press, 1995); Karl Jacoby, *Crimes Against Nature: Squatters, Poachers, Thieves, and the Hidden History of American Conservation* (Berkeley: University of California Press, 2001); Kathryn Morse, *The Nature of Gold: An Environmental History of the Klondike Gold Rush* (Seattle: University of Washington Press, 2003); Vera Norwood, *Made from This Earth: American Women and Nature* (Chapel Hill: University of North Carolina Press, 1993); Virginia Scharff, *Seeing Nature Through Gender* (Lawrence: University Press of Kansas, 2003); Mark David Spence, *Dispossessing the Wilderness: Indian Removal and the Making of the National Parks* (New York: Oxford University Press, 1999); Louis S. Warren, *The Hunter's Game: Poachers and*

Conservationists in Twentieth-Century America (New Haven, Conn.: Yale University Press, 1997); Marsha Weisiger, *Dreaming of Sheep in Navajo Country* (Seattle: University of Washington Press, 2009); Ari Kelman, *A River and Its City: The Nature of Landscape in New Orleans* (Berkeley: University of California Press, 2003); Marcus Hall, *Earth Repair: A Transatlantic History of Environmental Restoration* (Charlottesville: University of Virginia Press, 2005); Andrew Isenberg, *The Destruction of the Bison: An Environmental History, 1750–1920* (Cambridge: Cambridge University Press, 2000); Andrew Isenberg, *Mining California: An Ecological History* (New York: Hill and Wang, 2005); and Joseph E. Taylor, *Making Salmon: An Environmental History of the Northwest Fisheries Crisis* (Seattle: University of Washington Press, 1999).

22. For example, see Gregg Mitman, *Breathing Space: How Allergies Shape Our Lives and Landscapes* (New Haven, Conn.: Yale University Press, 2007); Linda Nash, *Inescapable Ecologies: A History of Environment, Disease and Knowledge* (Berkeley: University of California Press, 2006); Christopher Sellers, "Thoreau's Body: Towards an Embodied Environmental History," *Environmental History* 4, no. 4 (October 1999): 486–514; Edmund Russell, *Evolutionary History: Using History and Biology to Understand Life on Earth* (New York: Cambridge University Press, 2011); and Conevery Bolton Valencius, *The Health of the Country: How American Settlers Understood Themselves and Their Land* (New York: Basic Books, 2002).

23. For example, see Catherine Cocks, *Tropical Whites: The Rise of the Tourist South in the Americas* (Philadelphia: University of Pennsylvania Press, 2013); Annie Gilbert Coleman, *Ski Style: Sport and Culture in the Rockies* (Lawrence: University Press of Kansas, 2004); Susan G. Davis, *Spectacular Nature: Corporate Culture and the Sea World Experience* (Berkeley: University of California Press, 1997); Jane Desmond, *Staging Tourism: Bodies on Display from Waikiki to Sea World* (Chicago: University of Chicago Press, 1999); Finis Dunaway, *Natural Visions: The Power of Images in American Environmental Reform* (Chicago: University of Chicago Press, 2008); Andrew G. Kirk, *Counterculture Green: The Whole Earth Catalog and American Environmentalism* (Lawrence: University Press of Kansas, 2007); Frieda Knobloch, *The Culture of Wilderness: Agriculture as Colonization in the American West* (Chapel Hill: University of North Carolina Press, 1996); Gregg Mitman, *Reel Nature: America's Romance with Wildlife on Film* (Cambridge, Mass.: Harvard University Press, 1999); William Philpott, *Vacationland: Tourism and Environment in the Colorado High Country* (Seattle: University of Washington Press, 2013); Jennifer Price, *Flight Maps: Adventures with Nature in Modern America* (New York: Basic Books, 1999); Hal Rothman, *Devil's Bargains: Tourism in the Twentieth-Century American West* (Lawrence: University Press of Kansas, 1998); Marguerite S. Shaffer, *See America First: Tourism and National Identity, 1880–1940* (Washington, D.C.: Smithsonian Institution Press, 2001); David Stradling, *Making Mountains: New York City and the Catskills* (Seattle: University of Washington Press, 2007); Phoebe S. Kropp, *California Vieja: Culture and Memory in a Modern American Place* (Berkeley: University of California Press, 2006); and Joseph E. Taylor, *Pilgrims of the Vertical: Yosemite Rock Climbers and Nature at Risk* (Cambridge, Mass.: Harvard University Press, 2010).

24. Sutter, "The World with Us," 118, lists these as a sample of the variety of terms scholars have used to try and label things that contain both nature and culture.

25. Ibid., 95.

26. The following articles explore the differences between nature as structural context and nature as active agent: John Herron, "Because Antelope Can't Talk: Natural Agency and Social Politics in American Environmental History," *Historical Reflections* 36, no. 1 (Spring 2010): 33–52; Linda Nash, "The Agency of Nature or the Nature of Agency," *Environmental History* 10, no. 1 (January 2005): 67–69; Steinberg, "Down to Earth"; and Stroud, "Does Nature Always Matter."

27. Worster, "Transformations of the Earth," 1106, argued that the "blooming, buzzing, howling world of nature that surrounds us has always been a force in human life." In these forces of nature, he argued, "we encounter autonomous, independent energies that do not derive from the drives and intentions of any culture" (1089). Worster relied on definitions of nature and culture as oppositional: "Wherever the two spheres, the natural and the cultural, confront or interact with one another, environmental history finds its essential themes" (1090). Cronon questioned Worster's "potentially excessive materialism" asking for "subtler tools for building bridges among ecosystems, economies, and the cognitive lenses through which people view the world"; see Cronon, "Modes of Prophecy and Production," 1124, 1130. Worster countered that we did not need a return to "that old narrow focus on self-referential history of human ideas, society, and culture, with its tendency to dismiss nature as a mere epiphenomenon"; see Worster, "Seeing Beyond Culture," 1142. He cautioned against redefining the environment as cultural landscape, "a move that would encompass virtually every place on earth, even hospitals and military bases . . . and have us concentrate far more on telling how each social group . . . living in that landscape saw or felt about it" (1144). He concluded with a warning not "to reduce all landscapes to essentially social or cultural expression" (1147). This opening battle set the tone for the field, establishing a shaky relationship between nature and culture.

28. Elizabeth Blackmar, "Contemplating the Force of Nature," *Radical Historians Newsletter* 70 (1994): 1–5, quoted in Herron, "Because Antelope Can't Talk," 40.

29. Specifically Adsal argues that environmental historians turned to the science of ecology to tell the story of nature. This logic of ecosystems undergirded by scientific method and analysis took on an interpretive authority, what Adsal calls "an *a priori* source of explanatory power," that obscured not only the problematic history of ecology as a science but also the social, political, and historical relationships that inextricably link nature and culture. See Kristen Adsal, "The Problematic Nature of Nature: The Post-Constructivist Challenge to Environmental History," *History and Theory* 42, no. 4 (December 2003): 60–74, esp. 73.

30. Steven Lagerfeld, "Uncommon Ground: Toward Reinventing Nature by William Cronon," *Wilson Quarterly* 25, no. 1 (Winter 2001): 138–93.

31. See William Cronon, ed., *Uncommon Ground: Rethinking the Human Place in Nature* (New York: W. W. Norton, 1996); and William Cronon, "The Trouble with Wilderness," *Environmental History* 1, no. 1 (January 1996): 7–28. As Virginia Scharff noted in her review, "Cronon and his colleagues were denounced as pointy-headed city slickers who betrayed the movement by handing the enemy a potent argument: if nature isn't 'natural' why not carry on the process of invention by clear cutting, mining, paving, and polluting?" See Virginia Scharff, "Uncommon Ground: Toward Reinventing Nature, by William Cronon," *Journal of American History* 85, no. 1 (June 1998): 196.

32. James D. Proctor, "Resolving Multiple Visions of Nature, Science, and Religion," *Zygon* 29, no. 3 (September 2004): 649.

33. Ann Grodzins Gold and Bhoju Ram Gujar, *Time of Trees and Sorrows: Nature, Power, and Memory in Rajasthan* (Durham, N.C.: Duke University Press, 2002), 9, 11. Gold and Gujar also begin by accepting the central paradox that "any nature that it is possible for humans to know they have also produced, even as it has produced them" (7).

34. Worster, "Transformations of the Earth," 1089. Animal-studies scholars and the history of science have done more to challenge these boundaries. See Cary Wolfe, *Animal Rites: American Culture, the Discourse of Species, and Posthumanist Theory* (Chicago: University of Chicago Press, 2003); Kari Weil, *Thinking Animals: Why Animal Studies Now?* (New York: Columbia University

Press, 2012); and Donna Jeanne Haraway, *Simians, Cyborgs, and Women: The Reinvention of Nature* (New York: Routledge, 1991). For theory and method in environmental history, see Worster, "Transformations of the Earth," specifically his discussion of modes of production, 1090. See also Herron, "Because Antelope Can't Talk"; Nash, "The Agency of Nature"; and Steinberg, "Down to Earth." Stroud, "Does Nature Always Matter," questions the terms of the field—nature, environment, place—and calls for more specificity in terms. Stroud calls for a focus on nature—"the material, biological, and ecological components of the environments we study" (78).

35. Sutter, "The World with Us," 96.

36. Ibid.

37. Ibid.

38. Ibid., 119.

39. Nash, "Furthering the Environmental Turn," 134.

40. Claire Jean Kim and Carla Freccero, "Introduction: A Dialogue," *American Quarterly* 65, no. 3 (September 2013): 461–79, quotes from 471, 465, 461.

41. Julie Livingston and Jasbir K. Puar, "Interspecies," *Social Text 106* 29, no. 1 (Spring 2011): 4. For an overview of posthumanism, see Cary Wolfe, *What Is Posthumanism?* (Minneapolis: University of Minnesota Press, 2009); and Stefan Herbrechter, *Posthumanism: A Critical Analysis* (London: Bloomsbury, 2013).

42. Livingston and Puar, "Interspecies," 3. For an overview of the field of animal studies, see Jennifer Howard, "Creature Consciousness," *Chronicle of Higher Education*, October 18, 2009, http://www.chronicle.com/article/Creature-Consciousness/48804/ (accessed January 21, 2014). See also Cary Wolfe, "Human, All Too Human: 'Animal Studies' and the Humanities," *PMLA* 124 (March 2009): 564–75; Cary Wolfe, ed., *Zoontologies: The Question of the Animal* (Minneapolis: University of Minnesota Press, 2003); and Weil, *Thinking Animals.*

43. Livingston and Puar, "Interspecies," 3.

44. Ibid., 7.

45. *Oxford English Dictionary,* s.v. "render, v," http://www.oed.com.proxy.lib.muohio.edu /view/Entry/162386?isAdvanced=false&result=3&rskey=x86wEd& (accessed February 25, 2013).

46. Nicole Shukin, *Animal Capital: Rendering Life in Biopolitical Times* (Minneapolis: University of Minnesota Press, 2009), 23, 20.

47. Historians of science Donna Haraway and Bruno Latour offer compelling models for theorizing the narrative and cultural construction of science revealing the complex interplay between nature and culture. See Donna Haraway, "Situated Knowledges: The Science Question in Feminism and the Privilege of Partial Perspective," *Feminist Studies* 14, no. 3 (Autumn 1988): 575–99; Bruno Latour, *We Have Never Been Modern* (Cambridge, Mass.: Harvard University Press, 1993). For discussions of stories and narrative in environmental history, see William Cronon, "A Place for Stories: Nature, History, and Narrative," *Journal of American History* 78, no. 4 (March 1992): 1347–76.

Chapter 2. Beasts of the Southern Wild

1. The original version is *Slavery in the United States: A Narrative of the Life and Adventures of Charles Ball, a Black Man, Who Lived Forty Years in Maryland, South Carolina, and Georgia, as a Slave . . . Containing an Account of the Manners and Usages of the Planters and Slaveholders of the South, a Description of the Condition and Treatment of the Slaves, with Observations upon the State of Morals Amongst the Cotton Planters, and the Perils and Sufferings of a Fugitive Slave, Who Twice Escaped from the Cotton Country* (Lewistown, Pa.: J. W. Shugert, 1836). The short-

ened and, in some crucial respects, compromised version of the narrative reprinted in later decades as *Fifty Years in Chains* (in Norwich, England, in 1846; Edinburgh, Scotland, in 1847; Pittsburgh in 1853 and 1854; Wittenberg, Germany, in 1856; and in New York and Indianapolis in 1859) contains most but not all of the passages I analyze here. All citations to Charles Ball's narrative come from the most widely available edition: Charles Ball, *Fifty Years in Chains*, ed. Philip S. Foner (Mineola, N.Y.: Dover, 1970). Although this edition employs the title of the abridged version of Ball's narrative, the body of the text is actually drawn from the narrative's second edition: *Slavery in the United States: A Narrative of the Life and Adventures of Charles Ball, Black Man* (New York: John S. Taylor, 1837). Quotes in this paragraph are from Ball, *Fifty Years in Chains*, 3–4.

2. Here and elsewhere in the essay, I emphasize that humans are also animals. My intention is not to bestialize either slaves or slaveholders, but instead to forsake what the animal-studies scholar Paul Waldau calls "human exceptionalism." This perspective, Waldau argues, "has spawned great harms—to other animals, of course, but also to both our relationship with the more-than-human world and our own freedom, creativity, and imagination." See Paul Waldau, *Animal Studies: An Introduction* (New York: Oxford University Press, 2013), 8.

3. Ball, *Fifty Years in Chains*, 3–4.

4. Ball remained legally a slave, as he acknowledged at the conclusion of his narrative, when he explained that he used a pseudonym out of fear for his safety. On several occasions in the narrative, though, he described himself as a "freeman."

5. A very incomplete list might include Eugene D. Genovese, "Livestock in the Slave Economy of the Old South—A Revised View," *Agricultural History* 36, no. 3 (1962): 143–49; Robert Byron Lamb, *The Mule in Southern Agriculture* (Berkeley: University of California Press, 1963); Karl Jacoby, "Slaves by Nature? Domestic Animals and Human Slaves," *Slavery and Abolition* 15 (April 1994): 89–99; George B. Ellenberg, *Mule South to Tractor South: Mules, Machines, and the Transformation of the Cotton South* (Tuscaloosa: University of Alabama Press, 2007); S. Jonathan Bass, "'How 'Bout a Hand for the Hog': The Enduring Nature of the Swine as a Cultural Symbol in the South," *Southern Cultures* 1, no. 3 (1995): 301–20; John Campbell, "'My Constant Companion': Slaves and Their Dogs in the Antebellum South," in *Working Toward Freedom: Slave Society and Domestic Economy in the American South*, ed. Larry E. Hudson (Rochester, N.Y.: University of Rochester Press, 1994), 53–78; Marcus Rediker, "History from Below the Water Line: Sharks and the Atlantic Slave Trade," *Atlantic Studies* 5, no. 2 (2008): 285–97; and Walter Johnson, *River of Dark Dreams: Slavery and Empire in the Cotton Kingdom* (Cambridge, Mass.: Belknap Press of Harvard University Press, 2013).

6. On the performative aspect of slave narrative, see William L. Andrews, *To Tell a Free Story: The First Century of Afro-American Autobiography, 1760–1865* (Urbana: University of Illinois Press, 1986), 89.

7. The public historian Anne Dowling Grulich has corroborated many details of those portions of Ball's narrative relating to Calvert County, Maryland. See Grulich, *Putting Charles Ball on the Map in Calvert County, Maryland* (2008), http://www.jefpat.org/Documents/Grulich,%20Anne%20Dowling%20-%20Putting%20Charles%20Ball%20on%20the%20Map%20in%20Calvert%20County,%20Maryland.pdf (accessed October 21, 2014).

8. See Old Home Week Association, Huntingdon Pa., *Historic Huntingdon, Being a Brief Account of the History of Huntingdon from Its Earliest Settlements to the Present Day* (Huntingdon, Pa.: Press of the Monitor Company, 1909), 164; and J. Simpson Africa, *History of Huntingdon and Blair Counties, Pennsylvania* (Philadelphia: L. H. Everts, 1883), 11.

9. On Fisher's geological investigations, see *Gettysburg Republican Compiler*, August 22, 1837; and Isaac Fisher, "Essay upon the Geological History of Pennsylvania," *Atkinson's Casket*, no. 3 (March 1838): 121. Fisher was a candidate for Pennsylvania Supreme Court judge for the Free Soil Party in 1854; see *Pennsylvania Democrat-Sentinel*, May 25, 1854.

10. Virtually the only evidence documenting the creation of *Slavery in the United States* is contained within various editions of the book itself. From the first, the book's front matter included affidavits from two well-known public figures in southern Pennsylvania, both of whom attested that they had personally heard a slave recounting a life story identical in substance to the narrative presented in *Slavery in the United States*. In his preface Fisher described the book as an "unadorned detail of acts" and admitted that he had suppressed Ball's expressions of "bitterness" at the "unatoned injuries" he had suffered, both as a slave and as a fugitive. In the book's second edition, the New York publisher John S. Taylor related that Fisher had told him, "in a private communication, that many of the anecdotes in the book illustrative of southern society, were not obtained from Ball, but from other creditable sources." William Andrews, an authority on African American autobiographies, has speculated that many of these "anecdotes" offered "local color," focusing especially on the southern landscape and flora; see Andrews, *To Tell a Free Story*, 84.

We know that Isaac Fisher had traveled through portions of the South; he might also have obtained additional "facts" from books, periodicals, and even private correspondence detailing slavery. Yet there is no evidence to suggest that "Charles Ball" was only a creature of Fisher's imagination. Ultimately, *Slavery in the United States* relates "facts" that only someone who had experienced slavery firsthand could have grasped. The narrator, Charles Ball, in short, is best conceived of as the joint creation of Fisher and a fugitive slave whose story was known to other leading citizens of central Pennsylvania.

11. Marion Wilson Starling, *The Slave Narrative: Its Place in American History* (Boston: G. K. Hall, 1981), 106.

12. Andrews, *To Tell a Free Story*, 82, 62.

13. Starling, *Slave Narrative*, 227; Andrews, *To Tell a Free Story*, 82.

14. Peter Wheeler and C. Edwards Lester, *Chains and Freedom: Or, the Life and Adventures of Peter Wheeler, a Colored Man Yet Living . . .* (New York: E. S. Arnold & Co., 1839), 18.

15. To cite just a few prominent examples, see Walter Johnson, *Soul by Soul: Life inside the Antebellum Slave Market* (Cambridge, Mass.: Harvard University Press, 1999), 35, 60–78, 141, 66, 71, 74, 91, 96, 200, 18; Calvin Schermerhorn, *Money over Mastery, Family over Freedom: Slavery in the Antebellum Upper South* (Baltimore: Johns Hopkins University Press, 2011), chap. 1; Mark Fiege, *The Republic of Nature: An Environmental History of the United States* (Seattle: University of Washington Press, 2012), 108–9, 16, 25–29; Johnson, *River of Dark Dreams*, 152–53, 62–64, 66–67, 71, 77–79, 85–86, 90–91, 93, 98, 210–12, 15, 17–18, 24, 29–35, 37–38, 48; and Alan Taylor, *The Internal Enemy: Slavery and War in Virginia, 1772–1832* (New York: W. W. Norton, 2013), 59–60, 66, 69, 248–49, 65.

16. Ball, *Fifty Years in Chains*, 16–17; Ira Berlin, *The Making of African America: The Four Great Migrations* (New York: Penguin, 2010), 100.

17. Ball, *Fifty Years in Chains*, 18, 45–46. Ball—or perhaps in this case Fisher—propounded at length upon the poor condition of slave-cultivated lands from Virginia's tobacco regions southward (ibid., 18–30, 35–37).

18. A later passage in the narrative elaborated on the same theme: "In the plantation states . . . lands and slaves constitute the only property of the country that is worthy of being taken into an

estimate of public wealth. Cattle and horses, hogs, sheep and mules exist, but in numbers so few, and of qualities so inferior, that the portion of them, possessed by any individual planter, would compose an aggregate value of sufficient magnitude only to raise him barely beyond the lines that divide poverty from mediocrity of condition" (Ball, *Fifty Years in Chains*, 177–78).

19. Ball repeatedly reflected on these differences in ibid., chaps. 4 and 5.

20. For an overview of the diversification of slave plantations in the Upper South, see Lorena Walsh, "Slave Life, Slave Society, and Tobacco Production in the Tidewater Chesapeake, 1620–1820," in *Cultivation and Culture: Labor and the Shaping of Slave Life in the Americas*, ed. Ira Berlin and Philip D. Morgan (Charlottesville and London: University of Virginia Press, 1993), 184.

21. Peter Kolchin, *American Slavery, 1619–1877*, 1st rev. ed. (New York: Hill and Wang, 2003), 96–97. Note that Charles Ball joined many abolitionists in attributing Berlin's "second Middle Passage" to the destruction of the soil's fertility through the excesses of a slave-based tobacco economy instead of the progressivism of mixed husbandry in the Chesapeake.

22. On the internal slave trade, see Johnson, *Soul by Soul*; Steven Deyle, *Carry Me Back: The Domestic Slave Trade in American Life* (New York: Oxford University Press, 2005); and Michael Tadman, *Speculators and Slaves: Masters, Traders, and Slaves in the Old South* (Madison: University of Wisconsin Press, 1989).

23. Ball, *Fifty Years in Chains*, 81, 84.

24. Kolchin, *American Slavery*, 100. On Indian women prior to Native Americans' removal from their lands, see Kenneth M. Stampp, *The Peculiar Institution: Slavery in the Ante-bellum South* (New York: Vintage Books, 1989), 52–53. On black slaves, see James Adair, *The History of the American Indians, Particularly Those Nations Adjoining to the Missis[s]ippi, East and West Florida, Georgia, South and North Carolina, and Virginia . . .* (London: Printed for Edward and Charles Dilly, 1775), 230.

25. By the 1860s some four hundred thousand hogs were slaughtered in Cincinnati every year, amply justifying its claim to the title "Porkopolis"; see Brett Mizelle, *Pig* (London: Reaktion Books, 2011), 46. On Cincinnati, Chicago, and pork, see ibid., 47; and William Cronon, *Nature's Metropolis: Chicago and the Great West* (New York: W. W. Norton, 1991).

26. Quoted in Stampp, *Peculiar Institution*, 165.

27. Ball, *Fifty Years in Chains*, 46.

28. On livestock, slaves, and domination, see Jacoby, "Slaves by Nature."

29. Johnson, *Soul by Soul*, intro., drawing on James W. C. Pennington, *The Fugitive Blacksmith; Or, Events in the History of James Pennington*, 3rd ed. (London: C. Gilpin, 1850), vii.

30. Ball, *Fifty Years in Chains*, 46, 49, 53, 75.

31. Ibid., 46–47.

32. On "infrapolitics," see James C. Scott, *Domination and the Arts of Resistance: Hidden Transcripts* (New Haven, Conn.: Yale University Press, 1990).

33. Ball's narrative thus offers an important rejoinder to Robert Fogel's controversial conclusion that "the malnutrition of U.S. slaves was primarily a phenomenon of early life"; see Robert William Fogel, *Without Consent or Contrast: The Rise and Fall of American Slavery* (New York: W. W. Norton, 1989), 143.

34. Ball, *Fifty Years in Chains*, 9–10, 47–48, 57.

35. Ibid., 81.

36. Ball expressed his "opinion that our master lost money" by failing to provide his hands with meat after the harvest season (ibid., 126). Ball presented the same dynamic in a more scornful light elsewhere (77).

37. Ibid., 115.

38. My emphasis here on the interface between metabolic, social, and psychological processes complicates the hegemonic paternalism that Eugene Genovese famously conceived as the heart of southern slavery; see Eugene D. Genovese, *Roll, Jordan, Roll: The World the Slaves Made* (New York: Vintage Books, 1976).

39. Revealingly, Ball explained, "I was not a butcher by trade, but . . . had often assisted my master and others to kill hogs and cattle, and . . . could dress a hog, or a bullock, as well as most people" (*Fifty Years in Chains*, 119).

40. Ibid., 119–22, 124. Southern plantation owners almost universally marked holidays and "grand divisions of the labors" involved in growing cash crops for global markets by slaughtering livestock and giving their slaves meat. This practice, as Ball witnessed, often brought a modicum of joy to the slave quarters.

41. Ibid., 124, 126.

42. Ibid., 117–18.

43. Ibid., 119.

44. Ibid., 138, 142.

45. Ibid., 163, 116. Ball later claimed of the southern storekeeper that although he often "live[d] as well as" planters, "[t]he country has no hold on him, and he has no hold on the country. His habits of life are not similar to those of his neighbours—he is not 'one of us' " (178).

46. Ibid., 163. Ball even managed to fashion squirrel-skin moccasins to shield his feet "from the frost, which was sometimes very heavy and sharp, in the morning" (168).

47. Ball noted that despite the assumption that slaves lived "in a condition of the most perfect equality, yet there was in fact a very great difference in the manner of living, in the several families" (ibid., 171). More generally, see Ira Berlin and Philip D. Morgan, *The Slaves' Economy: Independent Production by Slaves in the Americas* (London and Portland, Ore.: Frank Cass, 1991); and Berlin and Morgan, eds., *Cultivation and Culture*.

48. Ball, *Fifty Years in Chains*, 172, 163.

49. Ibid., 172. See also Nicolas W. Proctor, *Bathed in Blood: Hunting and Mastery in the Old South* (Charlottesville: University of Virginia Press, 2002), 157; and Amy L. Young, Michael Tuma, and Cliff Jenkins, "The Role of Hunting to Cope with Risk at Saragossa Plantation, Natchez, Mississippi," *American Archaeologist* 103, no. 3 (2001): 699–701.

50. Ball, *Fifty Years in Chains*, 170–71.

51. Ibid., 172.

52. Ibid., 172–73.

53. Ibid., 173–74.

54. Ibid., 173–74, 182–83.

55. Ibid., 185–87.

56. Ibid., 187–88.

57. Ibid., 188.

58. Ibid., 187, 191.

59. Ibid., 189–90.

60. Ibid., 193–96. Previously in the narrative, Ball acutely dissected the social structure of the Deep South. "Those will fall into a great error," he declared, "who shall imagine that in Carolina and Georgia there are but two orders of men." He went on to point out that "there is a third order of men located there, little known to the world, but who, nevertheless, hold a separate station, occupy a place of their own, and who do not come into direct contrast [*sic*] with either the

master or the slave." Ball called the "poor cottagers" of Carolina "a separate and distinct race of men from the planters, and appear to have nothing in common with them. If it were possible for any people to occupy a grade in human society below that of the slaves, on the cotton plantations, certainly the station would be filled by these white families, who cannot be said to possess any thing in the shape of property" (ibid., 180–82).

61. Ibid., chap. 13.

62. For more on horses and dogs in the "carceral landscape" of the cotton kingdom, see Johnson, *River of Dark Dreams,* chap. 8. As noted earlier, Johnson makes heavy use of Ball's narrative in his analysis—though Ball probably never set foot in the Mississippi River Valley.

63. Ball, *Fifty Years in Chains,* 196.

64. Ibid., 196–97.

65. Ibid., 197.

66. Ibid., 197–99.

67. Ibid., 203–4, 246.

68. Ibid., 199–201.

69. On the six-mule team, see ibid., 213. On geographic details, see ibid., 214, 308. The county was not actually created until 1807.

70. Ibid., 215.

71. Ibid., 215–18.

72. Ibid., 219–20.

73. Ibid., 221–23.

74. Ibid., 222.

75. Ibid., 224.

76. Ibid., 222, 228.

77. Ibid., 231.

78. Ibid., 231–32.

79. Ibid., 232.

80. Ibid., 242–43, 245–46.

81. Ibid., 246.

82. Ibid.

83. Ibid., 246–48.

84. Ibid., 248.

85. Ibid., 248–49, 252–53. Ball sometimes regretted his dependence on the stars, as when severe cloudiness blocked his view of the night sky in South Carolina and made it impossible for him to determine which way to go, forcing him to stay put for almost two weeks. When he resumed his travels, he got lost but managed to retrace most of his steps before another spell of cloudy weather caused him to make camp for nearly a week (ibid., 264–66). On further troubles caused by cloudy nights, see ibid., 273, 279–80. Ball also described the ghostly remains of "several decayed beaver lodges" left behind by an "industrious little nation, which had fled at the approach of the white man," and a dark night on which he "slept but little; for it seemed as if all the owls in the country had assembled" at Ball's resting place "to perform a grand musical concert" (ibid., 249–50).

86. Ball, *Fifty Years in Chains,* 250, 254–55.

87. Ibid., 259–62. Ball also discusses hunger repeatedly at ibid., 251–52.

88. Ibid., 269–70.

89. Ibid., 271–79.

90. Ibid., 281–82, 286–88.

91. Ibid., 293.

92. Ibid., 295.

93. Ibid., 293–97.

94. Ibid., 297, 306.

95. Ibid., 306.

96. Ibid.

97. Ibid., 331.

98. See, for instance, Diane L. Beers, *For the Prevention of Cruelty: The History and Legacy of Animal Rights Activism in the United States* (Athens: Swallow Press/Ohio University Press, 2006).

Chapter 3. Stuffed

1. Comanche's status as the "lone survivor" is the key to his legend, but in truth many other horses (and a dog) survived the battle as well. As the battle mount of a well-known Seventh Cavalry officer, Myles Keogh, Comanche gets all the attention, though. A 1951 book by David Appel, a popular song by Johnny Horton, and a 1956 film starring Dana Andrews (and a 2000 film remake by Kris Kristofferson) have further solidified Comanche's status within the Custer myth. See Evan S. Connell, *Son of the Morning Star: Custer and the Little Big Horn* (New York: North Point Press, 1997), 296–98. For more information on the display of Comanche, including its recent restoration, see the Kansas Museum of Natural History, http://www.naturalhistory.ku.edu/explore-topic/comanche-preservation/comanche-preservation (accessed March 25, 2013).

2. My discussion of the panorama is drawn from William Sharp and Peggy Sullivan, *The Dashing Kansan: The Amazing Adventures of a Nineteenth-Century Naturalist and Explorer* (Kansas City: Harrow Books, 1990), esp. 66–78.

3. The *Kansas City Star* ran a number of articles about the panorama's creator, Lewis Lindsay Dyche, and the panorama before, during, and after the Chicago World's Fair. See, for example, articles and editorials from June 20, 1891; December 14, 1892; September 6, 1894; and April 1, 1895.

4. F. D. Palmer, "The Kansas Exhibit of Mounted Specimens of the Animals of the State," *Scientific American* 69, no. 3 (July 15, 1893): 41–42.

5. Hubert Howe Bancroft, *The Book of the Fair*, 2 vols. (San Francisco: Bancroft, 1893), 2: 818–19.

6. Ibid.

7. *Kansas City Star*, December 14, 1892, 4.

8. On the representational context of taxidermy displays, see Karen Wonders, *Habitat Dioramas: Illusions of Wilderness in Museums of Natural History* (Uppsala, Sweden: Uppsala University Press, 1993). Wonders's book is an excellent source for any scholar interested in taxidermy and diorama display. The idea of Victorian clutter has received much historiographical attention; for just one example, see Thomas J. Schlereth, *Victorian America: Transformations in Everyday Life, 1876–1915* (New York: HarperCollins, 1991).

9. Susan Leigh Star, "Craft vs. Commodity, Mess vs. Transcendence: How the Right Tool Became the Wrong One in the Case of Taxidermy and Natural History," in *The Right Tools for the Job: At Work in Twentieth-Century Life Science*, ed. Adele E. Clarke and John H. Fujimura (Princeton, N.J.: Princeton University Press, 1992), 281.

10. Steven Conn, *Museums and American Intellectual Life, 1876–1926* (Chicago: University of Chicago Press, 1998), 5; and Susan Stewart, *On Longing: Narratives of the Miniature, the Gigantic, the Souvenir, the Collection* (Baltimore: Johns Hopkins University Press, 1984), 162.

11. Lynn K. Nyhart, *Modern Nature: The Rise of the Biological Perspective in Germany* (Chicago: University of Chicago Press, 2009), 80, 117, 124, 196.

12. Conn, *Museums and American Intellectual Life*, 4–9. Conn labels such an approach "an object based epistemology." In brief, the idea is that the world could be understood through the proper display of appropriately arranged physical objects.

13. Hannah Rose Shell, "Skin Deep: Taxidermy, Embodiment, and Extinction in W. T. Hornaday's Buffalo Group," *Proceedings of the California Academy of Sciences* 55, no. 1 (October 18, 2004): 105.

14. Robert Rydell, *All the World's a Fair: Visions of Empire at the American International Expositions, 1876–1916* (Chicago: University of Chicago Press, 1984), 2.

15. See Amy Kaplan, *The Anarchy of Empire in the Making of US Culture* (Cambridge, Mass.: Harvard University Press, 2002). See also Conn, *Museums and American Intellectual Life*, 117–20.

16. William Temple Hornaday, *Taxidermy and Zoological Collecting* (New York: Scribner's, 1891), 111.

17. For more information on this larger discussion, see Jonathan Spiro, *Defending the Master Race: Conservation, Eugenics and the Legacy of Madison Grant* (Burlington: University of Vermont Press, 2009).

18. Shell, "Skin Deep," 100–101. The Hornaday quote comes from William Temple Hornaday to Lewis Lindsay Dyche, November 1, 1893, box 1, folder 3, Lewis L. Dyche Collection, University Archives, PP 66, Kenneth Spencer Research Library, University of Kansas Libraries (hereafter cited as Dyche Papers, Spencer Library).

19. Stephan Oetterman, *The Panorama: History of a Mass Medium* (New York: Zone Books, 1997), 49. See also Robert E. Kohler, *All Creatures: Naturalists, Collectors, and Biodiversity, 1850–1950* (Princeton, N.J.: Princeton University Press, 2006), 77.

20. James W. Cook, *The Arts of Deception: Playing with Fraud in the Age of Barnum* (Cambridge, Mass.: Harvard University Press, 2001), 228.

21. Ibid., 229.

22. See Miles Orvell, *The Real Thing: Imitations and Authenticity in American Culture, 1880–1940* (Chapel Hill: University of North Carolina Press, 1989), esp. 20–23. See also Sharp and Sullivan, *Dashing Kansan*, 73.

23. Lynn K. Nyhart, "Science, Art, and Authenticity in Natural History Displays," in *Models: The Third Dimension of Science,* ed. Soraya De Chadarevian and Nick Hopwood (Palo Alto, Calif.: Stanford University Press, 2004), 307–35, quotes on 308, 330. See also George W. Stocking, Jr., ed., *Objects and Others: Essays on Museums and Material Culture* (Madison: University of Wisconsin Press, 1985), 4.

24. Donna Haraway, *Primate Visions: Gender, Race, and Nature in the World of Modern Science* (New York: Routledge, 1989), 38–39.

25. Wonders, *Habitat Dioramas*, 115–23; Shell, "Skin Deep," 97.

26. The notions of illusion and representation are best explored by scholars of art history and visual culture. See, for example, W. J. T. Mitchell, *Picture Theory: Essays on Verbal and Visual Representation* (Chicago: University of Chicago Press, 1994); and Jonathan Crary, *Suspensions of Perception: Attention, Spectacle, and Modern Culture* (Cambridge, Mass.: MIT Press, 2001). See also Cook, *Arts of Deception*, 17–19.

27. Orvell, *Real Thing*, 35; Conn, *Museums and American Intellectual Life*, 15. See also Stewart, *On Longing*, 161.

28. The historiography on this topic is large, but as a small sample, see Dean MacCannell, *The Tourist: A New Theory of the Leisure Class* (Berkeley: University of California Press, 1999); George Stocking, *Delimiting Anthropology: Occasional Essays and Reflections* (Madison: University of Wisconsin Press, 2001); and Stewart's classic *On Longing.*

29. Nyhart, "Science, Art, and Authenticity," 308.

30. The historiography on naturalists and natural history is immense, but as a start consider the scholarship on the subject in an American context; see Keith R. Benson, "From Museum Research to Laboratory Research: The Transformation of Natural History into Academic Biology," in *The American Development of Biology*, ed. Ronald Rainger, Keith R. Benson, and Jane Maienschein (Philadelphia: University of Pennsylvania Press, 1988), 49–83, esp. 50–51; and Kevin C. Armitage, *The Nature Study Movement: The Forgotten Popularizer of America's Conservation Ethic* (Lawrence: University Press of Kansas, 2009).

31. Michel Foucault, *The Order of Things: An Archaeology of the Human Sciences* (New York: Vintage Books, 1970), 132.

32. Sue Ann Prince, *Stuffing Birds, Pressing Plants, Shaping Knowledge: Natural History in North America, 1730–1860* (Philadelphia: American Philosophical Society, 2003), 1–2.

33. Gary Cutting, *Michel Foucault's Archaeology of Scientific Reason* (Cambridge: Cambridge University Press, 1989), 162–69.

34. For more information on this idea, see Bruno Latour's classic *We Have Never Been Modern* (Cambridge, Mass.: Harvard University Press, 1993).

35. There are a number of ways to explore the connections between politics and nature display. Consider the following works on the American naturalist Charles Willson Peale: Charles Coleman Sellers, *Mr. Peale's Museum: Charles Willson Peale and the First Popular Museum of Natural Science and Art* (New York: W. W. Norton, 1980); and David C. Ward, *Charles Willson Peale: Art and Selfhood in the Early Republic* (Berkeley: University of California Press, 2004).

36. Philip J. Pauly, *Biologists and the Promise of American Life: From Meriwether Lewis to Alfred Kinsey* (Princeton, N.J.: Princeton University Press, 2000), 21, 45.

37. A number of scholars have taken up the theme of the biological turn, but I rely heavily on Nyhart, *Modern Nature,* esp. 18–24. Nyhart introduces several terms, including "civic zoology," "the biological perspective," and "the biological turn," that help explain the cultural dimension of animal display. Nyhart's earlier work *Biology Takes Form: Animal Morphology and the German Universities, 1800–1900* (Chicago: University of Chicago Press, 1995) was also helpful.

38. The negative press coverage of the panorama is covered in Sharp and Sullivan, *Dashing Kansan,* 67.

39. For more information on this topic, see David M. Lubin, *Picturing a Nation: Art and Social Change in Nineteenth-Century America* (New Haven, Conn.: Yale University Press, 1994), esp. 276–80, 309–18; Jonathan Crary, *Techniques of the Observer: On Vision and Modernity in the 19th Century* (Cambridge, Mass.: MIT Press, 1992); and Barbara Maria Stafford, *Artful Science: Enlightenment Entertainment and the Eclipse of Visual Education* (Cambridge, Mass.: MIT Press, 1996).

40. I am more indebted to Cook's *Arts of Deception* for my examination of the panorama and modernity than this single footnote suggests. His chapter on "Queer Art Illusions," especially 227–28 and 248–55, was especially insightful.

41. Bancroft, *Book of the Fair,* 818–19. C. Hart Merriam, chief of the Division of Economic Ornithology and Mammalogy within the Department of Agriculture, would also compliment Dyche for "perfection in the taxidermist's art"; see C. Hart Merriam to Lewis Dyche, July 10, 1888, box 1, folder 1, Dyche Papers, Spencer Library.

42. Clyde Kenneth Hyder, *Snow of Kansas: The Life of Francis Huntington Snow with Extracts from His Journals and Letters* (Lawrence: University Press of Kansas, 1953), 141. See also Sharp and Sullivan, *Dashing Kansan*, 10–11.

43. Francis Snow, "Report of the Professor of Natural History," in the *Biennial Report of the Board of Regents, 1877-1878* (Topeka: Kansas State Printing Office, 1878), 18.

44. One well-known popularizer of this classroom style was Louis Agassiz. The best source on Agassiz and his teaching methods is Edward Lurie, *Louis Agassiz: A Life in Science* (Chicago: University of Chicago Press, 1960). See also Louis Menand, *The Metaphysical Club: A Story of Ideas in America* (New York: Farrar, Straus, and Giroux, 2001), 100–101. The best-known natural scientist at the University of Kansas during this period was Francis Huntington Snow. The Massachusetts-born Snow did not study directly under Agassiz (although he did spend a study summer with Agassiz's son Alexander) but was influenced by his methods and brought such an approach to his classes at the University of Kansas. See Hyder, *Snow of Kansas*, 147–48.

45. Kohler, *All Creatures*, 227. I am heavily indebted to Kohler's description of the importance of collection and categorization. See also Sally Gregory Kohlstedt, "Museums on Campus: A Tradition of Inquiry and Teaching," in *American Development of Biology*, ed. Rainger et al., 15–47, esp. 16–17.

46. Kohler, *All Creatures*, 231–45. See also Wonders, *Habitat Dioramas*, 112.

47. Kohlstedt, "Museums on Campus," 19–21.

48. The quote and information about the growth of the Kansas collections come from a school newspaper, *Observer of Nature*, June 15, 1875, 4. More information can be found in Hyder, *Snow of Kansas*, 151.

49. "Snow Hall of Natural History at Lawrence, Kan.," *Science* 10 (December 30, 1887): 314.

50. Wonders, *Habitat Dioramas*, 111.

51. Francis Snow, "A New Natural History Building," in *Tenth Biennial Report of the Board of Regents and Chancellor, 1895-1896* (Topeka: State Printing Office, 1896), 22–23. A copy of the report is located in the Spencer Library.

52. Kohler, *All Creatures*, 236–39.

53. On Ward's establishment, see Sally Gregory Kohlstedt, "Henry A. Ward: The Merchant Naturalist and American Museum Development," *Journal of the Society for the Bibliography of Natural History* 9 (1980): 647–61; Mary Anne Andrei, "Nature's Mirror: How the Taxidermists of Ward's Natural Science Establishment Transformed Wildlife Display in American Natural History Museums and Fought to Save Endangered Species" (Ph.D. diss., University of Minnesota, 1996); Wonders, *Habitat Dioramas*, 110–15; and Mark V. Barrow, "The Species Dealer: Entrepreneurial Natural History in America's Gilded Age," *Journal of the History of Biology* 33 (2000): 493–534. In addition to Hornaday, future luminaries in the field including Frederic A. Lucas, Frederic S. Webster, Carl Akeley, and William Morton Wheeler all trained at Ward's establishment.

54. On his collecting tour, see William Temple Hornaday, *Two Years in the Jungle: The Experiences of a Hunter and Naturalist in India, Ceylon, the Malay Peninsula and Borneo* (New York: Scribner's, 1886).

55. Wonders, *Habitat Dioramas*, 121. Hornaday also brought back to Washington a live calf, which later died in captivity. See also William Temple Hornaday to Smithsonian Secretary Spencer Fullerton Baird, December 21, 1886, Smithsonian Institution Archives, Record Unit 305, Accession 18617, for a firsthand accounting of the hunt. In this letter Hornaday explains to Baird that "we killed very nearly all we saw."

56. See Hornaday, *Taxidermy and Zoological Collecting*, 160. Consider also William Temple Hornaday, "Common Faults in the Mounting of Quadrupeds," *Annual Report of the Society of American Taxidermists* 3 (1883): 67–71. The Society of American Taxidermists was a short-lived professional body of taxidermists organized by Hornaday; it sponsored competitions and issued annual reports in 1881, 1882, and 1884.

57. Hornaday, *Taxidermy*, 109–12, 139–41. The idea of a "buffaloness" comes from Shell's excellent essay on Hornaday in "Skin Deep," 97.

58. The University of Kansas is currently embarking on a fund-raising effort to restore many of the panorama mounts. See "One of America's Treasures," *Lawrence Journal-World*, August 25, 2013, D1–2.

59. Kohler, *All Creatures*, 83.

60. Quoted in Sharp and Sullivan, *Dashing Kansan*, 78.

61. Ibid., 139.

62. Hyder, *Snow of Kansas*, 111–12, 147.

63. For more information on Dyche's tenure as fish and game warden, see Sharp and Sullivan, *Dashing Kansan*, 155–82.

64. Nyhart, *Modern Nature*, 117.

65. For a discussion of children in museums, see Steven Conn, *Do Museums Still Need Objects?* (Philadelphia: University of Pennsylvania Press, 2010), 138–71.

Chapter 4. Digit's Legacy

Many people helped me to think through and understand the many perspectives that frame Digit's life and death. I am most grateful to Phoebe Young, who not only has worked with me over the long term to articulate the vision undergirding this essay and make this volume a reality but also has read and commented on multiple drafts of this essay. Her support and insight have been invaluable. I thank my colleagues in American studies at Miami University who read and commented on an early draft of the essay: Andrew Busch, Sheila Croucher, Sandra Garner, Kimberly Hamlin, Damon Scott, Helen Sheumaker, and Kristen Williams. In addition I would like to thank my writing support group for reading through this in multiple stages and providing helpful comments: Mary Jean Corbett, Madelyn Detloff, Elizabeth Hodges, Katie Johnson, and Tim Melley. Thanks go as well to my fellow Altman Scholars, especially the organizers José Amador and Amanda McVety at the Miami University Humanities Center, for providing a vibrant interdisciplinary context for this project.

1. Walter Cronkite, *CBS Evening News*, February 3, 1978, Vanderbilt TV News Archive, Nashville, Tenn. Cronkite reported the story as follows: "American zoologist Dr. Dian Fossey studies animal behavior in the African country of Rwanda; and for eleven years one of her favorite subjects has been a gentle and playful gorilla named Digit. Digit starred in film studies by Dr. Fossey shown round the world, as well as modeling for a Rwandan tourist poster. But now comes sad news from the World Wildlife Fund in Switzerland that reports that poachers have killed Digit and cut off his head apparently to sell as a trophy." Behind Cronkite is a map of central Africa highlighting the country of Rwanda. During the story, a film clip of Digit and Fossey shows Fossey lying on the ground with Digit sitting next to her. The camera zooms in for a close-up of Digit reaching out to touch Fossey and then pulls back out.

2. In an attempt to use Digit's murder to raise public concern about the plight of mountain gorillas, Fossey had a research assistant photograph his headless corpse, which she sent out for publication in a number of wildlife conservation newsletters. At one point she wanted to make a

poster using the image of Digit's corpse to draw attention to his death. See Farley Mowat, *Woman in the Mists: The Story of Dian Fossey and the Mountain Gorillas of Africa* (New York: Warner Books, 1987), 160–81. I think it is also important to note that Belgian colonizers in control of DRC and later Rwanda during the late nineteenth and early twentieth centuries amputated the hands of African workers as a standard punishment for insufficient work and productivity while under the direction of King Leopold II. Although Digit's hands might have been sold off as souvenir ashtrays, the link to this colonizing practice is a significant and often overlooked part of the story.

3. Bill Weber and Amy Vedder, *In the Kingdom of Gorillas: Fragile Species in a Dangerous Land* (New York: Simon & Schuster, 2001), 26.

4. Judith Butler, *Precarious Life: The Powers of Mourning and Violence* (London: Verso, 2003), argues that the public visibility and invisibility of death can be understood as a means of policing who counts as humans.

5. I describe the various human encounters with Digit as human-nature encounters rather than human-animal encounters because, as a "wild" mountain gorilla, Digit signifies an ideal of nature associated with pristine wilderness. Encompassed within this encounter are multiple binaries that have distinct but intersecting histories: nature/culture, human (or, as it used to be framed, "man")/nature, human/animal. The various encounters with Digit that are traced in this essay speak to all of these binaries in one form or another. Although I explore the human-animal encounter, most notably between Digit and Dian Fossey, the larger concern of this essay focuses on nature and culture.

6. Donna Haraway, *Primate Visions: Gender, Race, and Nature in the World of Modern Science* (New York: Routledge, 1989), 265.

7. Gene Eckhart and Annette Lanjouw, *Mountain Gorillas: Biology, Conservation and Coexistence* (Baltimore: Johns Hopkins University Press, 2009); "Year of the Gorilla," http://www.yog2009.org/index.php?view=article&catid=46%3Agorillaspecies&id=62%3Aelgspeciesinfo&option=com_content&Itemid=70 (accessed March 9, 2012).

8. Rebecca Rogers Ackerman and Jacqueline M. Bishop, "Morphological and Molecular Evidence Reveals Recent Hybridization of Gorilla Taxa," *Evolution* 64, no. 1 (January 2010): 271–90, quote on 275. Note that there is some discussion that the population of mountain gorillas living in the Bwindi Impenetrable Forest in Uganda constitutes a third subspecies of gorilla. But given the sparse data available on this population, scholars still include them with *g. b. beringei*. See Allison A. Elgart, "Are the Gorillas in Bwindi Impenetrable National Park 'True' Mountain Gorillas?," *American Journal of Physical Anthropology* 141, no. 4 (April 2010): 561–70.

9. Weber and Vedder, *In the Kingdom of Gorillas*, 197; "2009 Year of the Gorilla," http://www.yog2009.org/index.php?view=article&catid=46%3Agorillaspecies&id=70%3Amgspeciesinfo&option=com_content&Itemid=70 (accessed March 8, 2012). See also D. M. Doran and A. McNeilage, "Subspecific Variation in Gorilla Behavior: The Influence of Ecological and Social Factors," in *Mountain Gorillas: Three Decades of Research at Karisoke*, ed. Martha M. Robbins, Pascale Sicotte, and Kelly Stewart (Cambridge: Cambridge University Press, 2001). See also Eckhart and Lanjouw, *Mountain Gorillas*; and C. Groves, "A History of Gorilla Taxonomy," in *Gorilla Biology: A Multidisciplinary Perspective*, ed. A. Taylor and M. Goldsmith (Cambridge: Cambridge University Press, 2003), 15–34.

10. "Gorilla Taxonomy" (Web seminar about the mountain gorillas of the Viringas produced by Fathom), http://www.fathom.com/course/21701783/session1.html (accessed March 8, 2012). Note that the article indicates that at their 2000 meeting the International Union for Conservation

of Nature Species Survival Commission (IUCN/SSC) Primate Specialist Group proposed a revised gorilla taxonomy splitting the species into two species and four subspecies of gorilla. In this classification system *g. beringei beringei* is identified as a subspecies of the eastern gorilla, the other subspecies being Grauer's Gorilla, *g. b. graueri*. Primatologists are also debating whether or not *g. beringei beringei* should be further divided between those gorillas living in the Virungas and those living in the Bwindi Impenetrable Forest. Regarding the current estimated population statistics for the mountain gorilla, see http://www.igcp.org/gorillas/mountain-gorillas / (accessed March 9, 2012); and http://www.gorillacd.org/2010/12/15/mountain-gorilla-census -results-population-increases-by-263/ (accessed March 9, 2012). The International Gorilla Conservation Programme estimates a total of 786 mountain gorillas as a result of a census conducted in spring 2010.

11. Weber and Vedder, *In the Kingdom of Gorillas*, 197.

12. Elgart, "Are Gorillas in Bwindi Impenetrable Park True Mountain Gorillas."

13. "The Ecological Setting," session 1 of "Mountain Gorillas of the Virungas," Fathom: The Source for Online Learning web seminar, http://www.fathom.com/course/21701783/session1.html (accessed March 9, 2012). This Fathom web seminar was based on Kelly J. Stewart, Pascale Sicotte, and Martha M. Robins, "Mountain Gorillas of the Virungas: A Short History," in *Mountain Gorillas,* ed. Robbins et al., 1–26.

14. Eckhart and Lanjouw, *Mountain Gorillas*, 117–25.

15. See Dian Fossey, *Gorillas in the Mist* (Boston: Houghton Mifflin, 1983), 49. See also George B. Schaller, *The Mountain Gorilla: Ecology and Behavior* (Chicago: University of Chicago Press, 1963), 40–42; Eckhart and Lanjouw, *Mountain Gorillas*, 95–110; and Alastair McNeilage, "Diet and Habitat Use of Two Mountain Gorilla Groups in Contrasting Habitats in the Virungas," in *Mountain Gorillas*, ed. Robbins et al., 265–92.

16. From 1968 to 1969, with financial support from the European Development Fund, twenty-five thousand acres of forest land in the lower elevations of the Parc des Volcans were cleared and divided into five-acre plots to encourage the cultivation of pyrethrum for the global market. This program decreased the size of the protected habitat in the Parc des Volcans by 40 percent. See Weber and Vedder, *In the Kingdom of Gorillas,* 102. It is interesting to note that a milestone in the post–World War II environmental movement in the United States and other western countries, the banning of DDT in response to *Silent Spring,* would result in the destruction of wilderness and wildlife in Africa that would pose a significant threat to the mountain gorillas' survival.

17. Jean-Pierre Chrétien, *The Great Lakes of Africa: Two Thousand Years of History* (New York: Zone Books, 2003).

18. "2009 Year of the Gorilla," http://www.yog2009.org/index.php?view=article&catid=46%3 Agorillaspecies&id=70%3Amgspeciesinfo&option=com_content&Itemid=70 (accessed March 8, 2012).

19. Haraway, *Primate Visions*, 27.

20. Ibid., 31.

21. Ibid., 30.

22. See, for example, Cynthia Erb, *Tracking King Kong: A Hollywood Icon in World Culture* (Detroit: Wayne State University Press, 2009).

23. G. Scholl Bernard Pagés, *A Hamitic Kingdom in the Center of Africa: In Ruanda on the Shores of Lake Kivu (Belgian Congo)* (Brussels: Libraire Falk fils, Georges van Campenhout, Successeur, 1933), accessed through Human Relations Area Files, Inc. (HRAF) (New Haven, Conn.: HRAF, 2009), http://www.ehrafworldcultures.yale.edu.proxy.lib.muohio.edu/ehrafe/fullContext

.do?method=fullContext&forward=searchFullContext&col=collection('/eHRAF/ethnography /Africa/FO57')&docId=fo57-003&page=fo57-003-00698&offsetId=fo57-003-00719&tocOffsetId =tocfo5700300645&resultSelect=2 (accessed February 27, 2013).

24. Ibid. In particular, the Batwa were ostracized as "mutton eaters," indicating that they were willing to eat sheep meat, which was seen as uncivilized.

25. See Chrétien, *Great Lakes of Africa,* for a comprehensive history of the region.

26. Batwa peoples, also known as Twa (previously called Pygmies and forest people) were and are hunter-gatherers whose survival and culture depended on the montane forests. They hunted game, gathered fruit, and harvested honey, and their history and culture were intricately tied to the forest. During the mid-twentieth century, as colonial governments established national parks in DRC, Rwanda, and Uganda following the U.S. model, Batwa hunting and gathering were restricted. These restrictions further marginalized the Batwa, who were already being squeezed by local farmers and herders representing different ethnic groups and cultures. See Eckhart and Lanjouw, *Mountain Gorillas,* 122.

27. Fossey, *Gorillas in the Mist,* 26–41, provides a detailed but biased view of the motives that encouraged poachers, whom she identified as Batwa, to kill gorillas.

28. The only book-length study addressing the history of poaching is Edward I. Steinhart, *Black Poachers, White Hunters: A Social History of Hunting in Colonial Kenya* (Athens: Ohio University Press, 2006).

29. For an overview of accounts of gorilla-safari hunting, see Haraway, *Primate Visions,* 26–58. The most notable accounts are those of Carl Akeley and his wives: Carl E. Akeley, *In Brightest Africa* (Garden City, N.Y.: Doubleday, Page, 1923); Carl Akeley, "Hunting Gorillas," in *Wild Africa: Three Centuries of Nature Writing from Africa,* ed. John A. Murray (New York: Oxford University Press, 1993); Carl Akeley and Mary L. Jobe Akeley, *Adventures in the African Jungle* (New York: Dodd & Mead, 1930); Carl Akeley and Mary L. Jobe Akeley, *Lions, Gorillas, and Their Neighbors* (New York: Dodd & Mead, 1932); and Delia J. Akeley, *Jungle Portraits* (New York: Macmillan, 1930).

30. They still are valuable prey. In 2007 Congolese rebels invaded the Virunga National Park in DRC, and nine mountain gorillas were killed. See "Rebel Groups Invade Mountain Gorilla Park—Yet Another Gorilla Ranger Killed," May 2012, WildLife Extra.com, http://www .wildlifeextra.com/go/news/virunga-rebels.html#cr (accessed April 2, 2013). See also "Rebels Invade Congo Gorilla Sanctuary, Park Rangers Evacuated," September 4, 2007, mongabay.com, http://www.news.mongabay.com/2007/0904-gorillas.html (accessed April 2, 2013).

31. Jerome Lewis, *The Batwa Pygmies of the Great Lakes Region* (London: Minority Rights Group International, 2000).

32. Dian Fossey's characterization of the Batwa in particular identifies and condemns the Batwa as "gorilla poachers." For example, see Fossey, *Gorillas in the Mist,* 20–21.

33. Mowat, *Woman in the Mists;* Harold T. P. Hayes, *The Dark Romance of Dian Fossey* (New York: Simon & Schuster, 1990). Hayes uses the term "gorilla girl" (116).

34. A number of books document Fossey's life and work. See Fossey, *Gorillas in the Mist,* for an autobiographical rendition of her scientific career beginning in the 1950s and through 1982. Mowat, *Woman in the Mists,* provides a sympathetic biography based on Fossey's journals and letters. Hayes, *Dark Romance of Dian Fossey,* presents a more critical view of Fossey and her work based on interviews with colleagues. Sy Montgomery, *"Walking" with the Great Apes: Jane Goodall, Dian Fossey, Biruté Gladikas* (Boston: Houghton Mifflin, 1991), provides an analysis of the work of Louis Leakey's three protégés: Goodall, Fossey, and Gladikis. For a brief synopsis of Fossey's career and contributions, see John Sorenson, *Ape* (London: Reaktion Books, 2009), 66–69.

Other memoirs by Fossey's friends and colleagues provide information about her scientific career: See Weber and Vedder, *In the Kingdom of Gorillas*; and Rosamond H. Carr and Ann H. Halsey, *Land of a Thousand Hills: My Life in Rwanda* (New York: Viking, 1999).

35. Montgomery, *"Walking" with the Great Apes*, 104. Brian E. Noble suggests that Fossey's more intimate and subjective approach to habituation, what he calls "participatory engagement," is linked to Jane Goodall's earlier practice of observing the chimpanzees in Gombe, Tanzania. His analysis situates Goodall's and Fossey's novel approach to scientific observation in a historical, social, and cultural context of a "nexus of mediations" that defined a public and increasingly gendered primatology beginning in the late 1960s. See Brian E. Noble, "Politics, Gender, and Worldly Primatology: The Goodall-Fossey Nexus," in *Primate Encounters: Models of Science, Gender, and Society*, ed. Shirley C. Strum and Linda Marie Fedigan (Chicago: University of Chicago Press, 2000), 436–62.

36. Schaller, *Mountain Gorilla*, 22–23. See also George B. Schaller, *The Year of the Gorilla: With a New Postscript* (Chicago: University of Chicago Press, 2010), 112–13, for a description of his process of habituation.

37. Dian Fossey, "My Friends the Mountain Gorillas," *National Geographic* 137, no. 1 (1970): 51. It is interesting to note that during the late 1960s and early 1970s research on interspecies communication, specifically human-animal communication, was growing increasingly popular. Most notable are the stories of the chimpanzee Washoe, who during the late 1960s was taught to communicate with humans using sign language, and of Koko, the gorilla who during the late 1970s used sign language to communicate with humans. In the early 1970s the Mike Nichols film *Day of the Dolphin* explored the possibilities of human-dolphin communication. Regarding Koko, see Haraway, *Primate Visions*, 140–46. Regarding Washoe and other experiments with interspecies communication and language, see William A. Hillix and Duane Runbaugh, *Animal Bodies, Human Minds: Ape, Dolphin, and Parrot Language Skills* (New York: Kluwer Academic/Plenum Publishers, 2004).

38. Dian Fossey, "The Imperiled Mountain Gorilla," *National Geographic* 159, no. 4 (April 1981): 502–3.

39. In her first *National Geographic* article she explained that several of the gorilla groups "now accept my presence almost as a member" (Fossey, "My Friends the Mountain Gorillas," 49).

40. Mowat, *Woman in the Mists*, 73.

41. Haraway, *Primate Visions*, 149.

42. Brian Noble has called Fossey's controversial approach to habituation "participatory engagement" or "aping"; see Noble, "Politics, Gender, and Worldly Primatology," 439, 451. On women's place in nature, see Sherry Ortner, "Is Female to Male as Nature Is to Culture," *Feminist Studies* 1, no. 2 (Autumn 1972): 5–31.

43. Fossey, *Gorillas in the Mist*, 167.

44. Ibid., 172.

45. Ibid., 182.

46. Ibid.

47. Montgomery, *"Walking" with the Great Apes*, 46–66.

48. Fossey, *Gorillas in the Mist*, 199.

49. Mowat, *Woman in the Mists*, 140; Montgomery, *"Walking" with the Great Apes*, 63. On Fossey's relationship with Digit, see ibid., 46–66.

50. Fossey, "Imperiled Mountain Gorilla," 501; Montgomery, *"Walking" with the Great Apes*, 49.

51. Lynn White, Jr., "The Historical Roots of Our Ecologic Crisis," *Science* 155, no. 3767 (March 10, 1967): 1203–7. In the late 1960s this story of wildlife conservation took an interesting turn as women such as Jane Goodall and Biruté Galdikas along with Fossey gained celebrity status as iconoclastic global wildlife advocates. See Vera Norwood, *Made from This Earth: American Women and Nature* (Chapel Hill: University of North Carolina Press, 1993); Noble, "Politics, Gender, and Worldly Primatology"; and Karla Armbruster, "'Surely, God, These Are My Kin': The Dynamics of Identity and Advocacy in the Life and Works of Dian Fossey," in *Animal Acts: Configuring the Human in Western History*, ed. Jennifer Ham and Matthew Senior (New York: Routledge, 1997), 209–29.

52. William Graebner, "America's *Poseidon Adventure*: A Nation in Existential Despair," in *America in the Seventies*, ed. Beth Bailey and David Farber (Lawrence: University Press of Kansas, 2004), 158.

53. Fossey, *Gorillas in the Mist*, 183.

54. Schaller, *Year of the Gorilla*, 162.

55. Butler, *Precarious Life*.

56. Estimated subscription numbers for *National Geographic* in the early 1970s suggest that the magazine had a potential audience in the range of 6 million readers. See Meredith Ogburn, "The Life Cycle of National Geographic Magazine," in Association for Education in Journalism and Mass Communication, *Proceedings of the National Convention of the Association for Education in Journalism and Mass Communication* (74th, Boston, Massachusetts, August 7–10, 1991), part 7: Journalism and Media History, Section A (n.p.: 1991), ERIC, EBSCOhost (accessed April 2, 2013). Classic TV database indicates that 69.6 million households in the United States had TVs in 1975–76, with popular shows reaching an audience of between 14 and 20 million. See http://www.classic-tv.com/ratings/1975–1976-tv-show-ratings.html (accessed September 6, 2012).

57. For details on the first airing date and cast, see the official Web site of the producer David L. Wolper, http://www.davidlwolper.com/shows/EpisodeDetails.cfm?episodeID=360&showID=158 (accessed April 2, 2013).

58. Haraway, *Primate Visions*, 154.

59. It is interesting to note that following the film, Sigourney Weaver, who plays Fossey in the movie, took up Dian's cause. For an analysis of the film that focuses on Fossey, see Noble, "Politics, Gender, and Worldly Primatology." See also Diane Sippi, "Aping Africa: The Mist of Immaculate Miscegenation," *CineAction!* 18 (Fall 1989): 18–28.

60. Greg Mitman, *Reel Nature: America's Romance with Wildlife on Film* (Cambridge, Mass.: Harvard University Press, 1999); Finis Dunaway, "Gas Masks, Pogo, and the Ecological Indian: Earth Day and the Visual Politics of American Environmentalism," *American Quarterly* 60 (March 2008): 67–99.

61. Dian Fossey, "His Name Was Digit," *International Primate Protection League News* 5, no. 2 (August 1978): 7.

62. Note that by 1979 the African Wildlife Leadership Foundation would shift allegiance to the Mountain Gorilla Project.

63. Weber and Vedder, *In the Kingdom of Gorillas*, 149.

64. Alexander "Sandy" Harcourt arrived at Karisoke in the summer of 1971, just after finishing his undergraduate degree, to do census work. Fossey introduced him to her study groups and her habituation process. He would pursue his Ph.D. in zoology at Cambridge with Fossey under the direction of the same dissertation adviser. In the ensuing years, they coauthored a handful of scientific journal articles. Various sources suggest that they were entrenched in an intellectual

turf war over the mountain gorillas, each one wanting to secure the place as most acclaimed mountain-gorilla field researcher and scientist. See Mowat, *Woman in the Mists*; Hayes, *Dark Romance of Dian Fossey*; and Weber and Vedder, *In the Kingdom of Gorillas*.

65. Note that Weber and Vedder suggest that they gave Harcourt the idea for this multitiered plan and that he published it as his own without noting their contribution; see Weber and Vedder, *In the Kingdom of Gorillas*, 154.

66. Ibid., 23.

67. Amy Vedder and William Weber, "Rwanda: The Mountain Gorilla Project (Volcanoes National Park)," in *Living with Wildlife*, ed. Agnes Kiss (Washington, D.C.: World Bank, 1990), 85.

68. Weber and Vedder, *In the Kingdom of Gorillas*, 153.

69. Dian Fossey wrote to him suggesting he take only small groups; prohibit pointing, talking, and smoking; avoid surrounding the group; and not follow the group of gorillas once they moved off (letter quoted in Mowat, *Woman in the Mists*, 237).

70. Weber and Vedder, *In the Kingdom of Gorillas*, 193.

71. Ibid., 193, 184.

72. Ibid., 204.

73. Ibid., 133.

74. Ibid.

75. Ibid., 216.

76. Ibid., 218.

77. By 1989 Vedder and Weber noted that an average of five thousand tourists were visiting the park annually and paying approximately $200 each to see the gorillas, which generated $1 million in park revenues. They estimated that foreign tourists spent approximately $600 each while visiting Rwanda to see the gorillas, adding an estimated $3 million annually to the economy. In their 1990 report for the World Bank, they wrote, "With the gorillas thus leading the way, it is generally agreed that tourism has become the fastest growth sector in the Rwandan economy. Estimated revenues from all tourist-related sources total $6–8 million per year, moving tourism ahead of all but coffee and tea exports as one of Rwanda's principal sources of foreign exchange." See Vedder and Weber, "Rwanda," 88.

78. Donna Haraway, *The Companion Species Manifesto: Dogs, People, and Significant Otherness* (Chicago: Prickly Paradigm Press, 2003).

79. "Touched by a Wild Gorilla," YouTube, http://www.youtube.com/watch?v=hg2hCuDy2wg (accessed May 17, 2012). Note that the video is also showcased on the Bwindi National Park Web site, http://www.bwindiforestnationalpark.com/ (accessed April 3, 2013).

80. I have to note that the selection of this particular music from the biopic about Che Guevara cannot be coincidental since t-shirts sold in the village just down the road from the lodge sport portraits of mountain gorillas wearing Che-style berets and gun belts slung across their shoulders. In the DRC rebel guerrillas occupied the Volcan National Park in 2007.

81. Posted by dogvillaman, age thirty-two, from New Zealand; "Touched by a Wild Gorilla," YouTube, http://www.youtube.com/watch?v=hg2hCuDy2wg (accessed May 17, 2012).

Chapter 5. The Gulick Family and the Nature of Adolescence.

1. Jane Addams, *The Spirit of Youth and the City Streets* (New York: Macmillan, 1909), 3.

2. G. Stanley Hall, *Adolescence: Its Psychology and Its Relation to Physiology, Anthropology, Sociology, Sex, Crime, Religion and Education* (New York: Appleton, 1904).

3. Crista DeLuzio, *Female Adolescence in American Scientific Thought, 1830–1930* (Baltimore: Johns Hopkins University Press, 2007); Heather Munro Prescott, *A Doctor of Their Own: The History of Adolescent Medicine* (Cambridge, Mass.: Harvard University Press, 1998), esp. chap. 1.

4. I have used first names throughout this essay to avoid the confusion inherent in referring to all the principals as "Gulick."

5. For one of the clearest articulations of the connection between children and nature, see Charles B. Scott, *Nature Study and the Child* (Boston: D. C. Heath, 1900).

6. Sally Gregory Kohlstedt, *Teaching Children Science: Hands-on Nature Study in North America, 1890–1930* (Chicago: University of Chicago Press, 2012); Kevin C. Armitage, *The Nature Study Movement: The Forgotten Popularizer of America's Conservation Ethic* (Lawrence: University Press of Kansas, 2009).

7. Mrs. J. Ellen Foster, "The Conservation of Child Life," quoted in Laura L. Lovett, *Conceiving the Future: Pronatalism, Reproduction, and the Family in the United States, 1890–1938* (Chapel Hill: University of North Carolina Press, 2007), 110.

8. For discussion of the child as a natural resource, see Kriste Lindenmeyer, *A Right to Childhood: The US Children's Bureau and Child Welfare, 1912–1946* (Urbana: University of Illinois Press, 1997); and Theodore Roosevelt, "The Man Who Works with His Hands," in *The Works of Theodore Roosevelt*, ed. Herman Hagedorn, vol. 16 (New York: Scribner's, 1926).

9. John T. Gulick, *Evolution, Racial and Habitudinal* (Washington, D.C.: Carnegie Institute of Washington, 1905).

10. Ibid., 113, 257–59.

11. Addison Gulick, *Evolutionist and Missionary, John Thomas Gulick: Portrayed Through Documents and Discussions* (Chicago: University of Chicago Press, 1932).

12. Clifford Putney, *Missionaries in Hawai'i: The Lives of Peter and Fanny Gulick, 1797–1883* (Amherst: University of Massachusetts Press, 2010).

13. A. Gulick, *Evolutionist and Missionary*, 127.

14. Ibid., 53–55.

15. My understanding of the importance of active organism is based on Ron Amundson, "John T. Gulick and the Active Organism," in *Darwin's Laboratory: Evolutionary Theory and Natural History in the Pacific*, ed. Roy M. MacLeod and Philip M. Rehbock (Honolulu: University of Hawaii Press, 1994), 110–39.

16. A. Gulick, *Evolutionist and Missionary*, 144.

17. Ibid., 71–72.

18. Ibid., 149, 164, 183.

19. Leonore Davidoff, *Thicker than Water: Siblings and Their Relations, 1780–1920* (New York: Oxford University Press, 2012), 2. There has been a burst of recent scholarship on sibling relations. In addition to Davidoff, see Christopher H. Johnson and David Warren Sabean, *Sibling Relations and the Transformation of European Kinship, 1300–1900* (New York: Berghahn Books, 2011) and C. Dallett Hemphill, *Siblings: Brothers and Sisters in American History* (New York: Oxford University Press, 2011).

20. Christopher H. Johnson, "Sibling Archipelago: Brother-Sister Love and Class Formation in 19th Century France," in *Re-mapping the Humanities: Identity, Community, Memory and (Post) Modernity*, ed. Mary Garrett, Heidi Gottlieb, and Sandra F. Van Burkleo (Detroit: Wayne State University Press, 2008), 94–111.

21. Joy Schulz, "Crossing the Pali: White Missionary Children, Bicultural Identity, and the Racial Divide in Hawai'i, 1820–1898," *Journal of the History of Childhood and Youth* 6, no. 2 (Spring 2013): 209–35.

22. I do not mean to imply that there were never tensions in the siblings' interactions. For details of the brothers' sometimes fractious relationship, see Clifford Putney, "Luther Gulick: His Contributions to Springfield College, the YMCA, and Muscular Christianity," *Historical Journal of Massachusetts* 39, nos. 1 and 2 (Summer 2011): 144–69.

23. Frances Gulick Jewett, *The Next Generation: A Study in the Physiology of Inheritance* (Boston: Ginn, 1914), 188.

24. The Kallikaks had become virtually synonymous with questionable inheritance by the time Fanny was writing. See Nicole Hahn Rafter, *White Trash: The Eugenic Family Studies, 1877–1919* (Boston: Northeastern University Press, 1988).

25. Frances Gulick Jewett, *Luther Halsey Gulick: Missionary in Hawai'i, Micronesia, Japan and China* (Boston: Pilgrim Press, 1895).

26. Joy Schulz, e-mail correspondence with author, August 20, 2013.

27. Jewett, *Luther Halsey Gulick*, 185.

28. The concept of the "priceless child" is from Viviana Zelizer, *Pricing the Priceless Child: The Changing Social Value of Children* (New York: Basic Books, 1985). More recently scholars have elucidated the nineteenth-century antecedents of this concept. See Karen Sanchez-Eppler, *Dependent States: The Child's Part in Nineteenth-Century American Culture* (Chicago: University of Chicago Press, 2005); and Susan J. Pearson, *The Rights of the Defenseless: Protecting Animals and Children in Gilded Age America* (Chicago: University of Chicago Press, 2011).

29. Jewett, *Luther Halsey Gulick*, 130.

30. There is extensive literature on the convergence of Progressive thought and American eugenics. See, for example, Donald K. Pickens. *Eugenics and the Progressives* (Nashville: Vanderbilt University Press, 1968); Michael Freeden, "Eugenics and Progressive Thought: A Study in Ideological Affinity," *Historical Journal* 22, no. 3 (September 1979): 645–71; and Diane Paul, "Eugenics and the Left," *Journal of the History of Ideas* 45, no. 4 (October–December 1984): 567–90.

31. Fanny's connection to her uncle was personal as well as intellectual, and John was living in Oberlin, perhaps with Fanny and her husband, when he wrote his monograph on evolution. Cliff Putney, e-mail correspondence with author, April 11, 2013.

32. Jewett, *Next Generation*, 199.

33. Luther H. Gulick, Introduction to Frances Gulick Jewett, *Town and City* (Boston: Ginn and Company, 1906).

34. Ethel J. Dorgan, *Luther Halsey Gulick* (New York: Columbia University Bureau of Publications, 1934).

35. Stephanie Wallach, "Luther Halsey Gulick and the Salvation of the American Adolescent" (Ph.D. diss., Columbia University, 1989).

36. Gail Bederman, *Manliness and Civilization: A Cultural History of Gender and Race in the United States, 1880–1917* (Chicago: University of Chicago Press, 1995).

37. See Cynthia Eagle Russett, *Sexual Science: The Victorian Construction of Womanhood* (Cambridge, Mass.: Harvard University Press, 1989).

38. See Luther H. Gulick, *The Efficient Life* (New York: Doubleday, Page, & Company), 1907.

39. Susan A. Miller, *Growing Girls: The Natural Origins of Girls' Organizations in America* (New Brunswick, N.J.: Rutgers University Press, 2007); Leslie Paris, *Children's Nature: The Rise of the American Summer Camp* (New York: New York University Press, 2008).

40. Dorgan, *Luther Halsey Gulick*, 112.

41. A. E. Hamilton, "Putting over Eugenics," *Journal of Heredity* 6 (June 1915): 281–88.

42. Miller, *Growing Girls*, chap. 1.

43. Sandra C. Taylor, *Advocate of Understanding: Sidney Gulick and the Search for Peace with Japan* (Kent, Ohio: Kent State University Press, 1984), 16.

44. Ibid.

45. Lisa K. Langlois, "Japan—Modern, Ancient, and Gendered at the 1893 Chicago World's Fair," in *Gendering the Fair: Histories of Women and Gender at World's Fairs*, ed. T. J. Boisseau and Abigail M. Markwyn (Urbana: University of Illinois Press, 2010), 56–74.

46. Matthew Jacobson, *Whiteness of a Different Color: European Immigration and the Alchemy of Race* (Cambridge, Mass.: Harvard University Press, 1998); Noel Ignatiev, *How the Irish Became White* (New York: Routledge, 1995).

47. Gretchen Murphy, "How the Irish Became Japanese: Winnifred Eaton's Racial Reconstructions in a Transnational Context," *American Literature* 79, no. 1 (March 2007): 29–56.

48. Sidney L. Gulick, *American Democracy and Asiatic Citizenship* (New York: Scribner's, 1918).

49. Sidney L. Gulick, *The American Japanese Problem: A Study of the Racial Relations of the East and the West* (New York: Scribner's, 1914), 203.

50. Ibid., 8–9.

51. Sidney L. Gulick, *Evolution of the Japanese: A Study of Their Characteristics in Relation to the Principles of Social and Psychic Development* (New York: Fleming H. Revel, 1903), v.

52. Ibid., vi.

53. Ibid., 77.

54. Ibid., 73.

55. Sidney L. Gulick, *Mixing the Races in Hawaii: A Study of the Coming Neo-Hawai'ian American Race* (Honolulu: Hawaiian Board Book Rooms, 1937), iii.

56. Jane H. Hunter, *How Young Ladies Became Girls: The Victorian Origins of American Girlhood* (New Haven, Conn.: Yale University Press, 2002); Sarah E. Chinn, *Inventing Modern Adolescence: The Children of Immigrants in Turn-of-the-Century America* (New Brunswick, N.J.: Rutgers University Press, 2009).

57. The current preference appears to be for neurological factors, though undoubtedly this will soon change. See David Dobbs, "Teenage Brains," *National Geographic* 218, no. 4 (October 2011): 36–59, and a host of scientific and popular articles on teens and executive function.

Chapter 6. Children of Light

1. William Z. Ripley, *The Races of Europe: A Sociological Study* (New York: D. Appleton, 1899), 32.

2. On the relationship between race and culture, I am inspired by Ann L. Stoler, "Racial Histories and Their Regimes of Truth," *Political Power and Social Theory* 1, no. 1 (1997): 183–206; and Walter Benn Michaels, "Race into Culture: A Critical Genealogy of Cultural Identity," *Critical Inquiry* 18, no. 4 (Summer 1992): 655–85—not so much because I agree with their conclusions as because I agree with their premise that the two concepts are close cousins, not opposites. The shift I identify here encompasses the growing importance of the black-white binary ("race") and the corresponding demotion of differences among people of European descent ("ethnicity") that Matthew Pratt Guterl outlines in his *The Color of Race in America, 1900–1940* (Cambridge, Mass.: Harvard University Press, 2001). By the late twentieth century, advocates of culture asserted that

344 Notes to Pages 123-125

race was simply a scheme of cultural meanings assigned to otherwise meaningless variations in human bodies. This move, invaluable for highlighting the social construction of ideas about human difference, also further displaced explanations for human bodily variation into a realm of a biology shorn of social meaning. As Shaffer and Young note in Chapter 1 in this volume, expanding the realm of culture does not overcome the estrangement of nature and culture (nor, of course, does expanding the realm of nature). The difficulty of formulating an ethical environmental politics is the theme of a recent roundtable: "State of the Field: American Environmental History," *Journal of American History* 100, no. 1 (June 2013): 94–148. "Relational ontology" comes from Gregg Mitman, "Living in a Material World," *Journal of American History* 100, no. 1 (June 2013): 129.

3. On the possibility of such a nondeterminist, materialist history, see Christof Mauch, "Which World Is with Us? A Tocquevillean View on American Environmental History," *Journal of American History* 100, no. 1 (June 2013): 125; and Daniel Lord Smail, *On Deep History and the Brain* (Berkeley: University of California Press, 2008). One such philosopher-sunbather was Stuart Chase; see his "Confessions of a Sun-Worshiper," *Nation* 128, no. 3338 (June 26, 1929): 763–65. Notably, he was also a naturist, a more radical practice whose practitioners had to defend it; see Marguerite S. Shaffer, "The Environmental Nude," *Environmental History* 13, no. 1 (January 2008): 126–39.

4. A few good examples of the extensive literature on environmental determinism include Gary Y. Okihiro, *Pineapple Culture: A History of the Tropical and Temperate Zones* (Berkeley: University of California Press, 2009); David N. Livingstone, "The Moral Discourse of Climate: Historical Considerations on Race, Place and Virtue," *Journal of Historical Geography* 17, no. 4 (1991): 413–34; David N. Livingstone, "Climate's Moral Economy: Science, Race and Place in Post-Darwinian British and American Geography," in *Geography and Empire*, ed. Anne Godlewska and Neil Smith (Oxford: Blackwell, 1994), 132–54; and Warwick Anderson, "Climates of Opinion: Acclimatization in Nineteenth-Century France and England," *Victorian Studies* 32, no. 2 (1992): 135–57. David Arnold, "'Illusory Riches': Representations of the Tropical World, 1840–1950," *Singapore Journal of Tropical Geography* 21, no. 1 (March 2000): 6–18, traces the influence of these ideas into the twentieth century.

5. The classic elaboration of this line of thought came from Charles de Secondat, Baron de Montesquieu, *The Spirit of the Laws*, trans. and ed. Anne M. Collier, Basia Carolyn Miller, and Harold Samuel Stone (1748; Cambridge: Cambridge University Press, 1989), 232–33, 236, 246–52, 269, 271; see also the sources in note 4. The quotation is from Charles J. Kenworthy, M.D., *Climatology of Florida* (Savannah, Ga.: Morning News Steam Printing House, 1881), 17. See also Conevery Bolton Valencius, *The Health of the Country: How American Settlers Understood Themselves and Their Land* (New York: Basic Books, 2002).

6. Robert De C. Ward, "The Acclimatization of the White Race in the Tropics," in *Annual Report of the Board of Regents of the Smithsonian Institution, 1930* (Washington, D.C.: Government Printing Office, 1931), 561, repr. from *New England Journal of Medicine* 201, no. 13 (September 26, 1929): 617–27. These words are a close paraphrase of Ripley, *Races of Europe*, 560–61.

7. Lothrop Stoddard, *The Rising Tide of Color Against White World-Supremacy* (New York: Scribner's, 1920), 107–8.

8. Ward, "Acclimatization," 564.

9. Dane Kennedy, "The Perils of the Midday Sun: Climatic Anxieties in the Colonial Tropics," in *Imperialism and the Natural World*, ed. John M. McKenzie (Manchester: Manchester University Press, 1990), 118–40; Mark Harrison, "'The Tender Frame of Man': Disease, Climate, and

Racial Difference in India and the West Indies, 1760–1860," *Bulletin of the History of Medicine* 70, no. 1 (Spring 1996): 68–93; Simon Carter, *Rise and Shine: Sunlight, Technology and Health* (Oxford: Berg, 2007).

10. Charles Woodruff, *The Effects of Tropical Light on White Men* (New York and London: Rebman, 1905), 4, 323 (italics in original), 326, 328, 334–35, 340, 345–46. See also Warwick Anderson, "The Trespass Speaks: White Masculinity and Colonial Breakdown," *American Historical Review* 102, no. 5 (December 1997): 1343–70.

11. Tanning has only begun to attract serious historians, belatedly following up on James Walvin's pioneering "Selling the Sun: Tourism and Material Consumption," *Revista/Review Interamericana* 22 (Spring 1992): 208–25. See Kerry Segrave, *Suntanning in 20th Century America* (Jefferson, N.C.: MacFarland, 2005); Carter, *Rise and Shine*; Shaffer, "Environmental Nude"; and Daniel Freund, *American Sunshine: Diseases of Darkness and the Quest for Natural Light* (Chicago: University of Chicago Press, 2012), 97–133. I address the development of tropical resorts and the rise of tanning in Catherine Cocks, *Tropical Whites: The Rise of the Tourist South in the Americas* (Philadelphia: University of Pennsylvania Press, 2013), 41–72, 96–123. This essay focuses on the connections between tanning and shifting conceptions of race. Although tanning also was and is connected to issues of class, these issues are beyond the scope of this analysis.

12. See Cocks, *Tropical Whites*, 110–23; for the quotation, Stanley Hoffland, "Tan Is the Smart Shade This Summer," *Los Angeles Times,* July 18, 1926, B7; on primitivism, Marianna Torgovnick, *Gone Primitive: Savage Intellects, Modern Lives* (Chicago: University of Chicago Press, 1990); Phil Deloria, *Playing Indian* (New Haven, Conn.: Yale University Press, 1998); and Shari M. Huhndorf, *Going Native: Indians in the American Cultural Imagination* (Ithaca, N.Y.: Cornell University Press, 2001).

13. Ronald Millar, in collaboration with Dr. E. E. Free, *Sunrays and Health* (New York: Robert M. McBride, 1929), 6.

14. [Carita Dogget Corse], *Florida* (Tallahassee: Florida State Hotel Commission, 1930), 17, 19, 29, 33.

15. "In the Boudoir," *Chicago Daily Tribune*, August 9, 1907, 7.

16. Hazel Rawson Cades, "The Beautiful and Tanned," *Collier's* 79 (June 18, 1927): 14, 58.

17. Carter, *Rise and Shine*, 49–70; Freund, *American Sunshine*, 65–96. See also Margaret A. Cleaves, M.D., *Light Energy: Its Physics, Physiological Action and Therapeutic Applications* (New York: Rebman, 1904).

18. Peter C. Remondino, first typescript, p. 3, folder 10, box 4, Remondino, San Diego Historical Society, San Diego, Calif.; Peter C. Remondino, *The Mediterranean Shore of America: Southern California: Climatic, Physical, and Meteorological Conditions* (Philadelphia and London: F. A. David, 1893), 127.

19. W. A. Evans, "How to Keep Well," *Chicago Daily Tribune*, July 8, 1920, 8. Freund, *American Sunshine*, 98–99, portrays Evans as a sunlight enthusiast, but in this and other editions of his regular column, Evans was highly critical of sunbathing.

20. Edgar Mayer, *The Curative Value of Light: Sunlight and Sun-Lamp in Health and Disease* (New York: D. Appleton, 1932), 7–15; Rima D. Apple, *Vitamania: Vitamins in American Culture* (New Brunswick, N.J.: Rutgers University Press, 1996), 7–53; Freund, *American Sunshine*, 39–41, 146–47.

21. Michael F. Holick, "Sunlight, UV-Radiation, Vitamin D and Skin Cancer: How Much Sunlight Do We Need?," in *Sunlight, Vitamin D and Skin Cancer: Advances in Experimental Medicine and Biology*, ed. Jörg Reichrath, vol. 624 (New York: Springer Science & Business Media LLC, 2008), 1–15.

22. Apple, *Vitamania*, 7–53; Gregg Mitman, "In Search of Health: Landscape and Disease in American Environmental History," *Environmental History* 10, no. 2 (April 2005): 184–210. See also Claudia Benthien, *Skin: On the Cultural Border Between Self and the World*, trans. Thomas Dunlap (New York: Columbia University Press, 2002).

23. Apple, *Vitamania*, 7–53; Millar, *Sunrays and Health*, 82; Shaffer, "Environmental Nude"; Carter, *Rise and Shine*; Freund, *American Sunshine*, 65–133; Cocks, *Tropical Whites*, 110–23.

24. Millar, *Sunrays and Health*, 43. See also Leonard Falkner, "The Burning Question," *American Magazine* 110 (August 1930): 50.

25. Walter H. Eddy, "Nature Gives Us Sunlight—Let's Use It!," *Good Housekeeping* 107, no. 1 (July 1938): 51.

26. Josephine Hemenway Kenyon, "The Sun Cure and Rickets," *Good Housekeeping* 86 (March 1928): 106.

27. Ronald L. Numbers, *Darwinism Comes to America* (Cambridge, Mass.: Harvard University Press, 1998). Recent research has complicated this picture; see Nessa Carey, *The Epigenetics Revolution: How Modern Biology Is Rewriting Our Understanding of Genetics, Disease, and Inheritance* (New York: Columbia University Press, 2012).

28. Jonathan Peter Spiro, *Defending the Master Race: Conservation, Eugenics, and the Legacy of Madison Grant* (Hanover, N.H.: University Press of New England for the University of Vermont Press, 2009); Elazar Barkan, *The Retreat of Scientific Racism: Changing Concepts of Race in Britain and the United States Between the World Wars* (Cambridge: Cambridge University Press, 1992).

29. Henry Fairfield Osborn, preface to the second edition of *The Passing of the Great Race*, in Madison Grant, *The Passing of the Great Race: Or, the Racial Basis of European History*, 4th rev. ed., with documentary supplement (New York: Scribner's, 1923), xxix. The fourth edition included all of the prefatory material from earlier editions.

30. The scholarship on nationalism and the culture concept is enormous; among the works that influenced my thinking are Benedict Anderson, *Imagined Communities: Reflections on the Origin and Spread of Nationalism*, rev. ed. (1983; New York: Verso, 1993); Glenda Sluga, *The Nation, Psychology, and International Politics, 1870–1919* (New York: Palgrave Macmillan, 2006); Nancy Ley Stepan, *The Hour of Eugenics: Race, Gender, and Nation in Latin America* (Ithaca, N.Y.: Cornell University Press, 1991); Partha Chatterjee, *Nationalist Thought and the Colonial World: A Derivative Discourse?* (London: Zed for the United Nations University, 1986); Christopher Herbert, *Culture and Anomie: Ethnographic Imagination in the Nineteenth Century* (Chicago: University of Chicago Press, 1991); Adam Kuper, *Culture: The Anthropologists' Account* (Cambridge, Mass.: Harvard University Press, 2000); Mary Louise Pratt, *Imperial Eyes: Travel Writing and Transculturation* (New York: Routledge, 1992); and George W. Stocking, *Race, Culture, and Evolution: Essays in the History of Anthropology* (Chicago: University of Chicago Press, 1982).

31. Ripley, *Races of Europe*, 1. Though here and there Ripley mentions "intermarriage," one would otherwise never know from his account that women have anything to do with reproduction.

32. Grant, *Passing of the Great Race*, 18. Spiro, *Defending the Master Race*, traces the changes in the various editions of the book; with the exception of the addition of the documentary supplement, they were not substantive. See also Guterl, *Color of Race*, 27–51.

33. Osborn, preface, in Grant, *Passing of the Great Race*, xix.

34. Spiro, *Defending the Master Race*, surveys the institutions and policies of eugenics in the United States; see also Daniel J. Kevles, *In the Name of Eugenics: Genetics and the Uses of Human*

Heredity (Cambridge, Mass.: Harvard University Press, 1995). Wendy Kline, *Building a Better Race: Gender, Sexuality, and Eugenics from the Turn of the Century to the Baby Boom* (Berkeley: University of California Press, 2001), notes that eugenicists downplayed the old fear of unregulated sexuality in favor of a new bogey, unregulated reproduction. From this perspective birth control ceased to be a threat to the social order and became a tool for improving the stock.

35. Grant, *Passing of the Great Race*, 38; Spiro, *Defending the Master Race*, 153.

36. Weare Holbrook, "Tarred and Weathered," *Los Angeles Times*, January 6, 1929, H10; Stoddard, *Rising Tide of Color*, 107–8. It is curious that Holbrook's piece, so obviously written about East Coast, big-city apartment dwellers, appeared in the newspaper of a city built around public beaches, plentiful sunshine, and single-family homes in sprawling suburbs. Perhaps it was an exercise in self-congratulation.

37. Holbrook, "Tarred and Weathered," H10.

38. Ibid.

39. Ibid.

40. See Nina G. Jablonski, *Skin: A Natural History* (Berkeley: University of California Press, 2006), 65–96; and Nina G. Jablonski, *In Living Color: The Biological and Social Meaning of Skin Color* (Berkeley: University of California Press, 2012). Recent research indicates that diet played a key role in humans' changing skin color; see Michael Balter, "New Diet, Sexual Attraction May Have Spurred Europeans' Lighter Skin," *Science/AAAS I News* (March 10, 2014), http://news .sciencemag.org (accessed March 12, 2014).

Chapter 7. Dr. Spock Is Worried

This essay is based on material included in chap. 1 of Finis Dunaway, *Seeing Green: The Use and Abuse of American Environmental Images* (Chicago: University of Chicago Press, 2015).

1. SANE, advertisement, *New York Times*, April 16, 1962, 30.

2. Milton S. Katz, *Ban the Bomb: A History of SANE, the Committee for a Sane Nuclear Policy* (New York: Praeger, 1987), 75; Benjamin Spock, *Baby and Child Care*, rev. ed. (New York: Pocket Books, 1957), 3–4.

3. Often discussed by philosophers and political theorists, the concept of environmental citizenship has rarely found its way into historical studies of U.S. environmentalism. I use the term to denote the ecological rights and responsibilities of citizens: from state policies that promise to protect people from toxicity and other environmental risks to individuals engaging in ecologically responsible actions in daily life. Representative works by political theorists and other scholars include Andrew Dobson, *Citizenship and the Environment* (New York: Oxford University Press, 2003); and Andrew Dobson and Derek Bell, eds., *Environmental Citizenship* (Cambridge, Mass.: MIT Press, 2006). In addition the historian Michelle Murphy has defined "biocitizenship" as "a useful term naming efforts that take life—from human bodies to ecosystems—as points of entry into making demands of the state, and thereby articulating the terms of citizenship via health and living-being"; see Michelle Murphy, "Chemical Regimes of Living," *Environmental History* 13 (October 2008): 699. Murphy's article builds on the work of the anthropologist Adriana Petryna, *Life Exposed: Biological Citizens After Chernobyl* (Princeton, N.J.: Princeton University Press, 2002).

4. Michael Warner, *Publics and Counterpublics* (New York: Zone Books, 2002), 66; Robert Hariman and John Louis Lucaites, *No Caption Needed: Iconic Photographs, Public Culture, and Liberal Democracy* (Chicago: University of Chicago Press, 2007), 161. For an excellent overview of theoretical approaches to public culture, see Mary Kupiec Cayton, "What Is Public Culture?

Agency and Contested Meaning in American Culture—An Introduction," in *Public Culture: Diversity, Democracy, and Community in the United States,* ed. Marguerite S. Shaffer (Philadelphia: University of Pennsylvania Press, 2008), 1–25. See also Erika Doss, *Memorial Mania: Public Feeling in America* (Chicago: University of Chicago Press, 2010).

5. Martha C. Nussbaum, *Upheavals of Thought: The Intelligence of Emotions* (New York: Cambridge University Press, 2001); George E. Marcus, *The Sentimental Citizen: Emotion in Democratic Politics* (University Park: Pennsylvania State University Press, 2002), 7.

6. Rob Nixon, *Slow Violence and the Environmentalism of the Poor* (Cambridge, Mass.: Harvard University Press, 2011), 2.

7. For an important critique of the wilderness aesthetic, see William Cronon, "The Trouble with Wilderness; or, Getting Back to the Wrong Nature," in *Uncommon Ground: Toward Reinventing Nature*, ed. William Cronon (New York: W. W. Norton, 1995), 69–90.

8. On the atomic sublime and mushroom-cloud imagery as political pacification, see Peter B. Hales, "The Atomic Sublime," *American Studies* 32 (Spring 1991): 5–31; Scott Kirsch, "Watching the Bombs Go Off: Photography, Nuclear Landscapes, and Spectator Democracy," *Antipode* 29 (July 1997): 227–55; and Peter Bacon Hales, "Imagining the Atomic Age: *Life* and the Atom," in *Looking at Life Magazine,* ed. Erika Doss (Washington, D.C.: Smithsonian Institution Press, 2001), 103–19.

9. This military film clip is included in *The Atomic Cafe: Collector's Edition,* DVD, directed by Jayne Loader, Kevin Rafferty, and Pierce Rafferty (1982; New York: New Video Group, 2008). On the ecological body, see Maril Hazlett, "Voices from the *Spring: Silent Spring* and the Ecological Turn in American Health," in *Seeing Nature Through Gender,* ed. Virginia J. Scharff (Lawrence: University Press of Kansas, 2003), 103–28; and Linda Nash, *Inescapable Ecologies: A History of the Environment, Disease, and Knowledge* (Berkeley: University of California Press, 2006).

10. For background on *The Big Picture,* see Stanley Field, "The Big Picture," *Journal of Broadcasting and Electronic Media* 6 (Spring 1962): 125–27; J. Fred MacDonald, "The Cold War as Entertainment in 'Fifties Television," *Journal of Popular Film and Television* 7 (Spring 1978): 3–31, esp. 14; and Nancy E. Bernhard, *U.S. Television News and Cold War Propaganda, 1947–1960* (New York: Cambridge University Press, 1999), 142–43. The episode that I discuss can be found at http://www.video.google.com/videoplay?docid=-2149878949626814717# (accessed December 19, 2012).

11. "Color Photographs Add Vivid Reality to Nation's Concept of H-Bomb," *Life,* April 19, 1954, 21. See also Kirsch, "Watching the Bombs Go Off," 243.

12. SANE, advertisement, *New York Times,* November 15, 1957, 54.

13. Arno G. Huth, "Response to the First Statement Issued by the National Committee for a Sane Nuclear Policy, November 15–December 31, 1957: A Preliminary Analysis," January 1958, in Subseries B-1, box 4, folder "SANE, National Office—SANE Files of Norman Cousins, 1957–1958, Huth, Arno," Records of SANE, DG 58, Swarthmore College Peace Collection, quotes on 13, 14.

14. SANE, advertisement, *New York Times,* April 11, 1958, 15. On different conceptions of environmental apocalypse, see also Frederick Buell, *From Apocalypse to Way of Life: Environmental Crisis in the American Century* (New York: Routledge, 2004).

15. Wilma Holden to Norman Cousins, April 24, 1958, in Series B-1, box 2, folder "Correspondence of Norman Cousins (as editor of *The Saturday Review*), 'H,' 1958," Records of SANE, DG 58, Swarthmore College Peace Collection.

16. On images and democratic citizenship, see also Hariman and Lucaites, *No Caption Needed.*

17. Lauren Berlant, *The Queen of America Goes to Washington City: Essays on Sex and Citizenship* (Durham, N.C.: Duke University Press, 1997), 5.

18. SANE, advertisement, *New York Times*, April 16, 1962, 30.

19. Thomas Frank, *The Conquest of Cool: Business Culture, Counterculture, and the Rise of Hip Consumerism* (Chicago: University of Chicago Press, 1997), chap. 3.

20. On Arnold Newman and environmental portraiture, see Gretchen Garner, *Disappearing Witness: Change in Twentieth-Century American Photography* (Baltimore: Johns Hopkins University Press, 2003), 179–81; and Robert Sobieszek, introduction to Arnold Newman, *One Mind's Eye: The Portraits and Other Photographs of Arnold Newman* (Boston: David R. Godine, 1974), vi–xix.

21. First quote from an unnamed letter writer quoted in Nell Lee Litvak, Public Information Director of SANE, form letter to SANE members, April 21, 1962, copy in box 54, folder "Politics, SANE, Memoranda, Gen-1963," Benjamin Spock Papers, Syracuse University (hereafter BSP); second quote from Mary M. Grooms to Homer Jack, April 21, 1962, copy in box 10, folder "Correspondence, April 17, 1962–April 24, 1962," BSP; third quote from Mrs. John T. McClure to National Committee for a Sane Nuclear Policy, April 28, 1962, copy in box 10, folder "Correspondence, April 25, 1962–April 20, 1962," BSP; fourth quote from Mrs. J. F. Baglen to Benjamin Spock, April 16, 1962, in box 10, folder "Correspondence, April 1, 1962–April 16, 1962," BSP.

22. Jeanne S. Bagby to Benjamin Spock, April 20, 1962, in box 10, folder "Correspondence, April 17, 1962–April 24, 1962," BSP. On the politics of gender and antinuclear protest during this period, see Amy Swerdlow, *Women Strike for Peace: Traditional Motherhood and Radical Politics in the 1960s* (Chicago: University of Chicago Press, 1993); and Lawrence S. Wittner, "Gender Roles and Nuclear Disarmament Activism, 1954–1965," *Gender and History* 12 (April 2000): 197–222.

23. "SANE—and Others," *Time,* April 27, 1962, 22–23, quote on 22.

24. Dentists for SANE, advertisement, *New York Times*, April 7, 1963, 10. On Barry Commoner and the Committee for Nuclear Information, see Michael Egan, *Barry Commoner and the Science of Survival: The Remaking of American Environmentalism* (Cambridge, Mass.: MIT Press, 2007), chap. 2; and Kelly Moore, *Disrupting Science: Social Movements, American Scientists, and the Politics of the Military, 1945–1975* (Princeton, N.J.: Princeton University Press, 2008), chap. 4.

25. Dentists for SANE, advertisement, *New York Times*, April 7, 1963, 10.

26. For background on this commercial and the 1964 campaign, see Robert Mann, *Daisy Petals and Mushroom Clouds: LBJ, Barry Goldwater, and the Ad That Changed American Politics* (Baton Rouge: Louisiana State University Press, 2011); Kathleen Hall Jamieson, *Packaging the Presidency: A History and Criticism of Presidential Campaign Advertising*, 2nd ed. (New York: Oxford University Press, 1992), 198–202; and Edwin Diamond and Stephen Bates, *The Spot: The Rise of Political Advertising on Television* (Cambridge, Mass.: MIT Press, 1984), 127–34. The commercial can be viewed at *The Living Room Candidate* website exhibition maintained by the Museum of the Moving Image, http://www.livingroomcandidate.org/commercials/1964 (accessed December 19, 2012).

27. This commercial can be viewed at http://www.livingroomcandidate.org/commercials/1964 (accessed December 19, 2012). For background on the commercial, see Jamieson, *Packaging the Presidency*, 201.

28. Adlai Stevenson, as quoted in Egan, *Barry Commoner and the Science of Survival*, 52; Lyndon Baines Johnson, as quoted in ibid., 75.

29. On these issues, see also Paul Boyer, "From Activism to Apathy: The American People and Nuclear Weapons, 1963–1980," *Journal of American History* 70 (March 1984): 821–44; and

Kirsch, "Watching the Bombs Go Off," esp. 246–48, on how the treaty helped obscure ongoing health and environmental problems related to the arms race.

30. Rachel Carson, *Silent Spring* (Boston: Houghton Mifflin, 1962).

31. "Pesticides: The Price for Progress," *Time*, September 28, 1962, 45–48, quotes on 48, 45. On the gendered response to *Silent Spring*, see Michael B. Smith, "'Silence, Miss Carson!': Science, Gender, and the Reception of *Silent Spring*," *Feminist Studies* 27 (Fall 2001): 733–72; Hazlett, "Voices from the *Spring*"; and Maril Hazlett, "'Woman vs. Man vs. Bugs': Gender and Popular Ecology in Early Reactions to *Silent Spring*," *Environmental History* 9 (October 2004): 701–29. On gender and environmental politics, see also Adam Rome, "'Political Hermaphrodites': Gender and Environmental Reform in Progressive America," *Environmental History* 11 (July 2006): 440–63, esp. 456–57; and Adam Rome, "'Give Earth a Chance': The Environmental Movement and the Sixties," *Journal of American History* 90 (September 2003): 525–54, esp. 534–41.

32. Gordon Young, "Pollution, Threat to Man's Only Home," *National Geographic* 138 (December 1970): 758, photo by James P. Blair on 759; Don Moser, "A Lament for Some Companions of My Youth," *Life*, January 22, 1971, 52, photo by George Silk on 52.

33. Lynne W. Heutchy, letter to editor, *Life*, February 12, 1971, A14.

34. Environmental Defense Fund, advertisement, *New York Times*, March 29, 1970; Environmental Defense Fund, advertisement, *Audubon* 72 (November 1970): 109.

35. See Finis Dunaway, "Gas Masks, Pogo, and the Ecological Indian: Earth Day and the Visual Politics of American Environmentalism," *American Quarterly* 60 (March 2008): 67–99.

36. Susan J. Douglas, "Mass Media: From 1945 to the Present," in *A Companion to Post-1945 America*, ed. Jean-Christophe Agnew and Roy Rosenzweig (Malden, Mass.: Blackwell, 2002), 79.

37. See Finis Dunaway, *Seeing Green: The Use and Abuse of American Environmental Images* (Chicago: University of Chicago Press, 2015).

Chapter 8. Prototyping Natures

1. The *Atlantic*, for example, ran a series of articles reintroducing readers to the bizarre wonders of atomic history. See, for example, Alan Taylor, "When We Tested Nuclear Bombs," *Atlantic* (online), May 6, 2011, http://www.theatlantic.com/infocus/2011/05/when-we-tested-nuclear -bombs/100061/ (accessed April 6, 2012); and Michael Freedman, "Can We Unlearn the Bomb?," *Atlantic* (online), May 6, 2011, http://www.theatlantic.com/technology/archive/2011/05/can-we -unlearn-the-bomb/238460/ (accessed April 6, 2012). These wonderful articles showcased stunning atomic images with the same bias toward the atomic sublime as earlier journalists had demonstrated. Once again the Mojave and its people are dismissed as relics of the Cold War.

2. A wonderful example is the L.A. Museum of Contemporary Art's "Ends of the Earth" exhibit organized by Philipp Kaiser and Miwon Kwon, who also edited the exhibit catalog and collection of essays *Ends of the Earth: Land Art to 1974,* the Museum of Contemporary Art (Los Angeles and London: Prestel Munich, 2012); see in particular Emily Eliza Scott, "Desert Ends," 67–85.

3. The protagonists' use of art and other forms of visual representation to record their history and counter inaccurate perceptions of the Mojave is explained in many of the interviews by Mary Palevsky, Robert Futrell, and Andrew Kirk for the Nevada Test Site Oral History Project (hereafter NTSOHP), http://www.digital.library.unlv.edu/ntsohp/ (accessed September 13, 2014, and is also available in the collections of the National Atomic Testing Museum, Las Vegas, Nevada.

4. David Stradling uses these simple but still contested questions to launch his wonderful documentary collection *The Environmental Moment 1968–1972* (Seattle: University of Washington Press, 2012), 9.

5. No one has done more than Martin Melosi to look hard at the ugliest places and smelliest problems in order to understand better the links between nature and culture. See Martin Melosi, *Effluent America: Cities, Industry, Energy, and the Environment* (Pittsburgh: University of Pittsburgh Press, 2001); and Martin Melosi, *Garbage in the Cities: Refuse Reform and the Environment* (Pittsburgh: University of Pittsburgh Press, 2004).

6. On site choice and nuclear colonialism, see Valerie Kuletz, *The Tainted Desert: Environmental and Social Ruin in the American West* (New York: Routledge, 1998); Michon Mackedon, *Bombast: Spinning Atoms in the Desert* (Reno, Nev.: Black Rock Institute Press, 2010); and Robert Jacobs, "Nuclear Conquistadors: Military Colonialism in Nuclear Test Site Selection during the Cold War," *Asian Journal of Peacebuilding* 1, no. 2 (November 2013): 157–77.

7. Scott, "Desert Ends," 69. Emily Eliza Scott, "Wasteland: American Landscapes in/and 1960s Art" (Ph.D. diss., University of California, Los Angeles, 2010), does an excellent job synthesizing the scholarship on deserts and wastelands and explaining the relationships between art and cultural perceptions of deserts in American history and culture.

8. Finis Dunaway, *Natural Visions: The Power of Images in American Environmental Reform* (Chicago: University of Chicago Press, 2005); Finis Dunaway, "Cultures of Nature: Twentieth Century," in *A Companion to American Environmental History*, ed. Douglas Cazaux Sackman (Malden, Mass.: Wiley-Blackwell, 2010), 266–84.

9. On knowing nature through labor, see Richard White, "Are You an Environmentalist or Do You Work for a Living?," in William Cronon, ed. *Uncommon Ground: Rethinking the Human Place in Nature*, ed. William Cronon (New York: W. W. Norton, 1996), 171–85.

10. Michael Guggenheim, "The Long History of Prototypes," *ARC Studio*, http://www.anthropos-lab.net/studio/episode/03/ (accessed May 3, 2014); Claude Lévi-Strauss, *The Savage Mind* (Chicago: University of Chicago Press, 1966), 16–30. Lévi-Strauss defined bricolage as construction (of a structure or structure of ideas) achieved by using whatever comes to hand and also something constructed this way. A bricoleur is the opposite of an engineer; an engineer creates specialized tools for specialized purposes, while a bricoleur is a jack-of-all-trades who uses few, nonspecialized tools for a wide variety of purposes. A bricoleur is a person who accomplishes what has to be accomplished, when it has to be accomplished, with the tools and resources at hand. See also Glenn Adamson and Jane Pavitt, eds., *Postmodernism: Style and Subversion, 1970–1990* (London: Victoria & Albert Publishing, 2011), 113.

11. Lévi-Strauss, *Savage Mind*, 21.

12. Dan Flores, "Nature's Children: Environmental History as Human History," in *Human/Nature: Biology, Culture, and Environmental History*, ed. John Herron and Andrew Kirk (Albuquerque: University of New Mexico Press, 1999), 17.

13. Quote and paraphrase from Richard White, "From Wilderness to Hybrid Landscapes," in Douglas Cazaux Sackman, *A Companion to American Environmental History* (Malden, Mass.: Wiley-Blackwell, 2010), 183–90. White points to William deBuys, *Salt Dreams: Land and Water in Low-Down California* (Albuquerque: University of New Mexico Press, 1999), as an outstanding example of efforts to think of even the most tainted places as hybrid landscapes that might offer hope.

14. Militarized landscape scholars have done some of the most interesting recent research on similarly tainted hybrid landscapes. See Peter Coates, Tim Cole, Marianna Dudley, and Chris

Pearson, "Defending Nation, Defending Nature? Militarized Landscapes and Military Environmentalism in Britain, France, and the United States," *Environmental History* 16 (July 2011): 456–91. See also Ryan Edgington, *Lines in the Sand: An Environmental History of Cold War New Mexico* (Philadelphia: Temple University Press, 2012). For Cold War landscapes in general, see Maria Montoya, "Landscapes of the Cold War West," in *The Cold War American West*, ed. Kevin Fernlund (Albuquerque: University of New Mexico Press, 1998), 14. For an effort to study the NTS as a militarized landscape compared to more traditional parks and preserves, see John Wills, "Welcome to the Atomic Park: American Nuclear Landscapes and the Unnaturally Natural," *Environment and History* 7, no. 4 (November 2001): 449–72. On environmental history of the Cold War, see J. R. McNeill and Corinna R. Unger, *Environmental Histories of the Cold War* (Cambridge: Cambridge University Press, 2010). On testing specifically, see Toshihiro Higuchi, "Atmospheric Nuclear Weapons Testing and the Debate on Risk Knowledge in Cold War America, 1945–63," in the same volume, 301–22.

15. Rebecca Solnit, *Savage Dreams: A Journey into the Landscape Wars of the American West* (Berkeley: University of California Press, 1994), 47.

16. Tinguely's remarkable and widely publicized happenings are a central focus of Scott's insightful analysis in Scott, "Desert Ends," 68–69.

17. Mary Louis Pratt, "Fieldwork in Common Places," in *Writing Culture: The Poetics and Politics of Ethnography*, ed. James Clifford and George E. Marcus (Berkeley: University of California Press, 1986), 38.

18. For Fiege's argument about why it is worth considering the atomic scientists' views on nature and environment, see Mark Fiege, "The Atomic Scientists, the Sense of Wonder, and the Bomb," *Environmental History* 12, no. 3 (July 2007): 578–80; and Mark Fiege, *The Republic of Nature: An Environmental History of the United States* (Seattle: University of Washington Press, 2012).

19. On continental atomic testing, see Richard L. Miller, *Under the Cloud: The Decades of Nuclear Testing* (New York: Free Press, 1986); Howard Ball, *Justice Downwind: America's Atomic Testing Program in the 1950s* (New York: Oxford University Press, 1986); Phillip Fradkin, *Fallout: An American Nuclear Tragedy* (Tucson: University of Arizona Press, 1989); Barton C. Hacker, *Elements of Controversy: The AEC and Radiation Safety in Nuclear Weapons Testing, 1947–1974* (Berkeley: University of California Press, 1994); and A. Constadina Titus, *Bombs in the Backyard: Atomic Testing and American Politics*, 2nd ed. (Reno: University of Nevada Press, 2001). On more recent efforts to record and preserve NTS history in museums and through oral history, see Matt Wray, "A Blast from the Past: Preserving and Interpreting the Atomic Age," *American Quarterly* 58, no. 2 (June 2006): 468. Wray's pithy and insightful tour of the attempts to tell the story of the NTS through history, memory, and commemoration is the best introduction to the perils and opportunities of the topic. On "experimental landscapes" and their consequences, see Kuletz, *Tainted Desert*.

20. On the philosophy of the Shoshone protest, see Giovanna Di Chiro, "Nature as Community: The Convergence of Environmental and Social Justice," in *Uncommon Ground: Toward Reinventing Nature*, ed. William Cronon (New York: W. W. Norton, 1995), 313.

21. Solnit, *Savage Dreams*, 57.

22. On wild horses and perceived wastelands, see Leisl Carr Childers, "The Size of the Risk: An Environmental History of the Great Basin" (Ph.D. diss., University of Nevada–Las Vegas, 2011).

23. My analysis of NTS photography was published in an earlier version as Andrew Kirk, "Rereading the Nature of Atomic Doomtowns," *Environmental History* 17, no. 3 (July 2012): 635–47.

On visual culture and environmental history, start with Dunaway, *Natural Visions*; and Dunaway, "Cultures of Nature." Then visit or revisit Alan Trachtenberg, *Reading American Photographs: Images as History, Mathew Brady to Walker Evans* (New York: Hill & Wang, 1989). The gallery section of *Environmental History* has featured a fantastic selection of scholars who use visual sources to understand problems of environmental history. Particularly helpful for this essay were Virginia Scharff, "Where the Sea Used to Be," *Environmental History* 15, no. 2 (April 2010): 319–23; and Virginia Scharff, with Carolyn Brucken, *Home Lands: How Women Made the West* (Berkeley: University of California Press, 2010), which further looks at the work of the artist Buff Elting as part of a larger effort to use visual and material sources toward new perspectives on familiar topics. On reading industrial photo documentation toward environmental history insights, see Katherine G. Morrissey, "Rich Crevices of Inquiry: Mining and Environmental History," in *A Companion to American Environmental History*, ed. Douglas Cazaux Sackman (Malden, Mass.: Wiley-Blackwell, 2010), 394–409.

24. On visual analyses of atomic testing in particular, start with Peter Kuran, *How to Photograph an Atomic Bomb* (Santa Clarita, Calif.: VCE, 2006); and Kuran's related film, *Trinity and Beyond: The Atomic Bomb Movie* (Visual Concept Entertainment, 1995). Kuran's book details the history of photographic innovation required to capture atomic testing. The movie showcases Kuran's Academy Award–winning efforts to restore previously classified film footage of the testing era to new levels of clarity. Anyone who has seen the grainy footage in other forms will be stunned by Kuran's restoration efforts. Two important essays focus on atomic imagery: Peter Hales, "The Atomic Sublime," *American Studies* 32 (Spring 1991): 5–31; and Bryan C. Taylor, "Nuclear Pictures and Metapictures," *American Literary History* 9, no. 3 (Autumn 1997): 567–97, which analyzes the second-generation photography of nuclear opponents. Peter Hales's later *Atomic Spaces: Living on the Manhattan Project* (Urbana: University of Illinois Press, 1997), further explores the cultural landscapes of the Cold War and offers invaluable insights on how to "immerse ourselves" in pictures and their context. Both of these scholars rely on the earlier work of Spencer Weart and his study of atomic culture in *Nuclear Fear: A History of Images* (Cambridge, Mass.: Harvard University Press, 1988) and *The Rise of Nuclear Fear* (Cambridge, Mass.: Harvard University Press, 2012). Two early works combine oral history and documentary photographs to catalog atomic protagonists. Robert Del Tredici, *At Work in the Fields of the Bomb* (New York: Harper & Row, 1987), illuminates the national nuclear industrial complex through image and oral accounts. Carole Gallagher, *American Ground Zero: The Secret Nuclear War* (Cambridge, Mass.: MIT Press, 1993), offers a remarkable photo documentation and oral history of downwinders that also includes 1950s images by Dorothea Lange and Ansel Adams from their trip through the testing region during the height of the aboveground testing era. More recently several projects have documented the ruins of the nuclear West. See Peter Goin, *Nuclear Landscapes* (Baltimore: Johns Hopkins University Press, 1991); Tom Vanderbilt, *Survival City: Adventures Among the Ruins of Atomic America* (Chicago: University of Chicago Press, 2002); Richard Misrach, *Desert Cantos* (Albuquerque: University of New Mexico Press, 1987); and Richard Misrach, with Anne Wilkes Tucker and Rebecca Solnit, *Crimes and Splendors: The Desert Cantos of Richard Misrach* (Boston: Bullfinch Press, 1996). Both accompanying essays beautifully contextualize Misrach's photographs within the environmental context of the Cold War West. A disturbingly beautiful collection of historic blast images and the atomic sublime, Michael Light, *100 Suns* (New York: Alfred A. Knopf, 2003), lets the pictures speak for themselves with no interpretation whatsoever. On technology and photography, see David Nye, *American Technological Sublime* (Cambridge, Mass.: MIT Press, 1996). On thinking about the politics of photography and

atomic landscapes, see the excellent article by the geographer Scott Kirsch, "Watching the Bombs Go Off: Photography, Nuclear Landscapes, and Spectator Democracy," *Antipode* 29, no. 3 (1997): 227–55. He further explores the geography of testing in Scott Kirsch, *Proving Grounds: Project Plowshare and the Unrealized Dream of Nuclear Earthmoving* (New Brunswick, N.J.: Rutgers University Press, 2005).

25. On manifestations of atomic popular culture, see Paul Boyer, *By the Bomb's Early Light: American Thought and Culture at the Dawn of the Atomic Age* (New York: Pantheon, 1985); Allan M. Winkler, *Life Under a Cloud: American Anxiety About the Atom* (New York: Oxford University Press, 1993); Scott C. Zeman and Michael A. Amundson, eds., *Atomic Culture: How We Learned to Stop Worrying and Love the Bomb* (Boulder: University Press of Colorado, 2004); Macedon, *Bombast*; and Robert Jacobs, ed., *Filling the Hole in the Nuclear Future: Art and Popular Culture Respond to the Bomb* (Lanham, Md.: Lexington Books, 2010).

26. "New Atomic Ghost Town: Odd Shapes Arise from the Nevada Desert," CD, *Newspictures* 2, no. 5 (July–August 1957).

27. Of the many accounts of "Doom Towns," see the following important contemporary accounts: "Operation Doom Town," *Nevada Highways and Parks* 13, no. 2 (June–December 1953): 3–17; "Victims at Yucca Flats," *Life*, May 16, 1955, 58; "Real Folks Find Test Tribe Dead," *Las Vegas Review-Journal*, May 6, 1955, 1; "Federal Civil Defense Administration, Operation Doorstep," 1953. For analyses of Doom Towns and Civil Defense testing, see Joseph Masco, "Fantastic City," *Cabinet* 20 (Winter 2005/6): 1–6; and Joseph Masco, *The Nuclear Borderlands: The Manhattan Project in Post–Cold War New Mexico* (Princeton, N.J.: Princeton University Press, 1996). This is also discussed in Robert A. Jacobs, *The Dragon's Tail: Americans Face the Atomic Age* (Amherst: University of Massachusetts Press, 2010).

28. Masco, "Fantastic City," 1.

29. Brett Mizelle, *Pig* (London: Reaktion Books, 2011). For more on the cultural meaning of pigs and animal testing in Nevada, see Hugh Gusterson, *Nuclear Rites: A Weapons Laboratory at the End of the Cold War* (Berkeley: University of California Press, 1996), 108–9.

30. Hales, "Atomic Sublime," 8. Hales argues that the emerging iconography of the bomb from Japan to early testing "mediated the reality" of the bombs' human construction and devastating power to destroy. Kirsch, "Watching the Bombs Go Off," 229, too, discusses how photography and representations of testing in the media obscured the "wide-ranging human and ecological consequences" of testing in Nevada and the Pacific.

31. Ansel Adams recalled the experience of catching his most famous desert image, *Moonrise, Hernandez, New Mexico* (1941), as an example of the importance of fading or dawning light to the photographer's ability to convey an accurate sense of desert landscapes. More recently the landscape photographer Peter Goin intentionally used the bright light of day to highlight the most ruinous legacies of atomic testing in the West.

32. Vernon Jones, interview, October 4, 2005, NTSOHP, 49–53, http://www.digital.library.unlv.edu/ntsohp/ (accessed June 1, 2014). On oral history and environmental history, see Oral History Forum, "Talking Green: Oral History and Environmental History" (2010), http://www.oralhistoryforum.ca/index.php/ohf/issue/view/36. On oral history and atomic history, see Mary Palevsky's brilliant *Atomic Fragments: A Daughter's Questions* (Berkeley: University of California Press, 2000).

33. The atomic-blast photographers in action and especially their remarkable tools and new technologies are beautifully illustrated in Kuran, *How to Photograph an Atomic Bomb*.

34. "Operation Doom Town," 4.

35. For Cain Springs, see Frederick Worman, *Anatomy of the Nevada Test Site* (Los Alamos, N.Mex.: University of California and Los Alamos National Laboratory, 1965); and Frederick Worman, *Archeological Investigations at the U.S. Atomic Energy Commission's Nevada Test Site and Nuclear Rocket Development Station*, (Los Alamos, N.Mex.: University of California and Los Alamos National Laboratory, 1969).

36. For a summary of the Shoshone tribe's efforts to fight wasteland claims as part of Yucca Mountain protests, see http://www.nirs.org/radwaste/yucca/yuccaltrbycorbin102400.htm (accessed September 12, 2014); and Di Chiro, "Nature as Community," 313.

37. Mackedon, *Bombast*, 29.

38. On global testing, see Matthew Coolidge, *Nuclear Proving Grounds of the World* (Culver City, Calif.: Center for Land Use Interpretation, 1998); and Arjun Makhijani, Howard Hu, and Katherine Yih, *Nuclear Wastelands: A Global Guide to Nuclear Weapons Production and Its Health and Environmental Effects* (Cambridge, Mass.: MIT Press, 1995). The Kazakhstan "Polygon" test site is the most significant region of Soviet testing and the doppelganger of the NTS. For information on the history of the Soviet Polygon, see Kate Brown, "Gridded Lives: Why Kazakhstan and Montana Are Nearly the Same Place," *American Historical Review* 106, no. 1 (February 2001): 17–48; Christopher Robbins, *Apples Are from Kazakhstan: The Land That Disappeared* (New York: Atlas Books, 2008); and David Mould, "Warming to Life in the Hot Zone," *Times Higher Education,* January 12, 2012, http://www.timeshighereducation.co.uk/features/warming-to-life-in-the -hot-zone/418625.article (accessed October 13, 2014). Further insights into environmental/cultural history of Kazakh nuclear testing may be found in the oral histories and documentary footage generated during the "Nuclear Testing Legacies," a Museums Connect (MCCA) research project funded by the U.S. State Department from the summer of 2012, housed in the collections of the National Atomic Testing Museum and the http://digital.library.unlv.edu/ntsohp/ online archive. Also see the collections of the Ecomuseum in Karagada, Kazakhstan, http://www.eco museum.kz/ (accessed October 13, 2014).

39. Eugene Odum captured the ecologist's evolving view of the NTS in his immensely influential *Fundamentals of Ecology,* based in part on radioecology research conducted at the NTS under the auspices of the AEC and the National Science Foundation during the Doom Town tests of 1957–58; see Eugene P. Odum, *Fundamentals of Ecology,* 3rd ed. (Philadelphia: W. B. Saunders, 1971). For Odum's research at the NTS, see Betty Jean Craige, *Eugene Odum: Ecosystem Ecologist and Environmentalist* (Athens: University of Georgia Press, 2001), 66–73. Reflections on his life and work in Nevada are captured in a letter from his time there during the 1957–58 testing series (Craige, *Eugene Odum*, 69–70). For more on Odum's work in relation to larger trends in the history of science, see Peter J. Bower and Iwan Rhys Morus, *Making Modern Science: A Historical Survey* (Chicago: University of Chicago Press, 2005), 231–33; Peter J. Taylor, "Technocratic Optimism, H. T. Odum, and the Partial Transformation of Ecological Metaphor after World War II," *Journal of the History of Biology* 21, no. 2 (Summer 1988): 213–44; and Donald Wooster, *Nature's Economy: A History of Ecological Ideas,* 2nd ed. (Cambridge: Cambridge University Press, 1997), 345. For observations on nature appreciation while working at the NTS, see Robert Keller, interview with the author, Mercury, Nevada, February 9, 2012, http://digital.library.unlv.edu/ntsohp/ (accessed October 13, 2014).

40. More NTS participant views on nature and perceptions of the Mojave are revealed in many of the NTSOHP interviews; see the section "Contested Landscape," http://digital.library .unlv.edu/ntsohp/ (accessed October 13, 2014). NTS workers from scientists to maintenance workers described the testing region as diverse and beautiful and recalled the stark and even lush

beauty of sites such as Cain Springs. Quotes are from James Merlino, November 7, 2004, Tonopah, Nevada, and Sister Rosemary Lynch, June 8, 2004, Las Vegas, Nevada, http://www.digital.library .unlv.edu/ntsohp/ (accessed October 13, 2014).

41. Solnit's beautifully written *Savage Dreams* is a good example: poetic and fabulous on landscape and protest but no patience for conflicted workers and bureaucrats. Because of its proximity to larger population centers and agriculture centers, Hanford, Washington, has been the subject of a variety of recent studies. See, most recently, John Findlay and Bruce Hevly, *Atomic Frontier Days: Hanford and the American West* (Seattle: University of Washington Press, 2011).

42. The protagonists' use of art and other forms of visual representation to record their history and counter inaccurate perceptions of the Mojave is explained in many of the NTSOHP interviews, http://digital.library.unlv.edu/ntsohp/ (accessed October 13, 2014) and is available in the collections of the National Atomic Testing Museum.

43. For a recent example, see the posthumously published work from one of the great students of atomic pop culture, Ferenc Morton Szasz, *Atomic Comics: Cartoonists Confront the Nuclear World* (Albuquerque: University of New Mexico Press, 2012).

Chapter 9. River Rats in the Archive

Thanks to my excellent American studies colleagues at Notre Dame; to Peter Blodgett, Bill Frank, Alan Jutzi, and the Mead Foundation Fellowship, all of the Huntington Library; to Peggy Shaffer, Phoebe Young, and the other contributors to this volume; and to Craig Kinnear, Roy Webb, and Jon Coleman.

1. Barry Goldwater, journal typescript, July 9, 1940, Otis Marston Collection, Huntington Library, San Marino, California (hereafter referred to as Marston Collection), box 80, folder 2, 1.

2. Barry Morris Goldwater, *Delightful Journey: Down the Green and Colorado Rivers* (Tempe: Arizona Historical Foundation, 1970), 191. Otis Marston compiled this list from his research; it begins with the first Powell expedition in 1869 and does not count people who went down only partway through the canyon. It has since come under discussion. See Richard Quartaroli, "Docks Data of Navigational Numbers: The First 100 Grand Canyon River Runners," Guide Training Seminar (2009), http://www.gcrg.org/docs/gtslib/ (accessed October 14, 2014); and Tom Myers, "River Runners and the Numbers Game," *Boatman's Quarterly Review* 10, no. 1 (1997): 22–23, http:// www.gcrg.org/bqr.php (accessed October 14, 2014).

3. Goldwater, journal typescript, July 16, 1940, Marston Collection, box 80, folder 2, 9.

4. John Wesley Powell's book was published first as *The Exploration of the Colorado River of the West and Its Tributaries* (Washington, D.C.: Government Printing Office, 1875); then as a more popular account titled *Canyons of the Colorado* (Meadville, Pa.: Flood and Vincent, 1895); and its current edition is *The Exploration of the Colorado River and Its Canyons,* with an introduction by Wallace Stegner (New York: Penguin Books, 1997). Frederick S. Dellenbaugh published *The Romance of the Colorado River* in 1902 (New York: G. P. Putnam's Sons) and then *A Canyon Voyage,* which was more explicitly about the second Powell expedition (New York: G. P. Putnam's Sons, 1908). Ellsworth L. Kolb's book is *Through the Grand Canyon from Wyoming to Mexico* (New York: Macmillan, 1914).

5. Goldwater, journal typescript, August 22, 1940, Marston Collection, box 80, folder 2.

6. Cultural-studies scholars emphasize the process of making sense of the material world through symbolic practices and representation, while environmental historians pay most of their attention to the physical world around us. See Stuart Hall, ed., *Representation: Cultural Repre-*

sentations and Signifying Practices (London: Sage, 1997); Michael Lewis, ed., *American Wilderness: A New History* (New York: Oxford University Press, 2007); Ellen Stroud, "Does Nature Always Matter? Following Dirt Through History," *History and Theory* 42 (December 2003): 75–81; and David Demeritt, "The Nature of Metaphors in Cultural Geography and Environmental History," *Progress in Human Geography* 18, no. 2 (1994): 163–85.

7. For a discussion of what has become known as "the spatial turn" in American studies, see Karen Halttunen, "Groundwork: American Studies in Place," *American Quarterly* 58, no. 1 (2006): 1–15. For studies of the process of place-making, see John Wylie, *Landscape* (New York: Routledge, 2007); Tim Cresswell, *Place: A Short Introduction* (Malden, Mass.: Blackwell, 2004); Richard H. Schein, "The Place of Landscape: A Conceptual Framework for Interpreting an American Scene," *Annals of the Association of American Geographers* 87, no. 4 (1997): 660–80; and D. W. Meinig, ed., *The Interpretation of Ordinary Landscapes* (New York: Oxford University Press, 1979). Recent works that particularly influenced my analysis include Dianne Harris, *Little White Houses: How the Postwar Home Constructed Race in America* (Minneapolis: University of Minnesota Press, 2013); Elizabeth Kryder-Reid, "Sites of Power and the Power of Sight: Vision in the California Mission Landscapes," in *Sites Unseen: Landscape and Vision*, ed. Dianne Harris and D. Fairchild Ruggles (Pittsburgh: University of Pittsburgh Press, 2007), 181–212; and Keith Basso, *Wisdom Sits in Places: Landscape and Language Among the Western Apache* (Albuquerque: University of New Mexico Press, 1997).

8. Tim Ingold, *Being Alive: Essays on Movement, Knowledge and Description* (London: Routledge, 2011), xii, 12.

9. Powell, *Exploration*, x; Dellenbaugh, *Canyon Voyage*, vi. Otis Marston concluded that Powell did not keep a journal for the first part of the 1869 trip and that Sumner's journal and Powell's letters to the *Chicago Tribune* constitute the written record for the 1869 voyage. He makes reference to a journal kept by Bradley though does not cite it, and he says that Walter Powell wrote only one letter home. See Otis Marston to Harold Hutchings, November 19, 1973, Marston Collection, box 271, folder 1; and Otis Marston to Harold Hutchings, March 5, n.d., Marston Collection, box 271, folder 4.

10. Wallace Stegner, *Beyond the Hundredth Meridian: John Wesley Powell and the Second Opening of the West* (Lincoln: University of Nebraska Press, 1982), 136; Dellenbaugh, *Canyon Voyage*, vii, ix.

11. Ellsworth Kolb, *Through the Grand Canyon from Wyoming to Mexico* (New York: Macmillan, 1942; 17th printing, 1969), xiii–xiv.

12. Ibid., back cover.

13. Lance Newman, ed., *The Grand Canyon Reader* (Berkeley: University of California Press, 2011), 2.

14. John Wesley Powell, as quoted in Elizabeth C. Childs, "Time's Profile: John Wesley Powell, Art, and Geology at the Grand Canyon," *American Art* 10, no. 1 (Spring 1996): 19.

15. David Lavender, *River Runners of the Grand Canyon* (Tucson: University of Arizona Press, 1985), 22–32. Mile markers of inscriptions were culled from bibliographic data attached to digitized photos from the Marston Collection, http://www.hdl.huntington.org/cdm/landingpage/collection/p16003coll5 (accessed October 14, 2014).

16. For a brief history of river-running trips, see Lavender, *River Runners*.

17. Roy Webb, ed., *High, Wide, and Handsome: The River Journals of Norman D. Nevills* (Logan: Utah State University Press, 2005), 52, 67.

18. Hugh Cutler to Otis Marston, July 8, 1948, and interview notes with Hugh Cutler, October 1955, Marston Collection, box 37, folders 26, 27.

19. Dark Canyon Register, March 19, 1955, Marston Collection, box 309, folder 9.

20. As Judith Butler and others have established the notion of identity as performative, so too have Maurice Merleau-Ponty and other phenomenologists argued that a landscape's meaning derives from human movement through it, or as Tim Ingold puts it, through "productive engagement." See Judith Butler, *Gender Trouble: Feminism and the Subversion of Identity* (New York: Routledge, 1990); Maurice Merleau-Ponty, *Phenomenology of Perception* (London: Routledge, 1962); Erving Goffman, *The Presentation of Self in Everyday Life* (New York: Anchor Books, 1959); Ingold, *Being Alive*, 11; and Wylie, *Landscape*, 139–86.

21. See editors of *High Country News, Western Water Made Simple* (Washington, D.C.: Island Press, 1987); Philip Fradkin, *A River No More: The Colorado River and the West* (Tucson: University of Arizona Press, 1981); and Marc Reisner, *Cadillac Desert: The American West and Its Disappearing Water* (New York: Penguin, 1993).

22. Tom Martin and Duwain Whitis, *RiverMaps Guide to the Colorado River in the Grand Canyon*, 4th ed. (Flagstaff, Ariz.: Vishnu Temple Press, 2008), maps 7, 8.

23. See Leah Dilworth, ed., *Acts of Possession: Collecting in America* (New Brunswick, N.J.: Rutgers University Press, 2003), 3–13; and James Clifford, "Objects and Selves—An Afterword," in *Objects and Others: Essays on Museums and Material Culture,* ed. George W. Stocking, Jr. (Madison: University of Wisconsin Press, 1985), 236–46.

24. Andrew G. Kirk, *The Gentle Science: A History of the Conservation Library* (Denver: Denver Public Library, 1995).

25. Michel Rolph-Trouillot, *Silencing the Past: Power and the Production of History* (Boston: Beacon Press,1995).

26. Otis Marston, interview by P. T. Reilly, n.d., Marston Collection, box 420, reel 10, side 1; Otis Marston to Frank Dodge, December 1, 1947, Marston Collection, box 51, folder 18.

27. Otis Marston to Frank Dodge, May 18, 1952, Marston Collection, box 51, folder 1. He never explained why he spelled "Dock" with a "k."

28. Alan Jutzi, Avery chief curator, July 9, 2012, and Bill Frank, curator, July 10, 2012, interviews by the author, Huntington Library, San Marino, California.

29. Huntington online catalog, http://www.catalog.huntington.org/search~S0?/Xotis+r +marston&SORT=D/Xotis+r+marston&SORT=D&SUBKEY=otis+r+marston/1%2C63%2C63 %2CB/frameset&FF=Xotis+r+marston&SORT=D&2%2C2%2C (accessed October 14, 2014).

30. Jacques Derrida and Eric Prenowitz, "Archive Fever: A Freudian Impression," *Diacritics* 25, no. 2 (Summer 1995): 9–63.

31. For the sake of clarity I focus only on Marston's written materials here, rather than try to incorporate the enormous amount of photographic and motion picture material also in the collection. These materials function similarly to the written documents as texts but not quite as clearly, as they are organized separately and by format.

32. Frank Dodge, "The Saga of Frank Dodge: An Autobiography," compiled by the Tucson office of the U.S. Geological Survey (1944), Marston Collection, box 51, folder 17. For examples of correspondence, see ibid., box 51, folders 20, 22.

33. Marston Collection, box 124, folders 12–17. See also Marguerite Shaffer, "Playing American: The Southwestern Scrapbooks of Mildred E. Baker," in *The Culture of Tourism, the Tourism of Culture: Selling the Past to the Present in the American Southwest,* ed. Hal K. Rothman (Albu-

querque: University of New Mexico Press, 2003), 72–100. For an examination of gender as expressed in relationship to nature, see Susan Schrepfer, *Nature's Altars: Mountains, Gender, and American Environmentalism* (Lawrence: University Press of Kansas, 2005); and Annie Gilbert Coleman, "From Snow Bunnies to Shred Betties: Gender, Consumption, and the Skiing Landscape," in *Seeing Nature Through Gender,* ed. Virginia Scharff (Lawrence: University Press of Kansas, 2003), 194–217.

34. Marston Collection, box 15, folder 13.

35. Elzada U. Clover, "Danger Can Be Fun," *Quarterly Review of the Michigan Alumnus* 45, no. 4 (Winter 1944): 110, Marston Collection, box 32, folder 42; Elzada Clover to Otis Marston, December 3, 1947, Marston Collection, box 32, folder 44. Clover noted that she read Dellenbaugh's, Kolb's, and Eddy's books on their expeditions before starting down the river; along the way she commented on numerous inscriptions, including one by Bessie Hyde, who disappeared in the Grand Canyon with her husband in 1928.

36. Frank Dodge to Ian Campbell, August 3, 1938, Marston Collection, box 51, folder 20.

37. There is no direct evidence explaining how his organizational structure emerged, but it is clear that he was copying documents to be cross-filed from early on, and each section was developed to about the same extent when the Huntington Library accepted it. The archivists made a point to keep the original organizational structure rather than impose a new one, based on the standards of their profession. As stated in the glossary published by the Society of American Archivists, "Maintaining records in original order serves two purposes. First, it preserves existing relationships and evidential significance that can be inferred from the context of the records. Second, it exploits the record creator's mechanisms to access the records, saving the archives the work of creating new access tools"; see http://www2.archivists.org/glossary/terms/o/original-order (accessed January 10, 2014).

38. Marston Collection, box 269, folders 4–19.

39. Ibid., box 271, folders 2–5.

40. Otis Marston to Harold Hutchings, March 5, n.d., Marston Collection, box 271, folder 4; "Opinion to Darrah" and "Darrah's reply," Marston Collection, box 271, folder 6.

41. Bill Belknap, Buzz Belknap, Loie Belknap Evans, Lynn Evans Peesel, Wayne Ranney, Meribeth Riffey, and Douglas W. Schwartz, *Belknap's Waterproof Grand Canyon River Guide* (Evergreen, Colo.: Westwater Books, 2011), 13, 59; and Randall Henderson, journal typescript, 1947; notes from Hank Toll, interview by Otis Marston, October 2, 1958; clipping, Roderick Nash, "The Biggest Drop," *Mariah/Outside* (February/March 1979): 99, all in Marston Collection, box 341, folder 23.

42. Marston notes, "Lava Falls"; notes from Julius Stone, diary, November 10 and 11, 1909, 97; notes from Elwyn Blake, diary, September 18, 1923; notes from Birdseye and Moore, "A Boat Voyage Through the Grand Canyon of the Colorado," *Geographical Review* (April 1924): 192; all in Marston Collection, box 341, folder 23.

43. "ASB Ms Stanton," Marston notes, Marston Collection, box 341, folder 23, 262.

44. Elwyn Blake, diary, September 19, 1923, Marston Collection, box 341, folder 23.

45. Marston notes, "Lava Falls," Marston Collection, box 341, folder 23.

46. Ibid.; Joyce Hamilton, journal, June 23, 1960; clipping, Walter Kirschbaum, "Grand Adventure," *American White Water* (1960): 8, all in Marston Collection, box 341, folder 23. See also Goldwater, journal typescript, August 17, 1940, Marston Collection, box 80, folder 3, 41–42; and Webb, *High, Wide, and Handsome,* 91.

47. Library General Correspondence, Otis Marston, 1949–1960, Huntington Institutional Archives, Huntington Library, San Marino, California, 31.1.1.31.1. Quotes are from letters dated December 9, 1957, and December 12, 1957.

48. Peter Blodgett, H. Russell Smith Foundation Curator of Western American History at the Huntington Library, e-mail to the author, September 29, 2013. In this way Marston might remind one of Walter Benjamin and his *Arcades Project*, in which he lost similar power exploring the limits of collecting. See Dilworth, *Acts of Possession*, 6; Susan Buck-Morss, *The Dialectics of Seeing: Walter Benjamin and the Arcades Project* (Cambridge, Mass.: MIT Press, 1989); and Walter Benjamin, *The Arcades Project*, trans. Howard Eiland and Kevin McLaughlin (Cambridge, Mass.: Harvard University Press, 1999).

49. Brad Dimock, "David Lavender," *Boatman's Quarterly Review* 16, no. 2 (Summer 2003): 3, http://www.gcrg.org/bqr/pdf/16-2.pdf (accessed January 10, 2014); Blodgett, e-mail to the author.

50. Charles Richey to Otis Marston, June 5, 1959, Marston Collection, box 341, folder 23.

51. Kadin Henningsen, HEH Reader Services, e-mail to the author, July 9, 2012.

52. Webb is a multimedia archivist at the University of Utah's Marriott Library; Quartaroli retired as a special collections archivist at Northern Arizona University's Cline Library in 2011. Both have published books and articles in regional historical journals, given multiple public talks, and are active in the Grand Canyon River Guides professional association. Upon his retirement, Quartaroli said, "I'm going to be doing the 3 Rs—rivers, research, and (w)riting." Webb noted that he always keeps a journal on the river, because "it's so overwhelming it's the only way I can remember. I rarely look at them afterwards but I have shelves full of them." See http://www .yourwestvalley.com/topstory/article_b9610a16-8251-11e0-b672-001cc4c03286.html (accessed October 14, 2014); and Roy Webb, e-mail to the author, July 29, 2013.

53. Brad Dimock, "River Guide Quits and Tells Why," *High Country News*, December 21, 1998, http://www.hcn.org/issues/145/4682 (accessed October 14, 2014).

54. See http://www.gcrg.org/guide_resources_gtslib.php (accessed October 14, 2014); and Dimock, "David Lavender, 3."

55. See Marston Collection, box 17, folders 1–6; and http://library.nau.edu/speccoll/exhibits /belknap/bio4.html (accessed October 15, 2014). Rafting companies and amazon.com customers rank his guide highly.

56. "Recommended Reading," Marston Collection; box 380, folder 1; Barry Goldwater to Harry Aleson, February 26, 1956, Marston Collection, box 80, folder 8; http://www.gcrg.org/bqr .php (accessed October 14, 2014).

Chapter 10. Rocks of Ages

1. Patricia Nelson Limerick, *Desert Passages: Encounters with the American Desert* (Niwot: University Press of Colorado, 1989).

2. Dan Flores, *Horizontal Yellow: Nature and History in the Near Southwest* (Albuquerque: University of New Mexico Press, 1999).

3. See Marjorie Hope Nicolson, *Mountain Gloom and Mountain Glory: The Development of the Aesthetics of the Infinite* (Ithaca, N.Y.: Cornell University Press, 1959), repr. 1997 and 2011 in Weyerhaeuser Environmental Series through the University of Washington Press; and Gordon Davies, *The Earth in Decay: A History of British Geomorphology 1578–1878* (New York: American Elsevier, 1969). Thomas Burnet, *A Sacred History of the Earth* (London: Roger Norton, 1681), is a vivid expression of what came to be seen as "early" and discredited geology that relied on classi-

cal and scholastic sources. Stephen Jay Gould, *Time's Arrow, Time's Cycle: Myth and Metaphor in the Discovery of Geologic Time* (Cambridge, Mass.: Harvard University Press, 1987), offers a valuable glimpse of Burnet's work in comparison with the later work of James Hutton, the "discoverer" of geologic time, and that of Charles Lyell.

4. R. J. Chorley, Antony Dunn, and R. P. Beckinsale, *The History of the Study of Landforms*, vol. 1, *Geomorphology Before Davis* (New York: Routledge, 2009), 11. See also Alan Ford, *James Ussher: Theology, History and Politics in Early-Modern Ireland and England* (Oxford: Oxford University Press, 2007).

5. The spirit of Francis Bacon—deliberately taking down the hoary traditions of the past to build anew from nothing but his own wits in his *Great Instauration* (1620)—seems important to bear in mind. Newton's *Principia*, with its theorization of absolute time (independent of those things or processes that might embody or display it), appeared in 1687. See Mircea Eliade, *The Myth of the Eternal Return: Or, Cosmos and History* (New York: Bollingen, 1954).

6. See Chorley et al., *History of the Study of Landforms*, 1:11; and Nicolson, *Mountain Gloom and Mountain Glory*, 147–48.

7. Charles Lyell, *Principles of Geology*, vol. 1 (London: John Murray, 1830), 7.

8. Ibid., 15. It is interesting that this foundation, sifting through and organizing the rubble of history with remarkable sensitivity, is abridged out of the more easily available Penguin edition of Lyell, presumably because it is not necessary to understanding Lyell's "own" geological contributions.

9. Lyell, *Principles of Geology* (1830), 10.

10. Nicolson, *Mountain Gloom and Mountain Glory*, 83–88, 89.

11. Charles Lyell, *Principles of Geology*, ed. James Secord, vol. 1 (New York: Penguin, 1997), chap. 10, 115.

12. Ibid., chap. 25, 151.

13. Ibid., chap. 26, 178–79.

14. Ibid., chap. 4, 25.

15. Michel Foucault, *The Order of Things: An Archaeology of the Human Sciences* (New York: Vintage, 1994). Foucault's "archaeological" approach to knowledge suggests a seriously playful reckoning with other sciences that he did not investigate explicitly, including geology—epistemologically, we may all be "geologists" now.

16. That is a project well worth undertaking and forms part of the larger book whose approach this essay sketches. Romanticism is much more visible than decadence in environmental analysis but has become dismal shorthand for a form of nostalgia, or a critique lamenting losses of crucial things; merely an affinity for the sublime is enough to nod, say "John Ruskin, romanticism," and be done with it. Decadence, as an aesthetic (and I would argue an epistemological) approach, is at least as important. The relationship between romantics and decadents is already blurry enough not to be easily distinguished even in the career and life of one man, John Ruskin. Decadence was distinct enough from romanticism for some people to champion decadence as such. Ruskin was, incidentally, deeply interested in geology (among many things) and may well have devoted as much time as any other person to writing about it and drawing it. Walter Pater, whose notoriously appreciative description of the *Mona Lisa* as a vampire includes the sublime geology of the painting's background, was very interested in contemporary science. From the side of scientists, Darwin's thrill and disgust in the Galapagos sound remarkably decadent to me. Modernity spawned decadence as well as romanticism, whether the former is a subspecies of the

latter or distinct unto itself or not, and there is much more to say about the point of view of self-styled (and even reluctant) decadents in relation to modern science in general.

17. Walter Benjamin, "Paris, Capital of the Nineteenth Century," in *Reflections: Essays, Aphorisms, Autobiographical Writings*, ed. Peter Demetz, trans. Edmund Jephcott (New York: Schoken, 1986), 158.

18. Charles Baudelaire, *Les Fleurs du Mal* (1857), trans. Richard Howard (Boston: Godine, 1982). The poem is number 22 in the collection; Howard's verse translation appears on 28–29, and Baudelaire's original is on 206–7. The French sounds by turns guttural and sibilant and above all measured, an astonishing effect; the pedestrian prose translation is mine. My reading of Baudelaire's poetry and contexts obviously owes a great deal to Walter Benjamin, but I have elaborated emphases of my own.

19. Walter Benjamin, "On Some Motifs in Baudelaire," in *Illuminations: Essays and Reflections*, ed. Hannah Arendt, trans. Harry Zohn (New York: Schocken Books, 1969), 192–93.

20. The entomologist and philosopher Jeffrey Lockwood asked the first of these questions when I had a chance to present an idea of the "decadent desert" in a reading in November 2011.

21. Benjamin, "On Some Motifs in Baudelaire," 194. The "star without atmosphere" is Nietzsche's phrase. The star is doomed to darkness in an era overzealous about documenting a certain kind of history, celebrating science and utility, and offering the young a disgusting simultaneity of all the ages. See Friedrich Nietzsche, "On the Uses and Disadvantages of History," in Friedrich Nietzsche, *Untimely Meditations*, ed. Daniel Breazeale (Cambridge: Cambridge University Press, 1997), "star without atmosphere," 97.

22. Fredric Jameson, *Postmodernism, or, The Cultural Logic of Late Capitalism* (Durham, N.C.: Duke University Press, 1991), 382.

23. Benjamin was clear on the absence of Paris street crowds in Baudelaire's poetry—their conspicuous absence signified the ubiquity of the crowd.

24. Limerick, *Desert Passages*, 5.

25. Clarence Dutton, *The Tertiary History of the Grand Canyon District*, United States Geological Survey (1881), repr. with intro. by Wallace Stegner, foreword by Stephen Pyne (Tucson: University of Arizona Press, 2001), 1 (small capital letters in original).

26. Ibid., 62.

27. Wallace Stegner, *Beyond the Hundredth Meridian: John Wesley Powell and the Second Opening of the West* (1953), repr. with intro. by Bernard DeVoto (New York: Penguin, 1992), 168–69.

28. Donald Worster, *A River Running West: The Life of John Wesley Powell* (Oxford: Oxford University Press, 2001), 187.

29. Ibid., 188.

30. Ibid., 201. The characterization of King throughout the book as a libertine and a dandy is thorough.

31. The lavender gloves led me to Martha Sandweiss, *Passing Strange: A Gilded Age Tale of Love and Deception Across the Color Line* (New York: Penguin, 2009). King passed as a Pullman porter; he was married to a black woman who did not know his identity as a scientist and explorer.

32. Edward Abbey, *Desert Solitaire: A Season in the Wilderness* (1968; repr., New York: Simon & Schuster, 1990), 10.

33. Ibid., 5.

34. Ibid., 6.

35. Ibid., 211–13. Passages in square brackets indicate other impressions of the dead man's fate from the same attenuated episode. My juxtapositions do not preempt Abbey's but rather only underscore them. We do not know who this dead man was.

36. See Terry Tempest Williams, *Finding Beauty in a Broken World* (New York: Pantheon, 2008). About Rwanda she wrote, "All I can see are rivers running red, this time not with the blood of the people but the blood of the land. Steep mountainsides are cultivated clear to the summits. The green and yellow squares looked like a stretched quilt pulled apart by rain and gravity. Genocide is not just about the killing of people but the taking of the land. . . . Erosion—the other genocide in Rwanda, the one rarely mentioned. Rwanda is a country that is literally slipping away" (308).

37. Terry Tempest Williams, "Labor," in Terry Tempest Williams, *Red: Passion and Patience in the Desert* (New York: Vintage, 2001), 156.

38. Ibid., 160–62.

39. Terry Tempest Williams, "The Bowl," in Williams, *Red*, 32–35. Note the exotic and perishable lemon.

40. Bernard DeVoto, "To the Traveler's Eye," in *The Western Paradox: A Conservation Reader*, ed. Douglas Brinckley and Patricia Limerick, foreword by Arthur Schlesinger, Jr. (New Haven, Conn.: Nota Bene/Yale University Press, 2001), 192. The first part of this volume consists of articles reprinted from *Harper's* beginning in the 1930s; the rest is an unfinished manuscript of DeVoto's tenderly framed by his posthumous editors. DeVoto died in 1955. It is impossible not to see his conservation and desert-travel writings as a lost stratum in western (and environmental) history. Stegner knew DeVoto and chose not to finish the manuscript. The DeVoto of public record falls silent in 1955 to reemerge in 2001, eluding fifty significant years of American environmental politics and narrative. DeVoto's "señor" (an interlocutor who appears repeatedly) is reminiscent of some of Cormac McCarthy's characters in similar settings.

41. Henri LeFebvre, *The Production of Space*, trans. Donald Nicholson-Smith (Malden, Mass., and Oxford: Blackwell, 1991); Edward Soja, *ThirdSpace: Journeys to Los Angeles and Other Real-and-Imagined Places* (Malden, Mass., and Oxford: Wiley-Blackwell, 1996).

42. Catrin Gersdorf, *The Poetics and Politics of the Desert: Landscape and the Construction of America* (Amsterdam and New York: Rodopi, 2009), offers an array of obviously socially constructed desert spaces, from the desert as Garden to the desert as Heterotopia, the result of "a need to find new tropes and metaphors for the ongoing process of defining and redefining America" (19). The tropes are multiple, and her use of "Heterotopia" purposefully leaves room for multiply imagined "Americas" as well.

43. Walter Prescott Webb, *The Great Plains* (Boston: Ginn, 1931), 10.

44. See Charles Ferguson, "Geology of the Red Desert," the first chapter of his *Red Desert: History of a Place*, ed. Annie Proulx (Austin: University of Texas Press, 2008), 85–105.

Chapter 11. Winning the War at Manzanar

1. Terrence H. Witkowski, "World War II Poster Campaigns," *Journal of Advertising* 32, no. 1 (Spring 2003): 72, calculates that 11.8 percent of the war-time posters emphasized the conservation of materials.

2. William L. Bird, Jr., and Harry R. Rubenstein, *Design for Victory: World War II Posters on the American Home Front* (New York: Princeton Architectural Press, 1998), 20, 34. For other discussions of war-time propaganda efforts, see Susan A. Brewer, *Why America Fights: Patriotism and War Propaganda from the Philippines to Iraq* (New York: Oxford University Press,

2009), 87–140. For scrap drives, see Susan Strasser, *Waste and Want: A Social History of Trash* (New York: Henry Holt, 1999), 229–63; and Robert William Kirk, "Getting in the Scrap: The Mobilization of American Children in World War II," *Journal of Popular Culture* 29 (Summer 1995): 223–33.

3. Jake Kosek, *Understories: The Political Life of Forests in Northern New Mexico* (Durham, N.C.: Duke University Press, 2006), 193–202. For a broader discussion of racialized war-time propaganda, see John W. Dower, *War Without Mercy: Race and Power in the Pacific War* (New York: Pantheon Books, 1986).

4. Gary Y. Okihiro, *The Columbia Guide to Asian American History* (New York: Columbia University Press, 2005), 104.

5. My approach takes cues from Mark Fiege, *The Republic of Nature: An Environmental History of the United States* (Seattle: University of Washington Press, 2012). Fiege analyzes well-known episodes from American history through the lens of environmental history.

6. Hal K. Rothman, *Saving the Planet: The American Response to the Environment in the Twentieth Century* (Chicago: Ivan R. Dee, 2000), 82.

7. Richard West Sellars, *Preserving Nature in the National Parks: A History* (New Haven, Conn.: Yale University Press, 1997), 150–55. For the war's impact on wildlife conservation, see Robert M. Wilson, "Birds on the Home Front: Wildlife Conservation in the Western United States during World War II," in *War and the Environment: Military Destruction in the Modern Age*, ed. Charles E. Closmann (College Station: Texas A&M University Press, 2009), 132–49.

8. Sarah Elkind, "The Nature and Business of War: Drilling for Oil in Wartime Los Angeles," in *Cities and Nature in the American West*, ed. Char Miller (Reno: University of Nevada Press, 2010), 205–24. See also Gerald D. Nash, *The American West Transformed; The Impact of the Second World War* (Lincoln: University of Nebraska Press, 1985), 21.

9. John M. Findlay and Bruce Hevly, *Atomic Frontier Days: Hanford and the American West* (Seattle: University of Washington Press, 2011); Kate Brown, *Plutopia: Nuclear Families, Atomic Cities, and the Great Soviet and American Plutonium Disasters* (New York: Oxford University Press, 2013). For the Manhattan Project, see Peter B. Hales, *Atomic Spaces: Living on the Manhattan Project* (Urbana: University of Illinois Press, 1997).

10. The federal government's use of natural resources to promote political goals and reinforce ideals of American citizenship was not without precedent. For instance, the Civilian Conservation Corps enlisted young men to work in a wide array of conservation projects, mostly in the national forests and national parks, both to improve the American landscape and to create American workers who were invested in the nation, committed to conservation, and imbued with a sense of patriotism. See Neil M. Maher, "A New Deal Body Politic: Landscape, Labor, and the Civilian Conservation Corps," *Environmental History* 7, no. 3 (July 2002): 435–61; and Neil M. Maher, *Nature's New Deal: The Civilian Conservation Corps and the Roots of the American Environmental Movement* (New York: Oxford University Press, 2007).

11. Quoted in James T. Sparrow, *Warfare State: World War II Americans and the Age of Big Government* (New York: Oxford University Press, 2011), 3.

12. Ibid., 4–12.

13. Mark H. Leff, "The Politics of Sacrifice on the American Home Front in World War II," *Journal of American History* 77, no. 4 (March 1991): 1297.

14. Sparrow, *Warfare State*, 4–12. For another compelling discussion of home-front mobilization, see Robert B. Westbrook, *Why We Fought: Forging American Obligations During World War II* (Washington, D.C.: Smithsonian Institution Press, 2004).

15.Anne Marie Todd has also written about the rhetoric of environmental patriotism during World War II, but she focuses on conservation measures. See Anne Marie Todd, *Communicating Environmental Patriotism: A Rhetorical History of the American Environmental Movement* (New York: Routledge, 2013), 68–85.

16. See Alfred Runte, *The National Parks: An American Experience*, 3rd ed. (Lincoln: University of Nebraska Press, 1997); and Marguerite S. Shaffer, *See America First: Tourism and National Identity, 1880–1940* (Washington, D.C.: Smithsonian Institution Press, 2001).

17. Kosek, *Understories*, 202.

18. The social tensions caused by World War II have been well documented. See, for instance, John Morton Blum, *V Was for Victory: Politics and American Culture During World War II* (New York: Harcourt Brace Jovanovich, 1976); Heather Fryer, *Perimeters of Democracy: Inverse Utopias and the Wartime Social Landscape in the American West* (Lincoln: University of Nebraska Press, 2010); Thomas Guglielmo, "'Red Cross, Double Cross': Race and America's World War II–Era Blood Donor Service," *Journal of American History* 97 (June 2010): 63–90; and Elizabeth R. Escobedo, *From Coveralls to Zoot Suits: The Lives of Mexican American Women on the World War II Home Front* (Chapel Hill: University of North Carolina Press, 2013).

19. John Walton, *Western Times and Water Wars: State, Culture, and Rebellion in California* (Berkeley and Los Angeles: University of California Press, 1992); Marc Reisner, *Cadillac Desert: The American West and Its Disappearing Water*, rev. ed. (New York: Penguin Books, 1993); William L. Kahrl, *Water and Power: The Conflict over Los Angeles' Water Supply in the Owens Valley* (Berkeley and Los Angeles: University of California Press, 1982).

20. Robert L. Brown and Ralph P. Merritt, "Project Director's Report," in *Final Report, Manzanar Relocation Center*, vol. 1, Field Basic Documentation of the War Relocation Authority, War Relocation Authority Records, RG 210, microfilm C0053, roll 76, National Archives and Records Administration, Washington, D.C. (hereafter FBD-WRA).

21. Tom C. Clark to Ralph P. Merritt, March 7, 1942, box 21, folder 6, Manzanar War Relocation Center Records, collection 122, Special Collections, University of California, Los Angeles (hereafter Manzanar Records-UCLA); Brown and Merritt, "Project Director's Report."

22. H. A. Van Norman to S. B. Robinson, March 3, 1942, Water Executive Office, Administrative-Executive Files, Manzanar Relocation Center, Correspondence, May 1942–October 1943, WP14-1:3, Los Angeles Department of Water and Power Historical Records Program (hereafter LADWP Records).

23. "Proposal: Japanese Alien Problems," Los Angeles County, submitted by Wayne H. Fisher, Ed F. Williams, and L. A. Hauser, February 16, 1942, box 52, Fletcher Bowron Collection, Huntington Library, San Marino, California (hereafter Bowron Collection).

24. Mayor Fletcher Bowron, radio broadcast, Station KECA, Los Angeles, Thursday, February 19, 1942, 6:30 P.M., box 52, Bowron Collection. The WRA eventually established one relocation center, Poston (Colorado River), about twelve miles south of Parker.

25. "The Silverman Report," in *Final Report, Manzanar Relocation Center*, vol. 1, appendix 25, FBD-WRA, roll 76; H. A. Van Norman to S. B. Robinson, March 6, 1942, Water Executive Office, Administrative-Executive Files, Manzanar Relocation Center, Correspondence, May 1942–October 1943, WP14-1:3, LADWP Records.

26. Brown and Merritt, "Project Director's Report"; Harlan D. Unrau, *The Evacuation and Relocation of Persons of Japanese Ancestry During World War II: A Historical Study of the Manzanar Relocation Center*, vol. 1 (Washington, D.C.: United States Department of the Interior, National Park Service, 1996), 128; press release, March 7, 1942, FBD-WRA, roll 75; John L. DeWitt

to H. A. Van Norman, March 7, 1942, Water Executive Office, Administrative-Executive Files, Manzanar Relocation Center, Correspondence, May 1942–October 1943, WP14-1:3, LADWP Records.

27. T. Blevans to H. A. Van Norman, March 10, 1942, Water Executive Office, Administrative-Executive Files, Manzanar Relocation Center, Correspondence, May 1942–October 1943, WP14-1:3, LADWP Records. See also Kyle Palmer, "Proposed Owens Valley Camp for Japs Opposed," *Los Angeles Times*, March 7, 1942, 6.

28. H. L. Ford to Bureau of Power and Water, March 6, 1942, Water Executive Office, Administrative-Executive Files, Manzanar Relocation Center, Correspondence, May 1942–October 1943, WP14-1:3, LADWP Records.

29. Michael Rawson, *Eden on the Charles: The Making of Boston* (Cambridge, Mass.: Harvard University Press, 2010); David Stradling, *Making Mountains: New York City and the Catskills* (Seattle: University of Washington Press, 2008).

30. Nancy Tomes, *The Gospel of Germs: Men, Women, and the Microbe in American Life* (Cambridge, Mass.: Harvard University Press, 1998); Charles E. Rosenberg, *The Cholera Years: The United States in 1832, 1849, and 1866* (Chicago: University of Chicago Press, 1987).

31. Natalia Molina, *Fit to Be Citizens? Public Health and Race in Los Angeles, 1879–1939* (Berkeley: University of California Press, 2006), 1–2; William Deverell, *Whitewashed Adobe: The Rise of Los Angeles and the Remaking of Its Mexican Past* (Berkeley: University of California Press, 2004), 172–206.

32. "Placing Japanese in the Owens Valley," *Los Angeles Times*, March 7, 1942, A4.

33. H. A. Van Norman to H. L. Ford, March 10, 1942, Water Executive Office, Administrative-Executive Files, Manzanar Relocation Center, Correspondence, May 1942–October 1943, WP14-1:3, LADWP Records.

34. R. F. Goudey to H. A. Van Norman, March 10, 1942, Water Executive Office, Administrative-Executive Files, Manzanar Relocation Center, Correspondence, May 1942–October 1943, WP14-1:3, LADWP Records.

35. R. F. Goudey to H. A. Van Norman, March 24, 1942, Water Executive Office, Administrative-Executive Files, Manzanar Relocation Center, Correspondence, May 1942–October 1943, WP14-1:3, LADWP Records.

36. H. A. Van Norman to Lieutenant General J. L. DeWitt, March 25, 1942, Water Executive Office, Administrative-Executive Files, Manzanar Relocation Center, Correspondence, May 1942–October 1943, WP14-1:3, LADWP Records.

37. "Silverman Report."

38. Mayor Fletcher Bowron, radio broadcast, Station KECA, Los Angeles, Wednesday, May 19, 1943, 7:45 P.M., box 52, Bowron Collection. Bowron's anti-Japanese sentiments faded by 1944, and he apologized to Japanese Americans after the war; see Abraham Hoffman, "The Conscience of a Public Official: Los Angeles Mayor Fletcher Bowron and Japanese Removal," *Southern California Quarterly* 92, no. 3 (2010): 243–74.

39. Ralph P. Merritt to Fletcher Bowron, July 12, 1943, and Ralph P. Merritt to D. S. Myer, July 12, 1943, box 21, folder 8, Manzanar Records-UCLA.

40. Board of Water and Power Commissioners of the City of Los Angeles to Ralph Merritt, entry 48, box 224/43.120, War Relocation Authority Records, Record Group 210, National Archives and Records Administration, Washington, D.C. (hereafter WRA-NARA).

41. D. S. Myer to R. P. Merritt, November 11, 1943, entry 48, box 224/43.120, WRA-NARA.

42. C. G. Gillespie to Ralph Merritt, November 17, 1943, entry 48, box 224/43.120, WRA-NARA.

43. R. F. Goudey to J. K. Hoskins, December 3, 1943, Water Executive Office, Administrative-Executive Files, Manzanar Relocation Center, Correspondence, January 1944–September 1944, WP14-1:4, LADWP Records.

44. Dillon Myer to Ralph P. Merritt, December 22, 1943, entry 48, box 224/43.120, WRA-NARA.

45. Ralph P. Merritt to D. S. Myer, December 30, 1943, entry 48, box 224/43.120, WRA-NARA.

46. H. A. Van Norman to Dillon Myer, January 31, 1944, Water Executive Office, Administrative-Executive Files, Manzanar Relocation Center, Correspondence, January 1944–September 1944, WP14-1:4, LADWP Records.

47. Ralph P. Merritt to Board of Water and Power Commissioners, City of Los Angeles, April 17, 1944, entry 48, box 224/43.120, WRA-NARA.

48. H. A. Van Norman to Honorable Board of Water and Power Commissioners, April 24, 1944, Water Executive Office, Administrative-Executive Files, Manzanar Relocation Center, Correspondence, January 1944–September 1944, WP14-1:4, LADWP Records.

49. Ibid.; "Manzanar Hog Ranch Hit as Menace to City's Water," Los Angeles Times, May 4, 1944, A1.

50. Ralph P. Merritt, statement, n.d., entry 48, box 224/43.120, WRA-NARA; "Manzanar Hog Ranch Protest Hit as Politics," Los Angeles Times, May 5, 1944, A16.

51. Ralph P. Merritt to Gerald E. Kerrin, May 5, 1944, and Ralph P. Merritt to C. G. Gillespie, September 22, 1944, entry 48, box 224/43.120, WRA-NARA.

52. Floyd M. Hinshaw to W. W. Hurlbut, May 5, 1944, Water Executive Office, Administrative-Executive Files, Manzanar Relocation Center, Correspondence, January 1944–September 1944, WP14-1:4, LADWP Records; "City Asks Inquiry of Hog Ranch Plan," Los Angeles Times, May 6, 1944, 7; "Japs Pollute Water, Charge," Los Angeles Examiner, May 6, 1944.

53. Charles L. Senn to George M. Uhl, May 18, 1944, Water Executive Office, Administrative-Executive Files, Manzanar Relocation Center, Correspondence, January 1944–September 1944, WP14-1:4, LADWP Records.

54. Ibid.

55. Ibid.

56. H. A. Van Norman to the Honorable Board of Water and Power Commissioners, May 31, 1944, Water Executive Office, Administrative-Executive Files, Manzanar Relocation Center, Correspondence, January 1944–September 1944, WP14-1:4, LADWP Records.

57. Ralph P. Merritt to C. G. Gillespie, September 22, 1944, entry 48, box 224/43.500, WRA-NARA.

58. Horace R. McConnell and Henry A. Hill, "Agriculture Section," January 1946, 10, FBD-WRA, roll 78.

59. Mark R. Finlay, Growing American Rubber: Strategic Plants and the Politics of National Security (New Brunswick, N.J.: Rutgers University Press, 2009), 141.

60. Mark R. Finlay, "Behind the Barbed Wire of Manzanar: Guayule and the Search for Natural Rubber," Chemical Heritage 29, no. 3 (Fall 2011/Winter 2012), http://www.chemheritage.org/discover/media/magazine/articles/29-3-behind-the-barbed-wired-of-manzanar.aspx?page=1 (accessed April 1, 2012); Finlay, Growing American Rubber, 152–53.

61. Grace Nichols, "Guayule Research Project," August 1, 1942, Japanese American Evacuation and Resettlement Study, Bancroft Library, University of California, Berkeley, reel 157 (hereafter JERS).

62. Ibid. The WRA provided limited financial support to the guayule project.

63. Robert Emerson to Ralph Merritt, December 10, 1943, box 14, folder 6, Manzanar Records-UCLA; Finlay, *Growing American Rubber*, 153.

64. Nichols, "Guayule Research Project," JERS; Finlay, "Behind the Barbed Wire of Manzanar"; Finlay, *Growing American Rubber*, 153.

65. Neil D. Naiden, "Two Jap Nurserymen Experiment to Solve Rubber Shortage by Guayule Production," *Washington Post*, September 6, 1942, F6.

66. "Manzanar Will Contribute to Rubber Production as Guayule Cuttings Arrive," *Manzanar Free Press*, April 15, 1942, 4.

67. "Big Guayule Project Explained," *Manzanar Free Press*, August 10, 1942, 1, 3.

68. For WRA control of relocation-center newspapers, see Lauren Kessler, "Fettered Freedoms: The Journalism of World War II Japanese Internment Camps," *Journalism History* 15, nos. 2–3 (1988): 70–79; and Takeya Mizuno, "The Creation of the 'Free' Press in Japanese-American Camps: The War Relocation Authority's Planning and Making of the Camp Newspaper Policy," *Journalism and Mass Communication Quarterly* 78, no. 3 (2001): 503–18.

69. "Report on Guayule Project at the Manzanar Relocation Area, for Submission to the U.S. Forest Service and Bureau of Plant Industry, February, 1943," JERS. This research was later published in a scientific journal; see M. S. Nishimura, Robert Emerson, T. Hata, and Akira Kageyama, "The Propagation of Guayule from Cuttings," *American Journal of Botany* 31, no. 7 (July 1944): 412–18.

70. Finlay, *Growing American Rubber*, 199–200.

71. Ibid., 156.

72. Ibid., 200–201.

73. Ralph P. Merritt to Dillon S. Myer, August 29, 1943, box 14, folder 6, Manzanar Records-UCLA.

74. Ibid.

75. Ibid.

76. Ralph Merritt, untitled essay, n.d., box 14, folder 8, Manzanar Records-UCLA.

77. Alice Yang Murray, *Historical Memories of the Japanese American Internment and the Struggle for Redress* (Stanford, Calif.: Stanford University Press, 2008), 69–71.

78. Merritt was a friend of the photographer Ansel Adams, whom he invited to photograph Manzanar in 1943. Adams's impression of the Japanese Americans was similar to Merritt's. He noted how they had overcome their environment, making crops grow and gardens bloom while establishing "a democratic internal society." He wanted his photographs to convey that "the broad concepts of American citizenship . . . must be protected in the prosecution of war," implying that Manzanar had achieved that goal. See Ansel Adams, *Born Free and Equal: The Story of Loyal Japanese Americans* (Bishop, Calif.: Spotted Dog Press, 2001), 13.

79. Indeed, Brewer, *Why America Fights*, 110, suggests that government depictions of African Americans and Japanese Americans during World War II "emphasized loyalty, not freedom and equality."

Chapter 12. Unthinkable Visibility

1. Brett Mizelle, *Pig* (London: Reaktion Books, 2011).

2. Florida banned gestation crates in 2002, and California banned them in 2008 after the passage of Proposition 2, the Prevention of Farm Animal Cruelty Act. In 2009 Smithfield changed its stance, saying that because of financial hardships in the industry they would not be able to

phase them out within ten years, but then reversed the decision in 2011. See Philip Walzer, "Smithfield to End Gestation Crates by 2017," *Virginian-Pilot*, December 9, 2011, http://www.hampton roads.com/2011/12/smithfield-end-use-gestation-crates-2017 (accessed July 14, 2014). As of this writing, nine states have banned gestation crates, with a tenth (New Jersey) awaiting Governor Chris Christie's signature.

3. For a study of how industrialized agriculture has produced a desire for romanticized depictions of farming that have in turn been used to promote commerce, see Anna Thompson Hadjik, "Agricultural Romance: Constructing and Consuming Rural Life in Modern America" (Ph.D. diss., University of Texas, 2011).

4. Sidney W. Mintz and Christine M. Du Bois, "The Anthropology of Food and Eating," *Annual Review of Anthropology* 31 (October 2002): 99–119, quote from 102.

5. Lyall Watson, *The Whole Hog: Exploring the Extraordinary Potential of Pigs* (Washington, D.C.: Smithsonian Books, 2004), 92.

6. See, for example, Sam White, "From Globalized Pig Breeds to Capitalist Pigs: A Study in Animal Cultures and Evolutionary History," *Environmental History* 16, no. 1 (2011): 94–120.

7. Nathanael Johnson, "Swine of the Times: The Making of the Modern Pig," *Harper's* 312, no. 1872 (May 2006): 55. This domination is never total, of course. An industry analyst at the Pork Industry Forum told me that they have not been able to overcome seasonal fluctuations in breeding, for example. The problems posed by wild-living pigs (including feral domestic pigs, wild boars, and mixes of the two) are a reminder that pigs are not as much under our control as we might like. See Mizelle, *Pig*, 172–81.

8. For a compelling argument about our obligations to the domesticated animals we have created for our use, see Julie A. Smith, "Beyond Dominance and Affection: Living with Rabbits in Post-Domestic Households," *Society and Animals* 11, no. 2 (2003): 181–97.

9. For a pioneering exploration of our modern alienation from animals, one produced by industrial capitalism, see John Berger, "Why Look at Animals?," in John Berger, *About Looking* (New York: Vintage, 1980), 3–28. Berger claims that this loss is "irredeemable," although Nigel Rothfels, "Touching Animals: The Search for a Deeper Connection to Animals," in *Beastly Natures: Animals, Humans, and the Study of History,* ed. Dorothee Brantz (Charlottesville: University of Virginia Press, 2010), 48–49, has noted that "the quest for a connection to or communion with animals (or the restoration of that connection or communion, as some would see it) may be a distinguishing feature of the postmodern human relationship to animals."

10. Susan Hopmans, *The Great Murals of Farmer John Brand, Clougherty Meat Packing Co. in Vernon, California*, photographs by Peter Kenner (New York: Colorcraft Lithographers, 1971).

11. Sue Coe, *Dead Meat* (New York and London: Four Walls Eight Windows, 1996), 87–88.

12. The McRib was created by Rene Arend, the father of the Chicken McNugget, in 1981 because of a shortage of chicken nuggets for franchises. McDonald's "exploits the value differential between pork's cash price on the commodities market and in the Quick-Service restaurant market" in reintroducing the McRib. See Willy Staley, "A Conspiracy of Hogs: The McRib as Arbitrage," *Awl*, November 8, 2011, http://www.theawl.com/2011/11/a-conspiracy-of-hogs-the-mcrib -as-arbitrage.

13. "National Daily Hog and Pork Summary," March 1, 2013, http://www.ams.usda.gov/mn reports/lsddhps.pdf. The National Agricultural Statistics Service publishes a "Quarterly Hogs and Pigs" report; see http://www.usda.mannlib.cornell.edu/MannUsda/viewDocumentInfo .do?documentID=1086. As of the end of 2013, there were 65.9 million hogs and pigs in the United

States: a breeding inventory of 5.76 million pigs and a market inventory of 60.2 million. The average "pigs saved per litter" was a record 10.16.

14. National Pig Day was founded by sisters Mary Lynne Rave and Ellen Stanley, and their intent is described in Sarah Casey Newman, "Pig Day Hogs the Spotlight," *St. Louis Post Dispatch*, February 26, 2000, 43.

15. Anat Pick, *Creaturely Poetics: Animality and Vulnerability in Literature and Film* (New York: Columbia University Press, 2011), 1.

16. Timothy Pachirat, *Every Twelve Seconds: Industrialized Slaughter and the Politics of Sight* (New Haven, Conn.: Yale University Press, 2011), 3.

17. Charles Dickens, *American Notes for General Circulation* (New York: Harper and Brothers, 1842), 34–35.

18. John A. Duffy, *The History of Public Health in New York City, 1625–1866* (New York: Russell Sage Foundation, 1968), 11, 29–30.

19. Paul A. Gilje, *The Road to Mobocracy: Popular Disorder in New York City, 1763–1834* (Chapel Hill and London: University of North Carolina Press, 1987), 224–32; Hendrik Hartog, "Pigs and Positivism," *Wisconsin Law Review* 759, no. 4 (July-August 1985): 899–935.

20. Duffy, *History of Public Health*, 383–86. Small pigsties with no more than three pigs each were still allowed in the city, however. See also Catherine McNeur, "The 'Swinish Multitude': Controversies over Hogs in Antebellum New York City," *Journal of Urban History* 37, no. 5 (September 2011): 639–60.

21. See http://www.pikeplacemarketfoundation.org/faqs/ (accessed October 17, 2014); and Karen Sandstrom, "Going Whole Hog for Public Art: Painted Pigs Invade Cleveland," http://blog .cleveland.com/entertainment/2007/06/go_whole_hog_for_public_art_pa.html (accessed October 17, 2014).

22. An estimated 110,600,000 hogs and pigs will be commercially slaughtered in 2015; see Ron Plain, "September Quarterly Hogs & Pigs Report Summary," September 29, 2014, University of Missouri Agricultural Electronic Bulletin Board, http://agebb.missouri.edu/mkt/bull8c .htm (accessed October 17, 2014).

23. *Poulson's American Daily Advertiser*, December 20, 1820, [3].

24. *Philadelphia Gazette*, March 5, [3]; *Philadelphia Gazette*, March 12, 1821, [1].

25. See, for example, Margaret E. Derry, *Bred for Perfection: Shorthorn Cattle, Collies, and Arabian Horses Since 1800* (Baltimore: Johns Hopkins University Press, 2003); and Catherine E. Kelly, "'The Consummation of Rural Prosperity and Happiness': New England Agricultural Fairs and the Construction of Class and Gender, 1810–1860," *American Quarterly* 49, no. 3 (September 1997): 574–602.

26. *Poulson's American Daily Advertiser*, March 13, 1821, [3]. John Lewis Krimmel's April 1821 watercolor of the parade, currently owned by a private collector, was drawn on stone to produce a lithograph engraved by J. Yeager and printed by Charles Woodward Jr. in 1821. A copy of this lithograph is in the collections of the American Antiquarian Society, Worcester, Massachusetts. Louis Haugg redrew the Krimmel image on stone for a c. 1861 lithograph that is in the collections of the Library Company of Philadelphia. For the history of the publication of this image, see Milo M. Naeve, *John Lewis Krimmel: An Artist in Federal America* (Newark: University of Delaware Press, 1987), 104, 114–18.

27. Alexander Nemerov, *The Body of Raphaelle Peale: Still Life and Selfhood, 1812–1824* (Berkeley and London: University of California Press, 2001), 94. Nemerov provides one of the

few discussions of the parade of victuallers, using it to understand Peale's still-life paintings of meat.

28. *The Experienced Butcher: Shewing the Respectability and Usefulness of His Calling, the Religious Considerations Arising from It, the Laws Relating to It, and Various Profitable Suggestions for the Rightly Carrying It On: Designed Not Only for the Use of Butchers, but Also for Families and Readers in General* (London: Darton, Harvey, and Darton, 1816).

29. Robert Culff, *World of Toys* (Feltham: Hamlyn, 1969), 62. See also Lisa Hix, "Baby's First Butcher Shop, ca. 1900," *Collector's Weekly*, August 2, 2012, http://www.collectorsweekly.com/articles/babys-first-butcher-shop-circa-1900/.

30. See the essays in Paula Young Lee, ed., *Meat, Modernity, and the Rise of the Slaughterhouse* (Durham: University of New Hampshire Press, 2008).

31. See, for example, Margaret Walsh, *The Rise of the Midwestern Meat Packing Industry* (Lexington: University Press of Kentucky, 1982).

32. Frederick Law Olmsted, *A Journey Through Texas; or, A Saddle-Trip on the Southwestern Frontier: With a Statistical Appendix* (New York: Dix, Edwards, and Co., 1857), 9.

33. See William Cronon, *Nature's Metropolis: Chicago and the Great West* (New York: W. W. Norton, 1992).

34. Frances Trollope, *Domestic Manners of the Americans* (London: Printed for Whittaker, Treacher, & Co., 1832), 85.

35. Swift & Company, *Visitors' Reference Book* (1903), Duke University Libraries Digital Collections eaa_A0340.pdf, http://www.library.duke.edu/digitalcollections/eaa_A0340/. I am indebted to Nicole Shukin for calling this to my attention. See her important book *Animal Capital: Rendering Life in Biopolitical Times* (Minneapolis: University of Minnesota Press, 2009).

36. See, for example, Charlie LeDuff, "At a Slaughterhouse, Some Things Never Die: Who Kills, Who Cuts, Who Bosses Can Depend on Race," *New York Times*, June 16, 2000, A1; Pachirat, *Every Twelve Seconds*; and Steve Striffler, "Inside a Poultry Processing Plant: An Ethnographic Portrait," *Labor History* 43, no. 3 (2002): 305–13.

37. According to the *Oxford English Dictionary*, the term "factory farm" was first used in 1890 in a positive context when an economist urged experimenting with them. Critical use of the term "factory farming" seems to have emerged in 1964 in the United Kingdom, tied to efforts to amend the 1911 Protection of Animals Act to cover these newly intensified postwar techniques.

38. A 2007 study found that 95 percent of people surveyed said it was important to them how farm animals were treated and 76 percent said that animal welfare was more important than low meat prices. However, only 52 percent and 24 percent of respondents to those questions, respectively, thought that the average American shared this concern, indicating that people respond to these questions in a way that creates a favorable perception of themselves and thus "overstate their true concern for farm animal welfare." See Jayson L. Lusk, F. Bailey Norwood, and Robert W. Prickett, "Consumer Preferences for Farm Animal Welfare: Results of a Nationwide Telephone Survey," working paper, Department of Agricultural Economics, Oklahoma State University, August 17, 2007, http://www.asp.okstate.edu/baileynorwood/Survey4/files/InitialReporttoAFB.pdf (accessed July 14, 2014).

39. Johnson, "Swine of the Times," 56, quoting Paul Willis, a Niman Ranch farmer. Niman Ranch pork is available at http://www.nimanranch.com/pork.aspx. Jude Becker raises heirloom breeds organically outdoors in Dyersville, Iowa, and sells his pork in San Francisco and Chicago; see http://www.beckerlaneorganic.com.

40. Peter Kaminsky, *Pig Perfect: Encounters with Remarkable Swine and Some Great Ways to Cook Them* (New York: Hyperion, 2005).

41. Katie Zezima, "Push to Eat Local Food Is Hampered by a Shortage: Small Farms Are Increasing, but Slaughterhouses Are Not," *New York Times*, March 26, 2010, 16. See also John Eligon, "An Iowa Farmer's Quest for No Ordinary Pig," *New York Times*, February 28, 2013, A11.

42. R. W. Apple, Jr., "A Prince of Pork: In Seattle, Recreating the Perfect Ham," *New York Times*, March 26, 2010, F1.

43. Sarah Karnasiewicz, "Going Whole Hog," Salon, May 1, 2007, http://www.salon.com/2007/05/01/pork_review/ (accessed July 14, 2014); Jon Mooallem, "Carnivores, Capitalists, and the Meat We Read," *Believer* 3.8 (October 2005), http://www.believermag.com/issues/200510/?read=article_mooallem (accessed July 14, 2014).

44. Sarah Hepola, "Bacon Mania," Salon, July 7, 2008, http://www.salon.com/2008/07/07/bacon_mania/ (accessed July 14, 2014). See also Arun Gupta, "How the Food Industry Has Made Bacon a Weapon of Mass Destruction," Alternet, July 22, 2009, http://www.alternet.org/story/141498/gonzo_gastronomy%3A_how_the_food_industry_has_made_bacon_a_weapon_of_mass_destruction.

45. John S. Wilson, "Health Department," *Godey's Lady's Book* 60 (February 1860): 178. Meat consumption in the United States has declined in recent years. Annual average consumption of red meats and poultry fell from over 221 pounds per capita in 2007 to 198 pounds per capita in 2013. High feed prices, the recession, and drought are largely responsible. As a result, the U.S. meat industry is increasingly dependent on exports. See "USDA Agricultural Projections to 2021," February 2012, http://www.usda.gov/oce/commodity/archive_projections/USDAAgriculturalProjections2021.pdf. Americans still consume an average of 57 pounds of meat more than they did in the 1950s, with the majority of this growth taking place in the consumption of poultry.

46. See Rebecca Onion, "An Eccentric Millionaire's 1875 Pork Map of the United States," *Slate*, January 31, 2014, http://www.slate.com/blogs/the_vault/2014/01/31/pork_map_william_emerson_baker_s_porcinegraph_of_the_united_states.html (accessed October 17, 2014).

47. *The Daily Show*, February 25, 2009, Comedy Central.

48. The celebration of bacon and meat is also related to gender politics through the sexual politics of meat that links patriarchy and sexism with meat eating. See the generative work of Carol J. Adams, *The Sexual Politics of Meat: A Feminist-Vegetarian Critical Theory*, rev. ed. (New York: Bloomsbury, 2010).

49. Mark Bittman, "Banned from the Barn," *New York Times*, July 6, 2011, http://www.opinionator.blogs.nytimes.com/2011/07/05/banned-from-the-barn/. See also Cody Carlson, "How State Ag-Gag Laws Could Stop Animal-Cruelty Whistleblowers," *Atlantic*, March 25, 2013, http://www.theatlantic.com/politics/archive/2013/03/how-state-ag-gag-laws-could-stop-animal-cruelty-whistleblowers/273962/.

50. Pachirat, *Every Twelve Seconds*, 242. He goes on to note that "it is a risky strategy and one that always yields imperfect results" (253), in part because making the repugnant visible can equally produce apathy and inaction while requiring greater and greater "shocks" to gain the public's attention.

51. See, for example, Hal Herzog, *Some We Love, Some We Hate, Some We Eat: Why It's So Hard to Think Straight About Animals* (New York: Harper Perennial, 2011). As Julie Livingston and Jasbir K. Puar have written in "Introduction: Interspecies," *Social Text* 29, no. 1 (Spring 2011): 3, "Seeking to dismantle the binaries of self and other and their attendant violences, the most

compelling work in the field [of animal studies] challenges the instrumentalization of animals that is driven solely by effort to deepen the singularity of humanness or to enhance the capacities of human exceptionalism."

Chapter 13. "Bring Tent"

For help in sorting out the meanings of tents past and present, I would like to thank several people. I am in great debt to Peggy Shaffer for insisting that I attempt to write about Occupy, overcoming the historian's fears of trying to make sense of something not quite yet history, for pushing my analysis in productive directions, and for reading several drafts; Noah D. Finkelstein, Sarah Krakoff, and all the participants of the Third Nature symposium at Miami University and the University of Colorado Law School and Duke University Law School Climate Change Law and Policy Works-in-Progress symposium for fascinating and helpful discussions as I worked through the analysis; Vanessa Baird and Danika Medak-Saltzman for critical contributions; Michael Weeks for timely and skilled research assistance; and Elissa Guaralnick for her expert advice on writing and revision.

1. Laura Breeston, "The Ballerina and the Bull: Adbusters Micah White on 'The Last Great Social Movement,'" *Link,* October 11, 2011, http://www.thelinknewspaper.ca/article/1951 (accessed December 5, 2011); "Reasons to Love New York 2011: 2. Because It Started Here," *New York,* December 11, 2011, http://www.nymag.com/news/articles/reasonstoloveny/2011/occupy-wall-street/ (accessed January 24, 2012). For the purposes of this essay, "OWS" or "Occupy" references the broader protest movement, whether it took place on Wall Street or in other cities; references to specific organizations, such as Occupy Boulder or Occupy D.C. will be indicated in the text.

2. The movement did call some attention to sustainability, but there was less explicit focus on environmental issues than one might expect.

3. Marguerite S. Shaffer, *See America First: Tourism and National Identity, 1880–1940* (Washington, D.C.: Smithsonian Institution Press, 2001).

4. "#OCCUPYWALLSTREET: Yes We Camp," *Adbusters,* August 16, 2011, http://www.adbusters .org/content/occupywallstreet-yes-we-camp (accessed November 14, 2011) (Permission @ http:// www.adbusters.org/about/reprints).

5. Daryl Lang, "The Poster Art of Occupy Wall Street," *Breaking Copy* (November 20, 2011), http://www.breakingcopy.com/the-poster-art-of-occupy-wall-street (accessed January 19, 2012).

6. Paul Courson, "Federal Authorities Set to Crack Down on Camping at 'Occupy DC' Sites," *Cable News Network,* January 27, 2012, http://www.cnn.com/2012/01/27/us/camping-crackdown /index.html?iref=allsearch (accessed June 5, 2012).

7. Tavia Nyong'o, "The Scene of Occupation," *TDR: The Drama Review* 56, no. 4 (Winter 2012): 137–38; Hal Rothman, "Gates, Barriers, and the Rise of Affinity: Parsing Public-Private Space in Postindustrial America," in *Public Culture: Diversity, Democracy, and Community in the United States,* ed. Marguerite S. Shaffer (Philadelphia: University of Pennsylvania Press, 2008), 222. Well before Occupy appeared on the scene, Rothman argued that "[t]he battles over private and public space in American society [had] become the terrain on which the national definition is worked and reworked." Nyong'o noted that Zuccotti Park was privately owned space in which developers agreed to allow public access in exchange for the ability to "build higher than zoning laws permit (colonizing shared sky as well as land)." While she highlighted OWS's "decision to take a stand there—in a sliver of 'public' land carved out from rapaciously expanding privatized space," the potent and paradoxical meanings of "privatized public space" were key.

8. "#OCCUPYWALLSTREET: A Shift in Revolutionary Tactics" (blog), *Adbusters*, July 13, 2011, http://www.adbusters.org/blogs/adbusters-blog/occupywallstreet.html (accessed January 14, 2012).

9. Nathan Schneider, "Occupy Wall Street: FAQ," *Nation*, September 29, 2011, http://www.thenation.com/article/163719/occupy-wall-street-faq (accessed January 24, 2013).

10. Rebecca Schneider, "It Seems as If . . . I Am Dead: Zombie Capitalism and Theatrical Labor," *TDR: The Drama Review* 56, no. 4 (Winter 2012): 153; Judith Butler, "So What Are the Demands?," *Tidal: Occupy Theory, Occupy Strategy* 2 (March 2012): 9, http://www.occupytheory.org (accessed March 30, 2013). Butler goes on to identify how the attempts "to dismiss the Occupy movement as 'apolitical'" represented an attempt "to maintain a monopoly on the discourse of the political," properly construed, and to discredit OWS as "'beyond the pale,' 'misguided,' and 'impractical.'"

11. Anti-Apartheid shantytowns were most prevalent on elite college campuses in 1985–87, but occasionally such protests were held outside of corporate headquarters and banks, most notably Citicorp, the only U.S. bank to maintain a physical presence in South Africa at the time. The first "sit-out" occurred at Columbia University, and shortly thereafter Princeton hosted a "camp out," Harvard held a "sleep in," and students at Cornell, the University of Vermont, and Dartmouth built the first shantytowns, which were contentious, drawing both vandalism by other students and heightened national media—which spurred other campuses to try the same tactic. See Sarah A. Soule, "The Student Divestment Movement in the United States and Tactical Diffusion: The Shantytown Protest," *Social Forces* 75, no. 3 (March 1997): 855–82; and Tony Vellela, *New Voices: Student Activism in the '80s and '90s* (Boston: South End Press, 1988), 33–34.

12. The National Mall and other National Park Service grounds hosted other camping protests in the era, from Vietnam Veterans Against the War, who pitched camp on Lexington's Battle Green in 1971, to the 1979 Farmer's Vigil, which drew hundreds of rural Americans to Washington with trucks, tractors, and tents to call attention to troubled family farmers. The NPS largely tolerated the protests. See Lucy G. Barber, *Marching on Washington: The Forging of an American Political Tradition* (Berkeley: University of California Press, 2002); and Jill Lepore, *Whites of Their Eyes: The Tea Party's Revolution and the Battle over American History* (Princeton, N.J.: Princeton University Press, 2010), 67. In his testimony to Congress, Jonathan Jarvis, NPS director, mentioned both the Farmer's Vigil and Resurrection City as precedents (Jonathan B. Jarvis, "Statement of Jonathan B. Jarvis, Director, National Park Service, Department of the Interior, before the Subcommittee on Health Care, District of Columbia, Census, and the National Archives of the House Committee on Oversight and Government Reform, concerning issues surrounding the National Park Service's (NPS) handling of demonstrations at McPherson Square," January 24, 2012).

13. Todd DePastino, *Citizen Hobo: How a Century of Homelessness Shaped America* (Chicago and London: University of Chicago Press, 2002), 195–200. For additional discussion of the Bonus Army, see also Barber, *Marching on Washington*; Roger Daniels, *The Bonus March: An Episode of the Great Depression* (Westport, Conn.: Greenwood Press, 1971); and Paul Dickson and Thomas B. Allen, *The Bonus Army: An American Epic* (New York: Walker and Co., 2004).

14. "Hoover Orders Eviction," *New York Times*, July 29, 1932, 1; Phoebe S. K. Young, "Sleeping Outside: The Political Natures of Urban Camping," in *Cities and Nature in the American West*, ed. Char Miller (Reno: University of Nevada Press, 2010), 171–91.

15. Joe Richman and Samara Freemark, "The Bonus Army: How a Protest Led to the GI Bill," *Radio Diaries*, National Public Radio, November 11, 2011, http://www.npr.org/2011/11/11/142224795

/the-bonus-army-how-a-protest-led-to-the-gi-bill (accessed July 10, 2012); *The Rachel Maddow Show,* October 26, 27, 2011, NBC News, http://www.nbcnews.com/id/45065858/ns/msnbc-rachel _maddow_show/ (accessed July 10, 2012); Michael Lind, "Protests That Worked," *New York Times,* November 16, 2011, http://www.nytimes.com/roomfordebate/2011/11/16/does-congress-hear -occupy-wall-street/protests-that-worked (accessed January 24, 2012); Michael Hiltzik, "Occupy Wall Street Shifts from Protest to Policy Phase," *Los Angeles Times,* October 12, 2011, http://www .articles.latimes.com/2011/oct/12/business/la-fi-hiltzik-20111012 (accessed July 10, 2012). It is interesting that the interest in thinking with historic parallels clustered in October and November 2011, when the Occupy movement was beginning to gain momentum but with an as-yet-unclear outcome.

16. Barber, *Marching on Washington,* chap. 1; Carlos Schwantes, *Coxey's Army: An American Odyssey* (Lincoln: University of Nebraska Press, 1985); Martin Hutchinson, "Rebels Needing a Cause," *Reuters/Breaking Views,* October 12, 2011, http://www.breakingviews.com/occupy -wall-street-may-share-fate-of-coxeys-army/1610689.article (accessed July 10, 2012).

17. Stuart McConnell, *Glorious Contentment: The Grand Army of the Republic, 1865–1900* (Chapel Hill: University of North Carolina Press, 1992), 15, 24, 36–37.

18. John Emerson, "Take Back Wall Street," *Social Design Notes* (blog), October 7, 2011, http:// www.backspace.com/notes/2011/10/occupy-wall-street-posters.php (accessed January 20, 2012).

19. Charles R. Geisst, *Wall Street: A History, from Its Beginnings to the Fall of Enron* (New York: Oxford University Press, 1997).

20. Toronto resident and Occupy participant Ryan Hayes employed a different formula for a similar message: "(UN)OCCUPY CANADA: RESPECT INDIGENOUS SOVEREIGNTY." The artist was not advocating the end of Occupy but calling for recognition that "Canada is already 'occupied' land and that indigenous sovereignty has to be a foundational component of our work. Occupy sites can be an important, if challenging, place [*sic*] to have these discussions." Hayes put the abstract Occupy metaphor in service to a specific claim about indigenous sovereignty, rather than having images of indigenous people serve the broader cause of Occupy. See Ryan Hayes, "(Un)Occupy Canada," *Art & Social Movements* (blog), November 15, 2011, http://www.blog.ryanhay.es /unoccupy-canada/ (accessed January 20, 2012).

21. Emerson, "Take Back Wall Street"; Karen R. Humes, Nicholas A. Jones, and Roberty R. Ramirez, *Overview of Race and Hispanic Origin: 2010* (ser. 2010 Census Briefs), United States Census Bureau, March 2011, C2010BR-02.

22. In 2004 Lasn published a watch list purporting to detail the disproportionate preponderance of neoconservative, hawkish Jews in key State Department and other government positions and their influence on America's wars in the Middle East. He indicated which persons were Jewish by placing black dots next to their names on the published list. In a radio interview in 2011, when questioned about whether this position of "identifying who are Jews among prominent neo-conservatives" was out of bounds, Lasn replied, "some people think I'm way in bounds as well," and he expressed hope that the Occupy movement would not just oppose wealth inequality but also unify its message with broader critiques of military and foreign policy. Scattered evidence of anti-Semitic incidents appeared in various news outlets, although largely in conservative commentary seeking to discredit the Occupy movement. See Kalle Lasn, "Why Won't Anyone Say They Are Jewish?," *Adbusters* 52 (March/April 2004), http://www.adbusters.org/maga zine/52/articles/jewish.html (accessed July 8, 2012); Kalle Lasn, interview by Robert Siegel, "Adbusters Co-Founder Discusses OWS," *All Things Considered,* National Public Radio, December 6, 2011, http://www.npr.org/2011/12/06/143224364/adbusters-co-founder-discusses-ows (accessed

January 29, 2012); Joseph Berger, "Cries of Anti-Semitism but Not at Zuccotti Park," *New York Times*, October 21, 2011, http://www.nytimes.com/2011/10/22/nyregion/occupy-wall-street-criti cized-for-flashes-of-anti-semitism.html (accessed July 8, 2012).

23. Jonathan Neumann, "Occupy Wall Street and the Jews," *Commentary* (January, 1 2012), http://www.commentarymagazine.com/article/occupy-wall-street-and-the-jews/ (accessed July 8, 2012).

24. Marc Falardreau, "I Am Not Moving!!," Flickr.com, November 21, 2011, Toronto, http://www.flickr.com/photos/49889874@N05/6379327263/ (accessed January 19, 2012).

25. Schneider, "It Seems As If . . . I Am Dead," 153. See more on "precarity" below.

26. Tamara Audi, "Protesters, Homeless Share Turf—and Tension," *Wall Street Journal* (online), November 1, 2011, http://www.proquest.com/ (accessed January 30, 2012). For discussion of different cities' approaches to and connection of homeless issues and Occupy campers, see Tyler Kingkade, Hayley Miller, and Saki Knafo, "Occupy Wall Street and Homelessness," *Huffington Post*, November 27, 2011, http://www.huffingtonpost.com/2011/11/27/occupy-wall-street-and -homeless-evictions-cities_n_1111094.html (accessed March 30, 2013).

27. "5-6-10 Camping or Lodging on Property Without Consent," City of Boulder Revised Code, 1981, http://www.colocode.com/boulder2/chapter5-6.htm (accessed June 23, 2014); Jeremy P. Meyer, "Effect of Camping Bans Debated as Denver Considers Ordinance," *Denver Post*, April 22, 2012, http://www.denverpost.com/politics/ci_20452293/effect-camping-bans-colorado -debated-denver-ordinance (accessed December 14, 2012).

28. Nicholas M. May, "Fourth Amendment Challenges to 'Camping' Ordinances: The Government Acquiescence Doctrine as a Legal Strategy to Force Legislative Solutions to Homelessness," *Connecticut Public Interest Law Journal* 1 (Fall–Winter 2008): 113–35; Rob Tier, "Restoring Order in Public Spaces," *Texas Review of Law and Politics* 2, no. 2 (Spring 1998): 255–91; Harry Simon, "Towns Without Pity: A Constitutional and Historical Analysis of Official Efforts to Drive Homeless Persons from American Cities," *Tulane Law Review* 66, no. 631 (March 1992).

29. Heath Urie, "Boulder Council Strengthens No-Camping Law, Despite Push from Homeless Advocates," *Boulder Daily Camera*, April 20, 2010, http://www.dailycamera.com/ci_14925384 (accessed July 8, 2012); "City of Boulder v. Madison—Due Process," *American Civil Liberties Union of Colorado*, http://www.aclu-co.org/case/city-boulder-v-madison (accessed July 8, 2012).

30. Erica Meltzer, "Occupy Boulder Campers Plead Not Guilty, Ask for Jury Trial on Tickets," *Boulder Daily Camera*, December 6, 2011, http://www.dailycamera.com/boulder-county -news/ci_19480886 (accessed December 6, 2011); David Harris-Gershon, "From Igloos to Tents—PHOTO DIARY of the #OWS Encampments Still Standing Strong in North America," *Daily Kos*, December 20, 2011, http://www.dailykos.com/story/2011/12/20/1047386/-From-Igloos-to -Tents-PHOTO-DIARY-of-the-OWS-Encampments-Still-Standing-Strong-in-North-America (accessed January 23, 2012).

31. Gregory J. Hobbs, Jr., for the Supreme Court of Colorado, En Banc, The PEOPLE of the State of Colorado, Plaintiff-Appellant, v. Scott E. SCHAFER, Defendant-Appellee, no. 97SA142 (September 15, 1997).

32. Erica Meltzer, "Occupy Boulder: Police Violated Constitution by Opening Campers' Tent Flaps," *Boulder Daily Camera*, January 23, 2012, http://www.dailycamera.com/letters/ci_19801019 (accessed January 23, 2012); Heath Urie and Mitchell Byars, "Occupy Boulder Preparing for Possible Eviction Tonight," *Boulder Daily Camera*, January 6, 2012, http://www.dailycamera.com /boulder-county-news/ci_19688002 (accessed January 6, 2012); Meyer, "Effect of Camping Bans Debated."

33. "Hearing of the Health Care, District of Columbia, Census and the National Archives Subcommittee of the House Oversight and Government Reform Committee, Subject: 'McPherson Square: Who Made the Decision to Allow Indefinite Camping in the Park,' Focusing on the Impact of the Ongoing 'Occupy' Encampment on Public Health and Public Safety Inside and Outside the Park," January 24, 2012 Federal News Service, January 24, 2012. The encampment at McPherson Square began on October 1, 2011. Both Gowdy and Issa at different points insinuated that Jarvis was being instructed to ignore the law for political reasons, accusing the executive administration of giving Occupy unfairly favorable treatment, a conspiracy theory for which there was no evidence and which Jarvis adamantly denied. See Meredith Somers, "Issa Seeks Political Answers on Occupiers; Federal Decisions About Law at Issue," *Washington Times*, December 14, 2011, http://www.washington-times.vlex.com/vid/issa-seeks-answers-occupiers-decisions-338 643638 (accessed June 11, 2011).

34. Jarvis, Statement of Jonathan B. Jarvis. Jarvis suggested that the discretion and measured response the NPS employed in handling Occupy encampments within its jurisdiction had avoided some of the more volatile confrontations seen in other cities such as New York and Oakland. Rather the NPS aimed to bring any noncompliant features of the protest into compliance through communication with protesters and voluntary agreements rather than evictions or other heavy-handed tactics.

35. "Hearing of the Health Care, District of Columbia."

36. Ibid.

37. Ibid.

38. Ibid.

39. Young, "Sleeping Outside."

40. "Hearing of the Health Care, District of Columbia."

41. Martin Austermuhle, "Even Occupiers in D.C. Get Eviction Notices," *DCist.com*, December 6, 2011, http://www.dcist.com/2011/12/even_occupiers_get_eviction_notices.php (accessed June 8, 2012).

42. "Statement of Occupy D.C.," quoted in the testimony of Rep. Danny Davis (D-Ill.) in "Hearing of the Health Care, District of Columbia." No representative from Occupy was allowed to testify in person, but Representative Davis read the group's statement into the record.

43. Liz Farmer, "Turf War in McPherson Square," *Washington Examiner*, October 21, 2011, http://www.washingtonexaminer.com/article/119538 (accessed June 8, 2012); Meredith Somers, "For D.C. Occupy Camps, It's Divided They Stand," *Washington Times*, January 20, 2012, http://www.proquest.com (accessed June 8, 2012). At one point the NPS tried to negotiate a merger and move over to a single site at Freedom Plaza to simplify their protection efforts, but the protesters declined.

44. Dakota Smith, "Occupy L.A. Protest at City Hall Is Not Lawn-Abiding," *Los Angeles Daily News*, October 14, 2011, http://www.dailynews.com/politics/ci_19110153 (accessed June 10, 2012); Leo Stallworth, "Officials Want Occupy LA Protesters Off Lawn," KABC-7, Los Angeles, October 25, 2011, http://www.abclocal.go.com/kabc/story?section=news/local/los_angeles&id=8405818 (accessed June 10, 2012), emphasis added.

45. "City Hall Moves To Ban Tents, Overnight Camping After Occupy LA Damage," CBS-2, May 30, 2012, http://www.losangeles.cbslocal.com/2012/05/30/city-hall-moves-to-ban-tents-over night-camping-after-occupy-la-damage/ (accessed June 10, 2012); Emily Green, "Now, About L.A. City Hall's Lawn," *Los Angeles Times*, November 16, 2011, http://www.articles.latimes.com/2011 /nov/16/opinion/la-oe-green-lawn-20111116 (accessed June 10, 2012); Simone Wilson, "L.A. City

Hall Lawn Refurbishing Options Priced Between $350,000 and $1 Million (Really)," *LA Weekly*, January 11, 2012, http://www.blogs.laweekly.com/informer/2012/01/la_city_hall_lawn_price_occupy.php (accessed June 10, 2012).

46. Roy Rosenzweig and Elizabeth Blackmar, *The Park and the People: A History of Central Park* (Ithaca, N.Y.: Cornell University Press, 1992); Greg Hise and William Deverell, *Eden by Design: The 1930 Olmsted-Bartholomew Plan for the Los Angeles Region* (Berkeley: University of California Press, 2000).

47. Phillip Kennicott, "A Square Gets Hip: In McPherson Square, Occupy D.C. Creates a Vibrant Brand of Urbanism," *Washington Post*, "Style" section, November 10, 2011, http://www.washingtonpost.com/lifestyle/style/in-mcpherson-square-occupy-dc-creates-a-vibrant-brand-of-urbanism/2011/11/09/gIQAPBNa6M_story.html (accessed January 24, 2012).

48. "'Occupy' Is the 2011 Word of the Year," American Dialect Society, January 6, 2012, http://www.americandialect.org/occupy-is-the-2011-word-of-the-year (accessed July 10, 2012); "Reasons to Love New York."

49. "#OccupyCal Protesters Circumvent Order Not to Post Tents by Floating Them Above Sproul Hall," *abc7newsBayArea* (Twitter Feed), November 18, 2011, https://www.twitpic.com/7fmbla (accessed January 25, 2012).

50. Nicholas Ridout and Rebecca Schneider, "Precarity and Performance: An Introduction," *TDR: The Drama Review* 56, no. 4 (Winter 2012): 5–6; Lauren Berlant, *Cruel Optimism* (Durham, N.C.: Duke University Press, 2011), 192.

51. Schneider, "It Seems As If . . . I Am Dead," 152.

52. While public health challenges were real, discomfort with public displays of necessity highlighted how rats and sanitation issues were not unique to Occupy but "citywide problems" in need of public attention for residents in poor neighborhoods and the homeless. See Somers, "For DC Occupy Camps"; Somers, "Issa Seeks Political Answers."

53. Annie Gowen and Paul Duggan, "Occupy D.C. Protest Stays Peaceful as No-Camping Deadline Passes," *Washington Post*, January 30, 2012, http://www.washingtonpost.com/local/occupy-dc-prepares-for-park-service-deadline/2012/01/30/gIQAyojdcQ_story.html (accessed January 30, 2012); Katie Rogers, "Occupy D.C.: A Peek Inside the 'Tent of Dreams,'" *Washington Post* (Buzz blog), January 30, 2012, http://www.washingtonpost.com/blogs/the-buzz/post/occupy-dc-a-peek-inside-the-tent-of-dreams/2012/01/30/gIQAkYcscQ_blog.html (accessed January 30, 2012).

54. Urie and Byars, "Occupy Boulder Preparing."

55. Erik Devaney, "Occupy Providence Camp Unoccupied at Night? Police Use Infrared Technology to See How Many Protesters Stay Overnight in Tents," *New England Post*, November 9, 2011, http://www.newenglandpost.com/2011/11/09/occupy-providence-camp-unoccupied-night-police-infrared-technology-protesters-stay-overnight-tents/ (accessed January 25, 2012).

56. William Yardley, "The Branding of the Occupy Movement," *New York Times*, November 27, 2011, http://www.nytimes.com/2011/11/28/business/media/the-branding-of-the-occupy-movement.html?pagewanted=all&_r=0 (accessed January 20, 2012); Ben Davis, "How a Canadian Culture Magazine Helped Spark Occupy Wall Street," *Artinfo*, October 5, 2011, http://www.artinfo.com/news/story/38786/how-a-canadian-culture-magazine-helped-spark-occupy-wall-street/ (accessed January 19, 2012).

57. See, for example, Phoebe Kropp, "Wilderness Wives and Dishwashing Husbands: Comfort and the Domestic Arts of Camping Out, 1880–1910," *Journal of Social History* 43, no. 1 (Fall 2009): 5–29, and Rachel Gross, "Synthetic Wilderness: Gore-Tex and the Paths to Mastery in Outdoor Recreation" (M.A. thesis, University of Wisconsin, Madison, 2012).

58. William Cronon, "The Trouble with Wilderness; or, Getting Back to the Wrong Nature," in *Uncommon Ground: Rethinking the Human Place in Nature*, ed. William Cronon (New York: W. W. Norton, 1995), 69–90.

59. In the fall of 2012, members of New York's Occupy Wall Street reformed as Occupy Sandy in order to provide relief efforts to those affected by Hurricane Sandy when local and federal services failed to assist certain individuals, areas, and needs. See Alan Feuer, "Occupy Sandy: A Movement Moves to Relief," *New York Times*, November 9, 2012, MB1.

60. "Resist. Insist. Stand Together. Build. Never Surrender," *OccupyTheory.org*, n.d., http://www.occupytheory.org (accessed March 30, 2013); Butler, "So What Are the Demands," 11. The first issue of *Tidal* appeared in December 2011, and the three subsequent issues have been mass distributed for free as a protest action, with twelve thousand to fifty thousand copies per thirty-page issue being handed out on the streets and an open Web site for downloading. See Occupy Theory Group, "Tidal: Occupy Theory, Occupy Strategy," *Kickstarter.com*, September 11, 2012, http://www.kickstarter.com/projects/421440326/tidal-occupy-theory-occupy-strategy (accessed March 30, 2013).

Contributors

Thomas G. Andrews is Associate Professor of History at the University of Colorado Boulder. The author of *Killing for Coal: America's Deadliest Labor War* (2008), he is currently completing a book on the environmental history of the Colorado River headwaters. He is also hard at work on a project tentatively entitled "An Animals' History of the United States."

Connie Y. Chiang is Associate Professor of History and Environmental Studies at Bowdoin College. She is the author of *Shaping the Shoreline: Fisheries and Tourism on the Monterey Coast* (2008) and is currently completing a book manuscript on the environmental history of the Japanese American incarceration during World War II.

Catherine Cocks is Acquisitions Editor at the University of Iowa Press. She earned her Ph.D. at the University of California, Davis, and is the author of *Doing the Town: The Rise of Urban Tourism in the United States, 1850–1915* (2001) and *Tropical Whites: The Rise of the Tourist South in the Americas* (2013) as well as several articles.

Annie Gilbert Coleman is Associate Professor of American Studies at the University of Notre Dame. The author of *Ski Style: Sport and Culture in the Rockies* (2004) and more recently "The Rise of the House of Leisure: Outdoor Guides, Practical Knowledge, and Industrialization," *Western Historical Quarterly* (Winter 2011), she is working on a cultural history of professional outdoor guides in America since the nineteenth century.

Finis Dunaway is Associate Professor of History at Trent University, where he teaches courses in United States history, visual culture, and environmental studies. He is the author of *Natural Visions: The Power of Images in American Environmental Reform* (2005) and the recently published *Seeing Green: The Use and Abuse of American Environmental Images* (2015). In addition he has published articles in *American Quarterly, Environmental History, Raritan*, and other journals.

John Herron is Associate Professor of History at the University of Missouri–Kansas City. His research explores the intersection of natural science, cultural studies, and environmental history. His work includes *Science and the Social Good: Nature, Culture, and Community, 1865–1965* (2009) as well as two edited volumes currently in progress, *Heartland Green* and *Cowtown Cool*. His next monograph, an environmental history of taxidermy, builds on his essay for this collection.

Andrew Kirk is Professor of Environmental and Western History and Director of the Public History Program at the University of Nevada, Las Vegas. He is the author of *Collecting Nature: The American Environmental Movement and the Conservation Library* (2002), *Counterculture Green: The Whole Earth Catalog and American Environmentalism* (2007), *American Horizons* (2012), and numerous articles on environmental history. He is currently completing *PlumbBob 57: A Graphic History of Atomic Testing* (forthcoming, 2015).

Frieda Knobloch is Professor and Chair of the American Studies Department at the University of Wyoming, where she teaches courses in cultural theory and practice, environmental studies, gender and women's studies, and creative nonfiction in the M.F.A. writing program. She is the author of *The Culture of Wilderness: Agriculture as Colonization in the American West* (1996) and *Botanical Companions: A Memoir of Plants and Place* (2005).

Susan A. Miller is Assistant Professor of Childhood Studies at Rutgers University in Camden, New Jersey. She is the author of *Growing Girls: The Natural Origins of Girls' Organizations in America* (2007). Her current research is on children, patriotism, nationalism, and American civil religion.

Brett Mizelle is Professor of History and Director of the American Studies Program at California State University, Long Beach. His publications include the book *Pig* (2011) and numerous articles, book chapters, and reviews in the fields of nineteenth-century American history and the history of human-animal relationships. He is currently working on a book-length critical animal studies project on the discursive and material making and taking of animal life in American history.

Marguerite S. Shaffer is Professor of American Studies and History at Miami University, Oxford, Ohio. She is the author of *See America First: Tourism and National Identity, 1880–1940* (2001) and the editor of *Pubic Culture: Diversity, Democracy and Community in the United States* (2008). Her current work explores popular environmentalism.

Phoebe S. K. Young is Associate Professor of History at the University of Colorado Boulder, where she teaches courses in the environmental and cultural history of the United States. She is the author of *California Vieja: Culture and Memory in a Modern American Place* (2006) and has published articles in *Radical History Review* and *Journal of Social History*. She is currently writing a book on the history of camping and sleeping outside in American life since the Civil War.

Index

Page numbers in italics indicate figures and images.

284–85; slaves' consumption of, 31, 33–34. *See also* pigs, pork, and bacon (human-animal relationships and the meat industrial complex)

Bacon, Francis, 361n5

Bagby, Jeanne, 151

Baker, Mildred, 204–5, 208

Baker, William Emerson, 282

Bakhtin, Mikhail, 219

Ball, Charles, 13, 21–47; account of driving a mule team, 37–38; escape from Georgia to his Maryland family, 40–45, 329n85; family sold south, 45–46; hunting dog Trueman, 39, 41–42; and the internal slave trade, 25, 28, 37, 327n21; sale and forced migration from the Chesapeake to the Deep South, 24–26, 27; sale to a new Georgia plantation, 37–41; schemes to obtain and provide meat for his plantation slave household, 29–37, 38–39; slave narrative *Slavery in the United States* (1836), 21–47; work as butcher of animals, 28, 328n39. *See also* slavery, human-animal relationships in

Bancroft, Hubert H., 50

Batali, Armandino, 281

Baudelaire, Charles, 224–26

Beale, Edward F., 206

Beasts in the Jungle (Burroughs), 76

Beckmann, Robert, 170

Bederman, Gail, 113

Belknap, Bill, 205, 208, 216

Belknap's Waterproof Canyon River Guide, 215, 216, 217

Bell, Lorin, 205–6

Benjamin, Walter: *Arcades Project*, 360n48; on Baudelaire and decadence, 224, 226, 362n21, 362n23

Berg, Eric, 272

Berger, John, 369n9

Berlant, Lauren, 149

Best, James, 195

The Big Picture (army-produced television show), 144–45

biocitizenship, 347n3

biological turn, 60, 332n37

Bittman, Mark, 286

Blackmar, Elizabeth, 7

Blake, Elwyn, 209

Blake, William, 225–26

Blevans, T., 245–46

Bliss, Leslie, 213

Boatman's Quarterly Review (BQR), 214–17

Boddy, E. Manchester, 244

bodies, rendering of, 14–15; Progressive reformers' understandings of adolescence and childhood, 14–15, 99–121; suntanning by white North Americans after 1900, 15, 122–37; and visual media of American environmentalism, 15, 138–61

Bonus Army of World War I veterans, 294–95

Boulder City Council, 300–305

Bourdieu, Pierre, 107

"The Bowl" (Williams), 231

Bowron, Fletcher, 245, 248, 366n38

Boy Scouts: Colorado River registers of the 1950s, 198, 199; and recreational camping, 304, 306

Brand, Stewart, 170

Brewer, Susan A., 368n79

bricoleurs, 168–69, 351n10

Brown, Frank M., 195, *197*

Bureau of Plant Industry, 257

Burroughs, Edgar Rice, 76

butchers: model butcher shop carvings, 275, *276*; nineteenth-century celebrations of, 273–79, *274*, *276*, *278*, *284–85*; slaves' work as, 28, 328n39

Butler, Judith, 335n4, 358n20; on facial recognition and shared vulnerability/humanity, 85; on Occupy Wall Street, 316, 374n10

Bwindi Impenetrable National Park (Uganda), 73–74, 93–96, *94*, 335n8, 335n10

California Institute of Technology (Caltech), 253–54

California State Health Department, 252

Camp Fire Girls, 115–16

camping. *See* Occupy Wall Street (OWS); tents and camping

A Canyon Voyage (Dellenbaugh), 193, 201

Carhart, Arthur, 200

Carson, Rachel, 75, 157–59; *Silent Spring*, 75, 142, 157–59, 336n16

Chadbourne, Paul, 67

Charlotte's Web (White), 264

Chiang, Connie Y., 16–17

Chicago Daily Tribune, 127–28, 207

Tarzan of the Apes (Burroughs), 76
taxidermy and museum displays of animals,
    late nineteenth-century, 13–14, 48–69;
    appreciation as art, 50–51, 67; and the
    Chicago World's Fair (1893), 50–57, 60–61;
    children and natural history museums, 69;
    as civic biology, 59–60; the "Comanche"
    horse from Battle of Little Bighorn, 48,
    330n1; craft labor, 56–57; Dyche and the
    Kansas panorama, 61–69, 68; Dyche's skills
    of preservation and taxidermy, 64–67; early
    natural-history collection at the University
    of Kansas, 63–64; emphases on order and
    zoological classification schemes, 52–53,
    62–64, 331n12; Hornaday and taxidermy
    techniques, 65–67; Hornaday and the
    habitat group ("Buffalo Group"), 65–67,
    333n55; illusion and illusionism, 57; impact
    on viewers, 54–57; and the intersection of
    nature and culture, 50–61; and late
    nineteenth-century American life and
    political order/social context, 53–61; and
    late nineteenth-century biological turn,
    60–61; and late nineteenth-century shift
    from natural history to natural science,
    58–60; and modernity/modernization,
    60–61; mountain gorilla group diorama at
    Akeley African Hall, 75–76, 77; Natural
    History Museum at the University of
    Kansas, 48–50, 63–64; as natural science,
    50–51, 67–69; Panorama of North American
    Plants and Animals at the Kansas State
    Pavilion (Chicago World's Fair), 48–69, 49,
    51, 55, 56; panorama paintings of natural
    scenes, 54; popularity and praise for quality
    of, 50–51; racism and cultural nationalism,
    54; stuffing methods and Hornaday's
    improved technique, 65–67, 66; viewers'
    experience of authenticity, 56–57; and visual
    tradition of natural history, 58, 67–68
Taylor, John S., 326n10
tents and camping, 17, 287–317; anti-
    Apartheid shantytown demonstrations,
    293, 374n11; associations with recreation,
    288–91, 302–3, 306–9; associations with
    wealth, 288, 299, 315; Bonus Army of
    World War I veterans, 294–95; Coxey's
    Army (1894), 295; entanglement of nature
    and culture, 288, 317; expectations of
    privacy and protections against unreason-

able search, 303–4; Farmer's Vigil at the
    National Mall (1979), 374n12; as fulcrum
    for considering transience and perma-
    nence, 299–305; functional camping and
    associations with homelessness, 288,
    300–305; issues of shelter and sleep,
    300–304, 307; as meme, 314–15; at the
    National Mall in Washington, D.C.,
    293–94, 305, 374n12; National Park Service
    and the Occupy movement, 289–91, 305–11,
    374n12, 377nn33–34; and nostalgia, 315,
    315; Occupy D.C. and McPherson Square
    encampment, 305–9, 311, 312–13, 377n33;
    political, functional, and recreational
    modes, 288–91, 302–4, 306–9; and political
    protest, 292–99, 306–7, 374nn11–12; and
    precarity in modern life, 312–13; rendering
    a public place natural (public nature), 289;
    Resurrection City (1968), 293–94, 305,
    374n12; and Sukkot, 299; symbolic/
    performative tents, 311–15, 313, 315; and
    tacit dialogue about citizenship and access
    to nature, 305–11, 316–17; urban camping
    and municipal anticamping ordinances,
    300–305, 309–11; veterans of the Grand
    Army of the Republic (GAR), 295–96. See
    also Occupy Wall Street (OWS)
Tertiary History of the Grand Canyon District
    (Dutton), 227
The Theory of the Earth (Hutton), 220
Through the Grand Canyon from Wyoming to
    Mexico (Kolb), 193
Tidal: Occupy Theory, Occupy Strategy
    (journal), 315–16, 379n60
time: Carson's timeframe of fear and DDT
    hazards, 158–59; chronological files of
    Marston's Colorado River archive, 206–8;
    chronotopes, 16, 219; as cultural artifact,
    220–21; and deserts, 16, 218–34; and erosion,
    219, 227–32; geologic time, 194, 208–9,
    218–23, 232, 234; modern science and
    historical thinking, 223; reading geologic
    time in the Grand Canyon, 194, 208–13;
    sepulchral time and the decadent desert,
    219–20, 227–34; temporal framings of
    violence in 1964 presidential campaign ads,
    156–57; temporality ("slow violence") of the
    environmental crisis, 141–42, 156–57, 158, 161
Time magazine, 151, 158
Tinguely, Jean, 170

Acknowledgments

First and foremost, this volume is the byproduct of our friendship. We are grateful for the extended opportunities it has provided for us to meet, talk, and enjoy each other's company. Our conversations began in the stacks of the Huntington Library twenty years ago and have been nurtured over the years by other scholars and friends, most notably Hal Rothman, Susan Strasser, and Char Miller, among many others. We thank the Miami University Humanities Center, the Department of History, the American Studies Program, and the Program in Women, Gender, and Sexuality Studies for providing funds to support the scholars whose work is included in this volume. In addition, we thank the College of Arts and Science Dean's Office at Miami University for providing subvention funds for publication. Bill Deverell and Alan Jutzi at the Huntington Library provided us cogent advice and a congenial space to complete some of the final revisions. We would also like to thank Bob Lockhart, Acquisitions Editor at the University of Pennsylvania Press, who has provided unwavering support of this volume from its inception. His engagement every step of the way has helped us hone our central themes and intent while giving us the freedom to develop and explore our shared interests.

This volume would never have come to fruition without the support and encouragement of our respective partners and families. Ben, Callie, and Hugh Jacks not only celebrated birthdays and an anniversary on their own while Peggy Shaffer was off gorilla trekking in Uganda, but they also encouraged and humored her obsession with the everyday mishmash of nature and culture. Throughout this project, Phoebe Young's sons, Marlin and Darby, never failed to remind her that there was fun with nature to be had outside of her computer; Noah Finkelstein never let her forget the joys of discussing big ideas or get too far away from the hammock's-eye view on the world. We also honor our mothers, Marguerite J. Palmer and Gale Young, for cultivating our senses of exploration and engagement that sit at the root of this volume.